When Buildings Speak

:: **WHEN BUILDINGS SPEAK**

Architecture as Language in the Habsburg Empire and
Its Aftermath, 1867–1933

ANTHONY ALOFSIN

The University of Chicago Press   CHICAGO & LONDON

ANTHONY ALOFSIN is the Roland Gommel Roessner Centennial Professor in Architecture and professor of art and art history at the University of Texas at Austin. His books include *The Struggle for Modernism: Architecture, Landscape Architecture, and City Planning at Harvard*; *Prairie Skyscraper: Frank Lloyd Wright's Price Tower* (as editor); *Frank Lloyd Wright: Europe and Beyond* (as editor); and *Frank Lloyd Wright: The Lost Years, 1910–1922*, which was published by the University of Chicago Press. He was consulting curator to Frank Lloyd Wright, Architect, the major retrospective exhibition at the Museum of Modern Art. A contributor to the *Times Literary Supplement*, Professor Alofsin has published essays and articles in a wide range of other periodicals, including *Architect's Newspaper*, *Journal of the Society of Architectural Historians*, *Design Book Review*, *Harvard Design Magazine*, *Wright Studies*, and *Center: A Journal for Architecture in America*.

The University of Chicago Press, Chicago 60637
The University of Chicago Press, Ltd., London
© 2006 by Anthony Alofsin
All rights reserved. Published 2006
Printed in China

15 14 13 12 11 10 09 08 07 06   1 2 3 4 5

ISBN-13: 987-0-226-01506-4 (cloth)

ISBN-10: 0-226-01506-8 (cloth)

The University of Chicago Press and the author gratefully acknowledge the support of the Graham Foundation for Advanced Studies in the Fine Arts and of The Martin S. and Evelyn S. Kermacy Collection Endowment toward the publication of this book.

Library of Congress Cataloging-in-Publication Data

Alofsin, Anthony.
   When buildings speak : architecture as language in the Habsburg Empire and its aftermath, 1867–1933 / Anthony Alofsin.
       p. cm.
   Includes bibliographical references and index.
   ISBN 0-226-01506-8 (hardcover : alk. paper)
   1. Architecture—Europe, Central—19th century. 2. Architecture—Europe, Central—20th century. 3. Symbolism in architecture—Europe, Central. 4. Semiotics. I. Title. II. Title: Architecture as language in the Habsburg Empire and its aftermath, 1867–1933.
NA957.A44 2006
720'.9436'09034—dc22
                              2005021958

This book is printed on acid-free paper.

For Masaaki Sekiya
(1942–2002)
Masterful photographer,
kind and gentle man

Contents

Preface ix

INTRODUCTION

Issues of Architecture, Language, and Identity   1

1 The Language of History   17
2 The Language of Organicism   55
3 The Language of Rationalism   81
4 The Language of Myth   127
5 The Language of Hybridity   177

CONCLUSION

Continuities, Discontinuities, and Transformations   231

Appendix: Place-Names,
Educational Institutions, Translation of Secession   265
Notes   267
Selected Bibliography   295
Illustration Credits   311
Index   313

Preface

I can well imagine a religion in which there are no doctrines, so that nothing is spoken. Clearly, then, the essence of religion can have nothing to do with what is sayable.

Ludwig Wittgenstein

THERE ARE few trendy notions in what follows. Although I have attempted to benefit from the critical debates in architectural history of the late twentieth century and thirty years of poststructural thinking, I am neither following a preset agenda nor pushing a politically correct line of interpretation. My approach is somewhat similar to that of Roland Barthes in his *Mythologies*, a group of essays on diverse topics that examine how language operates in culture, but with an analytical apparatus underlying a series of accounts.[1] I also have benefited from the narratives of Italo Calvino, particularly *On a Winter's Night a Traveler*, and his self-consciousness of stories about stories. George Kubler's classic work, *The Shape of Time*, inspired me, like many others, to ask many years ago what meaning art has in cultures that have no historical record.

The architecture of the former Austro-Hungarian Empire embodies a history that is continually being written. Yet its buildings pale in black and white images; to appreciate the complexity and richness of the works discussed in this book, new color photography was necessary. Some scholars and architectural critics may lament the absence of floor plans, however. Their point is well taken, and I regret this disservice to my colleagues; but floor plans have not been included because many people in the broad readership sought here do not read them—and more significantly, floor plans do not speak to our experience in the ways that seeing, feeling, and moving through buildings do. As my intention here is to consider how buildings speak, it is their visual fabric that gets the most attention rather than the diagrams represented by plans and cross sections, though they are often helpful in understanding the processes of making buildings. Consequently, exploring extant buildings in situ and images of them became the main, though not exclusive, means of analysis.

I owe a particular debt to two preeminent photographers who provided the body of images for this book. Hans Engels contributed stunning photography that documents much of the architecture under discussion. He battled snowstorms and car theft to secure his beautiful images. Masaaki Sekiya, who devoted himself to the beauties of architecture, provided the incomparable images of Viennese architecture to which he dedicated much of his professional life. His sudden death was for me a personal loss, and a loss for the world of architecture. Both Hans and Masaaki had the eyes I needed to navigate the complex architectural languages of the former Austro-Hungarian Empire.

I have deduced the presence of these languages after studying these buildings for a number of years. My exposure to the architecture of Central Europe began in 1986, but only in 1990, while a Fulbright Professor in the Institut für Kunstgeschichte at the Vienna Academy of Fine Arts and after the fall of the Berlin Wall, did I realize that extraordinary, creative modern architecture dwelled behind the former Iron Curtain, and that almost all of it was unknown in the West. To further explore the architecture of the former Austro-Hungarian Empire and bring it to a wider audience, in 1992 I conceived, organized, and administered an international research consortium, "A Tense Alliance: Architecture in the Habsburg Lands, 1893–1928," which consisted of scholars from Austria, Croatia, the Czech Republic, Hungary, Italy, Poland, Slovakia, Slovenia, and the United States.

Generous institutions assisted this work. In the early phases of the Tense Alliance project, we received major support from the Internationales Forschungszentrum Kulturwissenschaft (IFK), Vienna; the J. Paul Getty Museum and Getty Research Institute, Los Angeles; and the Canadian Centre For Architecture, Montreal. The IFK also provided me with a fellowship to conduct research and to direct our project from Vienna. The central theme of my research was the role architecture in Central Europe played in the formation of national identity within the framework of an evolving alternative modernism.

My study draws on the discussions, expertise, and insights of colleagues who formed the international team of scholars of the Tense Alliance. To them I owe many thanks: Matúš Dulla, Bratislava; János Gerle, Budapest; Henrieta Moravčíková, Bratislava; Leszek Jodlinski, Cracow; Petr Krajči, Prague; Aleksander Laslo, Zagreb; Christopher Long, Austin, Texas; Marco Pozzetto, Trieste; Damjan Prelovšek, Ljubljana; Monika Platzer, Vienna; Jacek Purchla, Cracow; Rostislav Švácha, Prague; and Igor Zhuk, L'viv. Other individuals who contributed their insights to the project during the early research phases included Rudolf Klein, Ákos Moravánszky, and Ilona Sármány-Parsons. During this phase of work, Karen Koehler provided tireless administrative assistance.

The research we conducted became the basis of Shaping the Great City: Modern Architecture in Central Europe, 1890–1937, which opened in 1999 and traveled for two years. Curated by the members of its steering committee, this important international exhibition focused on urbanism and city planning in the well-established tradition of exhibitions examining the metamorphoses of the metropolis in the formation of modernism. The research conducted under the Tense Alliance had led me, however, in a different and independent direction to focus on issues of social, political, and cultural identity embodied in buildings themselves. I was less interested in drawings as aesthetic objects, though I appreciate them, than in the constituent factors that had made buildings meaningful, and ultimately in the languages used to convey their meanings.

My continuing research into issues of identity and language in the Austro-Hungarian Empire received subsequent financial support from the Graham Foundation for Advanced Studies in the Fine Arts, whose funds supported the photography for this book. The University of Texas at Austin provided leave and funding through its former University Research Institute, Dean's Leave from the School of Architecture, and two generous subventions from The Martin S. and Evelyn S. Kermacy Collection Endowment for the acquisition of photographs and support of research. Funds from my endowed position as Roland Gommel Roessner Professor of Architecture at the university further supported this ongoing research and writing.

In the concluding stages of work, numerous institutions and their staffs assisted in providing images for the book: Kupferstichkabinett, Akademie der bildenden Künste, Vienna; Cushing Memorial Library, Texas A & M University; Nancy Hadley, Library of the American Institute of Architects, Washington, DC; Dr. Margit Altfahrt, Univ.-Prof. Dr. Ferdinand Opll, and Univ.-Prof. HR Dr. Peter Csendes, Stadt Wien Archiv and Magistrat der Stadt Wien; Helmut Seltzer, Frauke Freutler, and Daniela Geist, Wien Museum; Tibor Sándor, Metropolitan Ervin Szabó Library, Budapest Collection; Alena Zapletalová, Museum of Decorative Arts, Prague; and the National Technical Museum, Department of Architecture and Civil Engineering, Prague.

Other individuals generously provided additional photographs and illustrations from their collections, including János Gerle, Antonia Graf, Rudolf Klein, Aleksander Lazlo, and Christopher Long. Each of them also shared their considerable knowledge with me. Isabella Croy provided much help with obtaining illustrations in Vienna. Additional assistance came from Matúš Dulla, Judit Gink, József Hajdú, Petr Krajči, Paul Robert Magosci, Henrieta Moravčíková, Tibor Sándor, Georg Schwalm-Theiss, Jindřich Vybíral, and Matthew Witkovsky. Anthony Burton and Sandra Hazel at the University of Chicago Press supplied prodigious expertise during production of the book.

My talented graduate assistants helped with this project as well. Danielle Langston worked during the continuing research phase, and Vladímir Kulić saw the project through to completion. Not only did he add some of his own photographs, but he took on any assigned task with humor and energy. Our discussions of the issues prompted by this book were always stimulating. Ivania Quesada-Lobo edited the final version of the bibliography.

I appreciate the efforts of the anonymous readers of the manuscript, all of whom provided wise and insightful suggestions. I warmly thank Paul Asenbaum, János Gerle, Otto Antonia Graf, Jutta and Wolfgang Fischer, Monika Knofler, and Eduard F. Sekler, who are not only colleagues but good and supportive friends. Susan Bielstein, my editor at the University of Chicago Press, deserves special recognition for her patience with this project and her long-term support of my work.

Finally, I owe a unique debt of appreciation to Patricia Tierney Alofsin, who journeyed with me from country to country on this long and challenging adventure.

Paris
December 2004

FIGURE I.1
Map of the Austro-Hungarian Empire, 1890; facsimile. Verlag G. Freytag & Berndt, Vienna. Author collection.

Introduction: Issues of Architecture, Language, and Identity

THIS BOOK investigates the assertion that architecture is a language. If architecture is a language analogous to text, then we can ask how buildings can be read. If it is analogous to speech, we can ask what architecture can say and cannot say. We can also ask what its means of communication are: abstraction, association, didacticism, or resonance with a deep structure of the human mind? Who reads buildings and for what purposes? Attempting to answer these questions suggests that architecture has limits in what it can say.

Though a long tradition in architectural theory associates architecture with language, the assumptions concerning how architecture speaks have rarely been scrutinized in depth or applied to individual buildings within a specific cultural context. When architectural historians write about the *architecture parlante* (literally, "speaking architecture") of late eighteenth-century France, they tend to associate it with political revolution, but they neither go into deeper questions of how buildings speak, nor look at architectural expression within the framework of language. How does the language of architecture convey meaning? Can it actually express identity or the society around it? Are there inherent limits to what architecture can say? If so, why are its possibilities limited? If we translate these large questions into personal experience, we ask after seeing a building: What did it say? How was it said? For what purpose did it speak? But if the building said nothing to me, then why was it mute? More broadly, we can ask if buildings convey national and personal identity. What are the means they use to communicate with a broad audience: motifs, ornaments, mass, color, light, shade, shadow? Are there innate limits to what architecture can express, or can architecture express unique meanings different from those expressed by literature, music, and other visual arts?

The subject for this study of language and architecture is based on buildings and unbuilt projects created in the late Austro-Hungarian Empire and its successor states (fig. I.1). The time frame of this book extends from the emergence of modernization, marked by the rise of industrialization in the 1860s and 1870s, to the economic and political crises of the early 1930s that foreshadowed the catastrophe of the Second World War.[1] Two sets of political boundaries delimit the geographic area being studied. The first set defined the empire, which after 1867 consisted of two states, Austria and Hungary, loosely joined by a common head and limited governmental bodies (fig. I.2). The second set of boundaries arose after 1918, when the empire dissolved and fractured into a number of smaller countries: a significantly reduced Austria and Hungary and newly formed Czechoslovakia and Yugoslavia, with parts of the Habsburg lands going to Romania and Poland.

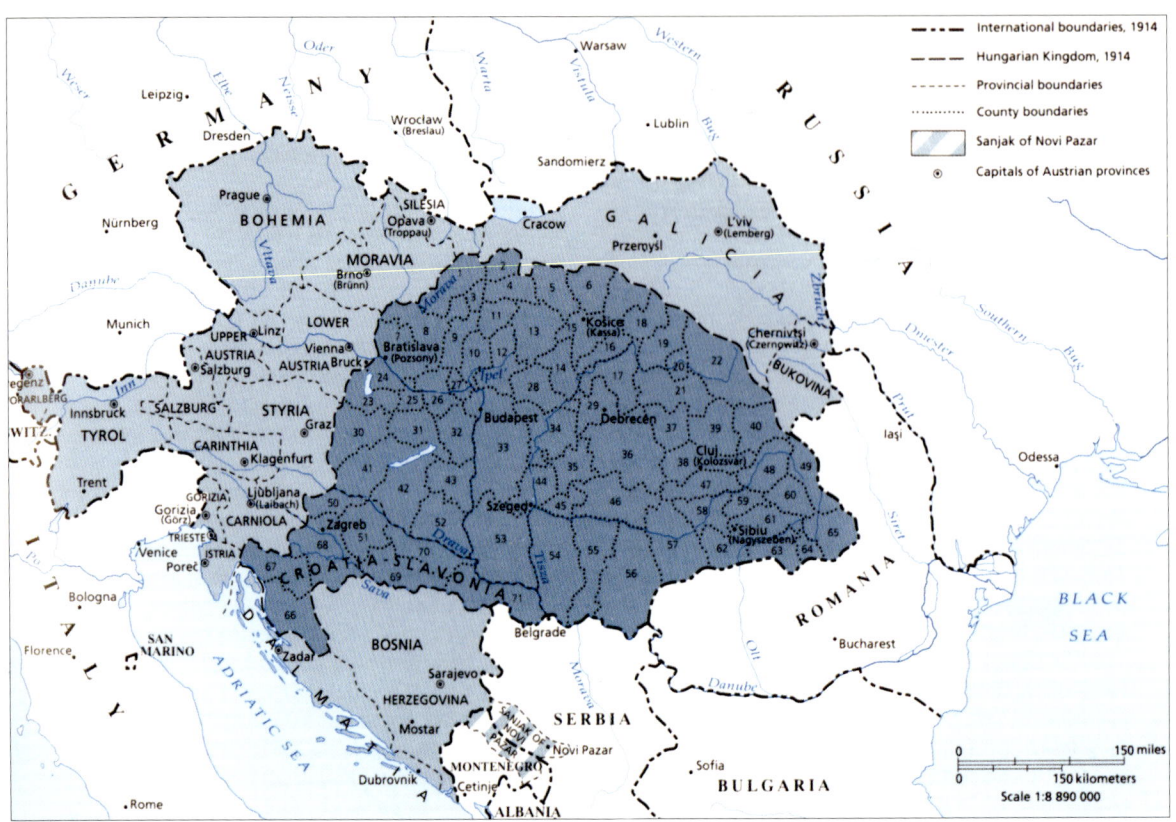

FIGURE I.2
Austro-Hungarian Empire, 1867–1914.

The Austro-Hungarian Empire was a collage of so many nationalities that it could never be transformed into a unified nation-state.[2] The expansions of the Habsburgs over four centuries had resulted in claims to a broad swath of lands, but control over a disparate and diverse realm created much tension. The conflict broke out with full force in 1848, when the wave of revolutions that shook Europe sparked similar developments around the empire. Turmoil was centered on contradicting demands for national autonomies, with the strongest revolt arising in Hungary. Partial resolution of the problem was not established until the Ausgleich (Compromise) of 1867, by which the empire was transformed into the Dual Monarchy, effectively consisting of two separate states. One monarch, who held the titles of the emperor of Austria and the king of Hungary, and only the common ministries of foreign affairs, war, and finance joined the two parts of the country.[3] The dividing line followed the little river Leitha. West of it lay Austria, comprising German-speaking Vienna, with its surrounding provinces and the Alpine regions further to the south and west; Czech-speaking provinces of Bohemia and Moravia to the north; Galicia and Bukovina in the northeast; Slovene provinces to the south; and Dalmatia on the Adriatic coast. To the east lay Hungary, which also incorporated Slovak-speaking areas, western Transylvania, and the Kingdom of Croatia-Slavonia.[4] In 1878, Austria and Hungary also jointly occupied the Ottoman province of Bosnia and Herzegovina, fully annexing it in 1908 (fig. I.3).

One of the reasons for the reorganization brought about by the Compromise was the emperor's hope that providing limited autonomy and sanctioning national cultural identity would consolidate the political loyalty of his subjects. But while the

FIGURE I.3

Central Europe, 1910.

Compromise accommodated the demands of Hungarians, other minorities remained empty-handed. In their desire to assert a unified national identity, Hungarians were particularly unwilling to grant to others any of the rights they had gained themselves. Nationalist movements remained active throughout the remaining life of the empire in both of its parts. Such historical factors are important in providing the context for looking at language and identity in the Austro-Hungarian Empire and its burgeoning cities.

The large urban centers of Vienna, Prague, and Budapest had all experienced varying degrees of political change, economic expansion, and population growth throughout the nineteenth century. In Vienna, the century began with political flux as Francis II declared himself emperor of Austria in 1804, relinquishing the former imperial crown of the Holy Roman Empire two years later. Strife followed as Napoleon's forces occupied the city twice, bringing subsequent inflation and state bankruptcy. Nevertheless, under the leadership of Prince Metternich, Vienna played a central political role in restoring European national integrity during the Congress of Vienna in 1814–15. By 1845, Vienna's population had grown to 430,000 inhabitants, and with expanding cultural interests its middle class delighted in the artistic expression of the simple and straightforward architecture and furniture of the Biedermeier style. Waltzes from Joseph Lanner and the elder Johann Strauss added to the cultural life of the city. But political tranquility was elusive: the revolution of March 1848 in Vienna ended Metternich's authoritarian control, and Emperor Franz Josef's army suppressed a second uprising in October of the same year.

The physical form of Vienna started to change as its inner ramparts began to be pulled down in 1857 and a new grand boulevard encircling the historic core—the Ringstrasse—opened on the cleared lands in 1865. Public buildings, luxurious apartment houses, and parks emerged along the boulevard over the years. New buildings replaced old ones in other parts of the city as well. Locks and canals controlled the Danube's floods, and gas and electricity became available. With free trade, the economy expanded and the city's population continued to increase. In 1861, Vienna became self-governing, with a freely elected city council that soon had a liberal majority. The city administration absorbed suburbs in 1890 and three years later constructed a second ring road, the Gürtel, which replaced the old Linienwall. Such expansions affected and reflected changes in identity, which in turn called upon architecture to speak effectively for its citizens.

Culturally and artistically, Vienna made major contributions to modernism. Throughout the nineteenth century, writers, artists, and composers—including such famous figures as Brahms or the Strauss family—gave shape to a specific Viennese bourgeois culture. But the period around the turn of the century was particularly radical, with many rebels against the established conventions. The most well known are architects such as Otto Wagner, Adolf Loos, Josef Hoffmann, and Joseph Maria Olbrich; painters such as Gustav Klimt, Alfred Kubin, Oskar Kokoschka, and Egon Schiele; musicians such as Arnold Schoenberg, Alban Berg, and Anton von Webern; and writers such as Arthur Schnitzler, Hugo von Hofmannsthal, and Karl Kraus. At the same time, Sigmund Freud and Alfred Adler were busy developing their influential psychiatric theories.

By the turn of the century, Vienna had almost 2 million inhabitants and an area of 105 square miles (272 square kilometers), spreading across the Danube canal to the river's left bank. Yet it was a place of tensions and paradox: its mayor, Karl Lueger, was a virulent anti-Semite, while at the same time it sheltered Theodor Herzl, the founder of Zionism.

Prague (Praha in Czech) was smaller than both Vienna and Budapest, and despite being as significant historically and culturally, it never achieved their status in the empire. Its history extended back one thousand years, during which time layers of tradition marked its many buildings and monuments. These range from the Charles Bridge over the river Vltava to a backdrop of its royal castle, the Hradčany, high on the left bank, to its great baroque palaces. During the eighteenth century, Prague's population had doubled from 40,000 in 1705 to more than 80,000 by 1771, and in 1784 the Old Town, the New Town, the Malá Strana, and the Hradčany complex administratively united into a single city. Its merchants and largely German, Spanish, and Italian nobility exerted much influence on architectural and cultural life. Outstanding architects created magnificent palaces and gardens, and churches in the Prague version of the baroque style sprang up throughout the city. Around the beginning of the nineteenth century, the Industrial Revolution began impacting Prague as the city made Karlín its first suburb in 1817. Factories opened to take advantage of nearby coal mines and ironworks. By 1837, the population exceeded 100,000, and establishment of the city's first railway in 1845 assisted this growth. Prague's cultural life continued a rich history marked earlier by Wolfgang Amadeus Mozart's residency there and the first performances of his Prague Symphony and the opera *Don Giovanni*. Lyric composers—Bedřich Smetana, Antonín Dvořák, and Leoš Janáček—would receive great acclaim, and the writings of Franz Kafka, which dwelled on the existential dilemmas of modernity, were inextricable from life in Prague.

Simultaneous with population increase, industrial expansion, and cultural flowering in Prague, a working class and strong nationalistic sentiments arose to play an important political role in city life. When the revolution of 1848 briefly erupted, artisans, students, and workers manned the barricades in opposition to the ruling Austrians. Nationalists pressed forward with the desire to establish autonomy, and by 1868 Czechs had achieved a majority on the city council. The effort to create a Czech renaissance that centered in Prague also saw the appearance of neo-Renaissance architecture as an idiom for its independent identity.

Budapest emerged as the capital of Hungary in 1872 with the amalgamation of the free towns of Buda, on the right bank of the Danube, and Pest on the left bank, along with the village of Óbuda. In the eighteenth century, Buda had been restricted to German Roman Catholic settlers and was an imperial garrison under scrutiny of the Habsburg monarchs. It remained aristocratic and found alien the idea of a native

Hungarian identity. On the other hand, Pest was a center of German commercial activity at that time, and attracted the gentry and intelligentsia who espoused nationalism; its nobility, though often of German ancestry, led the cause for Hungarian home rule. The two parts of the city thus represented different ideological and political allegiances as well as contrasting aristocratic and bourgeois social strata.

After the fusion of the towns, a dramatic increase in Budapest's population pressurized the contact of various ethnic groups and social classes. The city became ten times larger in area than its nearest Hungarian competitor, Szeged, and from a population of 100,000 in 1840 swelled to 1 million by 1918, at a rate of growth exceeding that of contemporary London.[5] Migration from villages and towns to the capital resulted in immense ethnic diversity, with specific groups tending to identify with sectors of the city. Germans and later Hungarians "ran" Buda; Germans controlled the government of Pest with Serbs dominating shipping, and "Greeks" (a term that applied to ethnic Greeks and others from the Balkans) were merchants there. Industrial workers were Germans and German speakers who had been imported as settlers from the West. These groups encountered a large population of Jews, expanded by immigration from eastern countries, which constituted one-quarter of Budapest's population by 1900. Within this social framework, Jews were predominantly professionals, and they administered much of the industrial and financial development in the country together with the gentiles and Germans who had become assimilated Hungarians. The non-Jewish middle class that could be identified as distinctly Hungarian was landowning, rural, small, and politically ineffective.

A second major pressure on both Budapest and Hungary itself was the mounting concern after the 1867 Compromise to establish a national identity that was distinctly Hungarian. Count István Széchenyi suggested the idea of a national style in 1838. The Hungarian art historian Imre Henszlmann later made similar calls. Intellectuals, fearful that Hungary's neighbors would cause the disappearance of its native language, reinforced the calls of Széchenyi and Henszlmann. One means of forming a distinctive identity within the Dual Monarchy was "magyarization," the process that confirmed a hypothetical "Hungarianness" by identifying with Hungarian ethnicity and by exclusive use of the Hungarian language.[6] Both ethnicity and language were associated with ancestors from Asia who had arrived in the ninth century; attached to these ancestors was a mythical aura and the assumption that a pure Hungarian stock existed and could still be identified.

The control of language was at the core of this process of identity formation in the Austro-Hungarian Empire. Spoken and written languages, in addition to being criteria of ethnicity, played critical roles throughout this period from the mid-nineteenth century to World War I as vehicles and mediators of political, social, and cultural conflict (fig. 1.4). For instance, the Austrian central government suppressed use of the Czech language for official purposes in order to assert a transnational imperial identity. The oppression rankled the Czechs, and the reintroduction of their language was part of the rise of the nationalist movement in Czech lands. Magyarization had as one

FIGURE I.4

Ethnolinguistic distribution, ca. 1900.

of its goals the replacement with Hungarian of the multiple languages spoken by the diverse groups of the region. Use of a single language was instrumental in creating and reinforcing a Hungarian national spirit as embodied in state institutions, such as schools and public administration. Despite the Nationalities Law, which intended to protect minority civil rights, minority languages were excluded from administrative and judicial arenas, and Hungarian became the nearly exclusive language of education in primary, secondary, and all state-run schools after 1870. Within thirty years, Hungarian had become the official language of the state. By 1900, most middle-class Jews, Germans, and many Slovaks and Ruthenes (who spoke a form of Ukrainian in Galicia) were magyarized. In a rural-urban split, the focus of the transformation occurred in central Hungary, while the periphery tended to retain native languages along with distinct ethnic and cultural identities. By converting people, magyarization worked against the grain of ethnic diversity. Similarly, the forced use of the Hungarian language in the towns along the shifting western borders of Slovakia juxtaposed one cultural identity against another.

In effect, Austria enforced the supremacy of German over Czech in Bohemia and Moravia, just as Hungary pushed for Hungarian over German, Slovak, Croatian, Serbian, and Romanian. The use of language became a powerful weapon and a necessity in political control. What could architecture say in this political and social climate? How well could it speak for itself and for the people who created it?

A RICH architectural polyglotism in Austria-Hungary paralleled the varied languages of its people.[7] Not only were many architectural languages expressed simultaneously, but they reflected various and even opposing issues of ethnic and national identities, as well as conservative or liberal ideologies.[8] Such complexity adds to the appeal of the buildings of the empire as excellent case studies of the limits of architecture as a language. These buildings are also relatively unknown outside Central Europe, and they do not fit into categories conceived by conventional historiography or within simplistic stylistic definitions. Moreover, they are contradictory. Straddling East and West, they contain enough elements of classical European traditions to identify them and locate them in the conventional history of art and architecture, yet they are so foreign, strange, and unexplored that layers of interpretation have not encumbered them. This book offers a look at them with fresh eyes—and indeed we must look at them freshly because almost all the buildings I discuss have been excluded from the canonical histories of modern architecture in the twentieth century. It is in part their foreignness and strangeness that excluded them as well as more recently their inaccessibility to western visitors during decades of Soviet control. That "otherness" plays a role in their limited ability to speak to us now.

The reader may say: yes, the architecture of Central Europe is unfamiliar, but isn't the debate about architecture and language an old discourse that is well established to the point that to re-engage it would be a tedious exercise? The analogy of architecture as language is, indeed, one of the oldest tropes in the traditions of western European architecture. Attempts to theorize architecture in linguistic terms extend from the rediscovery of Roman architect and encyclopedist Vitruvius in the early fifteenth century and the beginnings of historical consciousness in the Renaissance through the birth of the disciplines of history in the eighteenth century and its cousins, the history of art and architecture, into the twentieth. The topoi of history and theory of architecture assume that architecture "speaks," and that the visual language of architecture is comparable to the verbal language of words, involving vocabulary as well as structural syntax. Nonetheless, they still require investigation.[9]

The relationships and interactions between words and images, between architecture and language, go to the core mysteries of the human mind that still have not fully yielded to scientific investigation. These are issues that have preoccupied Western philosophy from its beginnings, and they are also central to Eastern traditions that find reality beyond the tangible.[10] For our purposes, we accept that images form in our brains—if not in words, then in their eidetic equivalents. And we know that in the minds of some people who tend to be visual, words may form images.

In a broad sense, we usually think of a "language" as human activity defined by the use of sounds, grammar, and vocabulary. The use of a language implies that people speaking the same one can communicate, but those who cannot read, speak, or aurally understand it, cannot. French speakers understand each other speaking French, but a German speaker may not understand French. Sometimes, two different languages are mutually intelligible. Norwegians and Swedes can understand each others' languages. And at other times, within one language, people speaking different dialects cannot understand each other: Chinese, although using the same writing system for all its variances, contains spoken dialects that are mutually unintelligible. The very concept of language, then, is marked fundamentally by its potential for multiple meanings. Here, I use the term *language* to include the simple sense in which people have the opportunity both to speak to each other with understanding and meaning and, within the same language, to speak without mutual misunderstanding.

The difficulty of applying the metaphor of language to architecture is immediately obvious: what are its equivalents to sounds, grammar, and vocabulary? Are its elements of communication—the parts and pieces that make up a building—equivalents to morphemes (meaningful linguistic units) and sememes (the meanings of morphemes), and their ordering analogous to sentences, paragraphs, and texts? It is those equivalents and the meanings they may construct that are central to this book. But the reader might ask: why even bother with these questions in the abstract? We bother because language not only creates basic means of communication, it is critical to creating identity; and the issues of identity are fundamental to understanding people, particularly in the complex social and political context of Central Europe.

Another point to bear in mind is that a *language* of architecture is different from a *style* of architecture, though the terms are often used casually as synonyms. A style is defined by a recognizable and repeatable set of motifs, organized by a conventional syntax. A stylistic sign of a neo-Gothic building is the presence of the pointed arch. Swirling curvilinear metal-skinned forms are a sign of the late style of Frank Gehry. Using stylistic terms to identify buildings has the advantage of quickly summing up in a generalized way an image of a building.

But the reliance on style as an aide-mémoire also makes it easy to forget the more complex meanings of buildings that are not visually apparent, particularly the social roles buildings play. Style is also used as a sieve to sort buildings that do or do not fit into a critic's worldview, and buildings that do not conform are often omitted from further consideration. Consequently, stylistic terms have immediate limits, particularly when architects have creatively transformed their material in ways that deviate from standard use. Style is a shorthand, a marriage of convenience between writings and their objects, but a reducer of meaning. In analyzing the transformative process that eludes simplistic stylistic analysis, looking at architecture and language becomes helpful.

No, the debate about architecture and language is not settled. The currency of interest in it rises and falls within the broad discourse about architecture. In the twentieth century, the ideology of functionalism rather than theoretical discussion dominated the middle decades, but with the appearance of postmodernism in the 1970s and 1980s, the issues of architecture and language reemerged. From the postmodernist perspective, architecture had its own language and structure, one rooted in the classical Western tradition; modernism had diverted our grasp of its independence and had corrupted it. Moreover, modernism had borrowed from the disciplines of sociology, psychology, and systems theory, which only increased the corruption of the pure language. According to postmodernists, architecture was linguistically autonomous and independent of social construction; consequently, it had no responsibilities to the society around it. Not only did this position make architects appear to be masters—finally—of their fate, but powerful ones at that. The proposition that architecture was an autonomous, self-reflexive system of signs, however, has never been proved, and architects' role as power figures within the larger society is questionable. Although postmodern classicism trickled down to become the idiom of the commercial mall of the 1980s, the public shared neither the zealous convictions of architects nor the insistence on one and only one kind of architectural language.

Postmodernism in architecture played out, along with its claims about architecture as an autonomous language. The discourse on semiotics had become so overlaid with poststructural analyses that its basic concepts were barely decipherable.[11] That this debate has not been active during the recent stylistic shifts to a revival of modernism and the emergence of blob architecture is worthy of contemplation. In the absence of polemics, a calm reassessment of the relationship of architecture to language is now possible. Some historians have begun this reassessment, and fresh approaches are still required.[12]

The approach used here to study the relationship of architecture to language results in a new kind of formalism—one that is at once deeply historical and relies on multivalent historical readings, but also one that confronts the physical reality of a building. I call this approach "contextual formalism." The methods of study involved differ from those used in the kind of historiography of modern architecture that dominated from the 1930s to the 1960s, but split apart thereafter. One direction of thought fixated on visual forces, particularly on modern architecture as the manifest destiny of the evolution of modernist space or technological teleology. This kind of formalism paralleled the formalism in art that is most associated with abstraction and the writings of critic Clement Greenberg: both art and architecture have an autonomy that lifts them above social purpose to the dictates of genius or to some innate impulses within themselves. Another direction led to the rejection of the formalist position and emphasized the social production of architecture. It opened sources of evidence for critical studies and an ever-widening range of neglected subjects. But positioning architecture in a sociopolitical context led historians, critics, and some practitioners to disparage and ignore the formal realities of their subjects. Postmodernists rejected both positions by proposing history as the repository of meaning and the source of archetypal forms, and by claiming that architecture was an autonomous language with its own rules. This unconscious revival of the nineteenth-century ideology of art for art's sake served in particular to vilify the social agenda of the modern movement.

The contextual formalism proposed here seeks to join these divergent paths by assuming that social and political forces of architecture are transmitted through its physical form and that the two inseparably create a dialectic realism. In other words, the visual manifestation of architecture—its space, light, color, texture, pattern—and its social and historical context must be considered inseparable if we, as receptors, are to grasp the messages of buildings, however limited they may be. Also, the approach of contextual formalism differs from other methods. The old formalism emphasized visual dynamics to the exclusion of cultural, social, and political considerations. Architectural theorists who appropriate linguistic models assume architecture is autonomous, its elements part of its own unique language system, its forms full of their own meanings. A more political viewpoint assumes that architecture is empty of meaning and that meanings come from the investment of history, culture, and memory into it. This study attempts to bridge these antithetical positions by putting buildings into the context of history and culture. It explores the possibilities and limits of architecture as a visual language in geographic and political arenas, questions assumptions about modern culture and constructions of national identity, and looks to see what the forms are saying as objects with aesthetic and physical presence.

Combining analysis and history, the method of contextual formalism uses descriptions and examinations of what is seen and places those observations in the context of the moment when the object was created. From the perspective of contextual formalism, *context* includes the historical, political, social, and cultural factors that gave meaning to the buildings and designs observed, and *form* includes the color, texture, mass, materials, and structure, as well as the images and symbols incorporated into the exterior and interior of the building. Historians have tended to focus either on the context or on the form, but this method attempts to correct the habit of emphasizing one mode of analysis at the expense of the other. I assume that instead of having a singular meaning, buildings have multiple meanings. Rather than placing buildings into neat categories, as reductive historians have done, this book emphasizes the range of meanings a building can convey. There are certainly other languages and other buildings in other places that have different languages. But the languages discussed here appear to provide the maximum opportunity for exploring the various relationships of the signs embedded in architecture. And rather than look for all-encompassing categories, I am interested in testing the consistency of an approach.

To further that goal, my purpose here is to outline a method of historical and critical analysis that can proceed without the burden of satisfying a fashionable ideology. Rather than assume it is a hopeless task to understand history because there are no absolutes, this method lays out a structure that has as its goal the optimistic effort to answer as many questions as possible and to engage many levels of interpretation. In that effort, it acknowledges the limits of objects to speak, our limits to hear them, and the viability of many different kinds of speech. Although we examine the particular context of the Austro-Hungarian Empire, my hope is that this approach could be tested across time and across cultures.

To get at these meanings of context and form, we need to look at several factors: political and social conditions; the building site; identities of the client and the architect, and the relationships between them; building program; design sequence, which is often deduced only from drawings, sketches, and documents; construction sequence; the building's fabric and its spaces; the interaction of the user and the object; movement patterns on the interior and exterior; and public reception of the building over time. The investigation and analysis of these factors leads from one inquiry to another, creating a net of inquiries that produces a narrative.[13] The net has no predefined edges, so the investigation appears limitless. There is no absolute or final word that defines all dimensions of an object's meaning, so the narrative appears open-ended. This open-endedness does not, however, invalidate the meanings of objects—instead, it makes their exploration a lengthy process requiring the careful application of multiple skills, close looking in particular. In the process of writing this book, I increasingly saw this method and the inquiry of language as a metaphor that talked about its subjects with differing intensities and differing depths of investigation. Some projects had more to say than others, so some buildings are treated in more detail and others in less. This unevenness turned out to characterize the flow of ideas that occurred in the geographic region itself. Some architectural explorations moved forward and then stopped; others moved forward and then regressed; still others moved forward and became transformed over time.

Rather than avoid the challenges of contextual formalism, this book reflects its approaches but varies the rhythm and scope of the dissections and analyses of the architecture it discusses. Attempting to produce complete studies of over forty buildings would be not only unwieldy, but contrary to the goal of outlining a direction of study instead of producing a finalized end product. Consequently, the material presented here consists of vignettes and narrative sketches for longer studies that look through the lens of contextual formalism and, it is to be hoped, reflect glimmers of the life that buildings represent.

Within these sketches are assumptions not only about language but also about multiple identities and contradictions. Multiple identities characterized most individuals, regions, and cities throughout the Austro-Hungarian Empire. For example, Hungary looked back to the East, whence the first Hungarians came, as well as toward western Europe, creating a preoccupation with identity.[14] To be a Jew and an Austrian or to live in the Czech lands and be a German established a condition of having at once several diverging religious, cultural, and political identities. The complex issues of identity are reflected in contemporary debates about what to call the area: Central Europe, eastern Central Europe, or Mitteleuropa.[15] The debate has been so contentious that one writer has considered sixteen definitions for *Central Europe* alone, and defining the region continues to have major political significance.[16] Cities in the empire also had multiple identities, as reflected in their many names: for example, the important city on the eastern border and the portal to Russia was L'viv in Ukrainian, Lwów in Polish, Lemberg in German, Lemberik in Yiddish, Lvov in Russian, and Ilyvó in Hungarian. The Slovak city of Bratislava, down the Danube from Vienna, was also called Pressburg in German and Pozsony in Hungarian. (To simplify this complexity, I use the names of cities most familiar to Western readers, but their multilingual variants can be found in the appendix.)

Furthermore, the concept of the empire as a dual monarchy is itself contradictory, as monarchs do not share realms, and such contradictions were all factors in a tense interplay of national and ethnic identity. Though these tensions might appear to have had long histories because they pressed so hard on the twentieth century and still continue to do so, in fact they have recent roots in the nineteenth century, as Eric Hobsbawm has shown in his masterful studies on the rise of nationalism. The intensity of nationalism added additional layers to an already highly complex fabric, making the buildings of the Austro-Hungarian Empire extremely difficult to read.

IN THE following chapters, I explore five languages of architecture found in the Austro-Hungarian Empire. These languages reveal aspects of nationalism, personal identity, politics, cultural expression, modernization, aesthetic fixations, nostalgia, returns to history, and hybridity; moreover, they can be interconnected or even contradict one another.

The *language of history* served to express imperial and national identities, and cultural and civic authority. Paradoxically, this historical language, expressed as a conventional style, sometimes served opposing identities. Czech architects identified neo-Renaissance architecture with the Golden Age of Czech Renaissance and used it as a symbol of national revival; at the same time, ethnically German architects saw it as the language of Austrian imperial identity. At other times, historical language was used solely for aesthetic delight or became emblematic of distinct political positions.

The *language of organicism* drew on analogies to nature, which Austro-Hungarian architects saw as legitimizing their efforts to define a modern vocabulary. Organic forms could refer to nature through analogy or through reference to its order and logic. Among the languages discussed, it is most familiar to readers and requires a somewhat shorter account.

The *language of rationalism* implied that new forms of architecture should have a scientific basis. Modern lives transformed by technology, logic, and order required an architecture that was similarly transformed. Geometric forms used purely and simply were the logical means of expressing rationalism, yet while they lent themselves to abstraction, they paradoxically had roots in ancient forms providing precedents from many cultures, including non-Western, "primitivist," and archaic sources; these sources allowed architects to return to pure origins before the blind following of historic styles corrupted architectural culture.

The *language of myth*, particularly myths of the origins of a nation, became another means for architects and clients to define themselves as modern and culturally different from other groups in the empire. This language turns out to be more complex and diverse than the others, with both cultural and political implications. It requires an extensive discussion to decode its symbols and to see how it operated.

A *language of hybridity* countered the organic, geometric, and rational trends by combining forms into new syntheses using history, the study of folk art and craft, vernacular architecture, classical forms, and innovative technology as a valid basis for a modern architecture. When we look closely, we see prodigious and creative transformations of architectural vocabularies in the works of many architects both before and after World War I.

After these investigations, I conclude by exploring how changes in architectural language resulted from the crises in identity that arose with World War I, the dissolution of the Austro-Hungarian Empire, and the formation of the successor nation-states of the region. Some languages of architecture ended, others continued, and some were subjected to transformation, but their movements were rarely parallel or even. The uneven trajectories reflect the strong ambiguity of identities in the empire that existed at its core. These jagged and contradictory pathways contributed to making this architecture seem so foreign to some contemporaries. When the authors of the first histories of modern architecture wrote their definitive works, the irregular and strange designs of practitioners of the Habsburg Empire had little place in them. The only buildings that could be included were those in line with the images of functionalism, which began to emerge in the early 1920s and would reach its ultimate manifestation as the International Style. Because modernist historiography dominated teaching, practice, and consciousness until the third quarter of the twentieth century—and witnessed a reemergence as a neomodernism in the 1990s that continues to the present—our grasp of the strange architecture of a broad expanse of middle Europe has eluded not only westerners but also the people of the region themselves.

My main point is that different languages can coexist in the same object. They form a series of interconnecting layers that I describe elsewhere as a net, and the nodes of intersection—where the grid lines of the net meet—are particularly interesting. Studying these buildings gives insight not only into the workings of architecture as language, but also into the culture, identity, and complex problems occurring in the empire's aftermath. In the end, we will see that the languages of architecture can say some things well and others less well, or not at all. This book attempts to explore what architecture can and cannot say, to point to the complex problems of past times, and possibly to provide lessons for our own time as well. This study concerns Central Europe, but it is also not only about Central Europe. It concerns something architects have had to reconcile across time and around the globe: the ability of architecture to express ideas—and the limits of that ability, which architects and their public continue to face.

THE LANGUAGE OF HISTORY

1

:: FROM THE outset, Austria and much of what would become the Austro-Hungarian Empire confronted foreign architectural idioms that it either copied or transformed for its own purposes. The process began when the area became a part of the Roman Empire, and the classical tradition provided early, if rudimentary, models for buildings and city forms, including Vindobona, the settlement that would become Vienna. After the fifth century, Germanic tribes occupied the area, and it eventually became a frontier in the empire of Charlemagne, a duchy and, in 1282, the seat of the Habsburg dynasty. Gothic architecture, with origins in France and variations from German states, provided other models, particularly for churches. Later, classical architecture, filtered through the Renaissance but more important through baroque architecture, eventually became the official imperial style.

While architects and their patrons transformed the models of Italian baroque and French Gothic, cultural undercurrents from the East surrounded them. The residue of Celtic invasions, the exoticism of Asia, and the resonance of Islamic architecture spread over centuries of Turkish control of the southeast sector of the region, and pockets of folk and native traditions from the Carpathian Mountains to the Tyrol formed part of the heritage and culture. Furthermore, from the early nineteenth century, the emergence of industry and expanded commerce altered society. Official architecture still relied on a narrow selection of historical styles, but after 1850, architects and critics increasingly asked: was the language of history alive enough to express a variety of emerging meanings and identities? The answers are complex and paradoxical.

While many buildings could represent the paradoxical use of the language of history, Friedrich von Schmidt's *Rathaus* (city hall) in Vienna, Josef Zítek's Czech National Theater in Prague, and Otto Wagner's Rumbach Street Synagogue in Budapest not only provide a range of civic, cultural, and religious buildings, but show depth and complexity. The Rathaus invokes a tension between religion and government, city and empire; the theater appropriates historical idioms of neo-Renaissance architecture to represent national identity; and the synagogue shows Otto Wagner, a pivotal figure, early in his career as he begins to transform history into a modern idiom while engaging the question of defining religious identity with forms borrowed from diverse cultures.

:: WHILE THE Gothic mode had provided models for earlier buildings, particularly religious ones in Austria, the neo-Gothic revival affecting architecture in western Europe throughout the nineteenth century had limited appeal, as preference for

FIGURE 1.1
Friedrich von Schmidt, Rathaus, 1893 historic view, Vienna, 1869–83. Copyright: Dr. E. Mertens & Cie., Berlin.

neoclassical styles and the Baroque remained dominant. So it was unexpected when, in 1869, the City of Vienna used Gothic architecture as a language of history for the design of its new city hall, the Rathaus (fig. 1.1). After the revolution of 1848, the middle class established itself as a powerful political and economic entity whose multiple needs for a comprehensive new bureaucratic government made the old city hall too small. To provide a home for the practical and ceremonial functions of the government of Vienna and all of its councils, departments, and agencies, a new building was needed.

The location of the new Rathaus would be somewhere on the Ringstrasse, the urban thoroughfare created in the 1850s and 1860s on the recently demolished old city walls. Its exact site, however, was determined only after much political and financial struggle, which yielded the decision to build on a roomy site at the former imperial parade ground. Part of the feasibility of this location lay in the fact that it was a public health risk that needed cleaning up anyway: often muddy, it was a hazard to cross and a breeding ground for infestations particular to swamps. Locating the primary object of civic pride on such a site was daunting, but it had potential because of its size and location near the city core, home of Vienna's royal and aristocratic legacies.[1]

Announcement in 1868 of the design competition for the new city hall elicited an international response, with sixty-four entries from France, Germany, Italy, and Austria. In October the following year, the jury selected a scheme coded as *Saxa Loquuntor*, or "the rocks are speaking," and named its German designer, Friedrich von Schmidt (1825–91), the winner. Designed in 1868–69 and constructed between 1872 and 1883, the new Rathaus was finally completed with furnishings in 1888.[2]

Schmidt wanted his rocks to say something specific: his goal was to have civic architecture "speak" on behalf of the citizenry with the propriety of the religion he espoused. Born a Protestant in Frickenhofen, Württemberg, Schmidt had attended trade school in Stuttgart. His apprenticeship as a stonemason included fourteen years of work on the renovation and expansion of Cologne Cathedral under its supervising architects and, more important, its ideological backer, August Reichensperger. He became a member of Reichensperger's Cologne Circle, a group in close allegiance with similar contemporary pro-Gothic associations in England.

In 1858, after converting to Catholicism, Schmidt moved to Milan and became a professor at the Milan Academy. But the next year, because of the outbreak of war between Austria and Sardinia-Piedmont, he moved to Vienna, arriving with the reputation of being one of Germany's most notable practitioners of the neo-Gothic. With the support of Emperor Franz Josef and Count Leo Thun-Hohenstein, the pro-Gothic education minister, he was appointed professor at the Vienna Academy of Fine Arts, the most prestigious school of art and architecture in the empire and its only institution at that time to offer instruction in architectural design.[3]

Schmidt brought to this prestigious post an ideological position supporting neo-Gothic architecture as espoused in Reichensperger's Cologne Circle. While Gothic architecture was traditionally seen as a sacred idiom, the Cologne Circle championed "profane" building in the neo-Gothic style. To its proponents, the neo-Gothic in Cologne was not a style that typified itself as "national," but was, rather, the bearer of a more general "Christian-Germanic" identity.[4] Reichensperger campaigned not only that the neo-Gothic should be the language of German reunification, but also that it be an international phenomenon. Through his writings and his role as a politician, he promoted a pure vision of the neo-Gothic with the fervor of a religious convert.

Schmidt absorbed from Reichensperger the idea not only that Gothic architecture *could* be re-created, but that the processes of medieval production used in earlier buildings *should* be re-created in contemporary practice. Ideally, private donations, a mass mobilization of the populace, and a building lodge, or *Bauhütte*, consisting of artisans instead of a businesslike firm of architects should be responsible for the financing, design, and construction of projects. This group of artisans would travel together, sketch, draw details, and work collectively as a small confraternity. Implicit

THE LANGUAGE OF HISTORY

in the *Bauhütte* tradition of Gothic construction is the idea of the "organic" building, which grows from the smallest detail to a totality in a coherent and natural fashion. The neo-Gothic was a style founded upon this idea of the organic, where in Reichensperger's terms "all aspects develop from one another, everything carries with it a deeply symbolic meaning, and nothing is merely decorative and meaningless."[5] In addition, Schmidt followed Reichensperger's principle that discipline, not invention, should guide the construction of contemporary neo-Gothic buildings. German Gothic architecture circa 1300 was their primary source of emulation.

As an emissary of the German neo-Gothic movement, Schmidt experienced mixed success in Vienna before he had won the Rathaus competition. His greatest early achievement there was replacing the iron spire on St. Stephen's Cathedral (the *Stephansdom*) with a stone version, which rendered the design less "modern" and more neo-Gothic.[6] But his efforts to introduce the neo-Gothic as a model of contemporary architecture in Vienna were largely unappreciated. To members of the Habsburg court and the bourgeoisie, the neo-Gothic was acceptable for religious buildings, but the classical language was thought to enunciate imperial identity and the new economic liberalism of the time. The rare exception was the *Votivkirche* (votive church 1856–79), designed by Heinrich von Ferstel, the only other major Gothic revival building on the Ringstrasse. Ferstel used French Gothic sources for the church, but the tastes of the Austrian capital were patently neo-Renaissance.[7] To the public, medievalism of the neo-Gothic style seemed antimodern. The editorial page of the *Neue Freie Presse* declared in 1869 that, having expelled the spirit of the Middle Ages in the revolution of March 1848, the Viennese should not "allow it to sneak in through the back door" in the guise of Schmidt's Rathaus.[8] In general, the neo-Gothic lacked support from the community of artists, clergy, and civic leaders, and had little of the political significance that had made it a unifying force in Germany. It faced opposition in Vienna, where the variety of buildings on the Ringstrasse built later in the 1870s and 1880s demonstrated that the Austrians were more interested in the political, social, and cultural associations of style than in doctrine or dogma.[9]

The new design of the Rathaus confronted not only a stylistic prejudice, but issues of its own identity. It was the representation of the city government, but the city of Vienna itself was the ultimate imperial representation of the Austro-Hungarian Empire. Could the city's identity emerge independently from that of the monarchy? Was there a difference between urban and imperial identity, and how was this difference conveyed architecturally? These questions were complicated by the use of the Gothic revival in the service of political agendas.[10] The Viennese viewed it as the "national style" of the newly unified Germany and also as a political statement of Bohemian aristocrats who opposed the Renaissance style as a reflection of the imperialism of Metternich and saw the Gothic as a reflection of their own taste and fashion.[11] Furthermore, the Gothic could be seen to represent the medieval era as a time when cities enjoyed a high degree of autonomy: the message would then be one of

FIGURE 1.2
Friedrich von Schmidt, Rathaus, historic view of the main arcade court, Vienna, 1869–83.

distancing from the imperial court, and reflect the fact that there were indeed significant differences between the politics of the Viennese citizenry and the emperor, dating back to 1848. Catholic reform efforts had a strong ally in the Austrian minister of education, Count Leo Thun-Hohenstein, and he supported Schmidt.

Schmidt's allegiance to the neo-Gothic both won and lost him allies in his new situation. Aside form Thun-Hohenstein, he had only one other major supporter, Cardinal Joseph Othmar Rauscher, the prince-archbishop of Vienna. In 1868, Schmidt wrote to his mentor Reichensperger: "I ask you to consider that, apart from His Eminence [Rauscher], I have no powerful patron here and that among the clergy—precisely because of my rigid views about religious art—I have mighty opponents. Furthermore, I do not have a single literary ally to stand by me."[12]

The battle to establish the neo-Gothic as a clear presence in Austria was an uphill one, but Schmidt's winning the new city hall competition was a reversal of his fortunes in that endeavor. Reichensperger and Schmidt communicated during the design process, ensuring that their shared ideology was reflected in the design of the Rathaus. Schmidt's scheme grew outward from an axially symmetrical plan to spaces developed in sectional drawings to elaborate façades, in contrast with other contemporary examples of neo-Gothic profane buildings, which were typically conceived as "exterior architecture."[13] He proposed a multistoried rectangular building containing a series of five interior courtyards symmetrically arranged around an arcade court (*Arkadenhof*) that would recall a cloister (fig. 1.2). The courtyards would provide air and light and an orderly separation of functional and representational aspects of the program. Towers at the corners and a great central bell tower at the main entry marked the front façade along the Ringstrasse.

Schmidt's models for the single-tower belfry of his new Rathaus had sources in the late Gothic Belgian town halls of Antwerp, Bruges, and Brussels. These towers were seen as icons of a free citizenry operating in what Schmidt identified as "the spirit of the new age."[14] High atop the pinnacle of the front tower was the special figure, the *Rathausmann*. Visible from afar, the iron sculpture embodied the citizen whom Schmidt apostrophized: "You, man of bronze and iron, keep an open eye as the true guardian of this city, which you also crown as a landmark. You are armored, and thus serve like citizens who should be armored against any assaults from whatever side they might come."[15] Schmidt also had contemporary city halls to draw upon as models, notably George Gilbert Scott's project for the Hamburg Rathaus (1854). An arcaded block with central clock tower and assembly hall, Reichensperger had cited the building as an example of how medieval architecture could serve modern times.[16]

Schmidt may have won the competition in 1869 in part because of his beautiful and detailed presentation drawings, which convey an idealized vision of the future building (fig. 1.3). The drawings include rendered and polychromed perspectives to describe the desired ambience and to communicate a cohesive and unified Viennese social structure that was strictly bourgeois, with no inflection of the ethnic and economic diversity existing in the city. Published in 1883 in the *Neue Illustrierte Zeitung*, vignettes of the *Volkshalle* (citizens hall) and the arcade court showed citizens strolling in an open vaulted space. Civic life was idealized in these images of discourse among small groups of well-dressed burghers and even their children, leisurely strolling through the great court and engaged in the conversations of city life: politics, culture, and gossip.[17]

Aware of the opposition to a purely German (or even Belgian-inspired) neo-Gothic design, Schmidt incorporated Italianate elements, including idealized Lombardesque paired windows with tympanum and arches in the façades and Lombardesque arcades. This treatment of the exterior appeased the public, who could recognize the distinctions, but he reserved an early Gothic treatment for the interior.[18]

The programmatic needs fulfilled by Schmidt's scheme were diverse. The scheme conveniently kept all major spaces on the same level, with the festival hall, formal staircases, and meeting halls of the city council and representatives taking on primary importance. His appropriate and clever partitioning of space and his plan, which gracefully accommodated all aspects of the program, won over the judges, who were allies and critics alike. His design contained highly ceremonial spaces with great representational value, as well as many smaller offices (including an unemployment office), waiting rooms, and circulation spaces required by the new bureaucracy of the

FIGURE 1.3
Friedrich von Schmidt, Rathaus, arcade court, competition drawing, Vienna, 1869.

civic authority. Of primary relevance in Schmidt's proposition was the separation of social strata and the distinction between ceremony and necessity. The public had access through four exterior arcaded entries on each side of the building. At ground level on the Ringstrasse side, pedestrians would pass under the bell tower and into the double-height *Volkshalle*. Directly in front lay the central court, with an arcade and chapel on the floor above. To the left and right of the main entry, Schmidt envisioned two ceremonial stair halls ascending four stories to a ceiling of ribbed vaults. They further led to a sequence of ceremonial rooms, including the Magistrates Room, the grand *Festsaal* (festival hall), the city council chamber, and several smaller rooms.

Centered between the two wings of city offices was the chapel, the most obvious connection between religion and good city government. But for citizens needing to conduct business, entry was from the rear on Rathausstrasse, which led to the offices of the bureaucracy. The arrangement resembled an office building. Not only were the wood-paneled offices of the mayor and councilmen and the buffet rooms located there, but also the simple offices of surveyors and cartographers, and even the apartment of the building concierge.

Schmidt refined these idealized visions between the time that he won the commission in 1869 and the start of actual construction in 1872, and he remained fully involved in every aspect of the building's construction. Meanwhile, he continued teaching at the Academy of Fine Arts and acted as the main supervisor of stonemasons for the restoration of the tower of St. Stephen's Cathedral. Building the Rathaus provided an actual opportunity to reinstate the medieval practice of the *Bauhütte* with a straightforward devotion to craft and life that was, at the time of construction, being threatened by the advances of the industrial age. Hired masons completed foundation work, and smaller local workshops carried out a very substantial component of cornices, door and window frames, columns, and revetments, but the master stoneworkers on site executed the building's upper floors with load-bearing stone walls. Instead of following the shop drawings, the masons designed the walls on-site under direct communication with the *Bauhütte*.

The Rathaus presented a dichotomy between the historical language on the one hand and its modern functional plan and the latest technology on the other. One of the very first buildings in Vienna wired for electrical lights, its infrastructure incorporated advanced heating and mechanical ventilation systems with a central steam system. The character of Schmidt's neo-Gothic details vanished inside the mansard roof terminations, which finished the building's profile: the roof structure consisted of modern iron trusses and diagonal iron bracing.

Modern political life also required accommodation. Although the burghers of Brussels still assembled to determine city affairs, the Viennese no longer convened to govern the city in a direct democracy, but through a representative one. Modern civic administration was an activity more akin to business than to the performance of pomp and pageantry. The ceremonial rooms of Schmidt's design may have contributed to his winning the competition, but they were not indicative of the actual processes of city government. Internal changes made during construction diminished his intended neo-Gothic spirit and reflected the confrontation between reality and idealized representation. As built, the original three ceremonial rooms of the festival hall along the front façade were combined into a single hall. The Magistrates Room and city council functions were united and shifted to a single council chamber located behind the chapel at the rear of the arcade court (fig. 1.4). This condensing allowed the conversion of two ancillary stair halls to internal courts, providing light and air to a total of seven courts.[19]

FIGURE 1.4
Friedrich von Schmidt, Rathaus, City Council chamber, Vienna, 1869–83.

Responding to the question of how the building should represent Vienna while the city itself was fashioned as the image of imperial identity required not only the communicative power of neo-Gothic details, but also complex programs of sculpture and painting. Austrian artists chosen through competitions similar to the one for the architect provided the painting and sculpture for the Rathaus (including decorative fixtures such as chandeliers) from 1877 to 1883. The iconographic programs for sculpture included allegories of civic life with typical representations of craft and trade, as well as crests of the regions.[20] Sculptures and reliefs on both sides of the main entrance under the tower portrayed allegorical themes of Strength and Justice; over this entrance were figures on horseback: Emperor Francis I as founder of the contemporary city of Vienna, Rudolf von Habsburg on his entrance into Vienna in 1278, and Rudolf IV as founder of the university and builder of St. Stephen's tower. On the rear

FIGURE 1.5
(*Facing*) Friedrich von Schmidt, Rathaus, detail of the loggia lunette in the City Council chamber, Vienna, 1869–83.

and side façades of the tower, allegories of civic life show typical representations of the citizen army, representatives of industry and trade, and figures bearing civic and imperial crests. In the courtyard alcove was an image of Henry II Jasomirgott, the Babenburg duke who transferred his court from Bavaria to Vienna in 1156; and Leopold IV, who conferred to Vienna its oldest known status as a city. Archways in the courtyard arcades contained medallions of famous men of Vienna.

The interiors were also highly elaborated. Between the columns in the festival hall were statues of Vienna's mayors and distinguished figures from the empire.[21] Large allegories in the loggia archways of the city council chambers attempted to balance major representations of the development of Vienna's culture within the history of Austria. The lunettes of the loggia showed the benefits of city expansion and development through allegories of education and training (fig. 1.5). On the right are Rudolf, the Founder, and his brother Albrecht III; their presence recalls placing the cornerstone of St. Stephen's, the founding of the university, and the sociopolitical changes of the 1300s, including the coining of money. On the left are Rudolf I von Habsburg and his son Albrecht I, who are identified with the arrival of civil rights.[22] At the right front are Emperor Friedrich III and Maximilian I to recall years of brotherly discord, siege of the emperor within the castle, bestowal of the city coat of arms, the occupation of Vienna by the Hungarian king Matthias Corvinus, and the descent of the traditional political status of Vienna at the beginning of the 1500s, which finally was embodied in the municipal laws of 1517. On the left front is Empress Maria Theresia and her family and court. And on the left of the main frieze: Emperor Leopold I and Prince Eugene, with representations of their successful wars against the Turks and the ascent of Austria to its position of great power, as well as Emperor Francis I and Archduke Karl. While these images are all about celebrating the Habsburgs, their location in a civic building adds to the layered readings of the building and its multiple obligations.[23]

The urban situation of the Rathaus helped Schmidt intensify its sacral associations as a rebuff to the secularization of contemporary life (fig. 1.6). Cloaked in neo-Gothic garb, the locus of city government occurred at the midpoint between the neoclassical Imperial Parliament building and the Votivkirche. Between the Votivkirche and the Rathaus lay the University of Vienna (1873–74), reminiscent of an Italian palazzo and also designed by the versatile Ferstel. The axial connection between the great tower of the Rathaus and the tower of St. Stephen's Cathedral at the historic center of the city—a symbolic link obvious to Schmidt, who had supervised the reconstruction of St. Stephen's tower—visually reinforced the connection between city and church. Directly in front of the Rathaus was the Hofburg Theater (later the City Theater) designed by Gottfried Semper and Carl Freiherr von Hasenauer (1874–88) in a neo-Renaissance style. The city hall, therefore, confronted its surroundings with its message of opposition to the loss of Catholic religiosity and opposition to neo-Renaissance and neobaroque styles that represented sanctioned tastes.

CHAPTER ONE

FIGURE 1.6
Ringstrasse (Dr. Karl-Lueger-Ring), view north, with the Rathaus on the left, Parliament in the foreground, university at center, *Votivkirche* behind, and City Theater right, Vienna, ca. 1905.

Vienna's Rathaus had no equal as a demonstration of the potential of the neo-Gothic in Central European public architecture. Moreover, it was the most technologically advanced city hall in Europe. Schmidt confronted Austrian style-consciousness, accommodated the programmatic demands of a public institution, and adhered to the lofty ideological precepts of a revived medievalism, and the result was functionally modern but cloaked in a neo-Gothic skin.

The language of the Rathaus had multiple, even contradictory readings: profane, yet layered with sacralizing intentions; medieval in spirit, yet modern in function; ceremonial, yet functional. The building read politically not only as opposition to the "official" neo-Renaissance style of Vienna but also as an unavoidable conflation of religion and civic activity. For those with a knowledge of the history of the Habsburg dynasty and regional history, the vast program of paintings and sculptures told the story of both the city and the empire. The building worked within a complex political matrix of bureaucratic, civic, and imperial interests. Opulent and large in scale, the main façade and spaces in the front of the Rathaus addressed the aristocratic demands of the program, whereas the bureaucratic interests were housed in the remainder of the building, in a far more staid and utilitarian fashion. The Rathaus attempted to embody the ideals and fulfill the needs of the entire city. Its

FIGURE 1.7
Friedrich von Schmidt, Rathaus, contemporary view with Christmas festival in preparation, Vienna.

program points to a diverse set of users that literally spans the strata of the populace, although the strict separation of spaces points to an extreme condition of social striation. At the end of the nineteenth century, people of the empire and Viennese citizens could read it as a combinatory sign of new civic power, imperial fortitude, urban revitalization, and sacred grandiosity. Today, while it houses many functions of city government, it reads as the locus of bureaucracy, a tourist Mecca, and a backdrop for festivals and events of city life (fig. 1.7). A knowledge of the complex history of the city and empire is largely absent among the contemporary users and viewers of the building. Its paintings and sculpture have moved from articulate forms to mute decoration.

THE CZECH National Theater in Prague harnessed the language of history to produce a building that became an outstanding representation of Czech identity in the late nineteenth century and was resistant to criticism even when new languages of national identity replaced its historicist vocabulary. Its language relied on a neo-Renaissance architectural vocabulary that used paintings and sculpture to illustrate the history and aspirations of the Czech people. The theater's ability to successfully communicate its message through architecture rested on three factors: the commission resulted from the efforts of the whole nation, whose public financial contributions came equally from major cities and the smallest villages; the idiom of the Renaissance, even in its neologic form, was equated with the rebirth of the Czech people in the nineteenth century; and paintings and sculpture in the building clearly conveyed the national mythology. The association of Czech nationhood with the theater was in fact so strong that the building was called the Cathedral of National Rebirth.[24]

The neo-Renaissance vocabulary was, however, transnational, so no nation or nation-state could claim it exclusively. How could it then serve as the language of a distinct national identity? For the Czechs, that identity was communicated less by specific architectural forms than by general associations with the Renaissance itself as symbolizing the pinnacle of artistic and cultural achievement and political independence attained under the reign of Emperor Rudolf II.

The building's long and complex history began in 1844 with efforts by intellectuals to establish a Czech national theater, but the cause took a political turn after the revolution of 1848, when intolerance between Czechs and Germans grew. The overall building organization was in the hands of the Association in Prague for Collecting Donations for the National Theater (a windy title cited hereafter as the Association). Upon its election in 1852, the building committee created a program for a National Theater and proceeded to purchase the former site of the Salt Works. Trapezoidal in shape, it was located in the district of Nové Město, at the foot of the Chain Bridge across the river Vltava (fig. 1.8).[25] Actual construction was decades away, and an immediate delay was caused by the Ministry of Interior in Vienna stifling cultural and political activities in Prague.[26] The project gained momentum in 1860 with a change of ministers in Vienna as a broad cultural and political effort arose to give an identity to the re-emerging Czech nation. Patriotic clubs opened as well as an artists' club in 1863, which included all branches of the arts. The music of Bedřich Smetana and Antonín Dvořák added to the enthusiasm for defining a Czech national identity.

This long gestation in the National Theater's history allowed two major political parties, the "Old Czechs" and the "Young Czechs," to use the construction of the theater as a platform for articulating their adversarial positions. The Old Czechs were conservative, and the Young Czechs more liberal, nationalistic, progressive, and appealing to students. Their constant attacks on each other, often published in their respective newspapers, inhibited what both parties wanted most: a united front for the Czechs of Bohemia and Moravia, to enter the government on an equal footing with Hungary and Austria. One of their disputes led to the Old Czechs' proposal to build

FIGURE 1.8
(*Facing*) Josef Zítek, Czech National Theater, exterior, seen from across the Vltava River, Prague, 1868–83.

CHAPTER ONE

a "Temporary Theater" while funds were raised for a larger structure. The effort succeeded over the opposition of the Young Czechs, and designs for a Temporary Theater were commissioned from Ignác Vojtěch Ullmann, a Prague architect, former student of Eduard van der Nüll and August Sicardsburg at the Academy of Fine Arts in Vienna, and first purveyor of Italian Renaissance architecture in Prague. His building opened in 1862 and, as the first Czech Theater, became a fledgling counterpart to the German-language Theater of the Estates, which represented the Bohemian estates. Executed in a neo-Renaissance style, the Temporary Theater provided an aesthetic that theatergoers could anticipate in the future building: white, blue, and yellow covered the walls and boxes, and a painted curtain included the Czech national emblem—a lion—and several of the monuments of national identity: Hradčany (Prague castle), the Old Town Square, Vyšehrad (the High Castle, the home of the first ancient princes of the Přemysl dynasty), Karlštejn castle (built in the fourteenth century as a safe repository for the Crown Jewels of the Holy Roman Empire and royal insignia of Bohemia), and Blaník (the mountain home of the mythical Knights of Blaník). However, the theater, with only nine hundred seats, was too small and uncomfortable, particularly in the summer heat.

The Association made immediate plans to launch a second competition for a permanent structure. It gave no specifics for the building program, save that it incorporate the existing Temporary Theater into any new design. After additional delays, a power shift within the Association allowed the Young Czechs to exert more influence in the selection of the architect. From the contenders who had submitted projects, the Association selected Josef Zítek in 1865 and gave him a provisional contract. Zítek, whom the Young Czechs favored, edged out Ullmann, who was popular among the Old Czechs. Next, the Association launched a widespread appeal for donations. The entire Czech nation responded, and construction began.

Josef Zítek (1832–1909) was born in the poor Prague suburb of Karlín, but benefited from the patronage of a wealthy state lawyer and Czech patriot, Adolf Maria Pinkas.[27] He studied architecture at the Prague Polytechnic from 1848 to 1851, but the curriculum was largely devoted to building sciences and construction and taught exclusively in German, the official language of the empire.[28] Ambitious to receive as complete an education as possible, Zítek went to Vienna in 1851 and simultaneously enrolled at the Polytechnic Institute in Vienna and the Academy of Fine Arts. His teachers, van der Nüll and Sicardsburg, not only taught Zítek, but employed him while they worked on the designs of the Staats-Oper (State Opera) in Vienna. Like most properly educated architects in the mid-nineteenth century, Zítek became conversant in a variety of architectural styles, including neo-Renaissance and neo-Gothic. His schooling concluded, he worked for a year in Vienna and received a scholarship to travel in Italy, where he spent two years making a tour of its great buildings and cities. He then visited the major cities of Europe before returning to Vienna to set up a practice.

The commission for the Czech National Theater brought Zítek back to live in Prague after a thirteen-year absence, during which he had been hired to design a new museum in Weimar. A local whose experience and success were by then international, the thirty-two-year-old architect found instant recognition in Prague for his artistic skills. During his time away, the conflicts between Germans and Czechs had intensified and had come to focus on the matter of language itself. The Czech language had been so suppressed during centuries of Habsburg control that it had fallen into disuse. Revitalizing it became a key goal in the emerging nationalism of the Czech people. A Czech National Theater would play a pivotal role of countering the German national theater and would, of course, be the venue for theatrical events produced in the newly revived Czech language. Cosmopolitan from his life abroad and speaking only German, Zítek tended to see the value of both cultural contributions, but he soon allied himself with the more progressive agenda of the Young Czechs.

Inspiration for the theater's design would come from multiple sources. Christian iconography found in baroque churches throughout the Czech lands was but one influence. Another source of national imagery was the city of Prague itself, with its monuments and topography: the Hradčany castle, the Vyšehrad, and the river Vltava, which provided picturesque settings and a main means of transport for the city.

There was also an extraordinary inspiration for the ideological program of Czech nationalism and the theater itself: the discovery in 1817 of "Manuscripts of the King's Court and the Green Mountain," allegedly written in an old medieval Czech dialect. Named for the site of their discovery in the small Bohemian town of Dvůr Králové (King's Court), the manuscripts consisted of six epic ballads, six songs, and two lyric-epic poems. Generally influenced by the epics from antiquity in which heroes fought tyrants in battles against foreign rule, the poems included "Libušin soud" (Libuše's Judgment), which told the story of Princess Libuše, the mythical founder of Prague. She had ruled with fairness, chosen a simple farmer as her mate (who later became king of the Czechs), and become the symbol of the Czech motherland, in contrast with the concept of a German fatherland.[29] The beauty of the manuscripts created a sensation, and the texts offered up symbols and mythic figures to inspire the Czech people and give its artists programs of imagery that they could claim as distinctly their own. However, doubts concerning the authenticity of the manuscripts had circulated from the mid-nineteenth century, and a professor of Slavic philology seriously challenged their validity in 1886, calling for scientific testing of them. Debates about their authenticity continued to swirl, and they were ultimately revealed as fakes created by someone who wanted to show that the Czech people had a literary history as rich as Germany or any other country. Despite the disappointing revelation, the documents and their themes continued to arouse intense patriotic admiration.

Zítek took up the themes of national identity and confronted the challenges of the site (fig. 1.9). For general strategies he drew on the plans of international theaters, including the State Opera in Vienna, inserting a U-shaped form around a public circulation system that included foyers and salons along the perimeter. But the site along the embankment of the Vltava was trapezoidal and relatively small. To accommodate the complex program, Zítek had to fill the site so much that critics complained he had

FIGURE 1.9
Josef Zítek, Czech National Theater, exterior, Prague, 1868–83.

exceeded its boundaries. The irregularity of the site also required that the geometry of the plan be slightly skewed (fig. 1.10).[30]

Work continued in heaves and pauses, as the advent of the Austro-Prussian War in 1866 temporarily halted construction.[31] During the lull, Zítek received his final contract for the theater in 1867 and set off that fall on a study tour to examine other European theaters, including stops in Munich, Leipzig, Dresden, Weimar, where his Weimar Museum remained under construction, and Zurich, where he met with Gottfried Semper, the widely renowned German architect and theorist.

Meanwhile, plans were made to lay the building cornerstone in May 1868. Instead of a single masonry block, seven stones from legendary locations in the Czech lands comprised the cornerstone. Included was a sacred rock from Mount Říp, a mountain fifty kilometers north of Prague where, according to myth, Great-Father Czech, ancestor of the Czechs, had settled. Each stone was welcomed with a public parade and festivities

34 CHAPTER ONE

as it arrived in the city, building the public's excitement and enthusiasm. The laying of the composite cornerstone became a widely publicized national event celebrated with a procession of flags and streamers in the national colors of red and white, which ultimately sent the message to the broadest reaches of the Czech lands that the National Theater would be a sacred symbol of the Czech nation.[32]

Despite the national enthusiasm over the project, construction was protracted and problematic from the start. Additional funding and the refinement of Zítek's drawings for construction documents were needed. The supply of face stone was often inadequate; German stone from Saxony was resisted as being unpatriotic but had to be used anyway. Water seepage at the foundation required constant pumping. In

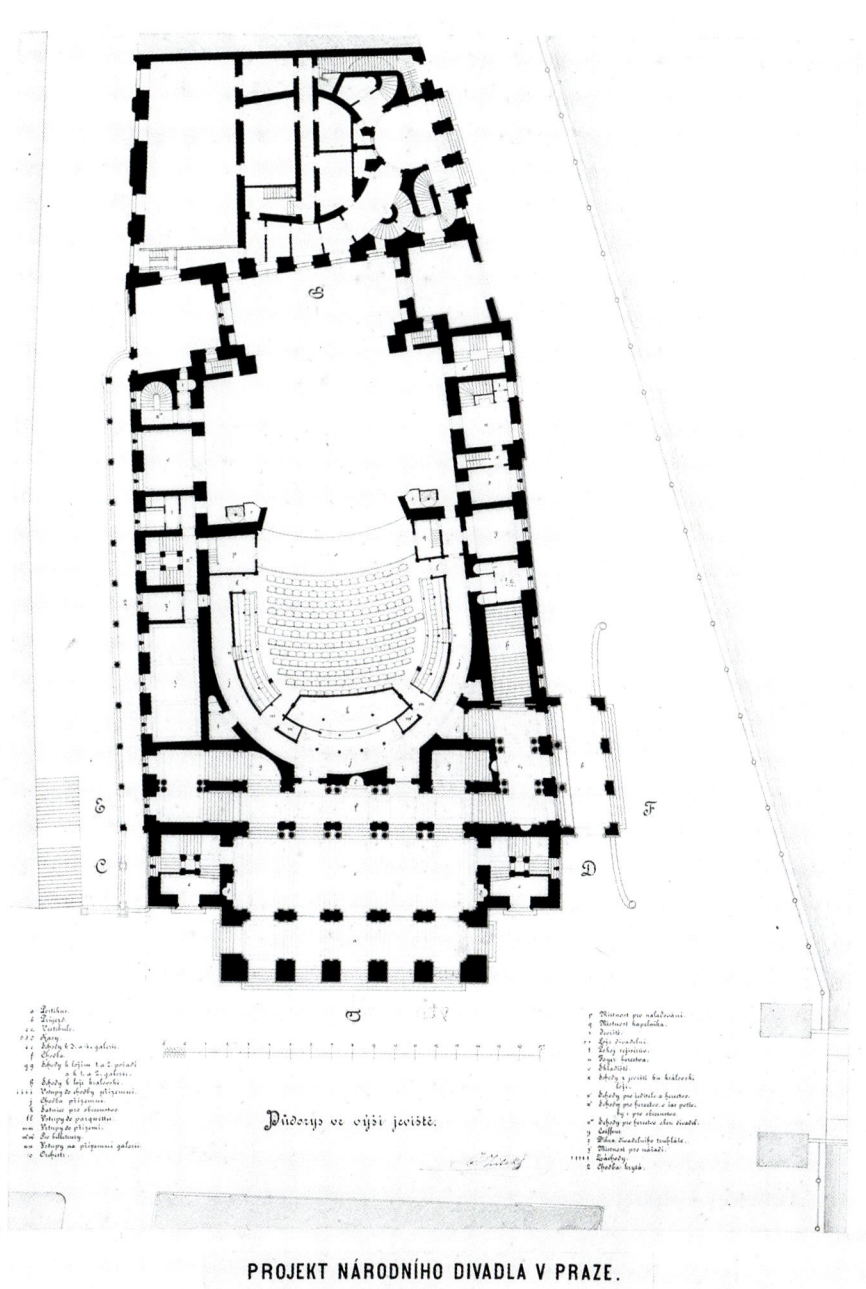

FIGURE 1.10
Josef Zítek, Czech National Theater, main floor plan, Prague, 1868–83.

addition to having his designs criticized, Zítek also came under fire for his teaching. The Prague Polytechnic had split into two schools, one in which German was the language of pedagogy, and another in which Czech was used. Zítek taught at the German Polytechnic, which his critics perceived as a lack of patriotism. Also, the Association had to deal with continuing political squabbles between the Old Czechs and Young Czechs. To compensate for construction cost overruns, the board of the Association made Zítek increase the number of seats in the auditorium in the hopes that increased ticket sales would eventually recoup expenses. Furthermore, several crises hit in 1873: financing slowed in response to the Viennese stock market crash that year, and although the building reached roof level in 1874, the contractor resigned, complaining of problems with funding and material deliveries.

Nonetheless, construction of the theater roof began only two years later. Its curved profile provided the visibility of a landmark from afar, and people liked its aesthetics (fig. 1.11). The local newspaper described its sloping ribs, cornice, and dormers of bronze, against which the green patina of the roof cladding nicely contrasted as a carpet of flowers woven into a background.[33] The high railing consisted of rods and circles with palmettes (the abstract palm motif from antiquity) while molded stars topped the rods. As work progressed bronze poles capped with globes were installed at the corners of the railings to serve as lightning rods, a cautionary move in response to recent theater fires. Gold plating picked out accents. Finally, the cornice balustrade would have statues and vases.[34] The overall visual effect was a colorful animation of the skyline.

Meanwhile, the Association prepared the iconographic program of sculpture and painting that would announce to the world the meaning of the theater. From spring 1871, it opened a series of commissions and competitions and provided an extensive program of exterior sculpture. Articulating the outline and surfaces of the theater, these sculptures are major signs in conveying the meaning of the building: they were the linguistic inflection over the neutral neo-Renaissance skin. The attic above the north main façade contains statues of Apollo and the Muses—Erato, Melpomene, Urania, Thalia, Polyhymnia, and Euterpe; two Winged Victories riding in three-horse chariots (trigas) were installed on their pylons later in 1911.[35] For the west façade facing the river, allegories of Drama and Opera with a supposed Slavic appearance rest upon the curving pediment above the entry behind the Temporary Theater, though discerning any specific features in these classical figures is difficult.[36] At the attic level are allegories of Dance, History, Music and Poetry. Along the sides of the building, statues of mythical heroes from the phony medieval manuscript, the Slavic poet Lumír and the hero Záboj, are placed in identical niches.[37]

The Association also commissioned an extensive program of paintings intended to celebrate Slavic character, history of the Czech nation, and mythology.[38] The competition for painters for the theater, announced in 1877, drew the attention not only of Prague artists but also of Czech painters throughout Europe. Special attention was

FIGURE 1.11
Josef Zítek, Czech National Theater, exterior, attic level, Prague, 1868–83.

paid to two rooms: the foyer, which was exposed to the public and therefore best suited to disseminate the message of the nation's rebirth; and the royal box, which had to remind the current Habsburg ruler of the historical importance of the Czech crown he held. František Ženíšek (1849–1916) and Mikoláš Aleš (1852–1913) received commissions to create paintings for the theater's foyer. The foyer featured a large cycle entitled *Homeland* by Aleš, showing mythic scenes from the imagined Czech past. This was accompanied by several smaller cycles, including Ženíšek's allegories of the *Golden Age of the Arts, Decline of the Arts*, and *Resurrection of the Arts*; significantly, the third painting shows the building of the National Theater itself, providing the historical key for the reading of the paintings that refers to the greatness of the Czech Renaissance Kingdom and its attempted resurrection in the present. In the stairway leading to the Royal Lounge, an allegory of Peace shows heroes of the nation giving a flag of national liberty to a blond female figure while a group dressed in Bohemian

FIGURE 1.12
František Ženíšek, *Resurrection of Art (Vzkříšení Umění)*, foyer painting, Czech National Theater, Prague, 1868–83.

and Moravian costumes represent the pacific people of the Czech nation. An allegory of the Czech Lands contains a female figure holding a symbol of Bohemia and embracing another figure who carries the emblem of Moravia. A young girl represents Silesia, alongside a lion and a peacock, the embodiments of strength and pride. Additional objects symbolize the material and spiritual wealth of the Czech nation.[39] Of particular relevance is František Ženíšek's *Vzkříšení Umění* (*Resurrection of Art*), which shows not only the symbolic figures representing painting and music soaring aloft to a clarion call, but an offering of the model of the National Theater itself as confirmation of artistic rebirth (fig. 1.12).[40]

Czech art critics saw Aleš and Ženíšek as representatives of the national spirit, but that did not apply to another painter, Vojtěch Hynais, who executed most of the program in the Royal Lounge itself. Hynais (1854–1925) was born of Czech parents but lived in Vienna, so his critics considered him much too influenced by Viennese, French, and Italian models. Hynais, however, rose to the challenge of providing national imagery in the Royal Lounge by painting images that confirmed the historical legitimacy of Czech rule over the country. His program included allegories of the Czech Lands—Bohemia, Moravia, and Silesia—and a cycle of historical landscapes, mythic and revered by the Czech people, including Vyšehrad, Hradčany, Mount Říp, and Mount Blaník.[41]

The richness of allegorical imagery was apparent to all those familiar with Czech political and cultural history, but how effective would the language of allegory be for the uninformed? This was the same dilemma confronting viewers of the Vienna Rathaus. What does an image convey to the untutored? An allegorical painting in the foyer entitled *History* raises the issue of the effectiveness of the visual program (fig. 1.13).[42] The uninformed viewer sees a centrally located bearded male figure writing something on a board; next to him sits a lion. In the front are a knight in medieval armor holding a wreath and a kneeling figure with a sinister look, trying to break a bundle of reeds. While the reading of the painting may be one of generic concepts, to the informed the iconographic interpretation is more specific and complex. The central figure is the chronicler of events, a scribe who is the symbol of history. At his feet sits a heraldic lion, the symbol of Bohemia. In the background is an idealized, romantic town of medieval origins. The blue banner with a golden star on the knight's spear identifies the knight figure as the victorious Jaroslav Sternberg, the Czech thirteenth-century nobleman who defeated the Tatars and stopped further invasions into Europe. The figure on the right is a "demon of evil" who unsuccessfully tries to break a bundle of reeds, a symbol of unity associated with the medieval prince Svatopluk (871–894). Svatopluk's rule was the high point of the great Moravian Empire, which at the time comprised not only Moravia, Bohemia, Silesia, and Slovakia, but also parts of Hungary, Lower Austria, and southern Poland; after his death, his sons engaged in a dispute that weakened the country, which was defeated by the neighboring Hungarian dynasty of Arpads between 904 and 907.[43] The appearance of Jaroslav suggests the Bohemian vanquishing of an old nemesis. Showing these figures in a national institution not only glorified the nation's past, but also offered a didactic message to the viewers, teaching them that its greatness can be regained only through its unity.

FIGURE 1.13
Mikoláš Aleš and František Ženíšek, Allegory of History, Czech National Theater, interior of foyer, Prague, 1887–88.

Completion of the pictorial program required several years. Interior decoration was still not finished when the Association and the Congress of Czech Lands (the regional authority) planned a provisional opening of the theater for May 1881, to honor the recent wedding of Austrian crown prince Rudolf to the Belgian princess Stephanie. It was intended as a demonstration of loyalty to Rudolf, who was not only the future emperor, but also heir to the crown of Saint Wenceslas, patron saint of Bohemia. But the event was disappointing: the imperial government would not allow major public welcoming ceremonies as it had in Budapest and Vienna, a slight that showed the inequality of the Czechs in the political sphere; and Princess Stephanie, ill, did not attend. Also, one local newspaper complained that though the National Theater had been built by and for the people of the nation, they were absent from the opening, while generals, privy councilors, and

FIGURE 1.14
(*Facing, top*) Josef Zítek, Czech National Theater, interior, Prague, 1868–83.

FIGURE 1.15
(*Facing, bottom*) Vojtěch Hynais, curtain for the National Theater in Prague, oil on canvas, 1882.

even aristocrats dominated attendance. Other newspapers, while praising the interior of the theater, criticized its auditorium as being drafty and the top galleries as too cramped. Nevertheless, artists and art critics saw the exteriors and interiors as having a transcendent aesthetic success that would be "the pride of Czech art and the ornament of our historical city."[44]

Disaster then struck on August 12, 1881, one month before the planned official opening. The building caught fire from a carelessly handled charcoal brazier on the roof and was entirely destroyed. The national reaction to the catastrophe was to rebuild the theater immediately. In response to pleas from the press, a huge outpouring of donations came from throughout the country, amounting to 600,000 florins, 75 percent of the cost of rebuilding. Yet the fabric of the building was not the only thing ruined; Zítek's reputation as its architect was destroyed as well. He became the focus of criticism for the fire, for design flaws, and even for marrying a "foreigner," his fiancée of ten years who was a wealthy German. Early on, Zítek had hired an assistant, Josef Schulz (1840–1917), a Prague architect who had also studied at the Academy of Fine Arts in Vienna in the early 1860s; their collaboration now continued on a more equal footing. Ultimately, Zítek was so harshly bashed that he resigned as architect in March 1882, and Schulz completed the reconstruction.

Among the items destroyed in the fire was the theater's curtain, which had contained symbolic figures representing Genius along with muses of music and drama, an allegory of the history of Prague, and classical pavilions associated with an enlightened civilization.[45] Hynais was appointed to design a new curtain that would speak not only of the history of the nation, but of the nation's building its own theater as well (figs. 1.14, 1.15). The curtain itself became a national emblem. Taking up the theater's motto, The Nation for Itself, it incorporates cultural, ethnic, and local references to convey its message.[46]

Hynais described his use of a historical allegory of the building of the National Theater itself to convey its significance as a temple for the arts: "In the picture, the main protagonist is Slavia—the embodiment of the nation's suffering—who is pleased by the enthusiastic gifts from the nation. . . . To the left of Slavia is the angel of glory, who encourages this immortal act."[47] The curtain also depicts the theater as it was being rebuilt, with workers, artists, muses, contributors, and the general populace depicted in this major community effort. Flags and banners of Bohemia are intertwined with figures. Genius hovers over the crowd, honoring artists and builders, and presents the flag as an act of national self-identity. This scene of rebuilding implies that the united community continually defines itself in a constant state of becoming like the allegory of Genius itself.

The curtain also registers on national, regional, and local levels. A two-tailed lion, symbol of the Bohemian kingdom, overlooks the scene from the top of the colonnade and acts as the protector of both nation and National Theater.[48] But the identification of the theater with the nation-state was problematic, because the Czech Lands

belonged to Austria. Instead of confirming one unifying symbol, regional shields of Bohemia, Silesia, and Moravia, bound historically under the Czech crown, are present. A common language that was a starting point for the Czech national movement joins them. Smaller figures also have symbolic meaning: for example, a falcon symbolized SOKOL ("falcon" in Czech), a pan-Slavic cooperative for physical and moral fitness and a popular movement that, like the National Theater, united people of all political backgrounds.[49]

After fifteen years of work, struggle, and a major rebuilding, the National Theater finally opened in November 1883 with a presentation of Smetana's opera *Libuše*. Immediate success and appreciation followed, but Zítek recieved little recognition for many years. The core of the theater's supporters had been ordinary citizens, and over the next several months special "Theater Trains" were organized to transport them from rural Bohemia and Moravia.[50] Over time the building took on sacred status for the Czech people.

The success of the theater as a national emblem resulted in the codification of the neo-Renaissance as the language of Czech nationalism, but its use took on new expression among the followers of Zítek and Schulz. One of Zítek's students, Antonín Wiehl, propagated the idea of transforming the international neo-Renaissance style into a Czech Renaissance mode by using domestic motifs. Other architects followed in these efforts: Antonín Balšánek wrote in 1902 that the original Czech Renaissance forms differed from those in Germany, Holland, and France, and that those details could be largely discerned in the gables of buildings, as seen in the houses of Staroměstske Náměsti (Old Town Square) or on the sgraffito façades around Hradčany castle. To this claim he added a warning against the "so called *moderna*" of the Vienna Secession overwhelming Czech architecture.[51]

The Czech National Theater provided a framework of identity nuanced by association. Its neo-Renaissance vocabulary of columns, arches, pilasters—elements that the rising bourgeoisie connected to the emerging capitalism of the Renaissance—gave identity to the class that was mainly responsible for the erection of the building. On the other hand, an iconography forming the equivalent of words that any informed citizen could read suggested national identity. Besides associating the rebirth of the Czech people with a generalized Renaissance vocabulary, individual motifs began to take on the character of signs. This identification of specific motifs coincided with research into what made Czech Renaissance architecture different from French, German, or Austrian Renaissance, and with research into vernacular Czech architecture. The use of the language of history, therefore, turned to an expanded set of signs for its expression and—for the moment—included the representational arts. Their common element was the perception of Czechness.

But the ironies and contradictions that pervade all uses of architecture and art as an analogy to verbal language are apparent here. From the perspective of cultural and political history, the Renaissance provides a frame for an idealized fantasy in which the unity of the arts existed somehow in a harmonious, lost Eden. Such thinking on the part of the Czechs—the romanticism of the past—is ironically a German contribution to Western civilization.[52] From the perspective of ethnographic history, the myths that inspired the paintings and sculpture were more powerful as symbols than any scientifically deduced fact about the origins of the Czechs. Their role in the self-identification of the nation, which saw itself as a leading but oppressed European cultural force, mattered more than historical accuracy.

:: FOR A culture within the larger nation-states of the Austro-Hungarian Empire, connections to history had further complications, particularly when it received much of its definition from religion. In the context of magyarization, Jews in Hungary experienced the pressures of defining multiple identities simultaneously, with inevitable tensions. The trend for progressive and reform Jews, particularly those who assimilated into the cultural mainstream, was to regard themselves as Hungarians first and as Jewish second. For more conservative and orthodox Jews, religious identity superceded national identity. But in both conditions, patriotism did not necessarily conflict with religious belief, and tendencies toward assimilation inevitably varied among individuals. To outsiders, the status of Jews was that of a people apart. A similar condition occurred in Germany, where Jews prided themselves on a Germanness held suspect by their fellow countrymen.

Architecture's role in the creation of religious and national identities was significant but problematic. For Jews, one issue revolved around the image of the synagogue. Solomon's Temple, the sacred site in Jerusalem described in evocative detail in the Pentateuch, served as a flexible precedent for historicizing styles. Johann Bernhard Fischer von Erlach, the preeminent eighteenth-century baroque architect of Austria, included a reconstruction of this temple, inflected with Roman details, in his *Entwurf einer historischen Architektur* (An Outline of Historical Architecture) of 1721, the first compendium of global architecture. But the question of how a synagogue should look remained without a definitive answer. The issue became more urgent from pressures induced by Jews' material prosperity and the threat of assimilation. The question of choosing a stylistic model was acute for the Jews of the Austro-Hungarian Empire, as it was for Jews everywhere, because their religion provided no standard building type for a place of worship. Moreover, Judaism had been shaped by the constant wandering of its people, induced by the Diaspora. Finding the identity of the synagogue and the architectural language of history that could support that identity was, therefore, a critical issue for Jews.[53]

Three divergent trends affected the language of history as it applied to Jewish sacred architecture of the nineteenth century. One direction was for Christian architects to design "orientalist" Jewish places of worship as modern equivalents to the Temple of Solomon. For example, the use of an Egyptian stylistic vocabulary reflected the early nineteenth-century view that the Phoenician architect Hiram built the temple in Jerusalem in this style.[54] A second direction saw Jewish architects, partly in confirmation of their Ashkenazi roots in Germanic Central Europe (including German, Polish, and Hasidic rites), espousing the virtues of a German-Jewish "national" style modeled on Gothic or Romanesque churches. A third direction was the use of Moorish architecture, with its possible reference to the Sephardim of Spain and Portugal and its roots in Islamic architecture of the Middle East and northern Africa. The style recalled the times when Jews had flourished in Moorish Spain (before the Christian reconquest in the late fifteenth century) as well as other areas of the Islamic world while facing persecution in Christian Europe.

A revival of the Moorish style had been used for secular buildings, first in English (and, later, German) garden pavilions around 1800, when whimsicality coincided with decorative freedom. Its use gradually widened into other "fantastical" yet pragmatic buildings, including market halls and train stations. Moorish-style architecture came into vogue at the same time that Gothic architecture was being revived; although they both employed pointed arches (but with differing shapes), they were often seen as opposed to each other. In this context neo-Gothic was viewed in a positive light for its sacred use in church architecture, whereas the Moorish style was regarded as its heathen cousin. Karl Schnaase, the German art historian and a leader in forming the scientific study of art history, denigrated the Moorish style. He believed its horseshoe arch to be ideologically opposed to its pointed Gothic counterpart; he also maintained even more broadly that Islamic architecture was atectonic and inefficient, and therefore lacking architectural integrity. Schnaase also attempted to link the architecture and ideology of Islam and Judaism and denigrate both by citing their shared Semitic roots.[55]

Some writers and architects viewed Moorish architecture differently, seeing Islamic and Gothic architecture as connected. Synagogue designer Max Fleischer believed Gothic was the only style appropriate for sacred architecture and gave it equal value and importance in both Christian and Jewish applications.[56] But generally the Moorish style had negative connotations as "fitting" for Jewish architecture in the service of German/Christian prejudices against Judaism. In the minds of many contemporary theorists, the main reason for the use of the Moorish style for synagogue architecture was the "Arabian heritage" of Judaism. The pairing worked well: in contemporary opinion a "second-class style goes with second-class program," so long as "higher" styles were not involved.[57]

The Moorish style had particular resonance in Austria-Hungary because of the empire's physical location as a bridge between East and West, but also because centuries-long Ottoman occupancy on its lower tier had made unavoidable cultural inroads. Familiarity allowed the style to serve political purposes, as it did when, after assuming administrative control of Bosnia in 1879, the Austro-Hungarian government approved construction of a new town hall in the central market district of Sarajevo. Built in 1896 from the designs of Alexander Wittek and Ciril Iveković, the structure's Moorish style was intended to appeal particularly to Bosnia's Muslim population, despite the fact that Bosnia consisted of Roman Catholics and Orthodox and Sephardic

Jews as well as Muslims; the collective presence in Sarajevo of all these faiths formed the identity of the community.[58] These religious groups worked together in mutual tolerance and also cooperated through a guild system that provided financial and professional collaboration in the daily life of the city. The assertion of the Moorish style for the town hall not only appeared to privilege one group over another, but also reinforced that the Austro-Hungarian government was in control through the politics of divide and conquer.

As a mode for religious buildings, the Moorish style began to dominate synagogue design in the large cities of the Habsburg Empire beginning in the 1850s. Before then, it had provided a "fairy-tale Oriental experience," a general mélange of Islamic decorative strains. Moorish mosques in Spain were unknown and therefore unavailable as precedents; in addition, little was known about specific Islamic sources.[59] This unfamiliarity was changed, however, when Owen Jones published two volumes in the 1840s on the Alhambra.[60] Because it was not bound to tradition like the Gothic, the Moorish style allowed for experimentation with modern materials and technologies, such as iron structure, gas, electricity, hot water, and steam heat. Generally, it was the most reformed and emancipated of synagogue clients who chose the style. As defined by Ines Müller, "the Moorish style was the hope, expressed in stone, that newly-attained civil rights, cultural integration and proud wealth could . . . educate the Christian society on tolerance."[61] Exotic and opulent buildings did not, however, increase tolerance or integrate Jews more deeply into society.

Using models of Islamic architecture for Jewish places of worship appears incongruous. But what mattered to many Jews was an association and perhaps a few details that "spoke" about the East, the origins of the Jews, and thereby acted as an expression of Jewish identity, more than historical reality based on archaeological evidence of early temples. Historical evidence was scant, ancient descriptions were vague, and traditional illustrations were either overwhelming or contradictory.[62] These circumstances introduced complexity into the application of history to synagogue design; the building became a constructed paradox. Its myriad forms mirrored the iconic forms of other religions and reconfigured history in doing so.

The complex uses of historical languages paralleled the complexity within Judaism itself. On the one hand, Orthodox Jews sought to adhere strictly to the laws and practices of tradition. On the other hand, the Conservative movement—begun in 1845 in Frankfurt as a reaction against Reform practices that had roots in the Enlightenment—attempted to keep the basic elements of these traditions but allowed for the modernization of religious practices in ways that were less radical than those promulgated by Reform Judaism.[63] The Conservatives saw their religion as a carrier of cultural and national identity, and despite diverging attitudes, beliefs, and practices, they valued continuity with the past. Even the terminology for the Jewish place of worship had complex nuances. While the terms *temple* and *synagogue* are often used as synonyms, the practice of calling places of worship temples arose from the preferences of Reform Jews in the second half of the nineteenth century. For them, a temple was a building that stood indefinitely for King Solomon's Temple.[64] Their temples were replete with organs, choirs, and pulpits. From the Orthodox perspective, there was only one Temple; it had served all Israelites and was holier than any synagogue. For them, *synagogue* was the term, though of Greek origin, that signified the place of religious assembly for Jews.

In Pest, the increasing Jewish population required more space for worship than its old synagogue provided, so a new one was built on a large site on the broad Dohány Street. Opened in 1859, it was designed to hold three thousand people and is the largest still in use of all of Europe.[65] The twin-towered façade sheltered a mixed congregation of Orthodox and Neologist Jews, as the Conservatives were called in Hungary. Ludwig von Förster, designer of the Moorish-style synagogue on Tempelgasse in Vienna, had won the competition for the building. A gentile, Förster saw church and synagogue architecture as equal in the eyes of God.[66]

Although its proposed details could be seen in the secular Alhambra in Granada and the Alcázar of Toledo, the design's Moorish idiom appealed to the selection committee, who saw it as an "oriental" style that linked the building to the Temple of Solomon. Other architects besides Förster were involved with construction of the building, and when completed, it included tracery that resembled Gothic details. As Carol Krinsky has observed, the Dohány Street Synagogue had multiple readings with diverse historical associations of Gothic architecture, Moorish aesthetics, and Western traditions, as well as "oriental" associations, which emphasized a separate national origin of Jews within the Austro-Hungarian Empire.[67] These Jews were subjects of a Dual Monarchy, but subjects with a national identity that was more "oriental" than European.

Despite the accommodations provided by the large new Dohány Street Synagogue, a group of twenty-four emerged that wanted its own combination of modernity and tradition.[68] For this splinter group, the Dohány Street rituals were too Reform, and the traditionalists, who remained in the old synagogue, too Orthodox. The group represented a faction of Conservatives who, while interested in traditional values, were not as Orthodox as those who had refused to go to the Dohány Street Synagogue, yet they were not as progressive as the majority that supported it. They also represented complex social, religious, and cultural overlays. Recent Orthodox arrivals from northern, northeastern, and western Hungary together with the traditionalists from Óbuda, they were artisans, intellectuals, and merchants who spoke Yiddish, German, and Hungarian.[69] Heterogeneous and polyglot, Hungarians yet traditional Jews, they were also like the rest of the general Hungarian Jewish community in seeking to establish their identity in a society made "tolerant" both by newly instated laws and general social tendencies. To address these complex, even contradictory, factors, they formed their own congregation and realized they needed their own building. The congregation wished to set itself apart from the Reform Jews and the strict Orthodox, and the medium for this distinction would be constructing their own synagogue. The raising of construction funds from the sale of 1,332 seats in a new synagogue and from private sources guaranteed its independence from Neological spiritual influence and financial control.

In October of 1867, the year of the revolution preceding the formalization of the Dual Monarchy, the group's building committee began planning for the construction of a new synagogue on Rumbach Street in Pest, on land purchased earlier in the summer.[70] Steering a middle ground between tradition and reform, the Jews of the Rumbach Street Synagogue would embrace old laws and traditions but also allow some more liberal ideas. Magyarized in custom and language, they would adhere to familiar, traditional ceremonies and local customs, including having two presiding rabbis, each with slightly differing views. The language used at the services was specific: Hungarian, German, and Hebrew would have assigned roles depending on the service and times. The congregation had other programmatic requirements for its new building that reflected its middle-ground position; for example, while there would be no organ housed in the new synagogue, a pulpit and space for a choir would be needed. It also deviated from strict Orthodox practices by specifying a loggia on the west side for a fifty-member choir and by having a pulpit (a copy of the one in the Dohány Street), both of which the Orthodox practice forbade. Furthermore, the traditional screen separating male from female worshippers, required by Orthodox practice, would receive only a symbolic treatment. Strong emphasis in the new synagogue would be placed on an elaborate decorative program encompassing both the main façade and worship space. The congregation was ready to spend what eventually added up to 350,000 florins (almost three times the amount spent on the contemporaneous synagogue in Győr) on 16-karat gold leaf and complex stucco relief panels throughout the building.[71] They wanted to rival the beauty, if not the size, of the Dohány Street Synagogue.

In December, the building committee initiated a private competition with entries submitted by invitation only, and on March 18, 1868, declared Otto Wagner, a young Viennese architect, the winner. The commission for the Rumbach Street Synagogue was one of the first large projects for the twenty-six-year-old Wagner (1841–1918). A huge boost to his career, it was also one of only three works of sacred architecture he would complete.[72] Wagner, who came from a family of wealthy bourgeois bureaucrats, had studied at the Vienna Polytechnic (1857–59) and the Academy of Fine Arts (1861–63), where he absorbed, as Zítek had, the lessons of history and utility and the refined skills of drawing from Sicardsburg and van der Nüll. He was developing an independent practice, the first phase of which had focused on speculative apartment buildings for Vienna's Ringstrasse development.[73] His theorization of modernism was already imminent, as he confronted in his new commission on Rumbach Street the challenges of using the language of history as a base for modern architecture.

Confronting the need to reconcile history with issues of Jewish identity, Wagner had much to consider in terms of sources and precedents, both built and unbuilt, sacred and profane, near and far.[74] Owen Jones's *Plans, Elevations, Sections and Details of the Alhambra* gave exact archaeological information on Moorish sources in Spain: wall-covering details illustrated in his folios became the direct models for Wagner's wall surfaces in the cupola zone. The Viennese journal *Allgemeine Bauzeitung* illustrated the archivolts of the Great Mosque of Cordoba in 1856; Wagner used their details on the side portals of his design.[75] Other inspiration similarly came from Toledo and Cairo.[76] Wagner could also reflect on the great Oranienburger Street temple in Berlin. Designed by Eduard Knoblauch and Friedrich A. Stüler (1859–66), it used Alhambra-inspired ornamental motifs, a double-tower façade, rectangular fields of façade ornament (bounded by ornamental bands), and an iron structural system. Its plan, spatial arrangement, and the character and color of ornament on its interior, which glowed from its gold leaf, were well known.[77] From Vienna, Wagner would have been familiar with Förster's synagogue in Leopoldstadt (1854–58), the Second District where most Viennese Jews lived.[78] It too used an iron structure, elaborate brick patterns, and a centralized façade with towers, cornices, and ornamental bands, as well as terra-cotta ornament using a color scheme of red, blue, and yellow from the Alhambra. Furthermore, Wagner would have seen how the synagogue fit into its urban context as it fell into the rhythm of surrounding buildings by continuing the street façade of these neighboring structures and retaining their scale.[79]

As he contemplated his design Wagner could also call on contemporary Hungarian works of sacred and profane models. In addition to Förster's nearby Dohány Street Synagogue in Pest with its pragmatic programmatic elements in front and its sacred space in the rear, the Györ Synagogue (1867–70), designed by Károly Benkó, provided a contemporary demonstration of the use of an octagonal worship space in a massive, rural synagogue with a dome over a square plan.[80] Profane examples demonstrated to Wagner how local architects combined and transformed historical tradition, freely combining classical elements with medievalizing references found in fortifications; one such case was Haus Unger (1852), where Miklós Ybl used a cornice with decorative crenellation. Wagner would also have seen the dramatic Pest Redout, by Frigyes Feszl (1859–64). Known locally as the Vigadó, it was built for festive occasions and musical entertainment. Combining Islamic tracery with neo-Renaissance arches and recollections of a defensive fortification, the building is an iconographic staging of Hungarian history, with Hungarian kings, notable historical figures, and dancers.

After sifting all this source material and confronting the demands of his building program and its irregularly shaped site, Wagner designed a "double" building, with a rectangular bar along the main street façade containing an administrative wing and apartments, and an octagonal worship space in the rear open yard (fig. 1.16). Though the separation between the two spatial volumes for worship and mundane activities is clear, they relate to each other perpendicularly. Entering through the main doors, a visitor bisects the orthogonal front wing and either proceeds directly into the octagonal sanctuary or follows staircases housed in the front building mass to the upper

FIGURE 1.16
Otto Wagner, Rumbach Street Synagogue, perspective-section rendering, Budapest, 1868–72. From Otto Wagner, *Einige Skizzen Projecte und Ausgeführte Bauwerke* (Sketches, Projects, and Executed Buildings), vol. 1 (October 1889), plate 53.

gallery. The building program directly determines the spatial formation and distinguishes functions, though the façade and entry sequences weave their functions into each other to some extent.

Krinsky suggests that the plan is a rare recall of the polygonal, Islamic Dome of the Rock in Jerusalem, but with its rectangular bays on east and west, a vestibule, and distinct façade treatments, the references are more associational than accurate.[81] Despite the illogic of using an Islamic model, its linkage to grandeur may have been more important than its incongruity for Jewish worship.

In the early part of 1870, Moritz Kallina, an Austrian collaborator and contemporary of Wagner's, became involved in the project as construction administrator. He was also largely responsible for production of the detail and construction documents and would stay in Budapest after the commission, eventually becoming a Hungarian citizen. Actual construction of the synagogue began in May 1870, and the building was consecrated on October 1, 1872. The blessing over the synagogue was given that day, with the lighting of the *ner tamid*, the Eternal Light, taking place, along with the installation of the Tablets of the Law representing the commandments Moses received from God at Mount Sinai. In the following months more pragmatic parts of the

FIGURE 1.17
Otto Wagner, Rumbach Street Synagogue, exterior façade along street, Budapest, 1868–72.

building (apartments and administration spaces in the wing running along the street) were completed, as were technical installations (heating, toilets). On May 1, 1873, the building was declared officially finished, and the full schedule of services began in Hungarian, except during the High Holidays, when the addresses were in German.[82]

Wagner's design provided an animated front façade, which measures approximately 21 meters in length (fig. 1.17). The composition of the façade is tripartite, with each part containing three sets of arched entries with double tiers of arches above. The center bay is higher and terminates at each corner with minaretlike turrets, named Jachin and Boaz, a biblical reference to the columns flanking Solomon's Temple. The open, domed, tripartite, double-height entry vestibule has slender paired columns leading to the sanctuary beyond. The side bays have square windows inserted at mezzanine level. The surface of the front façade is polychromed plaster over brick in which Wagner combined his literal use of Islamic motifs, existing details in other synagogues, with his own transformations of surface motifs.

Behind the façade was a residence for rabbis, a teacher training center, a study house for synagogue employees, and a girls' primary school, with rooms for study of the Talmud and Torah in the tower.[83] This wing of the building, provided with four sets of stairs, offered housing and space for social activities of the congregation that used the attached octagonal worship space. The entire complex extends about 32 meters into its asymmetrical site; the use of the octagon left open corners, permitting light, ventilation, and access to a small internal courtyard.[84]

The interior of the octagon reveals Wagner's response to the traditional values of the congregation and the requirements of Orthodox ritual. He located the *bimah*, the raised rostrum from which the Torah is read, in the center of the synagogue. The *Aron*, the ark which holds the Torah scrolls, is set against the east wall, so the congregation when praying will face east toward Jerusalem. A *dukhan*, or platform, sits in front of the ark to separate secular from sacred space. A most extraordinary Eternal Light, described generically in Exodus 27:20 and Leviticus 24:2, recalls the complex geometries of polyhedra that were basic to Wagner's design process.[85] According to tradition, women and men were separated, but the central plan and the light structural members supporting the roof and balcony open the space to a unified experience, joining the celebrants into one body. The structural system supports zones of decorative programs with surface treatments that show the direct transfer of motifs from Owen Jones onto precise archaeological revivals. However, the innovative use of cast iron and thin masonry walls instead of thick load-bearing ones reflects Wagner's modern approach to wall treatments and adaptation of the latest technology. He was also prolifically inventive in the midst of historical language. Ornament in combination with light structure creates an openness of space associated with modern innovation. The walls become tapestry held up by delicate columns, making the room a sort of tent (figs. 1.18, 1.19A–F).

As Ines Müller sums up this paradox, a Christian from Vienna designed a synagogue for Pest Jews in a Moorish style.[86] For Wagner, the commission was so significant that he listed the design of synagogues on his calling card for the next forty years.[87] Ludwig Hevesi, the leading progressive Viennese art critic of the time, eventually noted that though a youthful work, the building still possessed a spatial impact and impressive material treatment twenty-five years later.[88] Wagner's structure was not inflected with the Hungarian national style that would soon emerge, but demonstrated the transnational language of nineteenth-century synagogue architecture. In competition with the Reform temple on Dohány Street, it provided its members luxury, novelty, scale, and visibility. At the same time, its use of the language of history tells of contradictions inherent in late nineteenth-century Hungarian society.

FIGURE 1.18
Otto Wagner, Rumbach Street Synagogue, interior view into cupola, Budapest, 1868–72.

FIGURE 1.19A–F
(*Facing*) Otto Wagner, Rumbach Street Synagogue, composite views, Budapest, 1868–72.

The incongruity of Islamic models for Jewish worship seems to have mattered little to the designers and clients of numerous synagogues throughout the Austro-Hungarian Empire and Germany. Rather than assist in the assimilation of Jews into Austro-Hungarian culture, the language of history distanced them from it. It represented them, but was not uniquely their own. For non-Jews, the synagogue could be read as a Jewish building whose meaning was communicated by elements that were not Jewish. For Jews, the symbols of the Tablets of the Law, ark, *bimah*, and Eternal Light identified the building as Jewish. Yet these symbols existed embedded in the architectural fabric of Islam, a religion parallel and in competition with their own. Why would Jews settle for an architectural style that was not really theirs? Was their acceptance a function of the fact that, at the very least, the Moorish style gave them an identity, albeit a fictitious one? The Rumbach Street Synagogue presents the difficulty of reconciling these dichotomies. As the worshippers heard the words of history in their synagogue architecture, they used them to make sense of their heritage and define their identity while their fellow citizens saw a familiar but foreign dialect.

THE LANGUAGE OF ORGANICISM

2

THE PRESSURES of industrialization, political and social turbulence, and technological innovation in the nineteenth century challenged the use of history as an effective language to represent national and cultural identity. All forces of modernism, these pressures implied a misfit between contemporary life and the means of expressing it. As part of the search for a viable expression of modernity, architects began to explore other formal languages, and one that held much promise as the nineteenth century closed was an international language of organicism. In architecture, organicism has a long history extending back to antiquity, through the practices of medieval masons, and into the theories of Leon Battista Alberti, but its appeal in the nineteenth century lay in the central concept that nature provided an alternative to the models of history as a modern language of form. Generated as a result of biological processes, the forms of nature appeared pure, unlike the objects and buildings that were tainted by historical misunderstanding and the degradations of industrialization. Producing organic form was, however, more complex than simply imitating nature.

Nature's metaphor led in several directions: Nature could be imitated, but if literally copied, it only continued the traditions of mimesis, and its products rarely matched the real thing. Nature could be transformed, and its transformations could resemble natural objects, but differ from them by being more abstract. The approaches of both mimesis and transformation outlined a *biomorphic organicism* in which empathy between sensuous curvilinear and flowing forms, redolent in the vegetal shapes of flowers and leaves, created an association between natural forms and human emotion. Once again, abstraction was the guiding principle, but verisimilitude was to be avoided. Owen Jones advocated such abstraction—or "conventionalization"—in his *Grammar of Ornament*, which had widespread readership among designers and architects from its publication in London in 1856 up to World War I.

Nature also led in another direction, toward seeing a deeper rational structure that could produce new forms without the literal use of floral and vegetal references. These new forms were organic because they utilized the logic of natural growth. Multiplication and division of simple cells could produce larger ensembles, and the whole process had definable rules. We could call this approach *structural organicism*. In this approach the designer could discern in the patterns of Jones's polychromed plates of Chinese, Celtic, and Moorish ornament a compositional matrix whose subdivisions and permutations derived from similar design methods and procedures used by artists, artisans, and architects across time and cultures. In France, both Eugène-Emanuel Viollet-le-Duc and mid-nineteenth-century theorists at the École des Beaux-Arts in Paris saw the implications of this organicism for a structural rationalism in architecture.[1] At the same time, following these rational procedures could produce not only curved but also abstract nonrepresentational forms often expressed as rectilinear geometric shapes.

Using rectilinear configurations with analogies to structure produced forms that appeared at odds with the curving shapes of biomorphism, yet both shared the same motivations. At the core of these two approaches to the language of organicism was the shared desire to return to a state of purity. By leaping over the corruption of industrialized life, proponents of the organic believed that originary form could provide the basis for a new language to represent modern life. In this sense they attempted a more profound connection to the history of humanity itself than that provided by the history of styles.

These varying underlying motivations gave rise to equally diverse manifestations in architecture. Known as art nouveau in France and Belgium and *Jugendstil* (youth style) in German-speaking lands, it became the initial visual vehicle of the rebellious Secessionist movements that emerged throughout Europe. In France and Belgium, art nouveau found its expression in furniture, objects, and buildings of architects such as Victor Horta and Hector Guimard, who combined biomorphic and structural organicism into a single whole. Their innovative forms in stone, iron, and glass spoke of the "natural" tectonic laws of compression and tension, but they replaced Viollet-le-Duc's stylistic predilection for the Gothic with a preference for sinuous curves that resembled plants and insects. Similar in approach was the work of Antoni Gaudi in Barcelona, except that in his case the tectonics of stone structures were combined with an idiosyncratic language of forms resembling fantastic animals or rock formations. In German Jugendstil, which arose in Munich, artists combined diverse sources such as English Arts and Crafts movements and *Japonisme* (the predilection for Japanese aesthetics in western art). Darmstadt became another center of German Jugendstil around 1900, as seen at its Artists' Colony. The Belgian Henri van de Velde, who was influential in Germany, used sources in contemporary art that he tied to aesthetic and psychological motivations. His abstract curves, alongside his social considerations, also derived from Pre-Raphaelites and exoticism, and were less literally biomorphic.[2]

The influence of the Jugendstil with art nouveau variants soon spread throughout the Austro-Hungarian Empire, creating an "International Style."[3] However, some artists could rely directly on Belgian and French models as an attempt to assert an identity independent from the dictates of Vienna. Using Paris and Brussels as sources for a national identity occurred both in the Czech lands and Hungary, but in Hungary the wedding of organic form and nationalism became so strong that it took on its own character in the pictorial representation of a quasi historicism based on myths of Hungarian origins. In both cases the connection to art nouveau was a means of countering Austrian and German influence.

The early linkages between Austria and German Jugendstil were strong, but before Joseph Maria Olbrich (1867–1908) arrived in Darmstadt in 1899, he had already been active in establishing another movement for new art, the Vienna Secession. Born in Troppau, in the remote Austrian province of Silesia, Olbrich went to Vienna at the age of fourteen to study at the State Trade School (Staatsgewerbeschule) with teachers including Camillo Sitte. Then he returned home for practical experience, and later

FIGURE 2.1
Joseph Maria Olbrich, Secession Building, exterior, Vienna, 1898; contemporary view.

resumed studies at the Vienna Academy of Fine Arts under Karl von Hasenauer, an old-guard architect of the Ringstrasse era.[4] His skills in design and his draftsmanship brought awards and the attention of Otto Wagner, who hired him in 1893. Olbrich worked for Wagner from 1894 to 1898, and they developed the kind of rapport that existed between Frank Lloyd Wright, also born in 1867, and Louis Sullivan: the older architect became not only mentor to the younger protégé but also a surrogate father. But unlike Sullivan, Wagner encouraged his assistants to take on additional work.

In 1897 Olbrich and the architect Josef Hoffmann, along with two young painters, Gustav Klimt and Koloman Moser, founded the Vienna Secession as a revolt against academicism; it was one of many such movements that had originated in German-speaking lands. The Secession severed its ties with the exhausted academic tradition and looked for inspiration in nature and the origins of architecture. These origins found expression in the primary forms of geometry—circle, square, and triangle—and they provided the grammar of a language needed to rejuvenate contemporary art and architecture. Rejuvenation played a central role in the movement, as reflected in the title of its journal, *Ver Sacrum* (Sacred Spring).[5]

Also in 1897, Olbrich received the commission for the Secession Building, whose purpose was to provide a venue for the rebellious artists who had seceded from the salon of the Kunsthalle in Vienna (figs. 2.1, 2.2). For its design Olbrich utilized the language of biomorphic organicism to produce a building that resonated with history, but not historicism. The building was modern in its technology and spatial arrangement and

appeared to capture the enthusiasm and dreams embodied in the vitality of spiritual and artistic rebirth.

A visitor approaching the Secession Building is at once taken with the spherical dome of gilded wrought-iron laurel leaves. Shimmering in the light, the laurel wreath signifies the victory of art and its transcendence for those who both entered and participated. The triumph of art is literally spelled out above the door in a quote from the critic Ludwig Hevesi: "To every time its art, to Art its freedom." The motifs, both geometric squares and recessed grooves, gilt ribbons, abstracted flowers, and the portrait reliefs of the muses of painting, architecture, and sculpture, are consistent with the emerging Secession style. The building's interior, however, was highly functional. Supported by only six columns, its gallery space could be rearranged and the space altered for custom exhibitions, an approach that would have widespread influence. At the same time, the building's cubic massing, its structuring with base, middle, and top cornice, and its abstracted geometric moldings resurrected associations with classicism. But the history to which Olbrich, Wagner, and their circle referred went even further back in time. Egyptian motifs terminate the corners of the front cornice, and the canted walls resemble Egyptian pylons. Lest people not get the message, Koloman Moser designed a mural (now painted over) on the rear façade of the building with undulating Egyptians holding wreaths above their heads flanking the rear pylon portal.[6]

The Secession Building with its gaiety, recollection of the pure sources of art, and call for liberation evinced a scandalized reaction when it opened in 1898. Some called the building's dome the "Golden Cabbage," but the building itself announced with clarity the intentions of the Secessionists. While serpentine curves of Klimt's painting and floral ornament of Olbrich's Secession Building initially dominated the group's aesthetics, an insistence on geometry as a signifier of universal and primary values soon replaced biomorphic organicism. Hoffmann advocated this geometrical approach and gave it expression in the checkerboard patterns created by the Wiener Werkstätte (Viennese Workshops). Hoffmann and Moser, with the financial support of the industrialist Fritz Wärndorfer, founded the workshops in 1903, though their efforts to do so began earlier.[7] The building, however, had launched Olbrich's independent practice and a call to join the collectivist artists' colony in Darmstadt promoted by Ernst Ludwig, Grand Duke of Hesse. Olbrich's career flourished in Germany, but was cut short by his premature death in 1908.

The Czechs reacted by creating their own version of Secession, *Secese* in Czech, which combined the influences of Wagner and French art nouveau while retaining the original intentions to revive the arts through a rejection of historical references.[8] Other regions of the Austro-Hungarian Empire, from Slovenia to Galicia, made their own adaptations of the Jugendstil and Secession movements.[9] Hungary had its own particularly complex overlay, intertwining politics and aesthetics. A conservative mainstream had a stronghold among the professors of the Technical University in Budapest, who were skeptical of expressing national identity through architecture and

FIGURE 2.2
(*Facing*) Joseph Maria Olbrich, Secession Building, entrance, Vienna, 1898.

FIGURE 2.3
Otto Wagner, *Stadtbahn* Bridge "Über die Zeile" (Wienzeile Bridge), Vienna, 1894–98.

kept teaching positions for themselves, but other architects worked in the language of organicism; for example, the work of Emil Vidor shows such an approach filtered through French art nouveau and Jugendstil details.[10] There were also Hungarian Secessionists and emulators of Otto Wagner, like László Vágó and his brother József. In some of their works, the brothers followed the rationalism of Wagner's Postparkasse building, but in others they also used the imbricated square within a square, Hoffmann's emblematic motif.[11] A culminating example was József Vágó's design of the sumptuous Villa Grünwald (1914–16), a *Gesamtkunstwerk* (complete work of art) paralleling Hoffmann's Palais Stoclet in Brussels. Yet the Vágós were polyglots and occasionally also used abstract floral motifs whose origins reflect Hungarian folk crafts.

Though far older than the youth creating the new movements, Otto Wagner not only gave the movement his blessing, but fell under the spell of his young protégés. He had relied heavily on the language of history, but a review of his work reveals how his own language of organicism emerged in Vienna. By 1887, fifteen years after completion of the Rumbach Street Synagogue, he had amassed a considerable reputation as a builder of tenement houses in Vienna, and in 1894 received a professorial chair at the Vienna Academy of Fine Arts. In the same year he was awarded a series of commissions for developing the city railway (*Stadtbahn*), an immense undertaking that included forty-five kilometers of viaducts, bridges, and tunnels as well as thirty-four railway stations. His Wienzeile Bridge (1894–98) that opened to western Vienna provided not only transport but a monumental gateway, combining technical skill with artistic élan (fig. 2.3). But this apparent inclusion of Wagner into the officialdom of urban government did not mean he was either conservative or conventional: in 1899 he joined Gustav Klimt and other young artists after they had founded the Secession. By 1902, Wagner and the younger members of the Secession, along with his own followers, formed a camp that found itself in direct opposition to much of Vienna's public opinion.

WAGNER'S LANGUAGE of organicism emerged first as a manifestation of biomorphic form that resembled, yet differed from the international developments of art nouveau in altering proportions, expressing character of line, and emphasizing symmetry. Relying on the rationalism developed during his work on the *Stadtbahn*, he began to absorb the exciting work of his young colleagues. An early demonstration of how Wagner transformed historical form and iconography into a more biomorphic organicism can be seen in the special station on the city railway that he designed for the imperial court in 1898 (fig. 2.4).[12] Located in suburban Hietzing, at the edge of the Schönbrunn palace complex, the Imperial Court station resembled many of his others, with a pavilion located over the rail lines and access to each side of the tracks. The plan was square with an octagonal waiting room inserted in its center; subsidiary

FIGURE 2.4
Otto Wagner, Imperial Court Pavilion at Hietzing Station, exterior, Vienna, 1894–98.

rooms open off the octagon and to a parterre on the main level of the pavilion. The side opening toward the Schönbrunn palace has a porte-cochère that sheltered arriving imperial carriages.

Wagner's initial watercolor studies for the station suggest multiple readings: the court's favoring of the baroque style can be seen in the dome, which evokes the imperial crown, but Wagner treated the building surface with sinuous organic curves.[13] The forms of nature are also seen in the tall freestanding lamps that flank the pavilion at the street and in the details of grillwork that provide the structure for the porte-cochère with its curves, abstracted garlands, and floral motifs. In the built version, however, Wagner added oval windows, a baroque motif, to the dome's drum to reinforce the association of the station with imperial taste while he continued using floral motifs still connected to international art nouveau. The interior of the waiting room suggests multiple readings too: the octagon with dome is a typological form of ancient use, but its surfaces are covered in sinuous vegetal shapes and flowers.

Wagner focused on every surface detail and metal object at the Imperial Court station. Some forms have archetypal references to primordial forms, as seen in the pylon shapes—recollections of Egypt—found in the bases of the porte-cochère and lamp fixtures. Red flowers over green and gold backgrounds reinforce the shimmering effects of gold leaf. An interior wall featuring a painting of an aerial view of Vienna provides an allusion to space (fig. 2.5). From the wings of a hawk in the picture, a viewer sees the modernized city, with its Danube canal, green city parks along the Ring, the controlled Wienfluss (Vienna River), and the lines of the transport system, which owed their existence to Wagner's designs. At the same time, the building reveals tendencies associated with modernism: abstraction, spatial interplay of solid and void, and the exploitation of technology. Geometric rectangular grooves articulate the surface and recall the channels of classical triglyphs: their abstraction foreshadows Wagner's move toward a language of geometry. Iron structural systems and iron detailing demonstrate the efficient use of metal as a replacement for support systems of wood and stone as well as ornament, and the abstraction of floral forms utilizes the fluid possibilities of wrought iron and cast metal. Even the heating system is carefully worked into interstices of the wall, revealing Wagner's consistent approach of using technology to maximum benefit. Structure remains an end to the means of conveying a message of imperial dignity, efficiency of movement, and celebratory exuberance.

But did Wagner's language of organicism "speak" in a dialect different from that practiced elsewhere? On the one hand, his symmetrical floral designs on glass, carpets, and wall coverings have a crisp, delicate, calligraphic quality associated with *Japonisme* and the bold black and white treatments that were prevalent in international art nouveau. The delicate abstracting of floral forms into sinuous curves is also found in the cast-metal bronze fire-front surround in the waiting room of the

FIGURE 2.5
Otto Wagner, Imperial Court Pavilion at Hietzing Station, interior, Vienna, 1894–98.

Imperial Court station. On the other hand, though there are similarities in Wagner's graphism to works of international figures like Aubrey Beardsley and Charles Rennie Mackintosh, or to art nouveau artists in France or Belgium like Hector Guimard and Victor Horta, Wagner's biomorphic organicism tends more toward symmetry, shows more restraint in its curves, and represents a local iconography of swags, garlands redolent with baroque and imperial connotations, and the abstract geometric shapes of squares and rectangles on surfaces or cut in relief, a treatment that was particularly Viennese.

THE LANGUAGE OF ORGANICISM

THE RENTAL apartment houses that Otto Wagner designed and built as his own client in 1898 on Wienzeile, just below the Ringstrasse and the Academy of Fine Arts, provided an opportunity for further exploration of the language of organicism independent of the constraints of imperial iconography (figs. 2.6, 2.7).[14] The Wienzeile was a new avenue intended to link the center of Vienna, starting at the Ring, with the Schönbrunn Palace in a grand manner resembling Berlin's Unter den Linden.[15] Around 1897, Wagner began considering the design and construction of a complex of three rental buildings in the area, with two of them fronting the avenue and the third one standing on Köstlergasse, the side street.[16] The first building, no. 38 Wienzeile, occupies the prominent site at the corner with the side street and connects to no. 40 Wienzeile, which sits along the avenue nearly in the middle of the block. The third building, Köstlergasse 3, abuts no. 38. The buildings along the busy avenue still have commercial spaces on their first and second floors, with apartments on the remaining floors above. In plan, the retail spaces were two rooms deep, with one side along the street and the other opening into internal courtyards. In the corner building, the entrance is from the side street, but it leads to an oval staircase with an elevator; and at no. 40 Wienzeile, the entrance leads to stairs and an elevator directly through the center of the building. Beyond the communal spaces of these buildings' entryways are apartments efficiently and spatially organized to provide comfort and maximum rent per square meter. Every principal room in all three buildings has access to light and air.

FIGURE 2.6
Otto Wagner, apartment building, Linke Wienzeile 38, exterior, Vienna, 1898–99. From *Moderne Städtebilder: Abth. IV, Neubauten in Wien* (Berlin, 1900), plate 1.

Wagner confronted the issue facing all progressive architects: how to create a façade that would communicate a new message about contemporary life without falling back on the literal images of history? He began with a conventional approach drawn in 1897 that used Renaissance and baroque motifs, but the final design completed in 1898 with floral motifs executed in shiny mosaic tiles represented a complete iconographic rupture with precedent; Olbrich's simultaneous development of a new idiom for the Secession, the energies of his young students, and the burgeoning Vienna Secession assisted his leap forward.[17] Wagner envisioned a gradient of richness and complexity, with no. 40 exhibiting maximum exuberance and no. 38 gilt grandeur, since both were highly visible along the avenue. But as the buildings turned around the corner, Wienzeile 38's side façade was less ornate, and the rental house at Köstlergasse 3 was relatively plain, though it contained Wagner's own apartment.

FIGURE 2.7
Otto Wagner, apartment buildings on Linke Wienzeile 40, *left*, and 38, *center*, Vienna, 1898–99.

In Wagner's Wienzeile projects, the surface becomes the plane of communication, providing a screen for the projection of visual messages. The corner building has bands of bronze railing at the second and third floors. These bands are composed of vertical uprights flanked by flowers or circles rimmed with gold leaf. The surface of the building is dramatically flat. The only articulation of the window surrounds is a bottom cornice molding, with small drums resembling dentils and hemispheres below them. At the top of each window frame is an inset molding of abstracted leaves. The message of the façade starts to become apparent at the edges, where the engaged pylons are surfaced with a multitiered plant whose branches and trunk, as well as its flowers, are gilded. A nine-staged tree emerges from a planter to recall the Tree of Life. With origins in ancient Mesopotamia, the vegetal form symbolizes birth, growth, and fruition, and its presence here is a deliberate evocation of the life force. At the upper range of the top floors are nine gilt medallions, each of which contains a profile of a woman with hair treated as abstract striations, and each representing an aspect of human character and aspiration. Designed by Koloman Moser, the reliefs were named (from left to right) *Wissen* (Knowledge), *Frohsinn* (Cheerfulness), *Denken* (Thought), *Würde* (Dignity), *Ernst* (Seriousness), *Wahrheitsliebe* (Love of Truth), *Bescheidenheit* (Modesty), *Überzeugung* (Conviction), and *Kraft* (Power).[18] Behind these lunettes are bands extending from one window to another, and above them are pairs of palm fronds moving left and right. Beneath this ensemble a cascade of garlands

THE LANGUAGE OF ORGANICISM

FIGURE 2.8
Otto Wagner, apartment buildings on Linke Wienzeile 40, *left*, and 38, detail of the façades, Vienna, 1898–99.

FIGURE 2.9
(*Facing, top*) Otto Wagner, Majolikahaus (Linke Wienzeile 40), exterior, Vienna, 1898–99.

FIGURE 2.10
(*Facing, bottom*) Otto Wagner, Majolikahaus (Linke Wienzeile 40), detail of the cornice, Vienna, 1898–99.

composed of alternating gilt-edged disks, pairs of leaves, and pairs of small pods also refers to archaic plant forms. On the one hand, the sheer flatness of the façade reveals its straightforward purpose as the functional covering of a building and speaks of an incipient modernism; on the other hand, the language of plant forms and their organic references and associations with antiquity, along with the timeless associations of rebirth and fertility, proclaim the hopes and dreams of the Sacred Spring that appeared to emerge in the late 1890s in Vienna.

To announce the appearance of the new language and to make the message of artistic liberation even more literal, Wagner provided at the top of each curving corner a bust of a female figure. Designed by sculptor Othmar Schimkowitz, each figure has her open hands to her face and her mouth wide open, as if to announce the new language of architecture Wagner and his young colleagues were initiating.[19]

Wienzeile 40 connects to no. 38 through a transitional device consisting of a recessed strip of balconies (fig. 2.8). However, unlike the façade of no. 38, which uses symbolic figures to connote human qualities, the façade at Wienzeile 40 uses curvilinear and organic forms to announce nature as its theme. Composed in the modern hardy material of glazed ceramic tiles that give the building its nickname, Majolikahaus, the surface composition emanates from the central radiation of tendrils, curves, garlands, and abstracted plant forms (fig. 2.9). The façade glows with vibrant red, green, beige, and turquoise hues. At the balcony levels, shimmering plants on stands undulate between the windows. At the top floor, this floral field of curving lines interconnects with more leaf forms that surround green glazed lion heads. The lion, nearly a personal motif for Wagner and filled with associations of strength and courage, recurs later in other of his works. The cornice of the Majolikahaus exploits the forms of nature with rosettes and leaves, but also recalls the lozenges of classical moldings (fig. 2.10).

The language of organicism articulated on the Majolikahaus façade has stimulated different interpretations. Some writers see it as a textile, described in taxonometric terms by Gottfried Semper, or as a large carpet with holes cut into it for windows.[20] Others regard it following Semper's description of glazed ceramics of ancient Assyrians.[21] In any case, its organic antecedents are clear, and Wagner's motivations were not purely aesthetic, but aimed at a specific kind of liberation of the mind and spirit. His treatment of the façade also foreshadowed the tendency for surface ornament to become increasingly flat and two dimensional, presaging the evolution toward a structural organicism.

The interiors of both of Wagner's Wienzeile buildings continue the multiple message of abstraction, modern efficiency, and the life force contained within the references to primordial nature and its curvilinear floral forms. At the entry of no. 38 the striations on the floor, the grooves cut into the ceiling, and the lyre-like cartouches integrated with light fixtures recall classical traditions, yet they are abstracted to their essential qualities. Passing through the entryway, a visitor then sees the curvilinear shapes of the elevator (fig. 2.11) that can be readily identified with international art nouveau. The undulating forms organized around a central axis provide both the grill for the elevator entry and the motifs that define the stair railings of the build-

FIGURE 2.11
Otto Wagner, Apartment house at Linke Wienzeile 38, elevator and stairwell, Vienna, 1898–99.

FIGURE 2.12
Otto Wagner, Majolikahaus (Linke Wienzeile 40), elevator and stairwell, detail, Vienna, 1898–99.

ing. At the Majolikahaus (fig. 2.12), Wagner used a similar treatment for the entryway, though with a different color palette of light green with accents of red and dark green. These motifs of sloping leaves also form the surrounds of the light fixtures, and the wall treatments with their recessed grooves are analogous to those on the interior at no. 40. In both buildings, elevators received sumptuous elaboration. At Köstlergasse 3, though its façade was restrained, Wagner's own apartment had not only every surface covered with the organic forms, but also had floral motifs on rugs, tablecloths, bed linens, and wall surfaces as well as an ultramodern, all-glass bathtub and rectilinear glass cases with inlaid knobs of mother-of-pearl or ivory.[22]

:: THE LANGUAGE characteristic of biomorphic organicism spread into the centers of the Austro-Hungarian Empire. Friedrich Ohmann (1858–1927) worked in the idiom, and designed its first exemplar in Prague, the Café Corso (1897–98). Ohmann already had extensive experience designing a series of impressive neo-Renaissance buildings in Prague and was introducing the latest innovations from Vienna as he interpreted them. Born in L'viv on the edge of the empire, he had studied at the Polytechnic Institute in Vienna and at the Academy of Fine Arts. When his studies concluded, he taught in Vienna at the State Trade School and in 1889 received an appointment at the Prague School of Applied Arts. After almost ten years in Prague, Ohmann designed, with Bedřich Bendlmayer and Alois Drayak, the Hotel Central on Hybernska Street in the Nové Město section of Prague (1897–1901; figs. 2.13, 2.14). Here again the façade is the plane of action on which the language of organicism

FIGURE 2.13
Friedrich Ohmann, Hotel Central, exterior, Prague, 1898–1901.

plays out. The central bay windows of the building above the entry protrude and act as the visual center point from which plants symmetrically emerge along the building's surface. Bands with flowers horizontally wrap the first and top floors. The arched main entry has plants emanating from pots that flank the opening. Above the first-floor balcony, a face emerges from what appears to be a lyre. Light fixtures have curved mounts on floral foliated bases, and figural silhouettes in gold leaf on the top piers of the building catch the light. While the panoply of flowers, plants, and curvilinear shapes announces the building as organic, the subdivisions and partitioning of the façade remain conventionally neoclassical. Ohmann's organicism here lies only on the surface. The only apparent inflection of technological innovation is the cornice of translucent glass with metal struts that projects over the top floor and beneath the attic.

FIGURE 2.14
Friedrich Ohmann, Hotel Central, detail, Prague, 1898–1901.

Ohmann's subsequent career showed that an architect could pursue two languages at once: one of organicism and the other of history. In 1899 he was called back to Vienna to oversee construction of a new wing at the baroque Hofburg Palace, and though he resigned from the project eight years later, he designed numerous buildings in Vienna and other parts of the empire. Sometimes he used a neo-baroque idiom, representing the language of history; at others he relied on the language of organicism, as seen in his designs for the Vienna River Regulation project (1903–9), which controlled the overflowing Wienfluss. The latter designs differed from Viennese organicism by relying more on the formal and floral devices of art nouveau. In 1904, Ohmann became a professor at the Vienna Academy of Fine Arts, joining Otto Wagner, where both taught master classes. Ohmann found little conflict with modernity as represented by Jugendstil and the use of history; he also produced works in an Austrian vernacular.[23]

The preoccupation with organicism, reflected in the design of surfaces as well as in the use of figures (especially winged ones with symbolic content), flowers, and geometric forms, is also seen at the Angel Pharmacy in Vienna, designed by Oskar Laske (1901/1902) and built in 1907 (fig. 2.15).[24] For the façade of this small apartment building with a store at the ground level, Laske (1874–1951) drew two angels with a snake of the Greek god of medicine, Aesculapius, creeping up their arms to signify the purpose of the store as a dispensary. In Vienna's Fifth District, Laske also designed and built the Flora Hof (1901–2), an apartment block that used curvilinear forms of the Secession on its surfaces as well as abstracted wreaths along the cornice top.[25]

A final variation on organicism is exemplified by the apartment building and medical practice in Vienna that Otto Schönthal, a student of Wagner's, designed (1901–2)

FIGURE 2.15
Oskar Laske, Angel Pharmacy, exterior, Vienna, 1907.

FIGURE 2.16
Otto Schönthal, Villa Vojcsik, façade, Vienna, 1901–2.

for Ladislaus Vojcsik (fig. 2.16). Wagner recommend his twenty-two-year-old protégé for the commission to provide a residence and office for Vojcsik, his private physician and tarot partner. The motifs of the front entry portal include swags in Wagner's own manner, a triangular pediment above the entry gates, and a circular arch form that penetrates into the entry. A bulbous wrought iron balcony swells above the entry complex. Thin and spare, using the flexibility and strength of iron to its fullest capacity, the balcony nevertheless recalls the swelling forms of baroque architecture. In this instance Schönthal produced a building that is more three-dimensional than the two-dimensional façade treatments of the Hotel Central or the Angel Pharmacy. Its façade is also more restrained, and as Iain Boyd Whyte has pointed out, avoids a random application of Secessionist motifs while emphasizing the wall, roof, and window and door openings.[26]

THE LANGUAGE OF ORGANICISM

THE MOST complex and sophisticated transformation of the language of organicism into three-dimensional form remains Wagner's St. Leopold's Church at Steinhof in Vienna.[27] It also marks the transition from Wagner's language of biomorphic organicism to a structural organicism that uses natural forms but relies on the concept of organic organization. In this context, the total organism, relying on the integration of structure, surface, iconography, symbolism, and efficacy of the building, defined its organic presence. Its rational organicism was reflected in the building's imaginative synthesis of form and meaning, as well as in its character as a total work of art involving sculpture, stained glass, and murals of other artists, the use of historical narrative in symbolic representations, and increasing abstraction.

Wagner's involvement with the creation of what authorities saw as the "most modern" asylum in the Austro-Hungarian Empire began in 1902, when he designed a site plan for the "State Sanatorium and Home for the Mentally and Neurologically Ill at Steinhof" on the Baumgartner Höhe, a hill in the peripheral Fourteenth District of the city. Curves and floral aesthetics so dominant in his Wienzeile apartment buildings were still present in paths of the circulation.[28] Three years later, in June 1905, Wagner won the competition to design the focal center of the complex, a church at the summit of the hill (fig. 2.17). Fundamental to Wagner's conception of a sanatorium chapel for the mentally ill was a space of inspiration and lightness. Light itself was a theme, with its vital and salubrious effects on life and health. As a critic later noted, "Whoever believes that the mystical religious impulse within us is fostered in the semi-darkness of badly ventilated damp cold church rooms will find this notion brilliantly refuted by Wagner."[29]

The building is composed of primary shapes—a cube for the sanctuary, a cylinder for the drum, and a hemisphere for the crowning dome.[30] The regular shape of the cube was extended in plan into a Latin cross with a shortened extension behind the high altar. The entry is on line with the axis between the sanatorium buildings lining the hill. Seeing the front façade from below, but arriving at it sideways, a visitor encounters four columns mounted with angels and three portals. The side doors provided separate entries for men and women, while the center door was reserved for festive occasions. The five-centimeter-thick marble slabs on the façade appear to be attached by a series of aluminum rivets. Above the portal is a semicircular thermal window of stained glass designed by Koloman Moser.[31] Beneath the cornice, a series of wreaths, motifs of curvilinear, biomorphic organicism, alternate with abstracted crosses and squares. Above it, two towers, each composed of cubes superimposed one on top of the other, are bases for the thrones of the patron saints of Lower Austria. On the left, Saint Leopold holds in his left hand the model of the monastic church he founded in Heiligenkreuz, and in his right hand a staff.[32] Saint Severinus on the right holds a shepherd's crook in his left hand, a cross in his right. Behind the saints is the semicircular dome, whose ribbing, divided horizontally and vertically into layers of small squares, has rows of swags at its base along the drum. At its top is a lantern featuring wreaths, striations, and a cross.

FIGURE 2.17
Otto Wagner, St. Leopold's Church at Steinhof, exterior, Vienna, 1905–7.

Passing through the entry foyer, a visitor enters a vast space, whose proportion of width to height is 1:1. Light fills the white and gold void (fig. 2.18). The crystalline quality of both the massing and the space combine to communicate the purpose of the building, connecting its visitors with divine transcendence. The side apses contain stained glass designed by Koloman Moser, showing on the left *The Corporeal Works of Mercy* and on the right, *The Spiritual Works of Mercy*.[33] The central space was reserved for the ill and their caretakers, while employees and their dependents attended services in the gallery above the entry. Four clusters of electric lights with spherical bulbs descend from the ceiling. The floor tiles include patterns of leaves, which would have been curvilinear in Wagner's organic mode, but now are treated as abstracted, geometric rhomboids. The ceiling and soaring vaults are laid out as a taut skin behind

FIGURE 2.18
Otto Wagner, St. Leopold's Church at Steinhof, interior, Vienna, 1905–7.

a gilt grid of rectangles, with cells fastened to each other by pairs of gilt rectangles. Wagner used a double-dome system, one for the exterior to project its profile, the other, lower, for the space above the parishioners. But he reinforced the ethereal quality of the interior ceiling by inserting stained glass in the upper regions of the central vault space and along the barrel vaults, simulating the experience of perceiving the sky directly beyond.

Straight ahead are two side altars, a pulpit, and the glistening high altar with its baldachin. The use of mosaics and the extensive gilding on the pulpit and the front altar bring to mind Byzantine architecture in its most luminous examples, not only in the decoration but also in the spatial concept of a cube topped by a dome on a drum (fig. 2.19). A crucifix sits at the center of the high altar on a marble pedestal. Beneath are bronze doors with abstracted, geometricized flowers on the cabinet, which holds

CHAPTER TWO

FIGURE 2.19
Otto Wagner, St. Leopold's Church at Steinhof, detail of the altar, Vienna, 1905–7.

the utensils of the Blessed Sacrament and the monstrance designed by Wagner himself.[34] At the side of the altar are wreaths of victory. Behind the altar, Wagner added, as a backdrop, a mosaic consisting of imbricated squares, circles and squares, and Mycenaean wave motifs.

A comparison of Wagner's design drawings with the executed building reveals his movement from the vegetal curves of organicism to an increasing emphasis on abstract geometry, from the biomorphic to a language of rational organicism. In the studies his exterior façade includes the curves associated with biomorphic organicism; as built, rectilinear shapes dominate.[35] The baldachin, illuminated from within by electric light and featuring shimmering cherubim along its edges, corresponds to Wagner's earlier renderings of it, but borders of the altar base had been changed from circles with pendants, reminiscent of biomorphic treatments, to squares (fig. 2.20).[36]

THE LANGUAGE OF ORGANICISM

Moser's design for a glass mosaic mural behind the altar was not executed, but his initial proposal shows curving vines and grapes as the central motif of the design's bottom range.[37] After a provisional installation, a mural designed by Remigius Geyling, completed in 1913, has figures that have been changed from female to male. The mural's borders have become fully geometric fret keys, while the sun above the head of Christ radiates outward in lines rather than in a concentric pattern, as intended earlier by Moser—similar to the Klimtian quality of Moser's frontal figures, who have sinewy, serpentine gilt forms at their sides.[38]

The images of the exterior and interior of St. Leopold's Church at Steinhof are part of the intense iconography that creates the narrative of the church: angels at the entry, saints atop piers, swags and garlands, the huge stained-glass windows in the side niches showing fourteen saints and their attributes—all contribute to the synthesis that makes Steinhof a pinnacle of Gesamtkunstwerk, which required the collective efforts of seven artists and twenty artisans and firms.[39] The narrative, so critical for the Czech National Theater and even the Rathaus in Vienna, intermixes with the transformed language of Wagner's surfaces as they move from the curvilinear to the geometric.

While Wagner transformed his language of organicism, he still defined the modern through the dual characteristics of function and program. He seriously considered the inmates' physical condition and mental wellbeing by emphasizing cleanliness and hygiene. Designed for a total of eight hundred celebrants, the church contains seating for four hundred in short pews to allow for the assistance of patients who might be stricken with seizures; their care was supported by the provision of an emergency room in the church. Marble basins for holy water with dispensers of gilt metal replaced traditional open fonts to provide better sanitation. The floor, sloping to the altar, and a special treatment of corners made the central space easier to clean and limited the accumulation of dust. The building was also modern in practical and technical terms. Heating and ventilating were integrated into the three-meter-thick piers, which provided efficiency and cost savings. The electric light systems also were integrated into the fabric of the building, and an extensive use of iron in the light trusswork of the dome provided the double shell.

Despite its accomplishments, when the building opened in October 1907, some contemporary critics reacted negatively, even viciously, claiming that instead of a house of God, it resembled a "tomb of an Indian maharaja." One anonymous pamphleteer attacked Wagner as a traitor and corruptor of youth, who frequented Jews and freemasons. Others attacked the church as an example of "Assyrian Babylonian idiot style" and *"l'art juif."* [40] To the aristocracy, Wagner and the Secessionists were evil revolutionaries.

Neither evil nor corrupt, the Steinhof church marked the move from the organic in the biomorphic and natural sense to a structural organicism that would soon give way to an increasing abstraction, defining the last phase of Wagner's work and coinciding

FIGURE 2.20
Otto Wagner, St. Leopold's Church at Steinhof, baldachin, Vienna, 1905–7.

with a similar shift in the work of Josef Hoffmann and other members of the Vienna Secession. Some may see the change from the biomorphic organicism as a natural maturation.[41] Yet such shifts are complex and involve the interplay of taste, fashion, and even scientific developments. Suddenly, however, the preoccupation with biomorphic organicism generally disappeared in favor of an interest in crystalline form. The crystal and the pure geometric shapes of squares and circles became the correlative of a new language of rationalism.

3

CRYSTALS YIELDED to microscopy; iron and steel, to material testing and metallurgy; complex geometry, to mathematics; and everything solid, to X rays—all signs of the evolution of science and technology at the heart of modern life. Science and technology were in turn at the core of the broad force of rationalism that provided one pole of modernity and has its own history in philosophical positions on ethics, epistemology, metaphysics, and religion. Rationalism's central premise is reason as the main source and criterion of knowledge. By implication, reality has a logical structure, with truths and principles that the intellect can perceive directly. Reason not only refutes the idea that experience can test abstract knowledge, but also is superior to experience achieved through sensory perception. As such, rationalism is the enemy of emotion, esoteric knowledge, intuition, mystical experience, and the unconscious.[1]

Architecture has its own correlative to rationalism, which takes the form of a language. The formulation of the theoretical basis of that language began as early as the mid-eighteenth century and increased in momentum throughout the nineteenth. Its aesthetic would express logic, technology, principle, and truth. From the perspective of reformers, particularly followers of the Arts and Crafts movement, expressing the "truth" of materials was a rational pursuit in which form, function, and intrinsic properties made a harmonious whole. Objects in wood should express the qualities of wood; iron and steel had their logical expressions too. Not only was this pursuit rational, but it had moral overtones and declared itself to be superior to artifice. Just as nature had provided a model of organicism, it now provided a rational basis for architectural form as abstraction increasingly gained ground over mimesis and verisimilitude. Giving primacy to geometric forms facilitated the trend toward abstraction and ultimately produced a language of rationalism that differed from organicism both in appearance and in its emphasis on logic, science, and technology over association, emotion, and feeling. The circle, square, and triangle, the cube, sphere, and pyramid, could exist exclusively as visual stimuli void of meaning. This muteness facilitates abstraction. But while geometric shapes lent themselves to abstraction, practitioners and theorists could also see them as products of efficient industry, or as tectonic references to the structure of buildings or objects. They were also the primary forms of ancient art and architecture, providing precedents from many cultures, including non-Western, primitivist, and archaic sources. This created a split between architects who saw their rational pursuits based exclusively in a logic that purported to resemble science and those who saw rationalism in a return to pure origins of forms before historic styles had corrupted them. By going to origins they were going to the root sources of language.

The multiplicity of meanings attached to the language of rationalism resonated deeply in the Austro-Hungarian Empire, paralleling the existence of multiethnic populations and their competing languages. One distinguishing feature that separated them from their western European counterparts was the tendency for these multiple expressions

FIGURE 3.1
(*Facing, top*) Max Fabiani, Portois & Fix Store and Apartments, exterior, Vienna, 1898.

FIGURE 3.2
(*Facing, bottom*) Max Fabiani, Portois & Fix Store and Apartments, detail of the façade, Vienna, 1898.

of language to exist simultaneously and to move forward or backward, abnegating any sense of linear and progressive development.

Such jumpy movements can be seen in the work and career of architect Max Fabiani (1865–1962). Born in the Karst region of Istria, he inherited a cultural dualism connecting the Italian edge of the empire, which centered in Gorizia and Trieste, with the overlaying identity of Austrian citizenship. Studying in Vienna, he graduated from the Polytechnic Institute in 1892 and from 1894 to 1898 became a key figure in Otto Wagner's practice, collaborating with him and running the office.[2] Though highly experienced in construction, he was also appointed professor of art history at the Polytechnic. In 1898 his imperial pavilion at the jubilee exposition for Emperor Franz Josef revealed his familiarity with the language of organicism. However, in the following year he designed a building for the Portois & Fix furniture company that reflected the immediate lessons of Wagner's Majolikahaus and opened an immediate dialogue about the language of the surface of modern buildings (fig. 3.1).

The client, Herr Fix, required a typical Viennese building, with two floors of commercial space and apartments above.[3] Fabiani provided a plan beyond the ordinary: on the ground floor, showrooms with double-height spaces; at the rear, an interior open courtyard and furniture fabrication workshop (partially constructed of reinforced concrete); in the center, access to the apartments above through a separate entry; and the most modern façade in Vienna.

The façade makes a stunning statement of innovation with modern materials and new technology. Red-brown granite clads the lower levels, a shimmering array of light- and dark-green iridescent Zsolnay ceramic tiles covers the upper surface, and brown tiles molded in curves accent window surrounds and provide a drip course.[4] The whole treatment is antitectonic and nondecorative, as seen in the curving of the façade surface at its edges, as if the façade itself were a shallow tray with a curved lip. In addition to scintillation, the choice of glazed tiles reinforced the contemporary concerns for durability and cleanliness. Soot and other air pollutants wash off in the rain, so that the ceramics are in effect self-cleaning. Instead of a conventional cornice, a copper-clad, quarter-barrel vault dissolves the solidity of the building and leads to a flat roof, a contemporary technical innovation.

The surface presents visuality for its own sake, a stimulation for the eye that is neither narrative nor natural. It was conceived as an abstract play of visual forces: the surface composition is a series of figure-ground inversions, where patterns of two major motifs—one of dark-green crosses on a light field overlaid with an implied square, and the other of alternating beltlike courses of dark and light tiles—combine to resemble continuous printed rolls of textile fabrics. On the upper left of the façade, the tiles spell "P&F," for the names of the owners; and on the upper right, the Roman numerals MCM, the date of the building's completion, 1900 (fig. 3.2). At the roof, clawlike appendages, abstract wraiths in wrought iron, descend from the corners, and a wave motif with dots provides a linear band.

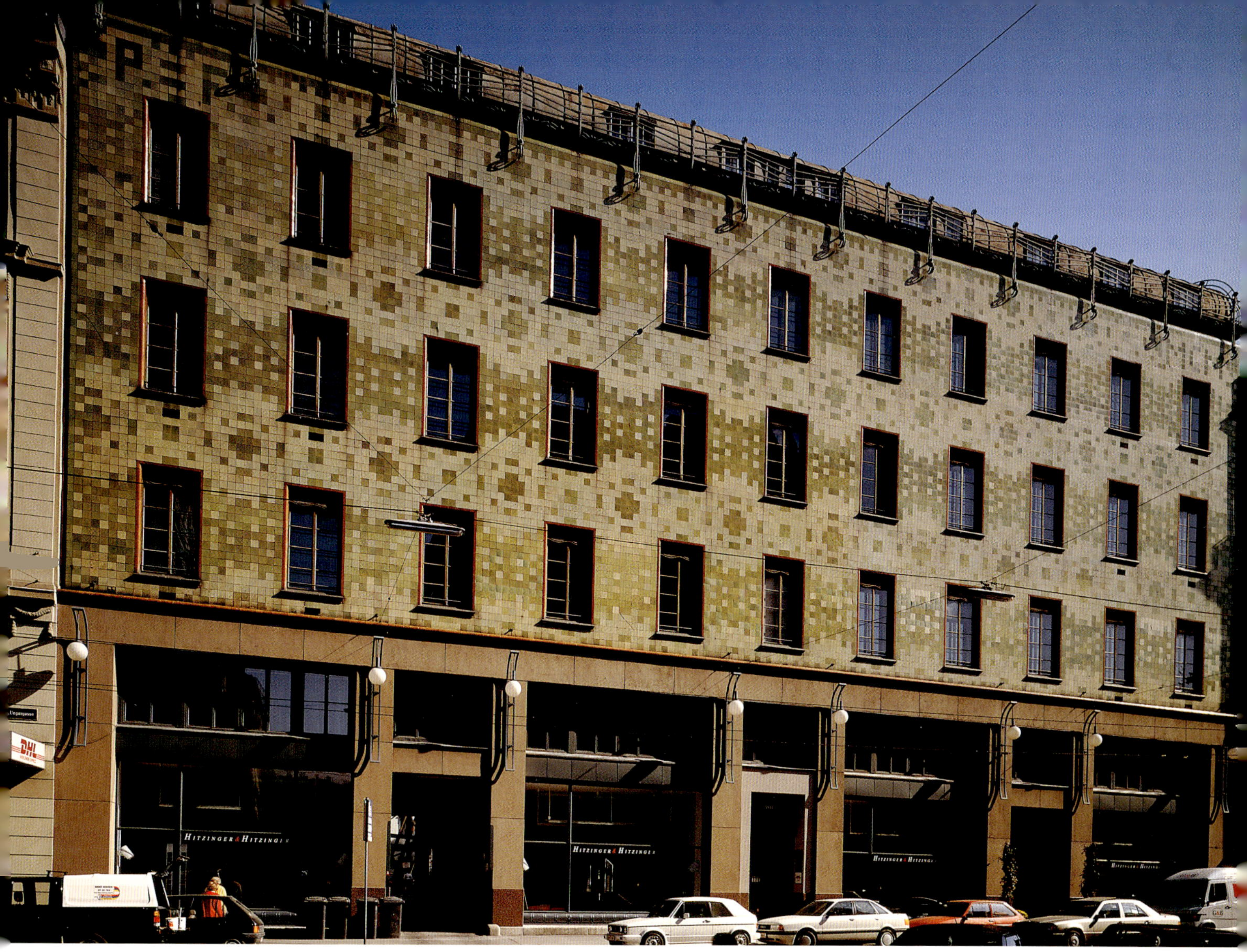

When finished, the building was widely published, and art critic Ludwig Hevesi lauded it in *Kunst und Kunstwerk* in 1901.[5] Not only did he praise the modernism of the building, its green and brown Zsolnay pyrogranite, but he also noted that the furniture in its showrooms ranged from imperial to Louis XIV, Queen Anne, and modern.

The plurality of styles of furniture offered at Portois & Fix, the coexistence of history and modernity, mirrored the cultural taste of the public at large—and Fabiani's own approach to architecture. Despite his obvious use of the language of rationalism, he simultaneously moved backward and sideways in his architectural modes as well. Immediately after designing the furniture building, he made a step in the opposite direction. In 1900 his design of a house in Ljubljana for Dr. Valentino Krisper, a commune council member, employed the floral language of organicism found in the Secession style. Fabiani's Artaria Building in the center of Vienna (1902) had an ingenious plan of interwoven yet separate functions, but its bay windows are reminiscent of the English Arts and Crafts tradition (fig. 3.3).[6] They are, however, pushed behind the façade surface, a gesture that accentuates the planarity of the surface skin. Flat panels on the façade have knobs that allude to rivets visually attaching a veneer to its structure, but the architect also used Secessionist details. Then, in 1905, Fabiani applied neobaroque swirls of stucco to the exterior of the building called Zum Roten Igel (At the Red Hedgehog) at the corner of Brandstätte Street; the treatment alluded to the emerging neobaroque gaining popularity at the time. He designed other buildings in an energetic baroque style that earned him the nickname "*baroccus fabianensis*."[7] Fabiani's designs for the Urania Theater (1908–9), highly visible on Aspern Place on the Ringstrasse, used a language of classicism inflected with baroque curves for a thoroughly modern program of a theater and astronomical observatory.[8] Fabiani's talent for straddling a position between rationalism, organicism, and historicism brought him to the desirable position of advisor to Archduke Franz Ferdinand. Later, after he returned south to Görz (Gorizia), he spent the rest of his career working in multiple modes while also producing numerous city plans in the region.[9]

In microcosm, Fabiani's inconsistency is rather consistent within the multilingual approach to architecture taken by Friedrich Ohmann and others, where a language of rationalism could be followed with a language of history, or a combination of both. Josef Hoffmann made a similar transit, and though he created powerful visual signs, his own work moved among various dialects.

Along with Fabiani and Joseph Maria Olbrich, Josef Hoffmann (1870–1956) formed a trio to whom Wagner owed many thanks.[10] Like his colleagues, Hoffmann was born outside the capital of the empire, in the Moravian town of Pirnitz (Brtnice, now in the Czech Republic), but Vienna transformed him.[11] After studying at the Vienna Academy of Fine Arts with Carl von Hasenauer and Wagner and graduating in 1895, Hoffmann traveled to Italy, and upon his return began working for Wagner. His designs for interiors and for the exhibitions of the Vienna Secession began to attract the

FIGURE 3.3
Max Fabiani, Artaria Building, exterior, Vienna, 1902.

attention of an artistic clientele. At the age of twenty-nine, Hoffmann was appointed professor at the Kunstgewerbeschule (School of Arts and Crafts) in Vienna in 1899.

Hoffmann drew on several currents around him for his language of form. From the Arts and Crafts movement and the ideas of John Ruskin and William Morris, he absorbed the concept of designing totally harmonious environments; from the work of Charles Rennie Mackintosh, who exhibited in Vienna, particularity and emotive power of abstract design; from the English architects Charles Robert Ashbee, M. H. Baillie Scott, and Charles F. A. Voysey, restraint and finesse. Hoffmann also responded to the calls for simplicity and truth articulated by Germans Alfred Lichtwark and Herman Muthesius, whose efforts would stimulate the formation of the German Werkbund in 1907. He also absorbed the efflorescence of his peer Olbrich, and the fundaments of Wagner, who had moved from the organic to a burgeoning expression of rationalism that focused on planarity and increasing rectilinearity.

Hoffmann made his own progression from the language of history—incorporated in the Beaux-Arts composition of his student projects—to the language of biomorphic organicism that he demonstrated in his designs for a candle shop in Vienna, an interior in Bergerhöhe, and some of his exhibition designs for the Secession. All this occurred in the brief period from 1895 to 1899. By 1902, however, he had produced two stucco reliefs for the fourteenth Vienna Secession exhibition that demonstrated an

THE LANGUAGE OF RATIONALISM

unprecedented abstraction and represented a shift from the language of organicism toward an abstract geometry.

Hoffmann's focus on geometry and matrices immediately found expression in items of everyday use made under the umbrella of the Wiener Werkstätte, whose purpose was to provide objects of simplicity needed in modern interiors. Fine craftsmanship would be the hallmark of jewelry, furniture, tableware, glassware, wallpaper, textiles, even book bindings. The enterprise preoccupied Hoffmann for thirty years beginning in 1903, although it was more an aesthetic than a financial success (figs. 3.4–3.6).

By 1904, Hoffmann and his colleagues from the Wiener Werkstätte focused on a language of geometric compositions that utilized color schemes of black and white, or white alone (figs. 3.7, 3.8). Interiors and a series of houses in the Hohe Warte area of

FIGURE 3.4
Salesroom of the Wiener Werkstätte at Neustiftgasse 32–34, Vienna, ca. 1904. Reprinted from *Deutsche Kunst und Dekoration* 15 (1904–5): 4.

FIGURE 3.5
(*Facing, top and left*) Josef Hoffmann, coffee pot, executed by the Wiener Werkstätte, Vienna, 1904. Asenbaum Collection.

FIGURE 3.6
(*Facing, top and right*) Josef Hoffmann, five pieces from the "flat model" flatware service, consisting of crab fork, sardine server, pastry serving spoon, cheese knife, and butter knife, executed by the Wiener Werkstätte, Vienna, 1904–8. Private collection. Used with permission. Photograph courtesy Neue Galerie New York.

FIGURE 3.7
(*Facing, bottom and left*) Koloman Moser, coffer (*Cassette*), Vienna, 1903. Collection Neue Galerie New York.

FIGURE 3.8
(*Facing, bottom and right*) Josef Hoffmann, inkstand (*Tintenzeug*), Vienna, 1905. Asenbaum Collection.

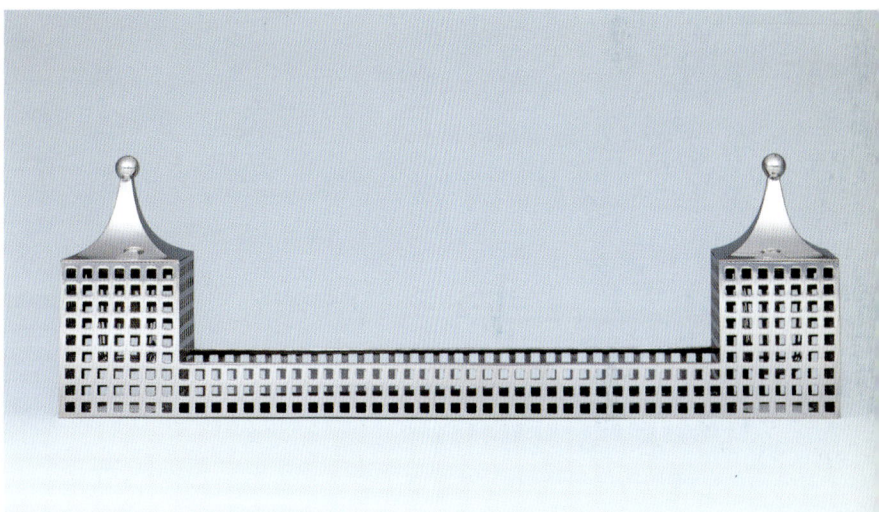

Vienna became a testing ground for this rectilinear vocabulary (figs. 3.9, 3.10). But Hoffmann's design of the Purkersdorf Sanatorium in 1904, with its cubic masses creating a flat-roofed building, confirmed the complete expression of pure geometry as a language of architecture (fig. 3.11). The square, which he had used earlier, became the sign of his work and that of the Wiener Werkstätte to such an extent that some called him "Quadratl Hoffmann."

With the square and grids, Hoffmann tapped two signs of modernism: monochromy in a palette of black and white, and abstraction. The square itself was ideal. A simple and pure shape, it could be replicated in series, laying one square within another to create imbricated or multiple frames; it could also articulate the blank surface of any

THE LANGUAGE OF RATIONALISM

FIGURE 3.9
Josef Hoffmann, dining room in the apartment of Dr. Hans Salzer, Vienna, 1902. From *Das Interieur* 4 (Vienna, 1903): 2.

FIGURE 3.10
Josef Hoffmann, salon in the apartment of Dr. Hermann Wittgenstein, Vienna, 1905. From *Deutsche Kunst und Dekoration* 18 (1906): 457.

FIGURE 3.11
Josef Hoffmann, Purkersdorf Sanatorium, exterior, Purkersdorf, near Vienna, 1904.

plane, creating an illusion of depth. Manipulating it was essentially a rational process: rotating one square within another produced a second square, whose area was one-half the outer square.

There are, however, multiple ways of reading this language of rationalism. These geometries may say nothing. Or they may engage in a visual interplay between figure and ground, affecting the "reader" at a subliminal level. Or they are "decoration," attachments to surface to alleviate boredom. The square itself seemed so modern, but the configuration had ancient precedents and existed far beyond the bounds of Greco-Roman culture. When replicated as a multiple frame, it had origins in the sacred architecture of the ancient Near East, as the sign of sacred temples.[12] Using the motif was in line with the effort to base a modern language of design on pure forms that leaped over historicism to the allegedly untainted originary forms of mankind. A similar motivation for these originary forms would stimulate investigations of folk art and the vernacular. Pure forms implied a consonance between art and life. But what, if anything, did these sacral associations mean for those eating fish with a beautiful Wiener Werkstätte knife and fork?

The complexity of interpreting the language of rationalism parallels the complexity of movements in Hoffmann's architecture. His work was inconsistent with any progressive model of modern architecture that outlined an unwavering movement toward increasing abstraction and a focus on function, but it was consistent within the polyglotism of architectural languages in the Austro-Hungarian Empire, and he soon returned to the language of history for his models. Usually identified as a return to classicism, Hoffmann's designs for the Vienna Kunstschau (1908) had classical pavilions (though interiors by others had imbricated squares). His art-exhibition buildings in Rome (1911) and at the Cologne Werkbund exhibition (1914) had classicizing features. Hoffmann even explored a language of folk traditions in his Primavesi house in Winkelsdorf (1913–14), but that gets us ahead of our story.

Before these moves to the language of history, Hoffmann created a synopsis of paradoxes of rationalism in the grand urban villa he designed for Adolphe Stoclet in Brussels (1905–11; figs. 3.12–3.15). This domestic palace summarized his ambitions to create the total work of art, bringing together painters, sculptors, and the full resources of the Wiener Werkstätte to produce a luxurious and sensuous ensemble. With apses and towers and an interior magisterial spatial sequence arranged around a central hall, the building is a secular equivalent of Wagner's St. Leopold's Church at Steinhof. Its pinnacle may be the Stoclet dining room, with Gustav Klimt's glistening mosaics. Every space and surface of its interior is treated to either pattern or rich material; but the exterior skin, stretched taut like a membrane, and its monumental cubic massing make a bold case for the language of rationalism.

However, as Eduard Sekler has perceptively observed, the use of moldings at the building's edges, the seemingly hovering connecting elements, and the windows appearing as dematerialized openings in the surface challenge reading the surface exclusively for its tectonic qualities, as if the building represents the idea of structure.[13] A paradox within rationalism characterizes much of Hoffmann's architecture. An "ambiguity" emerges between the simple and interlocked symmetries, between apparent tectonic expression and its denial through detail, between intention and effect. If Hoffmann attempted "to impart commonly understandable readability to architecture, to make it a vehicle of signification,"[14] then we should ask how readability is understood and what the vehicle signifies. The answers hover between cognition at a sensory level, stimulation of visual sensation in the eye of the beholder, the resurrection of cultural memory, and significance at a deep structural level that cannot be articulated, that is, a presence within the unconscious itself. Or readability implies boldness and clarity of perception independent of narrative content.

Along with simple cubic massing and the flat roof, the issue of tectonic expression became central to the language of rationalism as it increasingly became the defining condition of the modern movement. But in the countries of the empire, issues of tectonic expression and rationalism were highly complex. The work of the Czech Jan Kotěra (1871–1923) manifests this complexity, revealing a transit toward a language of rationalism in the Czech lands and its distinct inflection to issues of identity and modernism.

Born in Brno, Moravia, Kotěra played a formative role for Czech modern architects analogous to the role that Wagner, his mentor, played in the formation of Kotěra's

FIGURE 3.12
Josef Hoffmann, Palais Stoclet, exterior, Brussels, 1905–11.

FIGURE 3.13
Josef Hoffmann, Palais Stoclet, detail, Brussels, 1905–11.

FIGURE 3.14
(*Facing, top*) Josef Hoffmann, Palais Stoclet, interior, dining room with frieze by Gustav Klimt, Brussels, 1905–11. From *Moderne Bauformen* (1914), no. 1, plate 15.

FIGURE 3.15
(*Facing, bottom*) Josef Hoffmann, Palais Stoclet, interior, breakfast room, Brussels, 1905–11. From *Moderne Bauformen* (1914), no. 1, plate 24.

own generation of young moderns. Not only an architect, but a writer, theorist, teacher, and furniture designer, he became known as the father of modern Czech architecture.[15] After studying civil engineering in the German Industrial School in Plzeň (Pilsen) southwest of Prague, he went to Vienna and studied with Wagner from 1894 to 1897.[16] Like Wagner's other most successful students, Kotěra received a fellowship to Rome, a journey that still seemed to benefit a modernist's formation. Upon returning to Prague, he became a professor at the School of Applied Art in 1898, succeeding Friedrich Ohmann, and later professor of architectural composition at the Prague Academy of Fine Arts, a position he held until his death.[17] Significantly, he chaired the Mánes Artists' Association, a group of young artists promoting modernism and seeking true creative expression. These transfers between and ties to Vienna show how tightly knit was the network that allowed not only the transmission of architectural languages within generations but also from one generation to the next. At the School of Applied Arts, Kotěra trained architects who practiced throughout Bohemia and Moravia, both before and after the war. Among those was a generation of architects associated with Czech cubism, including Josef Gočár and Otakar Novotný. At the academy, Kotěra taught a generation of architects associated with functionalism, including Bohuslav Fuchs, Jaromír Krejcar, and Adolf Benš.[18]

But in order to mature, Kotěra had to separate himself from the shadow of Wagner and Vienna. That separation is conventionally described as his moving through a succession of styles and periods: from the Jugendstil or Secession period, to expressive rationalism, Czech cubism after 1910, and last, to a dry, neat classical phase. The trajectory is similar to the journey of some of his contemporaries and many of his followers throughout the Dual Monarchy. But a look at Kotěra's architecture through the lens of language adds dimensions that stylistic terms do not provide.

Kotěra's close collaboration with the founders of the Vienna Secession and his training under Wagner were reflected in his use of the language of organicism. The façade remodeling of an existing building for Franziska Peterka on Václav Square in Prague (1899–1900) is typical in its articulation of thin, curving, vegetal arabesques, flowers, and sculptural figures. Kotěra began to move from such conventionality in the Regional Authorities Building (1903) in the town of Hradec Králové.[19] Used for regional administration, the building had to communicate its purpose effectively to the public. Consequently, Kotěra added under the cornice a rampant lion and a frieze of flowers ringed with teardrop-shaped lozenges, a local floral folk motif familiar to Czechs of the area but not found in Vienna. Deviations from Viennese practice were also visible in the shallowness and the low arching of the cornice, a gesture to draw the eye of the citizen to the lion and the building's name, carved at the top of a protruding second-floor bay. In his pavilion representing the Imperial Royal School for Arts at the World Exhibition in St. Louis in 1904, Kotěra took a similar approach of combining Viennese Secessionist motifs, such as thin spirals, with floral folk motifs. This reliance on surface treatment diminishes in Kotěra's design (1905–7) for the National House in Prostějov (Proßnitz), the town with the largest Czech-speaking city board in Moravia. A cultural center in an industrial town, National House served the ongoing effort to

FIGURE 3.16
Jan Kotěra, City Museum, exterior, Hradec Králové, Bohemia, 1906–12.

express Czech national identity in a regional context. By providing a theater, restaurant, café, and intimate reception salons, the multipurpose building allowed people to meet in a place that resonated with their sense of being Czech. It also allowed Kotěra to begin uniting the language of organicism, replete with its representational iconography, with a new modeling of the building mass that moved his architecture beyond surface to treatment of volumes.

The monumental civic expression of Kotěra's move toward rationalism is seen in the City Museum for history and decorative arts that he designed in Hradec Králové (fig. 3.16). Known in German as Königgrätz, Hradec Králové was the capital of the Východočeský region and lies east of Prague, forming a rail junction at the confluence of the Elbe and Orlice rivers. Divided into an old town between the rivers and a new town on the west bank of the Elbe, Hradec Králové is situated at the meeting of the old trade routes from Prague to Cracow and from the Baltic Sea to the Danube River. It began as the settlement of Hradec in the tenth century, received the rights of a town in the thirteenth century, and became fortified in the fourteenth, when it fell under control of Elisabeth of Poland, the dowager queen who founded a Gothic cathedral in 1307. Since the town became known as the residence of dowager queens, Králové was added to its name, and it became "Town of the Queen."[20] Wars in the eighteenth century required more fortification, yet in 1866 its citadel could not resist the immense Battle of Königgrätz, in which the Prussians defeated the Austrians. The battle represented one of a series of defeats that both embarrassed the Austrian monarchy and showed its fundamental military vulnerability. At the end of the nineteenth century, the fortifications were removed, and the city was poised for urban redevelopment. By the turn of the century it was known as "the liveliest city in Eastern Bohemia."²¹ Town planning for one hundred thousand inhabitants would be in the hands of architects who would transform the city over the next three decades.

Several motivations were at work to create a new museum: the old museum in the city center was cramped, but also Hradec Králové wanted to compete with Prague as a center of arts and culture. In general, efforts to build a new museum were part of the social reaction against the elaborate and lavish new institutions of the National Museum, or the Museum of Decorative Arts, in Prague. However, the City Museum represented not only a reaction to an overly opulent language of history and the imposition of Austrian identity, but also a response to the perception that industrialization itself threatened regional traditions and cultural identity. Industrialization, the driving force of modernism, was double-edged. On the one hand, as a transnational force, it challenged the traditions of all inhabitants of the Dual Monarchy and disrupted the production of craft and handmade objects. That machines could sew more quickly than humans took work from people and disturbed the patterns of labor by which people defined themselves. On the other hand, industrialization provided material wealth that allowed Bohemia to prosper, reconfigure its cities, and build monumental works. In this context the museum's central importance lay in its function to preserve memory, so the people would not lose the connections to their past as they confronted the unknown world of the future.

The museum's board of trustees and the Hradec Králové city council resolved to commission Kotěra with his largest project to date, but the main mover and Kotěra's patron was František Ulrich, who saw the building through completion.²² With Ulrich's support, Kotěra received the commission to provide a landmark for the burgeoning town, a building of such scope that it represented a major financial undertaking for the city. While Hradec Králové's city government realized that its funds were limited, it still sought to create a dignified building that would make a clear statement.²³

That statement marked a significant shift in Kotěra's work. Rostislav Švácha has noted that the "aesthetics of impression" of Kotěra's early career, which I have described as a language of organicism, gave way to the expression of an "aesthetic of truth."²⁴ In his terms, the museum became a "place of work" combining monumental qualities of a temple with industrial forms of the period.²⁵ The first phase of Kotěra's museum designs occurred between 1905 and 1907.²⁶ On the site, located below the historic center and facing the Elbe on a rectangle sheared into a triangle by two intersecting diagonal streets, the architect located his building facing the river and parallel to the bank.²⁷ In planning the site he also proposed adding a rectangular garden with a semicircular alley of trees behind to animate the awkward triangle. In this first phase, Kotěra fixed the organization of the building: an early sketch shows the basic configuration of the plan as a tripartite division consisting of entry, vestibule, and staircase; a long wing; and a short wing terminated with an apse.²⁸

While the functional organization of the building was fixed from the outset, its image went through a process of creative transformation. In early versions of the project,

Kotěra considered an organic vocabulary for the building exterior.²⁹ But using a language of organicism that could be associated with the Viennese Secession put the building in conflict with efforts to promote Czech identity. As the design developed in a second phase from 1908 to 1909, the plan and general massing remained fixed, but Kotěra found a new and distinct expressive language of rationalism for his designs, one that retains an elaboration of surface and figural representation while communicating its purpose through mass and material. This general organization remained unchanged in the completed building, whose construction took place from 1909 to 1912.

Yet in order to express the truthfulness of its design, the City Museum had to express modernity as well.³⁰ From the exterior, a viewer sees that the center of the building indicates the location of the vertical spine of circulation and provides a major representational message. A visitor immediately confronts two colossal figures flanking the parallel curving walls that "invite" entry (figs. 3.17, 3.18). Švácha identifies the two figures by sculptor Stanislav Sucharda as goddesses honoring Ulrich's role as a Pericles of modern Hradec Králové, a classical association reinforced by the figure on the right

FIGURE 3.17
Jan Kotěra, City Museum, exterior, Hradec Králové, Bohemia, 1906–12.

FIGURE 3.18
Jan Kotěra, City
Museum, detail,
Hradec Králové,
Bohemia, 1906–12.

that imitates Phidias's Athena Parthenos. But the figures are also personifications: the figure on the right was identified at the time as a representation of History, and the figure to the left personifies Industry.[31] The "conversation" between the two is central to the meaning of the building: the dialectic between past, embodied in handwork, and new forms of objects—and life—embodied in industry.

Kotěra modeled the exterior massing of the building to communicate zones of the activities within. He coded the function of these spaces by the selection of materials used on the exterior, so that a viewer can "see" that different activities within the museum are being defined. The library forms part of the base of the building and is clad in brick. On the front façade a bank of windows connects the second-floor gallery to the library, while no such windows appear on the garden façade. A white stone cladding around the gallery and windowless upper floor is the code for the unlit zones. Following this theme of form expressing function, the light monitor at the top of the building is set back from a projecting cornice and attic. It is articulated as if it were a small house or a pavilion, and recalls the light monitors of industrial buildings. The cladding of the curved apse of the theater is divided into zones. A lower zone of red brick is punctured by windows that illuminate the interior, and a broad band of white stone that wraps the entire volume like a taut sheet contrasts with both the texture and the color of the brick courses. On the interior, this is the zone where sound reverberates and light is not needed. On the exterior, this neutral zone is delimited by a wide, shadow-casting cornice with attic that follows the curve of the hall and marks the top zone. After soaring two and a half stories, the exterior once again opens to light the interior through a curving band of windows that forms a shallow-roofed light monitor over the hall. The smooth, continuous, unarticulated surfaces recall the

THE LANGUAGE OF RATIONALISM

smoothness and precision of a machine-made object—a drum turned on a mechanical lathe or milling machine—associated with modern production techniques.

Kotěra used, however, traditional optical refinements to make the building's form coherent. One of those refinements occurred when Kotěra pulled the band of rectangular panels separated by single mullions back from the cornice edge to reinforce the motif of stepping that operates throughout the building and leads to its central focus, the cylindrical tower. Another refinement can be found in the steps of the cornice attic that provide the transition between the height of the cornice and the central mass above it.

From a distance, a visitor can read that tall piers of brick and stone, rendered in contrasting colors and recessing into the mass of the building, indicate the circulation system at the center of the museum. Conveying abstractly a gesture of entry and welcome, the piers also frame the windows that illuminate the interior landings of the main staircase. A sign announces the purpose of the building in clear, gilt letters: Museum. In addition to their gestural function, these piers also form recessed planes in the shape of multiple frames, geometric motifs which appear in the work of Josef Hoffmann and the Wiener Werkstätte. In front of the piers are thrones for Sucharda's figures; these thrones also have multiple frames as chair backs, and the theme of the multiple frames is literally restated on the floor pattern inside the museum with one square recessed within another. However, Kotěra countered more literal Viennese associations with multiple frames by constructing broad, flat planes with brick and stone on the façade, a treatment not found in Secession and Werkstätte examples, which use flat bands instead.[32] He continued his transformation of the multiple frame by using the motif of horizontal layers, stacked and receding, to form the base of the drum that tops the building, but he changed their syntax by shearing off the corners of frames.

The drum is a pinnacle that signals the location of the museum to the city. A cylinder whose lower half is solid and upper half glazed, it is surrounded by gray columns that support a copper-colored cornice and a shallow dome. Pierced openings in the cylinder allow light to enter the top-floor vestibule through a double-domed central space. The upper dome provides a tall exterior profile and protection from the elements, and the lower dome completes the carefully proportioned interior space.

Having seen the building from a distance and having entered its portal, a visitor passes through a rectangular foyer and into a large, square vestibule that marks the center of the building and its major point of internal reference. Above it is a cylindrical dome atop the building. Directly ahead is a staircase, which leads to the museum's exhibition floors above and to the lower floor and basement below. On the ground floor to the left, off the vestibule, a wide corridor goes past the director's office to a library and a reading room. The two upper floors in this wing contain exhibit galleries, including a prehistoric ceramics gallery.[33] The top floor terminates in a double-height space illuminated by a large, pitch-roofed light monitor. This monitor floods the end of the top gallery with light. The other galleries have banks of double windows to provide side illumination.

On the right of the entry vestibule is a 182-seat recital hall and theater flanked by a passage that opens to a terrace facing the park. The auditorium occupies the entire wing of the museum, forming a rectangular volume that extends the length of the wing and up to its full height. Its stage end terminates in a flattened curve that neutralizes the sharp angle of the street cutting across the site, a gesture analogous to the baroque device of a partial circle mediating the irregularities of a site.

Moving up the stairs to the upper vestibule, the visitor sees that the dome interior consists of a series of concentric circles whose size gradually shrinks (fig. 3.19). The language is complicated, but if we look closely, we see that here again Kotěra transformed motifs that could be associated with Austrian practices by changing rectangular or square multiple frames into recessed, round frames or concentric rings. The lowest range of the dome has zones filled with a diamond-shaped lattice that echoes the lattice of the art glass in the windows below the drum. A band of curved forms in low relief terminates each zone. Partly shaped like segments of a volute, these curves, organic motifs ending in scrolls, with rows of holes following each curve and framing abstracted flowers, have no precedent; they are Kotěra's invention. He continued to transform and invent motifs, as seen in the band of scalloped-shaped curves he applied to the underside of each layer of the dome as it ascends in ever-decreasing concentric circles.

Not only are motifs transformed, but the evolution of the building captures a moment of transition from one language to another, showing how these languages overlap. On the one hand, the museum reads as a machine-made object composed of masses that respond to and express the function within, fulfilling a tenet of modern architecture. These masses define a complex, articulated space, another benchmark for modernist critics. On the other hand, the smooth, unadorned surfaces coexist with pattern, texture, and color that that do not fit within the conventional canon of modern architecture as form without ornament solely in the service of function.

When completed in 1910, the museum's austere image had no equal in the Austro-Hungarian Empire. Kotěra continued his experiment in the language of rational form in his own family house in Prague-Vinohrady (1908–9). Housing his family, his architectural studio, and briefly, after 1910, his classes at the Prague Academy of Fine Arts, the building organized its functions through spaces that revolved around the living quarters. On the exterior, an asymmetrical arrangement of geometric shapes expressed and differentiated the activities within. Kotěra located windows precisely where they were required, not as part of an overall compositional scheme. Floral motifs had disappeared, window openings had lintels of exposed concrete, and wall surfaces were exposed brick or coarse plaster.[34]

OTTO WAGNER'S Austrian Postal Savings Bank in Vienna paralleled Kotěra's City Museum as an exemplar of a complex language of rationalism (fig. 3.20). Selected from among thirty-seven architects to design the building, Wagner wrote a proposal, published in 1904, about the rational basis for the project, with details on the disposition of activities, their area allotments, construction methods, exterior appearance, and costs.[35] His first sketches depicted a six-sided polygon that corresponded to the splayed building site, which opened onto Georg-Coch Square and the Ringstrasse, while the splayed sides followed Biberstrasse. At the center of the scheme was a main banking hall with symmetrical wings lit by open courtyards. The public would see and use the hall and its spaces; the bureaucracy would occupy the offices and processing rooms of the side wings. The building went up quickly between July 1904 and December 1906; a second phase of construction was completed 1910–12.

When the first phase was completed, Wagner published another report that detailed its execution, noting the use of granite and marble, reinforced concrete, full electrification, and even an integral vacuum-cleaning system.[36] Some changes had occurred from his early design sketch. In the early competition version, the central façade had an arching pediment of sinewlike arcs and glass, surmounted by a huge imperial crest—all consistent with the language of biomorphic organicism—but, as built, a rectilinear cornice replaced the arch, and squares and grids replaced circles and curves (fig. 3.21).[37]

Generally, Wagner's concept sketch had remained intact, but the image of the building had moved from organic toward a rational expression of purpose seen in abstract, rectilinear geometry and innovative uses of technology. The façade was a billboard demonstration of such purposes: granite slabs, ten centimeters thick, clad the first and second floors, and panels of Sterzing marble, only two centimeters thick, covered the upper portion. Locating Wagner's work within the cladding theories of Gottfried Semper, Ákos Moravánszky suggests that the "wall displays its origins in woven hangings."[38] Pins appear to hold the stone plates in place and are often described as indications that the building is an early tectonic demonstration of modern rationalism.[39] Representing the means of attaching the stone to its frame, they are described as a testament of truth to materials and the honest expression of structure. However, Wagner suggested that the aluminum bolts, which he called rosettes, had precedents in the nail work of Spanish buildings and the tradition of nails bringing good luck. These rosettes, which appear as dots, were part of the visual game played by Wagner, an effort at readability, independent of tectonic expression of the building's structure, process, or material.[40] In fact, the veneer is held in place by cement and clips—the rosettes provide no structural function.

Wagner further pushed material innovation and responses to the pragmatics of users' needs and building efficiency to new realms. Not only did he identify reinforced concrete as the most efficient structural system for his modern architecture, but he explored aluminum for its plastic potential, lightweight structural abilities, and

FIGURE 3.19 (*Facing*) Jan Kotěra, City Museum, interior, Hradec Králové, Bohemia, 1906–12.

THE LANGUAGE OF RATIONALISM

FIGURE 3.20
Otto Wagner, Postal Savings Bank, exterior, Vienna, 1904–6. Photograph by Erich Lessing / Art Resource, NY.

FIGURE 3.21
Otto Wagner, Postal Savings Bank, detail of the front façade, Vienna, 1904–6.

scintillating visual effects. Six aluminum posts hold up the broad glass canopy at the entry of the Postal Savings Bank (fig. 3.22). For these posts, Wagner created a new unprecedented order. Aluminum also provides the material for the interior heating vents, which in Wagner's designs take on a totemic, anthropomorphic character (fig. 3.23). He used glass, like aluminum, as a material that reveals its own qualities of translucency, transparency, and lightness. A hovering glass ceiling illuminating the main public hall is flanked by tellers' windows on the sides; the arrangement resembles, as others have noted, a basilica, with nave and side aisles. Glass blocks on the floor allow light to the sorting room below (fig. 3.24). Materials, function, form still meld with the ideal of total design, as seen in the interior of the boardroom. Furniture, wall surfaces, floors, even a painting of Franz Josef by Wilhelm List, all interrelate to communicate a conviction in the validity of harmonious design (fig. 3.25).

However, rational expression, abstraction, and representation persisted in a dialectic that did not fit unilateral readings of modern architecture at the time. The simple, abstract forms of geometry coexisted with representations of the human figure and traditional symbol systems that were valid means of speaking. The Austrian Postal Savings Bank was not totally abstract. The theme of victory remained present in Wagner's standardized laurel wreaths and great winged Nike, executed by the sculptor Othmar Schimkowitz, which Wagner used as acroteria at the ends of the cornice. But to what does the victory refer? The triumph of an efficient postal banking system? The control of the empire itself as represented in its institutions? Was Wagner making a social or a political statement? Though he leaned toward a German-oriented nationalism, Wagner was apolitical. He focused on the reconciliation of art

FIGURE 3.22
Otto Wagner, Postal Savings Bank, entrance with aluminum columns, Vienna, 1904–6.

FIGURE 3.23
Otto Wagner, Postal Savings Bank, aluminum heating vent, Vienna, 1904–6.

FIGURE 3.24
(*Facing, top*) Otto Wagner, Postal Savings Bank, banking hall, Vienna, 1904–6.

FIGURE 3.25
(*Facing, bottom*) Otto Wagner, Postal Savings Bank, boardroom, Vienna, 1904–6.

and technology through the language of architecture, but without any political and social motivations. For Wagner, new construction methods would lead to new forms and gradually to a new style. Engineering alone—and by extension, a fixation on function—was inadequate. As he wrote in *Moderne Architektur*, which first appeared in 1896 and was expanded in 1902, "The engineer who does not consider the nascent art-form, but only the structural calculations and the expense will . . . speak a language unsympathetic to man."[41] Art was the necessary mediator to create a sympathetic language. His Nikes, then, announced the triumph of a new language of modern architecture.

Wagner's achievements in expressing a language of rationalism were not sympathetic enough for the complexities of Viennese social politics, however. St. Leopold's Church at Steinhof had elicited critical praise but also snide and cruel attacks. By the time of the Postal Savings Bank's completion, Wagner was becoming professionally marginalized. His proposals for a new Kaiser Franz Josef city museum (1903–09) next to Fischer von Erlach's venerated baroque church on the Karlsplatz in Vienna had met with negative reactions.[42] As Otto Graf has noted, the conflict came from within the Vienna University art history faculty, where Josef Strzygowski promoted Wagner's ideas for the museum and Max Dvorák objected. Hugo von Hofmannsthal called Wagner a barbarian, and the supporters who initially favored his chair at the Academy of Fine Arts remained disappointed, as they wanted their professor to follow classical and Renaissance ideas.[43] But even earlier, Wagner had a premonition of the nature of the resistance, as he noted in *Moderne Architektur*: "The main reason that the importance of the architect has not fully been appreciated lies in the store of forms employed by him up to now: that is, in the language he has directed to the public, which in most cases is completely unintelligible."[44]

From this point forward, major patronage eluded Wagner. His career spanned the period from the start to the completion of the Ringstrasse, when Vienna transformed itself, but the mixed acceptance of his work limited his achieving built works. He received only sixteen commissions throughout his entire career, though he designed visionary projects and built fifteen apartment houses and villas for himself. The latter provided not only the means of experimentation, but also to some degree the satisfaction denied by official broad acceptance. However, he trained 190 students during his twenty-year-long academic career, and published twenty-eight books, essays, and collections of drawings and over fifty-five commentaries. He created the Wagnerschule, a master class whose students and followers were the most talented young architects; many were to become teachers of other architects throughout the empire. He transformed the face of Vienna through his work on the *Stadtbahn* and the Danube canal. Toward the end of his career he had lost all interest in nineteenth-century architecture and even changed the name of his *Moderne Architektur* in 1913 to its fourth-edition title, *Baukunst unserer Zeit* (Architecture of Our Time). Wagner died in 1918 in his house on the Döblergasse in Vienna.

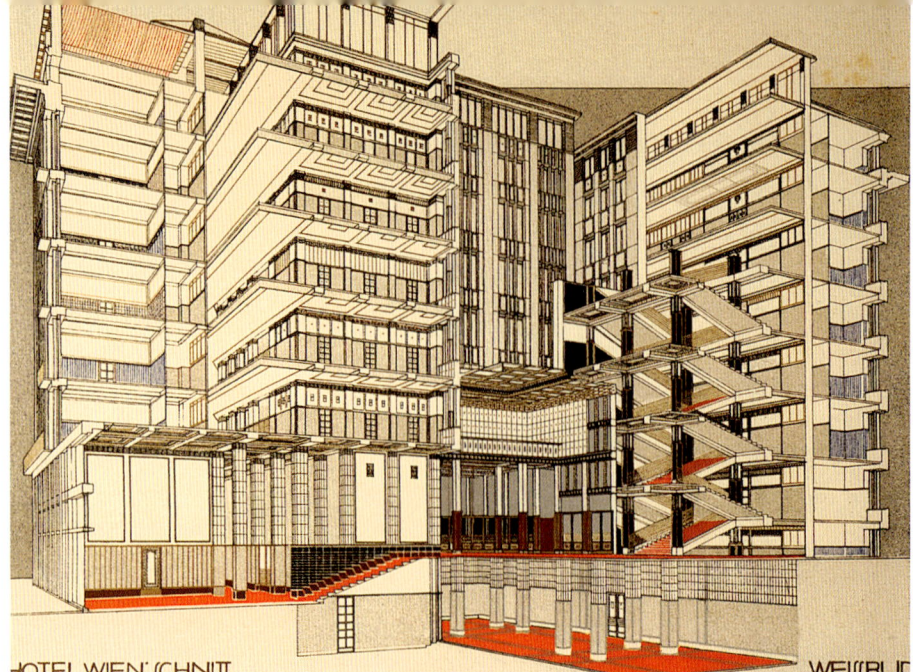

FIGURE 3.26
Rudolf Weiss, Hotel Wien, section, Wagnerschule project, Vienna, 1912. Reprinted from Otto Schönthal, ed., *Ehrenjahr Otto Wagners* (Vienna, 1912).

Just as Wagner's students had absorbed the language of organicism, they became highly proficient in producing the images of rationalism. Their student projects included series of building types, from tenement houses and department stores to artists' residences.[45] The hotel became an ideal building type appropriate for research in this direction. In noting the requirements of the modern hotel, the art critic Joseph August Lux asserted that it should operate "like a machine" with the same comfort found on the excellent wagon-lit of trains, and its "furniture and fittings of the dining and public rooms should be dominated not by high art, but by hygiene."[46] He also called for specifics: "well-lit hall of a functional height . . . club chairs and small tables . . . comfortable wickerwork chair from which to watch the world go by." The subject became a standard studio problem, and one Wagner himself took on (figs. 3.26, 3.27A–C).[47] Even Rudolf Schindler around 1912, while a student at the Wagnerschule before leaving for America, submitted a project entitled Hotel Rong.[48]

Some of Wagner's former students and important office assistants had moved from student projects to built work.[49] Marcel Kammerer, who had studied with Wagner from 1899 to 1902, followed the master's trajectory. Around 1900, he captured the organic moment in his study for a villa for a painter (fig. 3.28), but while still working in Wagner's atelier, he explored the potentials of rationalism when the Grand Hotel Wiesler in Graz commissioned him to design furniture and interiors in 1903–4, and provided a second commission that started in 1905. Though when published that summer in *Der Architekt*, the scheme still had organic tendencies, when finally completed in 1908, it showed Kammerer's absorption of the language of rationalism, described by Iain Boyd Whyte as a "crisp pared-down modernity" (figs. 3.29, 3.30).[50] The restraint on the façade, with its adroit corner, is paralleled by the interior of the entrance hall, which retains an organic vitality that is disciplined by the need to define the hotel as an artifact of modern life. Similarly, Kammerer's design for the interior of the *Festsaal*, dated 1909, is a stunning contrast of sensual materials of veined marble and geometric motifs in gold and white, balanced by animated surfaces, flat planes,

A

B

FIGURE 3.27A–B
(*Above*) Hans Fritz, Hotel Wien, hall and vestibule, interior studies, Wagnerschule project, Vienna, 1911. Reprinted from Otto Schönthal, ed., *Ehrenjahr Otto Wagners* (Vienna, 1912).

FIGURE 3.28
(*Right*) Marcel Kammerer, *Study for a Villa for a Painter—Perspective from 21 Meters Distance*. Watercolor, 1900. Collection Galerie St. Etienne, New York.

FIGURE 3.29
Marcel Kammerer, Grand Hotel Wiesler, Graz, exterior, Vienna, 1905–8.

FIGURE 3.30
Marcel Kammerer, Grand Hotel Wiesler, Graz, detail, Vienna, 1905–8.

and a rectilinear grid (fig. 3.31). At the same time, Kammerer accommodated the client's and his own interests in retaining associations with neo-Biedermeier comfort. Crisp modernity coexists with but does not dominate memories of the language of history. The same dualistic character informed his competition entry for the design of a country house in 1911 (fig. 3.32).

Wagner's other students also learned their lessons well. Wagner had used the designs of his numerous residences and ateliers as testing grounds suitable for rationalization—his last residence and studio on Döblergasse was his most severe—and the architect's residence became a typological exercise. Josef Hannich's design for such a villa demonstrates how effectively students absorbed Wagner's idiom. Hannich (1889–1962), who studied with Wagner from 1909 to 1912, executed a complete project, including perspectives, façade details, staircase, and section drawings. The result was a building of cubic masses and shear façades of applied stone set off with colored bands under the cornice and vertical panels, an architect's atelier that has a machinelike

FIGURE 3.31
Marcel Kammerer, study for the *Festsaal* of the Grand Hotel Wiesler, Graz, Austria, 1909.

FIGURE 3.32
Marcel Kammerer, study for a country house from the Austrian competition for the Rome Prize, 1911.

FIGURE 3.33
Josef Hannich, architect's residence at Hietzinger Haupstrasse—Auhofstrasse, perspective of the main façade, Wagnerschule project, Vienna, 1911.

FIGURE 3.34
Josef Hannich, architect's residence at Hietzinger Haupstrasse—Auhofstrasse, perspective of the Wagnerschule project, Vienna, 1911.

precision in its organization and sharp definition of cabinets, files, and drawers (figs. 3.33–3.35).[51] Both the aesthetics and the perfected methods of representation allowed Hannich to present the villa as classically restrained with its symmetrical projecting wings, yet enlivened by color and abstract ornament. Hannich articulated room interiors with framing bands connecting floor, rectilinear furniture, walls, and ceilings. Changes of color and material inflect each interior room's character: the dining room is gold and ochre, the office serious gray and white with black outlines; the bedroom has a red carpet and wall panels, and the atelier itself is nearly monochromatic except for a dark floor (figs. 3.36–3.38). The images are rational in their clarity and order, their control of surface, space, and volume, their absorption of technology, yet they emphasize sensuality through the persistent use of color, pattern, and materials themselves. In sum, the villa presents the architect as heroic and successful, an ambition that was already partly thwarted in Wagner's own career and that would elude most of his students, as the cataclysm of war lay three years away.

Kotěra's students in Prague were less predictable in their exploration of the language of rationalism. Not only were they more independent, but their immediate cultural, political, and social context elicited different responses to defining a modern architecture. Otakar Novotný (1880–1959), however, most closely followed Kotěra's leads.[52] His multifunctional building for the publisher Jan Štenc used Kotěra's structural concepts and treatment of brick and unplastered façades to provide the editor of art books with a residence, shop, offices, flats, and print works in one ensemble (figs. 3.39, 3.40). Designed and built from 1909 to 1911, the building used traditional brick load-bearing walls but included concrete for pillars, beams, and ceilings. The façade and massing of the building reflect the various functions within, yet they retain their

FIGURE 3.35 (*Top, left*) Josef Hannich, architect's residence at Hietzinger Haupstrasse—Auhofstrasse, Wagnerschule project, interior of the atelier, Vienna, 1911.

FIGURE 3.36 (*Top, right*) Josef Hannich, architect's residence at Hietzinger Haupstrasse—Auhofstrasse, Wagnerschule project, interior of the dining room, Vienna, 1911.

FIGURE 3.37 (*Bottom, left*) Josef Hannich, architect's residence at Hietzinger Haupstrasse—Auhofstrasse, Wagnerschule project, interior of the office, Vienna, 1911.

FIGURE 3.38 (*Bottom, right*) Josef Hannich, architect's residence at Hietzinger Haupstrasse—Auhofstrasse, Wagnerschule project, interior of the bedroom, Vienna, 1911.

FIGURE 3.39
Otakar Novotný, Jan Štenc House, exterior, Prague, 1909–11.

coherence. Novotný made brick the subject of the building, demonstrating how the nature of the material could be expressed horizontally in courses, vertically in striations, recessed to provide a variety of paneled motifs, extruded from the surface, and laid in herringbone patterns. Not only did he use unfinished brick as the material in its purest form, but he explored the nature of color contrasts with glazed breaks. On the front street façade, these white bricks form a flattened colonnade, with stepped pyramids to mark the columns and thrust the eye up into the façade. Novotný pushed brick to the extreme, beyond tectonic logic, to make a balcony on the fourth floor.

Although informed by Kotěra's example, Novotný had other inspirations contributing to his rationalist vocabulary. The Štenc House includes a quarter vault at the roof, resembling the curving cornice at Fabiani's Portois & Fix building in Vienna—here rendered totally in glass. Revealing the influence of Hoffmann and the Wiener Werkstätte in Prague, Novotný also used imbricated squares on interior walls and ceilings, and multiple frames in the arched openings at the attic level. He continued his demonstration in the rational variations of brick throughout the interiors and combined their visual mass with a conscious effort to link interior and exterior spaces, creating a startling contrast of mass and transparency. The interior graphic design studio opens to a glass wall that unites the studio with the interior courtyard around

FIGURE 3.40
Otakar Novotný, Jan Štenc House, detail, Prague, 1909–11.

FIGURE 3.41 (*Facing, top*) Josef Gočár, duplex at Tychonova Street, exterior, Prague, 1912–13.

FIGURE 3.42 (*Facing, bottom*) Josef Chochol, Hodek's Apartment Building at Neklanova Street, exterior, Prague, 1913–14.

which the building was erected. Not content to explore only functionality and materials, Novotný made the articulation of "the organism of space" and the "spirit of space" the subject of an essay, "Shody a rozpory" (Harmonies and Dissonances), that he published in 1915.[53]

By the time of Novotný's essay, Czech modernism had already moved from the rationalism of Kotěra to a radically new, vibrant, and constantly evolving style: Czech cubism. It had emerged and within a short period was already being revised, existing in a constant state of explorative flux. Largely an aesthetic movement with mythic overtones, it provides a foil for looking at the language of rationalism. Unlike much discussed here under the lens of language and architecture, Czech cubism has been the subject of international exhibitions and serious scholarship since the mid-1960s, when it was rediscovered as an important strand of modernism.[54] The outline of its history points to rumblings fueled by numerous factors: Edvard Munch's exhibition of expressionist paintings in Prague in 1905; the founding of the German Werkbund in 1907; the debates on art and production in industry and craft; and Viennese modernist developments that many knew firsthand. A break came in 1908, when in a protest against Kotěra a group of members of the Mánes Artists' Association formed their own Association of Architects within the organization. This marked the emergence of a cluster of young architects in their mid- to late twenties. The chief theorist and ideologue of the new movement was Pavel Janák, who had studied with Wagner from 1906 to 1908, and then worked in Kotěra's architectural studio from 1907 to 1909.[55] His early projects included the Hlávka Bridge in Prague (1909–12), water locks, and houses outside Prague. Josef Gočár, another member, had studied under Kotěra at the Prague School of Applied Arts from 1903 to 1905.[56] He would effectively actualize Janák's ideas in built form in Prague, most notably in the department store "By the Black Madonna" (1911–12) and a duplex on Tychonova Street (1912–13; fig. 3.41).[57] Josef Chochol, a third figure in the group, had studied at the Prague Technical University, worked for Osvald Polívka, architect of the Municipal House, and then resumed studies with Otto Wagner from 1907 to 1909.[58] The houses and Hodek's Apartment Building he would design below Vyšehrad Hill in Prague exemplified the faceted forms of the emerging style (fig. 3.42).[59] Others in the movement included Vlastislav Hofman (1884–1964) and Otakar Novotný, Kotěra's devoted follower, who eventually joined it.

Writing in 1908 in *Styl*, the magazine of the Association of Architects of the Mánes group edited by Zdeněk Wirth, Janák charted the new territory, yet acknowledged a debt to the rationalism of Wagner: "The spirit of the new style is already defined, and the road to its plastic means by penetration to the very nature of matter is clear: it includes geometric forms, prismatic and cubic, the most intrinsic essential of all forms, purged of everything secondary; the natural constructive arrangements are the new compositional principles, with the function of decoration transposed to only accentuating, which, like framing or underscoring, lacks all independent form. This is the state of Wagner's art today." Wagner was the source of "timeless and permanent

FIGURE 3.43 (*Facing, top*) Josef Gočár, Wenke Department Store (now city museum), Jaroměř, Bohemia, 1910–11.

FIGURE 3.44 (*Facing, bottom*) Josef Gočár, Wenke Department Store, interior, Jaroměř, Bohemia, 1910–11.

values" in a pure architecture that transcends a mechanistic connection between form and function and allows the emergence of the "healthy strong nature of the modern individual."[60]

But within two years, Janák put Wagner's ideas under siege. Taking up the motto of "function, construction, poetry," Janák claimed that the modern architecture under Wagner had focused on simplification, social purpose, and practicality at the expense of plastic development, "the problem of space or the problem of matter and form . . . and it was not sufficiently theoretical."[61] The crystalline prism and pyramid would be the forms for reengaging poetry, and theory would be its guide. For Janák, cubist architecture allowed the expression of spirit to emerge from inert matter.

With their emphasis on individual expression, the efforts of Czech cubists ran a deliberate attack on rationality. While Wagner's students in Vienna like Hannich were dutifully following his language of rationalism, young Prague practitioners had launched a bold countermovement focusing on the pyramid and the crystal. Expressing form defined by dynamic diagonals became ornament itself, an ambition perhaps more completely achieved in furniture and objects than in buildings. Revising the geometry of space to understand its composition became a goal in line with Guillaume Apollinaire's statement in *Les Peintres cubistes*: "It is space as such, the dimension of infinity; it is this which gives plasticity to objects."[62] An additional impetus for Czech cubism came in 1911, when a group of young Czech architects, painters, sculptors, and theorists formed the Group of Plastic Artists (also known as the Cubist Group of Visual Artists), marking its entry onto the European stage and beyond the confines of Austro-Hungary and forming a self-conscious avant-garde. Theirs was a revolt against harmony and taste, a deliberate move outside the language of rationalism to a language of feeling, emotion, and subjectivity.

Gočár's work shows the suddenness and drama of the shift from rationalism to feeling. His design of the Wenke Department Store in Jaroměř (1910–11) brings the language of rationalism to a provincial center (fig. 3.43).[63] Built for the trader Joseph Wenke, the building used modern materials: reinforced-concrete construction, steel, glass, ceramics, and interior railings of nickel-plated brass. The suspended glass front not only allowed for generously lit interiors and gives maximum exposure of the store's dry goods, which ranged from ceramic vases to baby strollers, but also demonstrates one of the earliest uses of the curtain wall, a surface of glazing that carries no load. A huge chandelier forming part of the motif of a circle in a square illuminates the interior of the central display area and speaks of clarity, function, and rationality (fig. 3.44). The building was designed as an efficient machine for commerce and brought what had been the latest Czech interpretations of the Vienna Secession to the provinces. However, Gočár's buildings completed shortly thereafter were seminal demonstrations of the different linguistic approach of Czech cubism. Comparison with Gočár's own duplex on Tychonova Street (1912–13) or with Chochol's Hodek's Apartment Building (1913–14) below Vyšehrad makes the Wenke Store's aesthetics instantly outmoded.

MĚSTSKÉ MUZEUM
VYSTAVNÍ SÍŇ

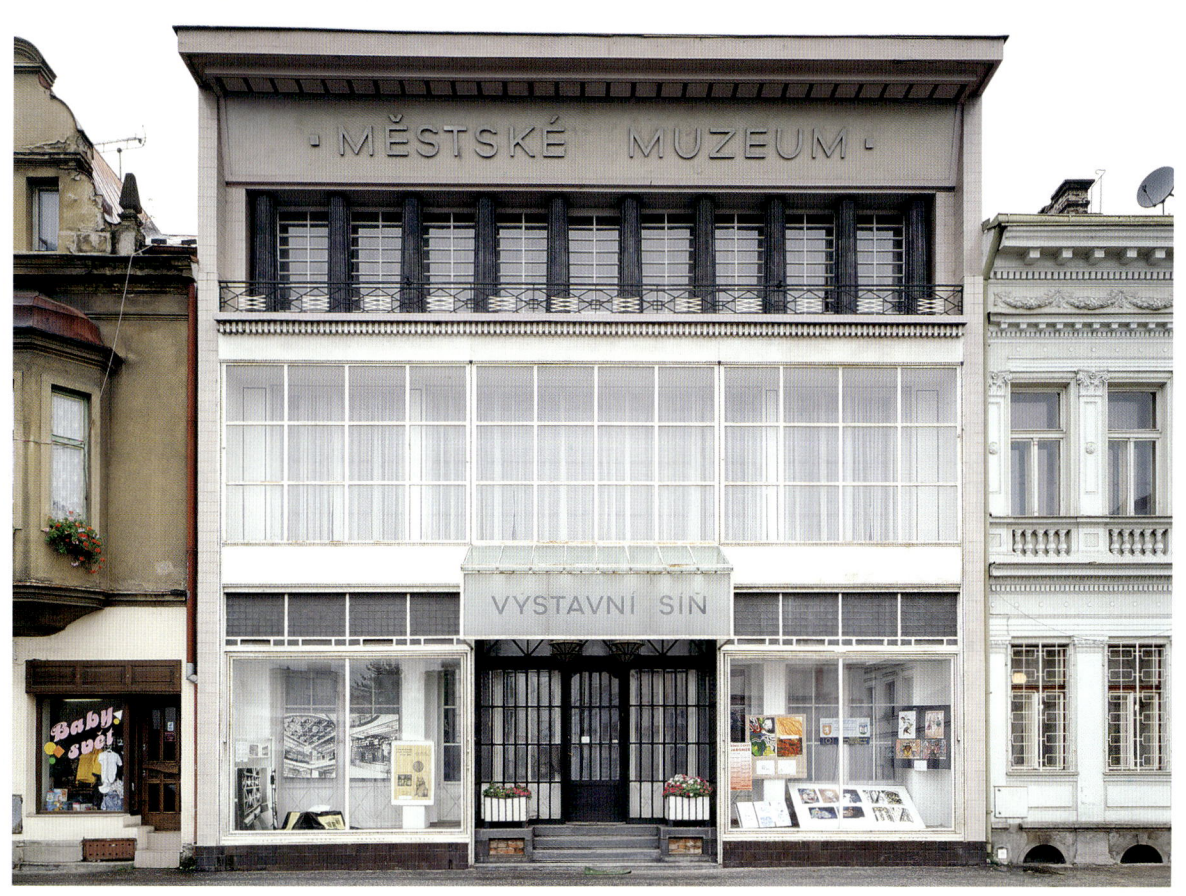

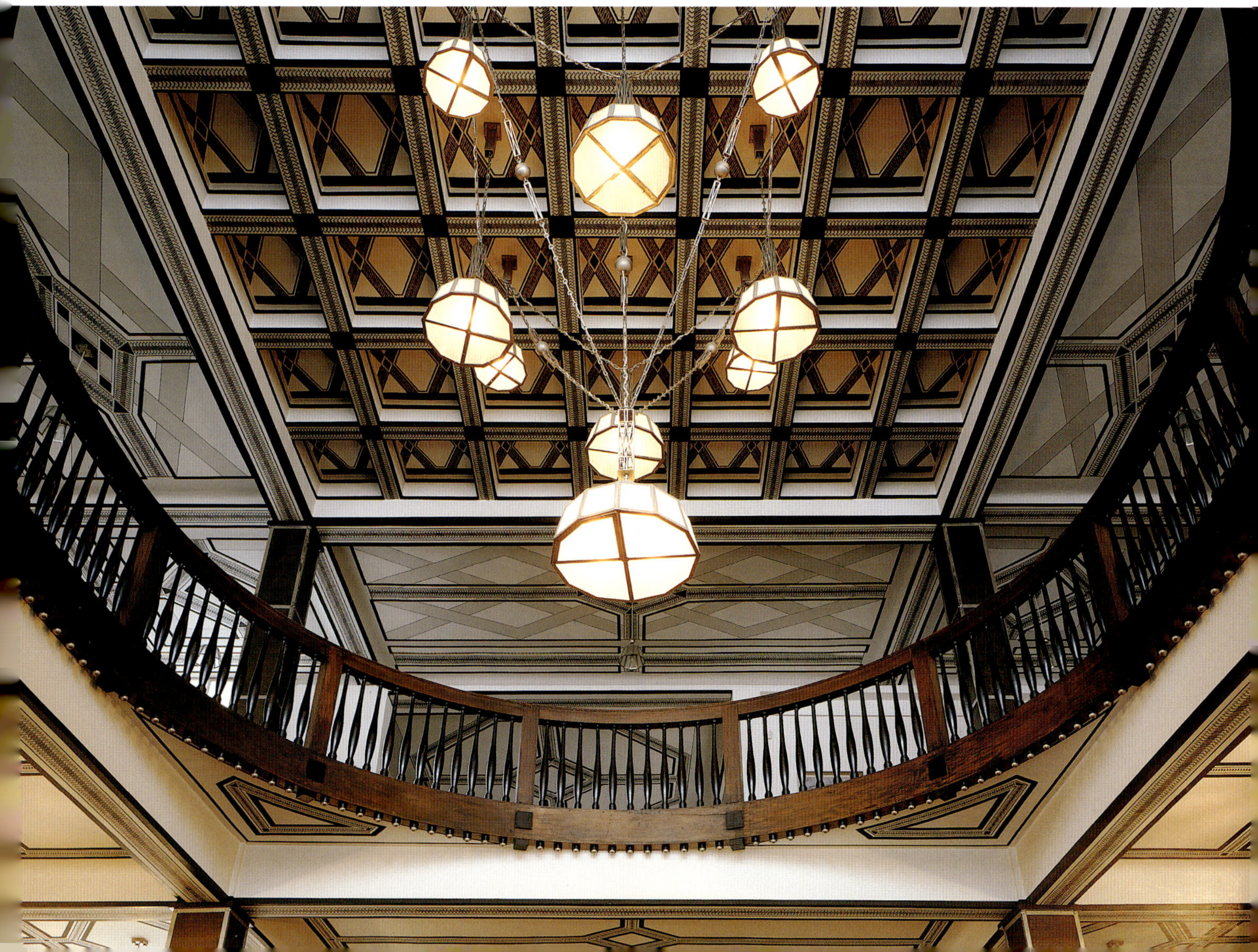

FIGURE 3.45
(*Facing, top*) Josef Gočár, main building of the spa, Bohdaneč, Bohemia, 1911–13.

FIGURE 3.46
(*Facing, bottom*) Antonin Brunner, *The Municipal Mud Baths Bohdaneč*. Poster, 1913. Museum of Decorative Arts, Prague.

What does the architecture of Czech cubism "say"? On one level, it seems to tell us that we are looking at the built forms of cubism that emanate from Picasso and Braque, forms that automatically place Czech artists within the center of the European avant-garde. Along with the numerous calls for the exploration of space as such, their effort would appear to be part of the mainstream of modern art history. Turning to France was also a deliberate turn away from Vienna. But the actual message is even more complex and more specific to Czech culture and history. Though Picasso's and Braque's cubist work was important to the Czechs, the conflation of forces around 1910 was broad and regional: the historical architecture found in the late Gothic diamond-patterned vaults of southern Bohemia and Moravia and the early eighteenth-century Czech amalgamation of baroque Gothic both added specific cultural referents. And unlike the European avant-garde that appeared to reject history, Czech cubist architects of this first phase showed a respect for history and a self-conscious interest in having Czech cubist buildings fit within revered urban contexts. References to the Middle Ages recalled an era of Bohemian Czech independence. Instead of breaking with history, the message of Czech cubism appealed for emotional expression manifested within historical consciousness. The art critic Václav Vilém Štech claimed that this effort was a culmination of the development of national culture over the previous century.[64] This duality of innovation and historical consciousness characterized the efforts of the emerging avant-garde—revolutionary to outsiders, yet subtly connected to context and tradition from within. Also, Czech cubism had additional political implications: its "Gothic" elements recalled the medieval period, when Bohemia was an independent kingdom, not yet conquered by the Habsburgs—and hence represented the political independence desired by the modern Czech nationalists. At the same time, by adopting cubist elements, which could be seen as a "French" style, the architects were indirectly saying that they were *not* going to look to Vienna for artistic inspiration.

Furthermore, the vocabulary of Czech cubism tells an incomplete story. It did not provide a complete architectural system: its forms applied to façades and altered building mass, but the floor plans of its buildings tended to be conventional and rectilinear. The plan of the Bohdaneč spa—a municipal facility for curative mud baths and rest—shows a utilitarian arrangement of cells on a rectilinear grid dedicated to the simplest functional arrangement of bedrooms, sitting areas, and treatment rooms; the plan is in no way informed by the crystalline quality of the exterior, though some details in stairwells and their railings have prismatic shapes (fig. 3.45). The floral surroundings and anachronistic rendering of figures on a bench in Antonin Brunner's poster of 1913 for the mud baths deflate the drama of the building's cubist façades (fig. 3.46). Furniture and objects, not floor plans, spoke most effectively for the new Czech cubist style and were its greatest efflorescence.

The early phase of Czech cubism in architecture was only a beginning of Czech modernism. In the 1900s, the reaction embodied in Kotěra had been against historicism in favor of practicality, society, and function in the service of the modern. In the 1910s

CHAPTER THREE

the reaction, identified with Czech cubism, was against practicality, society, and function in favor of spirit. Even this position would be revised and challenged before and during World War I to produce an eclectic language that historian Marie Benešová labeled "Rondo-cubism"; as we shall see, it produced a different amalgam of history and identity motivated by the liberated Czech nation.[65] In the 1920s, the reactions continued as an evolving Czech modernism identified with international *Neues Bauen* (the New Building) which opposed spirit and history in favor of function.

Paralleling the Czech reactions to what appeared as outmoded languages of architecture were the ideas of Adolf Loos (1870–1933). Born in Brno, Moravia, the son of a stonemason, Loos attended college in Liberec (Reichenberg), Bohemia, and studied architecture at the Polytechnic in Dresden for three years. In 1893, he left for three years in the United States, where he learned about the works of Louis Sullivan and other progressive American architects. Loos is the arch champion in the modernist attack on ornament and a forerunner of rationalism and abstraction that would define a principal functional line of the modern movement. But his ideas have been largely misinterpreted and misrepresented.[66] Though he indeed vigorously opposed Jugendstil, Hoffmann, and the Wiener Werkstätte as antithetical to the essence of modernity, his version of the

THE LANGUAGE OF RATIONALISM

language of rationality was tempered by a pluralism that extended back into history to moments of congruence between society and art, such as occurred in the Biedermeier period of the early nineteenth century, and forward in response to contemporary conditions. Loos advocated an ornament that connected form to the simpler facts of everyday life, embodied in the Biedermeier, to the celebration of materials, to simplified configurations, and to more canonical practices of history found in classicism. His use of coffering (recalling the dome interior of the Pantheon in Rome) for the ceiling of his Kärntner Bar (1907) is only one small example of materiality and tradition put into contemporary practice.

Drawing on the writings on linguistics and ethics of Karl Kraus, Loos posited that architecture needed to provide both material comfort and appropriateness. Within this framework, his architecture could be monumental and functional, yet simple and comfortable as required by the necessity of building program and social context. Fitting into this rubric was classicism in its essential linguistic expressions of column, capital, trabeation, coffering, and proportion. Not only did classical forms enter his buildings, but ornament did as well. Contrary to the general misconception of Loos's view, casually assumed from the title of his book *Ornament and Crime*, Loos did not oppose ornament, but only inappropriate ornament, particularly surface treatments that he saw as disconnected from the real expression of the contemporary.[67] His diatribe against local ornament was very much a direct attack on the Viennese scene. For his own ornament, Loos replaced the styles of surface treatments found in the Secession with materiality itself. The sensuality of marble, the abstracted molding of granite, the warmth of wood, became the linguistic equivalents of the old ornament. Had polemicists of the modern movement perceived this nuance, modern architecture might have avoided some of the functionalist austerity and lifelessness produced from the late 1920s onward. But, of course, this was an impossibility: the total rejection of ornament became a battle cry.

Loos's language of rationalism is therefore a complex amalgam. The branch of the Anglo-Austrian Bank on the commercial Mariahilferstraße in Vienna's Eighth District demonstrates the architect's approach to rationality, language, and ornament (fig. 3.47).[68] The building, constructed in 1914, is little known, unlike his often reproduced buildings, such as the Goldman & Salatsch store (1910–11) or the Steiner and Scheu houses. However, it shows the appropriateness of the language of history, embedded here in classicism and even in representational elements. The portal on the shopping street, with monumental proportions of nine meters in height by five meters in width, has pilasters and architrave of black granite. From the portal a visitor moves through a small dark anteroom and, passing the vault, emerges into the clear interior of the top-lit banking hall. It is in the interior that Loos expressed his rationalist vocabulary. The walls are covered with book-matched white marble panels to create a butterfly figure (fig. 3.48). Marble is hard, permanent, and sensual—an appropriate material for a place charged with safeguarding the assets of clients. Panels of mirrors, located at wall tops, create both the illusion of continuous space and, as seen in the beveling of the individual sheets, represent a transformation of stone into glass. Like dressed stone, each

FIGURE 3.47
Adolf Loos, *Zentralsparkasse*, interior, Vienna, 1912.

FIGURE 3.48
Adolf Loos, *Zentralsparkasse*, interior, Vienna, 1912.

mirror retains its integrity and announces itself. The bank's role as trustee is literally spelled out, as Loos had inscribed his own words on the wall:

The Bank must say
Here is your money
Firmly and well guarded
By honest people.[69]

WHEN WE look eastward across the domain of the Dual Monarchy to scan developments in the language of rationalism, we see a divergence of approaches to expressing modern life and cultural identity through architecture. In Zagreb, Croatia (Agram in German), these dynamics played out often in the shadow of the larger metropolitan centers of Vienna and Budapest.[70] Ignjat (Ignatz) Fischer's design for Dr. Joković's Sanatorium in Zagreb (1908–10) shows a duality between inner rational functionalism and outer historicist exterior (fig. 3.49).[71] Fischer (1871–1948) was a local architect, born in Zagreb, who had studied in Vienna and Prague. The facility he designed reflects the broad interest in finding modern forms for the needs of health care and hygiene, a theme we have heard elsewhere (in Wagner's Steinhof church and briefly at

FIGURE 3.49
Ignjat Fischer, Dr. Roko Joković's sanatorium, exterior, Zagreb, Croatia, 1908–9, from *Sanatorij u Zagrebu* (Zagreb, 1909), 3.

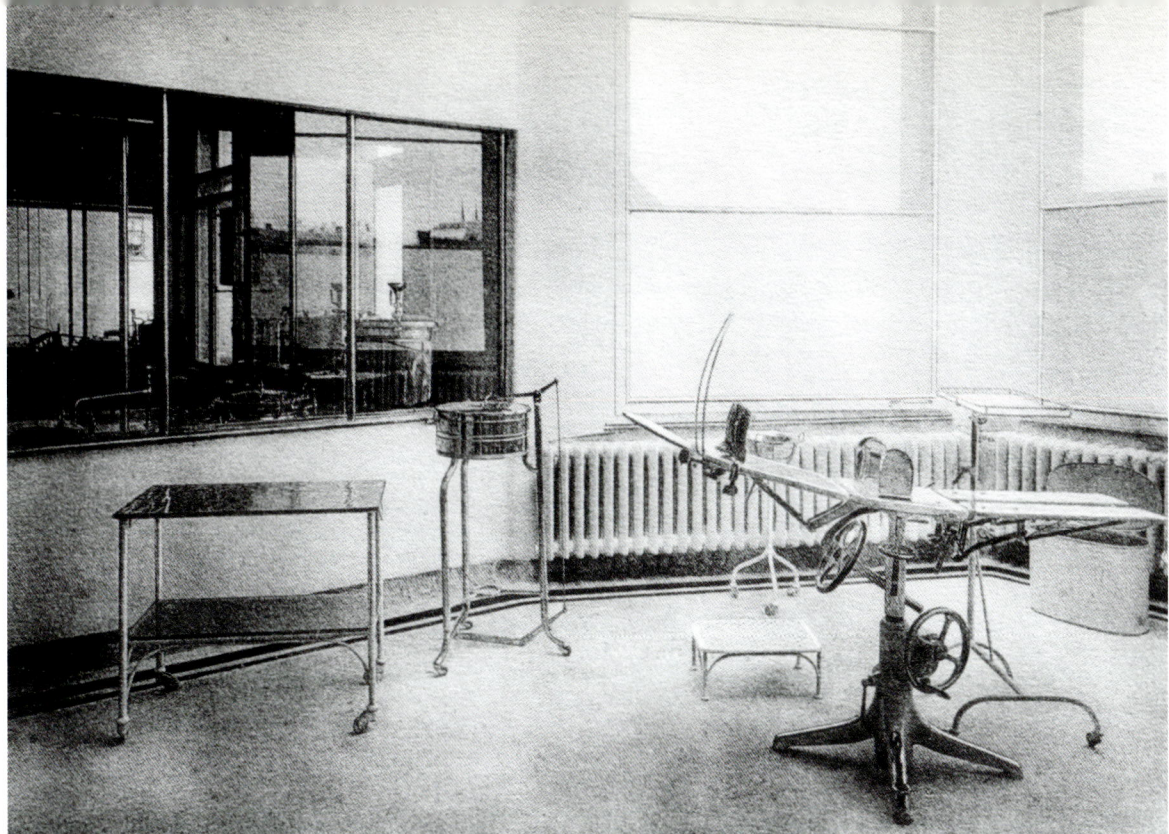

FIGURE 3.50
Ignjat Fischer, Dr. Roko Joković's sanatorium, operation room, Zagreb, Croatia, 1908–9. From *Sanatorij u Zagrebu* (Zagreb, 1909), 19.

the sanatorium at Bohdaneč). A booklet advertising services of the sanatorium shows an interior explicitly designed for medical function: patient rooms are oriented to obtain maximum sunlight, furniture has simple rectilinear shapes, functional fittings for bathing and medical procedures are void of elaboration, and hygienic ceramics cover surfaces (figs. 3.50, 3.51). Judging from the interior alone, the facility would appear to be a paragon of rationalism: a clear protofunctionalist plan with oblique wings of patient rooms for catching the most of sun and air, and a rear annex with two skylit bay-windowed operating theaters and therapy rooms below. However, the rationalist rear elevation contrasts dramatically with the street front exterior of the building, which was intended to front an extensive but never completed School Forum (intended as a campus). This façade uses some Secessionist motifs but reverts to a language of history with a tripartite façade organization of base, middle, and top, rusticated corners, colossal columns, and a flat projecting plane as cornice, as if the exterior requires classical motifs for the building to "speak" to the public.

In Hungary, the thriving economy, large industrial base, and extensive building industry assisted some architects in finding a more integral language of rationalism. In 1909, Zsigmond Sziklai designed the Grand Magasin Parisien (Párizsi Nagy Áruház), a department store for Sámuel Goldberg on Andrássy Street, one of the main new thoroughfares of Pest (fig. 3.52).[72] Constructed in 1912, it not only produced elegance but revealed how reinforced-concrete construction could open the exterior as well as the interior for the display of goods and services. While the exterior with its soaring arch motif dramatically drew the attention of passersby and visually announced its independence from the thin-mullioned window wall behind, a masonry veneer in blown-

FIGURE 3.51
Ignjat Fischer, Dr. Roko Joković's sanatorium, hydrotherapy room, Zagreb, Croatia, 1908–9. From *Sanatorij u Zagrebu* (Zagreb, 1909), 33.

FIGURE 3.52
Zsigmond Sziklai, Grand Magasin Parisien, exterior, Budapest, 1909–12. Reprinted from *Architektur des XX Jahrhunderts* (1912), plate 93.

up ashlar pattern still covered it. The conflict between form and expression of material was less evident in the vast sky-lit interior galleria, where shoppers could peruse goods along the sides of five floors and peer out through the hall. The framing of the floors and the arched bridges connecting them show a straightforward use of reinforced concrete. At its prime the store, as its name implies, was a deliberate rival of the best Paris had to offer.

An even more perfected expression of the language of rationalism is the monumental industrial hall designed by Árpád Gut and Jenő Gergely around 1912–13 and built 1913–14 as one of the most successful tectonic expressions of reinforced concrete found anywhere in Europe and a rare example of using the technology of reinforced concrete to explore both technical and aesthetic ends (fig. 3.53). At the time, the architects maintained one of the most important engineering offices in the Dual Monarchy, designing numerous industrial and transportation projects.[73] Built for the Weapon and Machine Factory Corporation, the industrial hall reduces the dimensions of its exterior piers to the minimum necessary to bear requisite load, thus allowing maximum window openings to light the interior. At the same time, the façade is composed of a layer of arches superimposed over the columnar structural grid. On the long façade (facing

FIGURE 3.53
Árpád Gut and Jenő Gergely, Weapon and Machine Factory Corporation Building, exterior, Budapest, 1912–14.

Soroksári Street), two smaller arches flank a central arch, and along with the curved terminations under the shallow roof cornice provide a softening effect to the innate hardness of concrete.

All in all, a quest for clarity and logic, for the expression of materials and structure that somehow resonated with the contemporary times defines the language of rationalism as it existed on the eve of World War I. But the rationalism of science and philosophy did not dominate absolutely. The architectural language of rationalism was neither total abstraction nor minimal form driven only by functional demands. Its breadth still extended the definition of function to include the poetic and the spiritual. This condition existed not only in the Austro-Hungarian Empire but elsewhere in Europe and even in the emerging modernism of Americans like Frank Lloyd Wright. The Bauhaus had not yet been conceived, and Le Corbusier had only begun in 1914 to develop the pure forms of shelter and structure articulated by the column and plane construction of his Maison Domino. The world was still multilingual, still searching for the modern in a vibrant variety. For the moment, polyglotism in architecture still ruled.

THE LANGUAGE OF MYTH

4

THE IDEA of architecture as a language that represents the identity of a people was a widely shared assumption at the turn of the twentieth century. A singular identity for the whole Austro-Hungarian Empire, however, could not be defined: numerous ones coexisted, and their multiple presences worked against any possibility of unity. Imperial Austria saw its identity rooted in baroque architecture in the eighteenth century, a position that supported a baroque revival extending from the late 1890s to World War I. But Austrian baroque architecture had its origins in Italy, and its greatest practitioner, Fischer von Erlach, received his crucial formation during extended study and work in Rome. Despite its transformations across the Alps in Austria, the baroque had its roots in Italian culture and history and ultimately imperial Rome. But Germany also had a strong cultural influence from the eighteenth century onward through its music and philosophy.[1] Italy, German culture, and history itself mitigated against baroque being the unique expression of imperial Austria, so that official Austria's identity was associative.

Similarly, the *Moderne* that Wagner, Hoffmann, and their circles championed had its own problems in representing collective identity. Beyond an upwardly mobile bourgeoisie, the middle class did not identify with the objects of the Wiener Werkstätte. Despite the claim of wanting to transform popular taste and put it in harmony with the spirit of the age, the production of objects for everyday life catered to an elite, not the masses, and therefore had inherent limits as a vehicle of collective identity.

Architecture's ability to express identity had limited alternatives. It could express the idea of a nation or nation-state as long as the nation itself had an ethnic and social cohesion. It could partially express that identity, a condition that allowed for contradiction. It could express, within its own limits, the efforts of individuals—architects and their patrons and clients. Or it could express nothing at all intrinsically but act as a hollow vessel into which anyone could insert his or her own meaning.

Within these possibilities, architecture in Austria retained an ambiguity. Vienna, the imperial center, enjoyed the illusion of control through the widespread use of the German language and official styles, formerly of the neo-Renaissance and more recently of the neobaroque. In their own way, these styles were assertions of a national myth. In reality, the empire was tense, multilingual, multiethnic, with a hugely varied architecture that had no unique origins. The quest for unique origins pressured progressive intellectuals, including artists, writers, and architects, to confront its conflicted position.

The need to develop a language of national identity in the Hungarian domain of the empire took on increasing urgency throughout the nineteenth century. By the

1890s, architectural developments in Hungary provided a rich ground for observing the unfolding of a language characterized by multiple readings: at first glance, a new architecture with curvilinear forms appeared to be a manifestation of organicism, but closer investigation shows it was also one of many strands of modernism. Not only did a small cluster of Hungarian architects develop their own interpretation of the biological metaphor of organicism, but for a brief period they tied their efforts to the emergence of a language of national identity, an architecture that was purported to be uniquely Hungarian. Hungary had a legacy of medieval, Gothic, Renaissance, and baroque architecture, and in the nineteenth century Miklós Ybl had provided masterful demonstrations of neo-Renaissance and *Rundbogenstil* (round arched style) buildings, while Imre Steindl designed a monumental neo-Gothic style Parliament building (1854–1904).[2] General opinion associated the Gothic with German origins, and the style of the Parliament building created controversy; but when Hungarians identified it with the British House of Parliament, the building became one more protest against Austrian hegemony and a claim for Hungarian sovereignty, as if the nation were more independent and more European than it was. Nevertheless, the effectiveness of the neo-styles to represent Hungarian identity was limited: the styles of Gothic and Renaissance were transnational in use, and no nation owned them exclusively.

A language of myth in Hungary grew out of a reaction against the languages of history and emerged in the 1890s, but its impetus began earlier. Count István Széchenyi and the art historian Imre Henszlmann began to call for the creation of a Hungarian national style around 1840. Occurring in an era of reform, their efforts were part of a rising nationalism that opposed the dominance of the Austrian crown and the German language. Some forty years later, the Transylvanian propagandist and art teacher József Huszka advocated the study of folk art as the best way to recall traditional Hungarian roots.[3] Not only did Huszka collect, publish, and lecture on Hungarian folk designs, but he urged architects to found a national style based on ethnographic investigation. He claimed that the purest forms of Hungarian cultural artifacts were preserved on the periphery of the country, in Transylvania. This could be seen, for instance, in the palm tree ornaments of the Székely wooden gates, which, in Huszka's opinion, resembled ancient Persian motifs. Furthermore, he insisted that to find the purest sources of national forms, one had to go back beyond Arabic Persian art to its precedents in the Sassanian culture of Turan.

In identifying Sassanian culture, Huszka was referring to the ancient Iranian dynasty (224–651 CE) whose empire at one point extended north to present-day Georgia, south into the Arabian Peninsula, eastward to the Indus River, and westward to the upper Tigris and Euphrates river valleys. Under the Sassanids, art, architecture, metalwork, and gem engraving had flourished. *Tūrān*, the Persian word for Turkistan, the land north of Iran, was a desert lowland in present-day southwestern Kazakhstan, northwestern Uzbekistan, and Turkmenistan. Implicitly present in the reference to Turan, however, was Pan-Turanism, the late nineteenth- and early twentieth-century movement to unite politically and culturally Turkic, Tatar, and Uralic peoples living in Turkey and across Eurasia from Hungary to the Pacific.[4] Intellectuals promoted the theory that Turkish, Mongol, Finnish, Hungarian, and other languages (the Ural-Altaic languages) allegedly shared common roots. Some saw Pan-Turanism as a means of uniting Turks and Hungarians in opposition to Slavs and Pan-Slavism, but the movement was minor.

This casting back to find the origins of Hungarian art and architecture and their legacy in folk art accompanied a basic narrative about the alleged origin of the ancient Turanian Magyars. By the late nineteenth century, the origins of the Hungarian people had assumed a mythic status, focusing on Arpad, chief of the Magyar tribes, forbearer of the nation's kings and leader of the seven tribes that comprised the Magyar people. The Magyars were believed to have settled in the area of modern Hungary—the plains of Pannonia—between 880 and 900. In this version of the foundation myth, the Magyars, whose language had Finno-Ugric roots, emanated originally from western Siberia and in the mid-ninth century settled between the lower Danube and southern Carpathian Mountains. A strong tribal order governed, but in 904 Arpad and his clan took over as supreme leaders. Their emblem became a falconlike bird, in Turcic *Turul*. Arpad, as founder of the nation, and his six tribal chieftains took figural form in popular imagination. All clothed in tribal cloaks, helmets with feathers, and flowing full moustaches, they became the focus of a grandiose monument constructed in Budapest in 1896 for the great Millennial Celebration of one thousand years of the Hungarian conquest.[5]

Upon their arrival in Pannonia, the Magyars created a unique synthesis of their own building traditions with whatever they may have confronted, including Greco-Roman and Christian traditions.[6] This synthesis of disparate elements was visible in the additional combination of battlement cornices in northern Hungary, brought by Italian fortress engineers, with motifs found in the ancient Székely and Kalotaszeg peoples of Transylvania. However, Turkish occupation, which lasted for about 150 years until 1686, hindered Magyar cultural development, as did the Habsburgs, who eventually established the dominance of baroque as the favored imperial style.

The discovery of the folk art of Kalotaszeg had a great impact on the nationalist discourse in Hungary starting in the 1870s. Similar to regions in other European countries that became identified with the folk traditions of their respective nations, like Brittany in France and Karelia in Finland, Kalotaszeg eventually became central to an emerging Hungarian ethnography. Enthusiasts like the writer Etelka Gyarmathy promoted objects of Kalotaszeg embroidery, woodcarving, ceramics, weaving, and other genres at such major national events as the 1885 National Exhibition and Fair and 1896 Millenary Exhibition. Painters such as Aladár Körösfői-Kreisch, composers such as Béla Bartók, and architects flocked to Kalotaszeg around the turn of the century seeking inspiration; visitors also came from abroad, including the English painter Walter Crane. At the same time, the region developed a rising cottage industry,

FIGURE 4.1
Embroidery of a *szűr*. Such patterns representing flower bouquets were applied around the lower end of the coat, in the corners of the collar, and on the sleeves; Bihar County, Hungary.

FIGURE 4.2
(*Facing, top and left*) Detail of chest, Hódmezővásárhely, Csongrád County, Hungary. The front of the chest is elaborately decorated and the principal ornament, a vase of flowers, is set in a field framed with carving, against a dark-blue background with red, white, yellow, and green colors. The main color, however, as on other specimens of the older style, is red.

particularly of embroidery and ceramics, that found its way into Hungarian middle-class homes.

Clothing became both the legacy and the source of Hungarian national identity as well as a basis for a new form of language while the main themes of Hungarian folk art—abstracted hearts, flowers, and birds—became central to the iconography of the Hungarian national styles. Because connections to folk embroidery and pottery played an increasing role in this iconography, it is helpful to briefly examine objects and techniques of folk art to help in reading their use in architecture. As animate forms, they were by definition organic and works of nature, though subjected to processes of abstraction and conventionalization in their execution. Materials, technique, and traditional processes dictated their production and use (figs. 4.1, 4.2). The stylized ceremonial knots of the Hungarian hussar cavalry uniform had already provided a motif that Frigyes Feszl used on his Vigadó concert hall in Budapest (1859–64). The *suba*, a sleeveless sheepskin coat, and the *szűr*, with its white background with islands of ornamental pattern, were embodiments of traditional clothing. The *szűr*, an embroidered woolen cloak worn by shepherds, contained other characteristic motifs suitable for integration into art and architecture (figs. 4.3, 4.4). The general morphology of surface treatments, as seen in the *suba* or *szűr*, consisted of a trim for defining edges, a filled pattern along the trim, a void area of neutral background, and islands of pattern within the void, providing visual balance (fig. 4.5).[7] Embroidery encompassed a variety of decorative designs with plain or fancy stitches. Especially important were different techniques of decorating garment openings and edges, such as welting, piping, or braiding, as well as appliqué, where decorative motifs were created by sewing one material over another.[8] The techniques of piping and welted edges, the themes of hearts, birds, and animals, as well as the morphology of pattern-making that characterized shepherds' cloaks, would be deftly appropriated by the emerging generation of Hungarian nationalist architects for their ornament. Reds and greens were national colors used in deeply saturated combinations. Dots became common motifs, often associated with embroidered patterns. They could even be seen on special bakery confections.

The calls for national identity, the exhortations to look back to the Magyars, and the emergence of a language of myth to express them in architecture found fruition in

FIGURE 4.3
(*Top, right*) Herdsmen from the Hungarian Great Plain. The *szűr*, a cloak made of rough, heavy cloth, is thrown over the shoulder. The feather affixed to the hat represents the profession of the wearer: the herdsman on the left wears a crane feather, the shepherd on the right the feather of a bustard, a game bird related to cranes and plovers.

FIGURE 4.4
(*Bottom, left*) Fancy *szűr* from the Great Hungarian Plain.

FIGURE 4.5
(*Bottom, right*) Sheepskin cloak, Hódmezővásárhely, Csongrád County, Hungary. The sheepskin is dyed yellow, cut in a sleeveless cape style, and decorated on the edges and shoulders with leather appliqué and colorful wool embroidery. The collar is made of black lamb hide.

the work and writings of Ödön Lechner (1845–1914).[9] With its curves and flowing forms, the architectural language he ultimately produced appears highly organic—it could have been discussed as an example of the language of organicism—but his work differed significantly from early Hungarian followers of art nouveau and Jugendstil as he moved from the realm of empathy, emotion, and art for art's sake to his own idiom of national identity. Furthermore, his innovative use of a language of myth actually preceded the radical Secessionists and Jugendstil in Vienna and Prague.

Study, travel, and passion motivated Lechner to explore Hungarian folk art and to investigate Hungarian identity. Born in Pest, he studied at the Technical University in Budapest and the Berlin Academy of Architecture (Bauakademie).[10] After finishing his studies and traveling in Italy in the late 1860s, he designed apartment houses, and worked in Paris from 1875 to 1878, contributing to the building and restoration of castles and being impressed with early French Renaissance architecture; he later traveled to England, where he studied the polychrome ceramics found at the South Kensington Museum in London.[11] Observing the remarkable Persian pottery at the museum reminded him of his father's own pottery factory, which had produced geometric and glazed bricks for the Dohány Street Synagogue in Pest. His companion on this first trip was Vilmos Zsolnay, the inventor of pyrogranite, a durable water-resistant ceramic produced at Zsolnay's factory in Pécs; their friendship, together with Lechner's own family tradition, later became decisive in the formation of his unique modern style.[12] Lechner made another trip to England to explore the "Indian style" architecture that had been in vogue at the beginning of the nineteenth century. From these travels, as Lechner declared later in his "Autobiographical Sketch," "Studying our folk art led me to the art of Asian peoples, for some striking similarities are immediately apparent. This Eastern relationship, which shows up primarily in Persian and even more in Indian art, was of particular interest because these peoples invested their art with monumentality, and I wished to find some guidance on using the folk motifs in monumental architecture."[13] Success in establishing the new architecture was not easy: native Hungarian architecture, "the mother of the arts," was buried deep in the past, and as Lechner wrote in 1902, "the only national characteristics that could not be encountered in the streets of Budapest were Hungarian ones."[14]

Lechner elaborated this theory in an essay in the journal *Művészet* (Art) in 1906, the same year that Frank Lloyd Wright published his own manifesto, "In the Cause of Architecture," in *Architectural Record*. Lechner's text opens with a salvo: "There has been no Hungarian language of architecture, but there will be!"[15] For Lechner, the establishment of a Hungarian national style of architecture was a necessary political goal, because without one, the nation would disappear. He insisted that authentic national cultures have never copied styles from others, but that "races" created their styles in terms of their own distinct spirits, which are most manifest at the level of surface decoration. Although Lechner noted that architects should study history, he found historical styles, including Hungarian neoclassicism and neo-Gothic, inappropriate for modern life.

Lechner's theory also emphasized language and its relationship to architecture and identity. Foremost was the parallel between identity and the Hungarian language. The Hungarian language had fallen into disuse a hundred years earlier (the gentry spoke German, while the Parliament used Latin, a practice that the people ridiculed), but it had been revived as an expression of national identity. Lechner's hope was that Hungarian architecture would become as accepted and commonly used as the Hungarian language itself. Just as German was the language of business and government, homogenizing the different entities of the Austro-Hungarian Empire and thus ought to be opposed, Lechner hoped historical styles of neo-Renaissance and neo-Gothic would be rejected too. While the Hungarian language expressed identity by providing Hungarian words for names and places, architecture must reinforce this sense of identity as well, a principal source of which could be found in Hungarian folklore, particularly in clothing. Echoing Huszka, Lechner observed that clothing had already found its way into the expression of national spirit, as seen in folk costumes. He also claimed that the language of form could exert a greater impact than even the spoken language. Magyar was "exotic and hard to understand for outsiders," whereas a new language of national forms would be more comprehensible.[16] Furthermore, the successful development of a Hungarian architectural language could be a better unifying force than the spoken language itself. It could uplift the minorities who had opposed Magyar being imposed on them in schools, offices, and the army.

Lechner's theories met resistance, and the road to the new expression was challenging. To move forward, people would need to reject the connection of the architecture of national identity to the Secession, with its implications of something unserious and rude and Viennese. They would also need to create a broad-based conscious nationalism beyond the confines of an intellectual elite. And architects would need to overcome their own reluctance to use the new forms out of fear of the financial costs involved. Lechner also saw that the new organic language had limitations: while he found the new form operating in two dimensions, that is, on the surface, he realized that two dimensions were inadequate for the creation of great architecture. Nevertheless, treating the surface was better than merely copying the past, and technical innovation could assist new solutions. But technology, which seems to be so equated with rationalist modernism, was for Lechner a means of creating a language dedicated to national architectural expression, not an end in itself.

Lechner's first great opportunity to demonstrate and transform the grammar of Hungarian folk art into an architectural language of myth was his commission for the Museum of Applied Arts in Budapest (1892–96; fig. 4.6). The design marked the shift from his own historicism—Lechner had a broad-based practice and had designed schools and city halls throughout Hungary—to a new, distinctly recognizable vocabulary of nationalism. Moreover, the museum commission appropriately coincided with the great Millennial Celebration of 1896.[17] The celebration confirmed, at least in some degree, that a mythic past could serve as the basis for a modern identity; and the creation of a national school for the study and training in decorative arts was a corollary to such acknowledgment.

FIGURE 4.6
Ödön Lechner, Museum of Applied Arts, exterior, Budapest, 1891–96.

The rationale for establishing the museum was similar to that for the South Kensington Museum in London (1857, later the Victoria and Albert Museum) and the Museum of Art and Industry in Vienna (1864, later the Museum for Applied Art). These institutions allowed designers, craftsmen, and manufacturers the opportunity of studying historical forms and materials as they sought the basis for new, modern designs. The museums were intended to support the reform of national industrial production in order to increase the competitive edge of one country over another. However, in the case of the Budapest museum, that conviction was combined with more specific nationalist ambitions.

The commission for the museum enabled the first blossoming of Lechner's artistic maturity and the construction of the first museum built in Europe outside the limits of traditional historical styles.[18] Designed in 1891 in conjunction with his partner Gyula Pártos and completed in 1896, it spoke of a history that located the origins of the Hungarian people in Persia and India and in the clothing and objects of folk arts. It also utilized innovative construction techniques and new materials.

To achieve these ends, Lechner began by using a series of open courtyards to occupy the irregularities of a trapezoidal site. He then laid out the plans to include not only gallery spaces, but also apartments, offices, and a school. He clad the exterior basement with stone, the first story with pyrogranite, and faced the two floors above with glazed brick that allowed dramatic contrasts with the main articulating motifs of the surface: the treatment of window surrounds with ogival arch motifs that recall Indian traditions. These arches, executed as stone moldings around windows, also recall welted stitches on the *szűr*, the traditional coats of Hungarian shepherds, thus allowing the curving forms to serve double duty.[19] At the upper wall termination, a series of arched openings have blind panels filled with ceramic glazed flowers. A cresting of stone above this parapet also uses the ogival motif. Punctuating the façade is a series of engaged columns terminating in finials with multiple shafts that recall similar treatments in Indian architecture. The green and yellow of the roof resembles the colors found in Persian ceramics. The drama of the building's exterior revolves around the central entry pavilion and corner tower, each of which has soaring apsidal domes topped with cupolas. Zsolnay tiles in a field of green overlaid with a diamond lattice of ochre articulate every surface of the domes and the roofs; Ákos Moravánszky has compared them with "rug-covered tents of the Orient."[20] Yet these domes hover beyond finite nomenclature. Their pronounced verticality recalls the shape of a helmet. With its cupola, the central dome also resembles a crown, yet one very much associated with the crown of Saint Steven, a national treasure; moreover, it has vague associations with Indian temples. At the same time, the apsidal form with its pronounced ridges corresponds rationally and precisely to the internal steel structure of trusses which provide the support for the dome itself.[21] This multiplicity of meaning and its multiple linguistic interpretations characterize Lechner's entire treatment of the building.

The themes of dancing, colorful Persian and Indian motifs announced on the exterior can be seen close up as visitors enter the building. The handrail of the stairs consists of serpentine ogival forms, which are nearly identical to the uppermost cresting of the roof ridge; they are executed in a thick, vibrant Zsolnay glaze in ochre with white accents (fig. 4.7). Flanking the sides of the entry stair are arched openings, also with ogival moldings in stone, and glazed brick surfaces with red crowns and blue hemispheres. Both the ogives and trefoils recall Persian motifs resembling those readily available for adaptation in the plates of Owen Jones's *Grammar of Ornament*.[22]

Passing through a windbreak and into an octagonal entry, visitors enter a forecourt, at the center of which is a lobed opening in the floors above with a skylight of colored glass (fig. 4.8A–B). The opening recalls an *opaion*, a hole in primitive structures like tents that allowed the escape of smoke. This primitivist association coincides with extraordinary formal and technical finesse. The shape of the opening is composed of four arched motifs, two of which have pointed arches and two opposing ones with round arches. Approached from an angle and seen from either above or below, the shape has a dynamic diagonal quality. At the same time, its framing is a tectonic expression of the steel beams emanating from the entryway and surrounding all sides of the opening. Yet these beams, rather than being exposed, are covered with stucco floral motifs reminiscent of those from the plates of Jones's Moresque ornament.[23]

THE LANGUAGE OF MYTH

FIGURE 4.7
Ödön Lechner, Museum of Applied Arts, detail of the railing, Budapest, 1891–96.

FIGURE 4.8A–B
(*Facing*) Ödön Lechner, Museum of Applied Arts, opening in forecourt, Budapest, 1891–96. *B*, detail.

Beyond the foyer at the entry level is the glass-lit museum space itself (figs. 4.9, 4.10). A rolled steel framing supports the glass roof and fully participates in the iconographic program of the building. Its webs are perforated with circles and multifoliated forms, creating an impression of lacy flowers, delicate entities rendered in a hard material. Stained glass forms a transition from the translucent glass of the vault to the steel girders and walls that support it. Unfortunately covered in white in the 1970s, the vertical surfaces originally had colorful painted flowers. At the edges of the hall are the most literal references to Indian architecture: two sets of superimposed arches defined by piers of multiple columns, foliate capitals, and arches with cusps.

Lechner's language shows a panoply of Indian forms pressed into the service of giving identity to the new Hungarian national architecture. Cusped arches and the grammar of Indian architecture overall have highly complex systems with long histories and their own technical names, but Lechner would have had access to the numerous publications on Indian architecture that abounded in the late nineteenth century, including James Fergusson's *A History of Indian and Eastern Architecture* (London, 1876), revised in 1891, as well as Fergusson and J. Burgess's *The Cave Temples of India* (London, 1880).[24]

While the language of the museum spoke to its visitors with organic shapes, referring to flowers of Hungarian folk art and Indian architecture as the purported origins of the Hungarians, it also spoke of the innovative use of materials. Glazed ceramics not only provided an opportunity for the richest iconographic development, but also,

FIGURE 4.9
Ödön Lechner, Museum of Applied Arts, main hall, Budapest, 1891–96.

in Lechner's terms, were a quintessentially modern material. They resisted soot and urban smog and were hygienic, washable, and colorfast. Also, modern manufacturing techniques using majolica compensated for the fact that stone of good quality was not available in Hungary. Further, this efficient and highly malleable material connected contemporary use to the traditions of folk ceramics.

Lechner's incipient modernism is also revealed in the uncovered steelwork in the interior of the roof of the exhibition hall. Though general construction consisted of brick walls covered with ceramic plates, steel framing provides the building's support and props for its extraordinary stucco detailing. The existence of extensive static analyses shows that Lechner's solution for the main glass hall and its ornamental beams, as well as consoles, was among the most up-to-date technical achievements of the time. In addition, the structural system of the entry includes a three-dimensional riveted

FIGURE 4.10
Ödön Lechner, Museum of Applied Arts, main hall, detail of the top floor, Budapest, 1891–96.

steel frame extending from the front façade to the main exhibition hall and carrying the skirting beams of the *opaions*.[25] However, as in the main exhibition hall, the steel is perforated with patterns resembling lace or abstracted flowers instead of emphasizing its structural function.

Lechner's treatment of structure represents an attitude of modernism that differs from the functionalist and aesthetic languages that would emerge in the next decade in western Europe. For Lechner, structure was a means to provide efficient construction, spatial drama, and a framework for what the building needed to say to its public. It was neither a symbol of progress nor an end in itself. However, his new language of Hungarian national identity executed with curvilinear shapes loaded with references had a difficult reception. Critics called the museum building "the Palace of the Gipsy King." Even Lechner himself thought it overstated, with its references to India.[26]

FIGURE 4.11
Ödön Lechner, Hungarian Geological Institute, exterior, Budapest, 1896–99.

The opportunity to further explore the language of mythic national identity linked to modern technology arose with the announcement of a competition for a new Hungarian Royal Geological Institute (fig. 4.11). A scientific institute for research and documentation, it was one of the facilities that started appearing around Europe in the mid-nineteenth century in response to the needs of industrialization.[27] The first institute was established in England in 1835 and the second in Austria in 1849, with similar organizations in Prussia, France, and Italy following soon after. The Hungarian Royal Geological Institute had been founded in 1869, but for the next twenty-five years had no permanent home until it received a substantial private donation of one hundred thousand crowns, and the City of Budapest set aside land for a new building. The new building would provide free access to the public and house samples of minerals; financial support came from the state treasury as well as from other public contributions.

The site selected was 2–4 Stefánia Street, a street formed after the unification of Pest, Buda, and Óbuda, when the periphery of the city began to develop. The government mounted a competition for the institute building in 1896. The jury's minutes, which announced Ödön Lechner as the first prizewinner, praised the clarity of his design and, in particular, his concept for allowing future expansion of the building on its site. The plan was a simple square with central court. As built, it would contain an area of 2,165 square meters on three floors. Public spaces were located in the center, stacked one upon the other, and corridors had offices on a single side, allowing natural light to penetrate from the court into hallways and rooms.

Conscious of criticism leveled at the Museum of Applied Arts, Lechner provided a more modest and reserved competition entry.[28] Like the museum, the Geological Institute has a pronounced verticality to it and uses engaged piers to accentuate its height of forty-two meters. The roof provides a visual lure for visitors, with its dazzling light-blue Zsolnay ceramics (fig. 4.12). Open arches alternating with abstracted anthemia, which guide the eye toward a globe at the top of the central apex, articulate the ridges of the roof's pyramidal forms. The globe represents the narrative of geology, as the earth itself became the subject for the building. Descending from the roof to the façades, the eye encounters two shades of blue: a light-gray "Prussian" blue for joinery and an ultramarine blue for other glazed ceramic elements within a field of yellow bricks. The cartouche-like outlines of brick with floral motifs in their centers recall the motifs of folk art.[29] The front façade also conveys the purpose and function of the building: two floors of offices are identified by single windows framed by stone moldings, while triple windows that form a bracelet around the top of the building announce the museum on the third floor. The national significance of the institution is reinforced by the Hungarian coat of arms, executed in ultramarine-blue glazed majolica and located above the entry portal.

FIGURE 4.12
Ödön Lechner, Hungarian Geological Institute, detail of the roof and top floor, Budapest, 1896–99.

Despite establishing similarities to the Museum of Applied Arts, at the Geological Institute Lechner toned down the more overt references to Indian and Persian architecture. The main entry above a basement no longer has cusped arches with their Indian reference, but soft curves that ascend toward the midpoint along with a fanlight divided by undulating floral forms (fig. 4.13). The carvings on the entry doors have white "braided" ornaments, and flower motifs in their panels (now gone) had curved tops. A visitor enters from the street through a screen of wood and glass that acts as a windbreak before the main vestibule. The upper portion of the screen has curved terminations mirroring the entry that reverberate with associations of international art nouveau. But unlike his European peers, Lechner filled the screen's upper range with a globed fretwork and floral designs of an interlaced lattice of curves that still make some reference to Persian and Islamic patterns.

FIGURE 4.13
Ödön Lechner, Hungarian Geological Institute, entry, Budapest, 1896–99. From *Budapester Neubauten* (Vienna: Verlag Anton Schroll, 1910), plate 33.

FIGURE 4.14
Ödön Lechner, Hungarian Geological Institute, view of the interior vestibule, Budapest, 1896–99. From *Budapester Neubauten* (Vienna: Verlag Anton Schroll, 1910), plate 34.

Having passed into the foyer, a visitor sees a broad stair leading up to a simple arrangement of common rooms, vestibules, library, and meeting rooms (fig. 4.14). On the north side, a gray-colored marble stair leads to the office of the director, the laboratories, and storage rooms. A lecture hall, reading rooms, and research rooms for geologists are located in the side wings. The floor above the entry contained the exhibition hall of geological specimens. Lechner himself designed the mahogany vitrines and added running bands of trefoils at their top edges to reinforce the motif of the building. The ceiling of the hall has fretwork executed with lobed forms. However, the lobed arches resonating with Indian forms found at the museum are replaced here with a wave motif that undulates under the arched openings of the entry vestibule. This lobed fretwork with flowers at the center became a sign that could be varied throughout the building; such linking and transforming a motif reflected the idea of Gesamtkunstwerk and organic wholeness. At the same time, Lechner's treatment of surfaces reflects a shift from Indian connotations at the museum toward more pronounced folk motifs.

THE LANGUAGE OF MYTH

Though less overt than at the museum, references to India and Persia are nonetheless present in the institute's architecture. The engaged columns in the entry vestibule are based on the Persepolitan column type, as seen in columns of the free-standing stupa hall at Karli (78 BCE), where bases have inverted forms and the capitals are transformed into elephants. Lechner could have had access to many sources on Persian architecture that were published after the mid-nineteenth century.[30] Since the forms of Persepolis migrated with time eastward to India, the iconography of Persepolis in particular serves dual purposes: not only does it refer to Persia, but also to India as the sources of originary form of the Hungarian nation.

Lechner, however, transformed his material as he substituted and reassembled motifs to create a mythic language of identity. In the vestibule, he replaced the cusps in every arch with a wave motif. The undersides of these arches were surfaced with rosettes and rows of dots shaped as hemispheres in an octagonal pattern. He altered the engaged column shafts of octagons in the Indian model, or the narrow vertical slots in the palace model, by adding additional rows of semispherical knobs. On the one hand, these knobs can be interpreted as metaphorical rivets, which refer to the steel construction embedded in the walls of the vestibule and the modern means of supporting its open space. On the other hand, these dots can refer to those frequently found in folk designs.

A dual reading of architectural language is again present in Lechner's treatment of the structure. As at the Museum of Applied Arts, steel supports allow for the open spaces of the entry and the halls. The dichotomy between structure and imagery is seen in that Lechner used riveted steel arches to divide the vestibule vault, yet instead of leaving it bare, he articulated the steel structure with wave forms, with rivet knobs executed in stucco. The vestibule ceiling has a shallow, scalloped flat dome at whose center is a descending protuberance used for hanging a chandelier. This protuberance also has the rivet dot, but at the same time it recalls a stalactite, a geological formation relevant to the purpose of the institute itself. The narrative of geology is further articulated in the stalactite-like portions of the capitals. Similar shapes support the central chandelier.

The opening of the Geological Institute in 1899 did not cause the uproar that greeted the debut of the Museum of Applied Arts, though it, too, embodied paradoxes. It relied on folk arts to create an iconography of national identity. However, the massing of its interior spaces, its placement within the cityscape, and the expression of its functions conveyed a functional approach that responded to the need to attract visitors to the institute's museum and satisfy the modern requirements of geologists in the pursuit of their scientific research. With its minimized literal associations with the architecture of India, the Geological Institute provides a transition to the third and final major building of Lechner's career, the Hungarian Royal Postal Savings Bank in Budapest.

FIGURE 4.15
Ödön Lechner, Postal Savings Bank, exterior, Budapest, 1899–1901.

The Austro-Hungarian Empire's first post office savings bank was opened in Vienna in 1883.[31] Although post offices throughout the empire were part of the same service network arising from the Compromise of 1867, the new Postal Savings Bank in Budapest was established in 1885 with an emphasis on its role as a people's bank. Its founding prospectus announced it would collect deposits "not from the surpluses of the rich, but from the pennies of simple farmers, workers and children, saved often with great difficulty, with great sacrifice and self-discipline."[32] Lechner won the competition in April 1900, work was completed quickly, and the building was opened with much ceremony in November 1901 (fig. 4.15). Even seven years later, a commentator noted that more often than small depositors visiting the bank, the building's supporters and opponents flocked there to comment on its architecture.

With the completion of the Postal Savings Bank, Lechner's language of myth now was put to practical and popular use in a location at the back of a block facing the splendid new Szabadság Square. A consistent treatment of single windows on the façade implies the functions of the building, with mostly offices and apartments on upper floors.[33] Brick veneer frames windows and composes the vertical piers that outline the central entry and corners of the building; light-cream stucco fills in between the bands of brick. Green and yellow Zsolnay ceramics comprise the decorative elements,

THE LANGUAGE OF MYTH

FIGURE 4.16
Ödön Lechner, Postal Savings Bank, exterior, Budapest, 1899–1901.

particularly on the roof. Lechner used ogival arches, signs of the national style, in the vertical piers, with finials outlining flat fields resembling shields. The shield motif runs the length of the top floors and forms an interlacing pattern with the top row of office windows. These shields, like much of Lechner's detailing, have multivalent connotations. Comblike and forming a screen, they resemble flat curvilinear battlements. They also bring to the viewer's eye recollections of cartouches, and the welted edges around the floral decoration found in folk-art clothing (fig. 4.16). These framing outlines became a hallmark of Lechner's approach, as were the brightly colored ceramic tiles in ochre, blue, and green, colors found in the folk traditions of the countryside. One commentator saw the hood moldings surrounding the windows as a recollection of the "Hungarian rhythm of line . . . a crowning of all striving after a Hungarian decorative art."[34]

Lechner's vocabulary at the Postal Savings Bank was the subject of fantastical invention. The central bay is emphasized by tiers of interconnected shields and piers topped with beehives. The ochre revetment of Zsolnay ceramics on the central pavilion gives the appearance of visual icing. Beyond the apex of the central bay, a soaring, mansard-like pinnacle covered in blue-green ceramic tile, pierced with openings framed by ochre shapes, is surmounted by an extraordinary termination. At the top of the tent-like middle pinnacle are two bulls' heads; an enlarged motif of Hungarian sheep-coat embroidery is located between them. While the embroidery motif refers to folk art, the bulls' heads have multiple associations: the form recalls the Persian treatment found at Persepolis in columns with two bulls' heads looking in opposite directions, an image confirmed by the presence of horns; and they resemble a blown-up detail from a drinking cup that was part of the Nagyszentmiklós treasure, named for the province where it was found but more commonly known at the turn of the century as Attila's Treasure.[35] Lechner specifically invested this motif with a symbolic message to refer in this context to the ancient national treasure and the continuity between the Huns and the Magyars.[36]

The roof also features other imaginary figures that contribute to the meaning of the building and interact with the sky. Lechner's drawings of the façade show ceramic figures at each end of the steeply sloped roof, perched upon a globelike element, resembling dragons with outstretched wings.[37] As executed, these terminations evolved into an abstract interlacing of winged serpents, hovering over the building as if they were guardians of treasures within.[38] The octagonal piers hold beehives at their tops, symbols of accumulation and diligence typical of many savings banks, and lines of bees can be seen moving up the piers toward them.

At the core of the interior is the banking hall (fig. 4.17). Its columns swell with entasis, while their capitals, referring to Persian precedents, are flattened on their fronts and waved on their sides; rivet-dots, as seen in the Geological Institute, stud their full lengths. Flat wall surfaces between the column capitals are covered with flower motifs. The columns and walls support a pierced clerestory consisting of pairs and triads of oval shapes, many in the form of teardrops. On the one hand, they recall French and Belgian art nouveau, and on the other, the lobed fretwork that by that time had become synonymous with Lechner's vocabulary. Not only was this motif used to articulate the clerestory below the glass brick ceiling, but its curvilinear forms were repeated in the original chairs at the tables of the banking hall.[39] Instead of a double roof for glazing, the postal hall ceiling consists of only a single layer of hollow glass bricks that allow external light to pour through the glittering glass lenses, a bold and defiant gesture ignoring the risks of weather and age.

The Postal Savings Bank in Budapest summarized the motifs of Lechner's organic national style and the dualism of his approach that exploited the latest developments in technology, yet covered that technology with a linguistic treatment intended to speak to the Hungarian nation. Like his two other major works, the Postal Savings

FIGURE 4.17
Ödön Lechner, Postal Savings Bank, banking hall, Budapest, 1899–1901. Reprinted from *Budapester Neubauten II* (Vienna: Verlag Anton Schroll, 1910).

Bank demonstrated the paradox of his language. The building was technologically and conceptually modern, yet its ornament spoke of a language of myth, enlisted to communicate a vision of national identity at a time when ornament would soon be seen by an emerging avant-garde as antimodern. The Postal Savings Bank had multiple significances: it marked the end of historicism, maturely stated Lechner's language of national identity, and paralleled looser interpretations of Hungarian art nouveau. It also exemplified the latest developments in technology: its steel structure allowed for the artistic deployment of space, and majolica ceramics, a material developed by a national industry, provided both a cladding material and a linguistic tour de force.

Lechner's major works all involved public institutions through which he intended to establish a national character: the Museum of Applied Arts promoted domestic applied arts, the Geological Institute furthered the exploration of natural resources on Hungarian soil, and the Postal Savings Bank sought to stimulate economic growth through savings as "a national virtue."[40] Their language shared the references to Asia and folk art, from embroidery to wood carving, although mixed in different proportions. Though specific to Hungary and Lechner, these efforts occurred while other neologisms emerged elsewhere in a search for folk architecture's national characteristics, in neo-German, neo-Norman, neo-Byzantine, or neo-Russian vocabularies. But Lechner's approach differed in both perpetuating and transforming craft traditions while seeking a functional modern approach to structure and use.

Although Lechner's language of myth achieved its definitive refinement in the Postal Savings Bank, the building also undermined his future. The Hungarian minister of culture criticized it as too Hungarian and too Secessionist, and government support of Lechner permanently ceased with a parliamentary ban in 1902. Ironically, while he was trying to create an authentic architecture for the nation, the nation preferred more conventional representation. Flower motifs, undulating curves, vibrant colors, and sensual majolica threatened the tenuous control exerted by the Hungarian governmental officialdom.[41] The criticism was doubly damning in that it associated Lechner's work with the Secession movement (which Lechner had lamented), and it revealed an innate conservatism lodged within the bureaucratic mindset of government that refused to accept the romantic myths of the nation's origins. By the time Lechner died in 1914, the neobaroque style had become a fashionable and dominant mode of Hungarian architecture, despite its overt connections to Austrian imperialism. Writing in 1918 in "Hungarian Architecture," one commentator lamented: "[Lechner] created a most constructive, expressive architecture, answering the needs of absolutely new tasks. . . . Looking for national, he found the international; looking for Asian, he found the European, looking for the specific, he found the universal and looking for ancient, he found the modern, the-up-to-date."[42]

Lechner's failure to ensure an architectural language of national identity had many causes. In addition to official condemnation at the hands of conservatives was the question of how craft traditions could be at the center of national identity when machine technology had already fundamentally altered the relationships of production to market and to everyday use. Furthermore, the political reality of the times did not support Lechner's theories. The conviction that the language of myth in architecture could mediate social tensions of differing ethnic groups and produce a unified Hungarian nation was not viable. Rising internal tensions from Slavic and Romanian nationalists could in no way be neutralized by an architectural style. In addition, being Hungarian was not a "racial" issue at that time as it later became, but, rather, concerned the acceptance of "imperial" thought, which was equated with Hungarian nationhood and also contained the core of modernization itself. Even the basic assumption of the mythic origins was shaky: Pan-Turanism's belief in the common origin of the Ural-Altaic languages ultimately proved untenable and is now largely discarded.

Lechner did have followers whose positions were liberal, modern, and in search of collective identity through architecture. But there were also opponents to the Lechnerian position who claimed that his "Hungarian style" missed capturing the racial character of the people. Károly Kosch (later magyarized to Kós) led the opposition and claimed that the love of the race had superseded the old idea of national pride.[43] Whereas the liberal position saw Hungarian identity amalgamated in the multiethnic mix of Germans, Slavs, and Jews, Kós and the group around him saw the real Hungarian spirit, its pure forms of the race, embodied in the eastern reaches of the nation, in Kalotaszeg in Transylvania, whose undiminished vernacular buildings he documented and published as models of the true Hungarian architecture (fig. 4.18).[44] The stance of Kós and his group, Fiatalok (the Young Ones), was antiliberal

FIGURE 4.18
Transylvanian church, from Károly Kós's *Erdélyország népének építése* (1907), n.p.

and antimodern, yet their architecture flourished alongside other movements, and its proponents built churches, schools, and the extensive housing estate of Wekerle, one of the biggest garden city housing estates in Central Europe (1908–26).[45] Standing in a more neutral and not overtly political position were other factions, such as the Gödöllő Artists Colony, an experimental commune located near Budapest. Its members were part of the "life reform" movement, whose adherents sought an alternative lifestyle between cultural elitism and proletarian socialism. Calling for a return to a "natural life," they worked collectively. They united elements of the English Arts and Crafts movement with Hungarian and Scandinavian nationalistic motifs, with weaving receiving major emphasis.

Despite official censure, proponents of Lechner's language of myth still sought to promote his vocabulary as a vehicle of national identity with cultural and religious inflections. Among his most devoted followers were Flóris Korb and Kálmán Giergl as well as Desző Jakab (1864–1932) and Marcell Komor (1868–1944). After graduating from the Technical University in Budapest in 1893, Jakab worked in the offices of Samu Pecz, Korb, and Giergl in Budapest, as well as at the city engineer's office and for the Hungarian Railways Company. After working as a designer of the Millenary Exhibition in 1896, he entered Lechner's atelier. Like Jakab, Komor had graduated from the Technical University in Budapest (in 1891) and worked in the city engineer's office before joining Lechner's office, where he worked on the interior of the Museum of Applied Arts and on the Hungarian Royal Geological Institute. He also wrote for a weekly magazine, *Vállalkozók Lapja* (Journal of Entrepreneurs). Komor and Jakab opened their joint office in 1897.[46] During a decade of practice, their City Hall and Palace of Culture in Marosvásárhely (now Tirgu Mureș, Romania; 1906–10) and their City Hall in Szabadka (now Subotica, Serbia; built in two phases, 1908–10 and 1910–12) in southeastern Hungary used mythical, historical, and Lechnerian motifs to propagate an image of national identity. Moravánszky asserts that even though the firm used Lechner's "ribbon ornamentation" and other stylistic elements, they "lacked their master's originality, freshness, and richness and fantasy."[47] But they were working within a self-conscious movement, and both complexes are prodigious accomplishments in scale and detail for their provincial environments.

The Reform synagogue that Komor and Jakab designed in Szabadka (Subotica) in 1900 had a particularly broad impact on the surrounding region (fig. 4.19). It was not only their first major building in the Hungarian national style, but also the first Hungarian synagogue in that style and an example that melded "Jewishness" and "Hungarianness."[48] To satisfy the need of the Szabadka's Jewish community for a building with twelve hundred seats, they provided a slightly elongated rectangular

FIGURE 4.19
Marcell Komor and
Desző Jakab, Reform
synagogue, exterior,
Szabadka (Subotica,
Serbia), 1900–1903.

FIGURE 4.20
Marcell Komor and
Desző Jakab, Reform
synagogue, detail of
the façade, Szabadka
(Subotica, Serbia),
1900–1903.

floor plan with the sanctuary and the main entry at opposite ends. A second-floor mezzanine held seats for additional worshippers, and the central space focused on a double dome. Built from 1901 to 1903 by local contractors, the building has concrete foundations for the central piers, brick masonry walls, steel columns and ceiling trusses, and timber trusses in the roofs and dome. Brick was also used for the ribbonlike moldings, window framing, and cornice details, along with flowers, vegetation, and Stars of David in terra-cotta (fig. 4.20). These elaborated elements offset the flat voids of stucco, an iteration of Lechner's figure-void system. Changes occurred after the initial design, and as built, simpler round arched windows replaced numerous cusped and welted arches, a curved and billowing roof structure replaced shear and angled roof planes, and the rose window had its cusped motifs and concentric circles replaced with a shell-like composition. Komor and Jakab retained the cusped arch in the central bay of each façade, and they carried the motif into the interior of the central worship space, thus uniting interior and exterior.

As for the interior, the focus is on the *bimah* and the sanctuary, which features folk motifs of hearts, abstracted plants, six-pointed Stars of David, two menorahs, and torchères with

FIGURE 4.21
Marcell Komor and Desző Jakab, Reform synagogue, interior view toward ark, Szabadka (Subotica, Serbia), 1900–1903.

FIGURE 4.22
(*Facing*) Marcell Komor and Desző Jakab, Reform synagogue, entry, Szabadka (Subotica, Serbia), 1900–1903.

leaflike detailing. Flanking the sacred Ark of the Covenant with its Torahs are two engaged columns, each topped with a capital consisting of bands of vegetation and tall, waving palm fronds symbolically associated with the Temple of Solomon (and the motifs of ancient Mesopotamia) (fig. 4.21). Uniting the columns is an ogival arch with scalloped underside. At its pinnacles are a pierced Star of David and Tablets of the Law. The architects mirrored the altar's engaged columns with palm fronds and an ogival arch at the entry, thus creating symmetry of form with an inversion of solid and void: a visitor enters through the opening of the door to confront the solidity of the altar at the opposite end of the synagogue (fig. 4.22). From the gallery at the entry end, the visitor not only focuses on the altar but has his or her gaze gradually

lifted upward through a lattice of arches and arched windows. These windows are layered in zones, which decrease in size and increase in number as they ascend; those in the drum of the dome contain art-glass compositions of floral designs (fig. 4.23). The visual movement upward culminates in a segmental dome outlined with frames of flower motifs and capped in the center by a filamentous chandelier (fig. 4.24). Along with the vaulting that recapitulates the cusped arches of the exterior, all these details confirm the movement of motif from exterior to interior, uniting form and structure into an organic whole. The building speaks of a successful melding of the identities of being Jewish and being Hungarian, yet the "otherness" of the building reinforces the existence of the Jews as a people apart.

THE NEED for an expression of distinct identity and opposition to a domineering power pressed more intensely on the peripheries of the Austro-Hungarian Empire as people felt controlled within a shifting framework of oppression. Austrian hegemony pressured the Czechs, as well as in different degrees the Hungarians and Galicians. Hungarian royalists and conservatives pressured Hungarian nationalists, who pursued national identity in indigenous architecture and folk art. Simultaneously, Hungary pressured Slovaks, Croats, Serbs, and Romanians to assimilate. The result was the eruption of multiple efforts to forge a language that associated national identity with definable ethnic and historical origins, and to attribute architectural forms to those origins so that they uniquely represent a people. Lacking scientific ethnographic bases rooted in sociological and anthropological history, these efforts created additional languages of myth. By expressing that uniqueness in a language of myth, nationalists hoped to resist foreign domination and to assert their independence.

In Poland, independence was only a memory. From the eighteenth century, Russians, Prussians, and Austrians had repeatedly absorbed and divided the country. To suppress national identity, the occupiers suppressed the use of the Polish language and hindered the teaching of its history and literature. Austria, controlling Galicia in the former southern Poland, continued to assert its hegemony, and as a reaction to this suppression an art movement called Mloda Polska (Young Poland) emerged in the 1890s to reconstruct a Polish national identity. Architects, graphic artists, painters, and writers led in this endeavor, with the old Polish capital of Cracow still playing the role of cultural and spiritual center and source of an emerging modernism.[49] Ironically, in the visual arts the language they first drew on to assert their autonomy was art nouveau's international language of organicism rather than forms that could be defined as uniquely Polish.

However, an effort to create an architecture that spoke of a uniquely Polish identity emerged as a new style, derived from the vernacular of the eastern highland region, the Podhale. Stanisław Witkiewicz (1851–1915), a multitalented art critic, theoretician, architect, painter, novelist, and journalist, drew on the regional art and architecture to invent what became known as the Zakopane style, named for the mountain resort.[50] His first venture was the Villa "Koliba" (1892–94), but his best-known building was "Dom pod Jedlami," or "the House under the Firs" (1897), in Zakopane, where the style started (fig. 4.25).[51] Built for Jan G. Pawlikowski by local folk craftsmen, the house has a rusticated stone base, timber construction, wooden relief panels of carved floral motifs, and wooden shingles (fig. 4.26). The canted stone base negotiates a sloping site, and arches provide access to storage and a basement and introduce a cavelike theme. The overall wooden construction of the house counters the heaviness of the stone. The walls are dark timbers with chinking, but railings, balustrades, and areas under the eaves are a contrasting lighter wood, with carvings and appliqués of strips that define the motifs associated with the style. The eaves contain sunbursts, abstracted into linear rays, a motif also found on the interior woodwork. Designed as a consummate Gesamtkunstwerk, the chairs, tables, cabinets, and textiles form a synoptic statement of Polish identity embodied in folk motifs and vernacular traditions (fig. 4.27).

FIGURE 4.23
(*Facing, top*) Marcell Komor and Desző Jakab, Reform synagogue, interior, Szabadka (Subotica, Serbia), 1900–1903.

FIGURE 4.24
(*Facing, bottom*) Marcell Komor and Desző Jakab, Reform synagogue, interior of the dome, Szabadka (Subotica, Serbia), 1900–1903.

THE LANGUAGE OF MYTH

FIGURE 4.25
(*Facing, top*) Stanisław Witkiewicz, "Dom pod Jedlami" (House under the Firs), exterior, Zakopane, Poland, 1897.

FIGURE 4.26
(*Facing, bottom*) Stanisław Witkiewicz, "Dom pod Jedlami" (House under the Firs), detail, Zakopane, Poland, 1897.

FIGURE 4.27
(*Above*) Stanisław Witkiewicz, "Dom pod Jedlami" (House under the Firs), dining room, Zakopane, Poland, 1897.

Witkiewicz had high aspirations for the Zakopane style:

The idea was not to build yet one more beautiful, typical house. The focus was something else entirely: to build a home which would settle all existing doubts about the possibility of adapting folk architecture to the requirements deriving from the more complex and sophisticated needs of comfort and beauty. To design a home that would inherently withstand all common grievances and undermine all customary prejudices. To erect a house that would prove that one can have a home, a dwelling in the dominant style of Zakopane and yet be confident that this home will not disintegrate, that it will effectively protect one from storms, gales and the cold, that it will possess the full range of comforts yet simultaneously be beautiful in a fundamentally Polish way.[52]

As a result of his efforts, the village of Zakopane became identified as the spiritual center of the Polish national movement, and the style influenced other Polish architects. Already in 1900, Franciszek Mączyński had won an international architectural competition organized by the Paris-based magazine *Moniteur des Architectes* to design a villa in the newly developed Zakopane style.[53] In the following decade, Witkiewicz and Mączyński collaborated in the creation of the Dr. Tytus Chałubinski's Tatra Mountains Museum in that style. Constructed in 1913–22, it was a new building for one of Poland's oldest regional museums, founded in 1888 by its namesake, a physician, botanist, and public figure who celebrated the beauty and nature of the highlands culture. Its extensive collections of plants, animals, fish, birds, and geological specimens represented the identity of the region.[54] From the Polish perspective, the inflections of folk architecture spoke of the efforts to reestablish their own identity. But how unique were the motifs and elements they used?

It turns out that the vocabulary of folk motifs had a transnational existence, a fact that continued to deny any single group a unique claim to flowers, rustic furniture, and handmade textiles. Movements to preserve and promote regional identity, from Germany to Britain, Finland, and beyond, had sprung up toward the end of the nineteenth century, and were defined by the concept of *Heimat* (literally, "homeland") as an attempt to delineate architectural and artistic regionalisms.[55] A *Heimatstil* (literally, "homeland style") began to emerge in villas and recreational architecture found in rural settings, often taking the form of the "Swiss House" or "Tyrolean House."[56] While calling attention to vernacular architecture, the style ironically reflected a generally positive reaction to industrialization, the preferences of city dwellers instead of rural people, and capitalistic opportunity. It was a style of the urban elite characterized by an appropriation of rural vernacular forms put into use as decorative motifs for vacation hotels, spas, and villas out in the countryside. Villas and hotels made use of the "fretwork style" (*Laubsägestil*), which was positively identified as a "ruralizing style" and found in areas recently converted to vacation spots, becoming a means of localizing new tourism ventures. In the words of one historian, the style "was the icing on rural hotels, spas, baths, train stations and villas. It expressed the ill-conscience of the urbanites, who tried to speak to the locals in their rural dialect without having the slightest interest in the real workings of the place . . . the Lederhosen for the Notary [and] an international style of the landscape of recreation."[57]

The Heimatstil experienced its own reaction in a movement, *Heimatschutzstil* (literally, "homeland protection style"), that sought a more fundamental return to local form, means, and methods of production.[58] The movement intended to overcome the self-centered, arbitrary Heimatstil of the rich urban classes and replace it with "real, native building that speaks directly of its landscape."[59]

The efforts to create a Heimatstil and even a Heimatschutzstil were paradoxical and their own kind of myth. Intended for vernacular architecture to speak with the individuality and unique identity of a genius loci, they were neither unique nor individual, but an international idiom inflected only by small local variations. The paradox affected even perceptive critics who sought to occupy a carefully considered position of a middle ground between industrial/materialist international style and the conservative rejection of modern forms and methods of production. Adolf Loos,[60] who believed that rationality could conquer the excesses of the industrial age and that looking to history could solve the conundrums of the present, yearned for meaningful continuity, as he wrote in 1914:

Instead of using deceitful words like "Heimatkunst," one should decide to return to the only truth that I ever preach: to tradition. One should become accustomed to building like our fathers built, and not to be afraid of being "unmodern." . . . We work as well as we can, without wasting a second of thought on form. The best form is always already ready, and no one is afraid to use it, even though it may have originated from another person. Enough of the original genius! Let us unceasingly repeat ourselves! One may not be published in "Deutsche Kunst und Dekoration," and may not become a professor at the School of Applied Arts, but one will have served his time, himself, his people and humanity well. And therefore his "Heimat"![61]

Just as the use of the language of organicism to establish national identity was limited because it was an international style, the use of the vernacular for a distinct regional or national identity was also paradoxical. Claims of a unique Polish national style existed more as a myth than a reality; its forms lacked uniqueness and authority.

In Slovakia, a somewhat more authentic initiative to create a language of national identity began to emerge at the turn of the century. At its core was the belief that Slovaks had a definable identity, differing in degree both from other Slavs and from their neighbors across the borders with Hungary, Austria, and Galicia. The Slovak language itself provided some of the criteria of difference—certainly with respect to German and Polish, though less so with Czech—but creating a language of architecture provided larger challenges. Dušan Jurkovič (1868–1947) addressed those challenges.[62]

One year after the Austro-Hungarian Compromise had established Hungary's authority to suppress the minorities, Jurkovič was born in Turá Lúka, a village on the border of Slovakia and Moravia which became a center of resistance to Hungarian domination. His father, an evangelical Christian and ardent Slovak nationalist, imbued him with the importance of reviving Slovak national identity. After his early studies, Jurkovič entered the State Trade School in Vienna in 1885, where he received practical training in building, developed an interest in the artistic traditions of crafts, and became aware of Austrian Tyrolean folk architecture. Upon his return to Slovakia at the age of nineteen, he found an inspiration that would direct his own efforts to create a Slovak national idiom: an exhibition of Slovak embroidery. He also began to perceive that industrialization was threatening the crafts of embroidery and lace-making. Moving from studying textiles, Jurkovič began to study wooden Slovak folk architecture and its characteristic motifs. He then moved from Slovakia to Moravia, where minorities, under Austrian control, were less suppressed than they were under Hungarian administration. In Vsetín he helped a local architect prepare artistic and ethnographic exhibitions that included folk designs from the remote Walachian area on the Slovakian border whose inhabitants originally came from Romania and brought Transylvanian building traditions with them.[63] Jurkovič's expertise landed him an assignment to design Walachian buildings for an exhibition in Prague in 1895; in preparation for making these replicas, he traveled to northern Slovakia to study existing old houses. His success at the exhibition led to commissions in Moravia for neofolk designs, including a resort in Pustevny on Mount Radhošt, a site of pagan worship and mass meetings of Moravian nationalists. Although he used a vernacular vocabulary in these early projects, Jurkovič had already begun to transform their motifs, claiming to search for the principles that would express a unique regional identity.

The next phase of Jurkovič's work began when he moved in 1899 to Brno. There he continued to use the compositions and wood construction of his previous projects, but he started changing them as he became aware of international developments, particularly in British domestic architecture, which he had discovered from reading issues of *The Studio*. Jurkovič integrated the plans of the English "free style" and interiors by C. F. A. Voysey and M. H. Baillie Scott into his use of folk motifs. He also drew on the language of organicism that emerged from Prague, via the Czech Secese style with its inflections of Munich and Vienna. The amalgam was seen in his design for a spa at Luhačovice in Moravia from 1901, where the main building, Janův dům (Jan's House), demonstrated his evolving approach. It paralleled that of Károly Kós, but while Kós's appropriation of folk forms remained literal, Jurkovič gradually absorbed and transformed vernacular and folk idioms. Jan's House resembles the German-inspired Heimatstil buildings found throughout the Austrian part of the monarchy, but Jurkovič's use of a pitched jerkin-head roof with sunbursts over the entry is Slavic, particularly Moravian.[64] Aware of the evolving context of modernism in Central Europe and England, he continued to explore the transformation of Slovak folk motifs in subsequent projects, including a clubhouse at Skalica whose assembly hall used exposed rafters simplified from Arts and Crafts practice, rectilinear interior bays in grids of lattice and glass recalling Macintosh, and carved columns with folk details.[65]

Jurkovič conducted fieldwork at sites throughout Moravia to inform his research. Considering it not merely a reference for architectural designs, he began publishing his documentation of folk painting, lace, woodcarvings, furniture, and cloth in fourteen large-format folios that first appeared in 1905. Containing drawings and his own photographs, the collection was titled *Práce lidu našeho: Lidové stavby, zařízení a výzdoba obydlí, drobné práce* (The Works of Our People: Folk Buildings, Interiors, and Handicrafts), with texts in Slovak, German, and French.[66]

In the next phase of his development, Jurkovič began utilizing the language of rationalism, as filtered through Josef Hoffmann, Koloman Moser, and the Wiener Werkstätte, in conjunction with folk motifs. His work became more abstract, as reflected in the dining room he designed for historic Molitorov castle (1909). The rectilinear geometries of the room provided a framework, but Jurkovič made his folk forms more referential than dominant. This direction characterized an evolving modernism that also drew on his commitment to create a cultural context for national identity. However, by the time the last folio of his massive documentation appeared in 1913, Jurkovič had moved increasingly away from literalism, though he fervently believed in the necessity of preserving popular art—and the Slovak language—as key to national identity and the necessity of countering Hungarian dominance. As he had written earlier, "The Slovak who has renounced his nationality is more accessible to magyarization in both language and politics. . . . This popular art is a precious heritage whose mysteries the child drinks in with his mother tongue and the popular poetry of the race."[67]

The most potent examples of Jurkovič's vision for a modern architecture of national identity appeared in a series of cemeteries in Galicia that he designed during World War I. Galicia, on the northern slopes of the Carpathian Mountains between the upper Wisla and Prut rivers, had been a region laid waste by centuries of battle, and included Slovak territory under Hungarian control on the south. Russia, including part of former Poland, bordered on the north and east; Moravian Austria, to the west; and Moldavia, in the far southeast. The area became a part of Austria after the partitioning of Poland in 1772 and 1795, but shortly after the onset of World War I, Russia attempted to annex most of Galicia. With German support, the Austrians pushed back the Russian assault, with huge casualties on all sides. In May 1915, as the Russians retreated east, the military command in Cracow began dividing up the area into ten districts in which it planned to build hundreds of cemeteries and mass graves. Of the 60,829 listed casualties, two-thirds were exhumed and interred in new cemeteries. The graves contained the remains of soldiers from all parts of the Austro-Hungarian Empire (from Tyrol in the far west to Bosnia-Herzegovina in the far southeast), soldiers of German and Russian armies, as well as Poles, who served in all three armies and had the ignominy of opposing their own countrymen on the battlefields.

To accomplish its task, the War Graves Department of the Military Command in Cracow used its own military teams of eight architects, five sculptors, twenty-three painters, and two builders.[68] The command considered 600 cites, ultimately constructing 378 cemeteries, identified by number and location. The scale of operations was so large that storage depots—11,188 wrought-iron crosses were needed for use as grave markers—and regional workshops were maintained for the fabricating of wooden markers and the crosses.

The military command meticulously published its efforts in *Die Westgalizischen Heldengräber aus den Jahren des Weltkrieges 1914–1915* (The West Galician Heroes' Graves from the Years of the World War 1914–1915), documenting not only the cemeteries, but expenditures for all materials, including wood, stone, gypsum, wrought iron, land purchase fees, and amounts to subcontractors. With over four hundred illustrations accompanying the text and directions by rail and road to the obscure locations of the cemeteries, the book provided nothing less than a guide for the living to the graves of their dead, as if the detail and attention given by the whole enterprise ennobled the deaths of so many. This was a last gasping breath of an empire that itself had all but expired.

As a member of the team of architects, Jurkovič chose for his projects the First District in the southeast of the region along the Carpathians, where the Russian Army had attempted to enter the Slovak territory of Hungary.[69] The main battles had occurred in 1914–15 and had ravaged the hilly and mountainous area, furthering the poverty of its inhabitants, many of whom were Greek Catholics who had built wooden churches. Jurkovič photographed the original cemeteries and local churches, symbolic forms, and views of the countryside. The architect made his designs in consort with

FIGURE 4.28
Dušan Jurkovič, cemetery Magóra-Höhe, western Galicia, 1914–15. Reprinted from Rudolf Broch and Hans Hauptmann, eds., *Die Westgalizischen Heldengräber aus den Jahren des Weltkrieges 1914–1915* (Kraków: K. u. K. Militärkommando Krakau, 1918), 39, no. 60.

the landscape, often on hill sites. For him, wood was the material that best conveyed a sense of primordial value; it was abundant and a part of the existing landscape. He also used stone extensively in the cemeteries he designed, conveying what Matuš Dulla has described as a dialogue continuing over centuries between human labor and materials, one soft and pliant, the other hard and intractable.[70] Wood lent itself to the embellishment of ornament and composition at a human scale, while stone was treated as a raw mass of undifferentiated material.

To these simple materials Jurkovič brought a profound grasp of folk traditions, embodied in construction techniques, floral and abstract motifs, and regional details, and created a mythic language that transformed materials and motifs into a national symbolism replete with ancient Slavic references. While he modified some of his previous forms from early designs, Jurkovič devised two types of wooden crosses: one for single graves, a simple cross, and another for mass graves, with multiple vertical elements to abstractly represent the multiple corpses. He also designed innovative capitals and arches of variety and elegant simplicity. His large crosses assumed an anthropomorphic character, and his occasional pillars resembled, in Dulla's terms, "abandoned human silhouettes."[71] The roofs over entry gates, crosses, and boundary walls conveyed primordial shelter. The result was a mythic presence, a transformation from local identity to the universal.

Jurkovič designed a total of thirty-two cemeteries, a sampling of which embodies his synoptic and transformative language of myth.[72] The material he used was primal and folk, but the total impression of his designs tended toward abstraction. Cemetery 60, Magura (Magóra-Höhe), at Małastowska pass, was one of Jurkovič's first designs, prepared in April 1916 (fig. 4.28). The perimeter fence is a broken ellipse of three courses of red stones upon which lay massive, debarked tree trunks sheltered by a continuous pitched roof. A triangular roof with open wood framing marks the entry, and the roof motif is repeated not only on the sixty-three single graves and four mass graves, but also at the center chapel. Jurkovič used brute and primal logs for the chapel base, wood shingles for its double-sloped roof, and wood for the interlacing of crosses beneath the top roof.

Cemetery 51, called the Rotunda after the hill of the same name on which it sits, lies near the village of Regetów Niżny (fig. 4.29). Access to it required a journey on foot, which was typical of many of the cemeteries: at the end of the village, a visitor walks through pastures and then a valley, enters into a rocky ravine, passes through a forest, and climbs up four hundred meters to find the cemetery in a meadow on the prominent hill.[73] Designed and built in 1916, the Rotunda contains a combination of mass and individual graves for Austrian and Russian soldiers. A circular rubble stone wall, one and a half to two meters high, defines its perimeter. Five tall, shingled pyramids, each topped with a large metallic cross mounted with a curving tin cover, are grouped at the center. In their grouping, they recall an Eastern Orthodox church with

FIGURE 4.29
Dušan Jurkovič, cemetery Rotunda (Regetów Niżny), model of original design, western Galicia, 1914–15. Reprinted from Rudolf Broch and Hans Hauptmann, eds., *Die Westgalizischen Heldengräber aus den Jahren des Weltkrieges 1914–1915* (Kraków: K. u. K. Militärkommando Krakau, 1918), 49, no. 51.

FIGURE 4.30
Dušan Jurkovič, cemetery Gładyszów, western Galicia, 1914–15. Reprinted from Rudolf Broch and Hans Hauptmann, eds., *Die Westgalizischen Heldengräber aus den Jahren des Weltkrieges 1914–1915* (Kraków: K. u. K. Militärkommando Krakau, 1918), 43, no. 55.

its combination of domes, an appropriate association, as the cemetery was intended largely for fallen Russians. Also, anthropomorphic and abstract, the crosses stand as figural witnesses. An inscription at the base of the central cross announces:

Don't complain of the storm that wails on your grave,
in these deserted heights far away from any man.
We are close to the call of eternal times,
and the early sun spreads its purple veil over us.[74]

Cemetery 55 is located on a small hill on the road from Małąstowska pass to Gładyszów (fig. 4.30).[75] The plan, a square with a polygon forming a truncated arrow, is outlined by a perimeter fence made of a pair of massive logs laid flat over rough rubble. On top of the logs sits cross members and a double-layered roof characteristic of Slovak folk architecture. Jurkovič applied the same roof treatment to the entry gate. Within the fence, a spire with four layers of shingled roofs sits on an octagonal stone base. At its peak is a cross covered with a circular band of metal while individual graves have wooden crosses. The cemetery contains the remains of 93 Russians and 12 Austrians.

164 CHAPTER FOUR

After the war, Jurkovič's cemeteries were known to upcoming avant-garde architects because he described many of them in detail in an article in the Czech journal *Styl*. But as Galicia returned to Poland after the war, many of the cemeteries, not being exclusively Polish, were forgotten as they crumbled and forests engulfed them.

Like much of what we have seen, Jurkovič's language of myth contained paradoxes. A nationalist dedicated to defining an architecture representative of Slovaks, he found himself a member of the Austrian military, putting his vision to the purpose of designing cemeteries for the dead of all armies involved in the war—even those who suppressed the very identity he sought to establish. His exploration of a vocabulary of Slovak identity moved from a form language representing one people to a profound and timeless expression of the horror of war itself. His striding figures of wood silently testify to this in the midst of nowhere.

THE NEED for a language of myth was also felt along the southern periphery of the empire, where the Slovene population had been so encumbered by outside powers that by the nineteenth century they were considered, in Damjan Prelovšek's terms, "a people without a history," a people seeking fictional and romantic glorification of the past and legitimacy by association with larger Slavic enclaves.[76] In ethnographic and historical terms, the ancestors of the Slovenes were Alpine Slavs, who in the sixth century settled in the river valleys of the eastern Alps and the Karst region.[77] Bavarian and Magyar invaders eventually absorbed their Slavic kingdom in an area that became Austria, and western Hungary caused the further contraction of Slovene speakers toward the south. In the tenth century, the domain of the Slovenes became part of the German kingdom, which assigned them to various marquises or dukes. They subsequently fell under the control of various territorial dynasties, with Styria becoming acquired by the Habsburgs in the late thirteenth century along with the provinces of Karinthia and Carniola; Istria and the city of Trieste became Habsburg properties in the fourteenth century. Throughout this period, the Slovenes experienced increasing pressure to become more Germanic; they were also introduced to the Roman Catholic Church.[78] Slovene lands were attached directly to the Habsburg crown, which allowed them to escape some of the economic and political pressures that affected other southern Slavs. They were also closer to the urban and economic centers of the empire than were their neighbors. These factors allowed the Slovenes to become more literate, technically developed, and better integrated into the Habsburg market system than many people on the periphery, where illiteracy and backwardness persisted.

At the beginning of the nineteenth century, from 1809 to 1814, many of the Slovene lands became a part of the Illyrian provinces of Napoleon's Empire, along with Dalmatia, Trieste, and parts of Croatia. Though the French occupation was short, it did encourage the use of Slovene as the official language. A grammar of the Slovene language was published in 1808, and the first Slovene-language newspaper appeared in 1843. Local efforts arose to foster national self-awareness for Slovenes as well as

Croats, and aroused for intellectuals the notion of an Illyrian ideal that stressed a political and cultural bond among southern Slavs.

The revolutions occurring throughout Europe in 1848 stimulated the creation of a Slovene national program and efforts for the establishment of a unified Slovene province within the empire.[79] Merchants and a small elite still used German, but the Slavic bourgeoisie was expanding, and Carniola, the province containing Ljubljana, was largely Slovene by 1900. Among the political parties formed in the 1890s to push for Slovene identity, the Slovene Peoples' Party, which was closely linked to the Roman Catholic Church, had played a key role earlier in the century in creating large-scale cooperatives that provided credit, marketing, and other facilities to rural and urban artisans and peasants, efforts that also helped free Slovenes from dependence on German institutions.[80] The beginnings of the Slovene style in architecture—appropriated from floral patterns applied to objects such as painted eggs and embroidery—had appeared at the turn of the century in the work of Ivan Jager, who relied for his motifs on patterns from furs and painted Easter eggs. Lavishly illustrated compendia of Slovene popular ornament, published by Albert Šič, provided images representative of Slovene identity.[81]

Ljubljana (Laibach in German), capital of Carniola, became the center of Slovene self-awareness. Founded as the Roman colony of Emona by the emperor Augustus in 34 BCE, Ljubljana's role as a sleepy provincial town changed dramatically with the devastating earthquake of 1895.[82] The disaster allowed a rebuilding of the town as the expression of the awakening Slovene nationalist movement. By this time, the capital had a Slovene theater and societies for the promotion of science and literature, all of which conducted their affairs in the Slovene language. The use of the language tended to support the government's claim for a distinctive Slovene culture.

Jože Plečnik (1872–1957) was born in Ljubljana into this atmosphere of rising Slovene self-consciousness.[83] Uncomfortable with academic education, he attended a trade school in Graz with the intention of becoming a cabinetmaker like his father. The Graz venture marked the end of his formal education, and he began working after 1892 in a Viennese furniture factory, where he learned the historical styles of furniture.

Impressed with Plečnik's draftsmanship, Otto Wagner hired him to work in his atelier in 1895. Though Plečnik lacked the formal education in the humanities requisite for entry to the Academy of Fine Arts, Wagner admitted him to his master class, where Plečnik's intellectual universe expanded under his mentor's tutelage. As Prelovšek has demonstrated, the writings of Gottfried Semper, particularly *Der Stil in den technischen und tektonischen Künsten oder Praktische Aesthetik* (Style in the Technical and Tectonic Arts, or Practical Aesthetics) (1860–63), became the sole theoretical body upon which Plečnik would found his entire career. Semper's pronouncements on cladding and textiles, emphasis on the symbolism of ornament, and a quest for professional ethics became Plečnik's theoretical guides.[84] Plečnik graduated as one of Wagner's outstanding students, winning the Prix de Rome. His travels throughout Europe with a visit to England 1898–99 broadened his view of the world, previously gleaned only from the limited transit between Ljubljana, Graz, and Vienna. Rome in particular impressed him. He saw its architecture as the source of Wagner's genius, and it provided a permanent component in his vision of the essential qualities of architecture. In 1900, he visited Prague at the invitation of Jan Kotěra, an alumnus of the Wagnerschule and founder of Czech modern architecture. This visit not only introduced him to Kotěra and his progressive circle, but also reinforced his identification of Czechs as fellow Slavs. To the Slavs, Plečnik began attributing characteristic traits: "austerity," "astringency," and "lyricism," and for them he sought "a national art valid for the whole Slavic world."[85]

By the time he began his own independent architectural projects around 1900, Plečnik had a foundational knowledge of ancient Egyptian, Greek, and Roman art, which he studied in Viennese museums; his ideological guides were an ardent and ascetic Catholicism; his nationalism, which sought not only a Slovene identity, but also a transnational identification for all Slavs; and Semper as a theoretical guide.

Plečnik also had his own particular conception of the origins of the Slovene people that differed dramatically from the historical record. For Plečnik, the original sources of Slovene culture and identity lay in the ancient classical world of the early Etruscans, who he believed had settled the area of Slovenia. For him, a true architecture representing Slovene identity would refer to its roots in the Etruscan world, and these roots inspired his mythological language.

Within this framework, Plečnik began developing a vision of generalized Slavic identity and a particularized Slovene culture. He believed Slavs to be a civilizing factor in Europe and "God's elect."[86] Aiding Plečnik and his mission was his devotion to the Catholic Church, which he saw, along with architecture and design, as the basis for elevating the spiritual life of his countrymen.[87] For this Slavic identity, he postulated a mythic source of Slavic origin in the Etruria of central Italy. Consequently, Tuscan detail—columns, doorjambs, and tumuli, for instance—became the legitimate expressions of national Slovene identity as expressed in architecture. Unlike his peers elsewhere, including Ivan Jager, Plečnik rejected folk motifs and decorative arts as a source of national idiom and focused on the world of ancient history as "the expression of the unspoiled Slovene national art."[88]

Such views, along with his ardent devotion to Roman Catholicism, oriented him toward investing great symbolic meaning in architectural form, as can be seen from his earliest projects in Vienna. Between 1904 and 1906, Plečnik participated as a member of the Secession, designing exhibitions while preparing the impressive office and residential building designs for the industrial magnate Johannes Zacherl in Vienna's historic center. The project dealt with all of the architectural questions that Wagner was posing, from the treatment of the surface and the nature of materials to the role of iconographic form. Four years later, Plečnik's Church of the Holy Spirit (1910–13) in Vienna demonstrated a pioneering use of the tectonic expression of reinforced concrete for a monumental building, but its unconventionality and rough material elicited the disapproval of church authorities. In 1911, Plečnik was appointed professor at the Prague School of Fine Arts, thus beginning a long if somewhat rocky relationship with the Czech citizenry, who saw him at times as an interloper. Meanwhile, Plečnik was the academy's choice as Wagner's successor, but his appointment was twice rejected, and Leopold Bauer was appointed. Plečnik was certain the crown prince Franz Ferdinand blocked his appointment because he was a Slav, but the crown prince had an encompassing dislike for all progressives associated with the *Moderne*.[89]

Later, in Prague, Plečnik did have the good fortune of becoming a friend and beneficiary of the new president of Czechoslovakia, Tomáš G. Masaryk. Upon the founding of the new country in 1918, Masaryk commissioned Plečnik to restore and adapt the presidential residence at Hradčany castle in Prague.[90] The castle had its origins in the early Middle Ages, blossomed under the Czech king Charles IV in the fourteenth century, and entertained the luxurious court under the Habsburg ruler Rudolph II in the seventeenth century. The Czechs had long regarded it as a national shrine. By the time Plečnik started his work there, the castle had grown into a complex around three courtyards, along with subsidiary garden spaces and ramparts. Immediately after the establishment of the Czechoslovak state, the Czech people attempted to restore the palace after decades of neglect under the Austro-Hungarian monarchy.[91] Archaeological work and restoration commenced in 1920, and in March of that year Masaryk publicly stated his intention to make Hradčany castle a national monument. In Masaryk, Plečnik found an ideal patron, one from a similar modest background, but an admirer of antiquity; through Plečnik, Masaryk found an architectural expression that connected a new nation with the democracy of ancient Greece through the language of antiquity. Even though Plečnik officially returned to Ljubljana in 1921 at the invitation of Ivan Vurnik to assume a professorship at the newly founded School of Architecture, he worked on sections of the Hradčany castle restoration from 1920 to 1930, traveling there during the summers to supervise the project.[92]

Plečnik's work at the castle was detailed and complex, confronting not only architectural problems and questions of restoration, but also issues of how to represent national identity. His charge was to update a language of myth that bore on the history and identity of the Czech people. For the renovation of the first courtyard, Plečnik proposed an ingenious paving scheme with large granite slabs. He laid out two paths between the venerable Matthias Gate, the former main entry. The courtyard took on a symbolic cast, representing a portion of the globe, recalling "the time when Prague Castle was regarded as the navel of the world."[93] Plečnik intended to design a symbol of the Czech state to stand in the center of courtyard, but could not come up with a suitable symbol and abandoned the proposal. However, he placed two twenty-five-meter-high flagpoles, made of straight pines, in the courtyard (fig. 4.31). Originally, he wanted the poles to be entirely painted with the three colors of the Czech flag, but they were eventually left to their natural wood tone and texture. Plečnik mounted the masts on granite bases with massive, semicircular torus moldings, a motif he used in other capitals and wall details in the castle's Southern Garden. He himself contributed

FIGURE 4.31
Jože Plečnik, flagpoles at the first courtyard, Hradčany Castle, Prague, 1925.

much to the double meaning of the symbols; as Prelovšek has noted, Plečnik identified "Czech legends with Classical antiquity, regarding both as the elementary expression of the human soul."[94] The gilding at the masts' tops appears Egyptian, but the treatment also recalls the flagpoles in Saint Mark's Square in Venice. The association seemed appropriate, as the Matthias Gate was considered, erroneously at the time, the work of the Venetian architect Vincenzo Scamozzi.

The ongoing work at Hradčany castle involved complex changes in the circulation system, including transitions from the first to second courtyards, as well as access to the interior Spanish Hall, two tasks that Plečnik faced in 1927. While the Czech public watched with skepticism, he emptied out a part of the castle north of the Matthias Gate to create a solemn entry space with balcony and a grand staircase leading up to the Spanish Hall (fig. 4.32). Rows of columns hid the irregularity of the preexisting windows behind them. Portal, balcony, steps, and columns worked together to create the sense of a stately Greek temple. Plečnik had visited Athens and Delphi, and he emulated Greek Doric capitals on the two lower rows of columns. On the high ceiling

THE LANGUAGE OF MYTH

FIGURE 4.32 (*Facing*) Jože Plečnik, Hall of Columns at the Hradčany Castle, Prague, 1927–30.

he placed riveted copper plates, which added to the archaic effect and avoided the practical problem of cleaning or whitewashing such a broad expanse. Ionic volutes on the top-row columns marked a separation between the columns and metal.[95] However, when the Matthias Gate regained its role as main entry, the south door of what would become known as the "Plečnik Hall" became secondarily important and little used.

Parallel and contradictory visions inspired Plečnik: he appreciated modern industrial aesthetics and innovative technology, as seen in the precision of his forms and his use of concrete, but he also admired antiquity and age-old methods of construction. His combination of innovative technology and architectural history, religion, and national mythology provided an alternate modernism to the languages focusing exclusively on utilitarianism, technology, and standardization, which he saw as the "death of any art."[96] Consequently, he stood apart from many other architects, but he was not totally alone in these efforts.

Ivan Vurnik (1884–1971) was another young Slovene who inherited the mantle of national consciousness and sought its expression in a language of myth.[97] Born in the provincial town of Radovljica into a family of stonecutters and engravers, he studied at the Polytechnic Institute in Vienna and under Otto Wagner at the Academy of Fine Arts.[98] After graduating in 1912, Vurnik went on a study tour of Rome. He then returned to Vienna, where he worked for Ludwig Baumann, Friedrich Ohmann's successor, who was completing management of work on the new Hofburg Palace in Vienna. Though Baumann employed him, Vurnik began his first independent designs in church architecture. His interior for the bishop's chapel in Trieste (1913) was an effulgent demonstration of Gesamtkunstwerk, recalling with its glistening white and gold Wagner's St. Leopold's Church at Steinhof. Also in 1913, Vurnik married Helena Kottler, a Viennese painter and graphic artist who would become a collaborator in many of the paintings, mosaics, and interior designs of his later work. During the war, they returned to Radovljica, and Vurnik continued to work on projects for church architecture. In 1919, the couple moved to Ljubljana, where the first Slovene university, an ambition since 1848, had just been established. Appointed professor in 1920, Vurnik created the university's Department of Architecture within its Technical Faculty. To complement its faculty, he immediately invited the two leading Slovenes working outside the country, Max Fabiani and Jože Plečnik, to accept teaching positions. Fabiani declined, but despite disputes and delays over his appointment, Plečnik accepted and began teaching his own program in architectural composition while Vurnik taught technical courses. Vurnik's interest in folk motifs and colorful patterns gradually began to emerge in both his public projects and the religious buildings he designed in the early 1920s.

Vurnik's Cooperative Bank at Miklošičeva Street in Ljubljana, designed and built in 1921–22, exemplifies his interpretation of a language of myth dedicated to a Slovene national architectural style (fig. 4.33). The bank's plan is conventional, with entry on the ground floor, followed by the main banking hall, subsidiary offices at the rear, and

FIGURE 4.33
Ivan Vurnik, Cooperative Bank, exterior, Ljubljana, Slovenia, 1921–22.

four floors of apartments facing the street. The façade has rectangular windows set simply in the walls, projecting bay windows running vertically along each edge, and a series of bay windows at the top floor.

The message of the building comes from its painted surfaces and the iconography of its façade and interior public spaces (fig. 4.34). While Plečnik was looking to ancient architecture, particularly to Etruscan and Roman precedents, Vurnik looked, in addition to folk motifs, to Gothic and nonclassical traditions for his language of Slovene identity. A long tradition of abstract patterns in late medieval and Gothic architecture, including polychromed zigzags, and a number of other detailed treatments could be seen at Slovene churches at Dvor, Breg near Preddvor, and particularly the

FIGURE 4.34
Ivan Vurnik, Cooperative Bank, detail of the façade, Ljubljana, Slovenia, 1921–22.

reconstructed portal at Ljubljana castle. Zigzag painted strips, therefore, appeared a part of Slovene national heritage.[99] Vurnik drew on these sources to design the façade of the Cooperative Bank, but he limited himself to what he considered Slovene motifs, rejecting Viennese ornament and even motifs identified with Pan-Slavism. Onto a background painted salmon-pink and white, Vurnik overlaid the basic motif of the building's exterior, a simplified carnation known from embroideries.[100] To them he added vibrating abstracted medallions, bands of frets, and interlacing that juxtaposes blues, whites, reds, and yellow. Instead of three-dimensional moldings, Vurnik used running bands of blue, white, and red in a relaxed zigzag pattern to provide courses along the front.

FIGURE 4.35
Helena and Ivan Vurnik, Cooperative Bank, interior, Ljubljana, Slovenia, 1921–22.

On the interior of the banking hall, the entry has a scalloped archway recalling Lechnerian motifs, but the vibrant blues, reds, and greens come directly from folk art or images of folk art as reproduced in local publications (fig. 4.35). The columns within the banking hall, surfaced with the zigzag pattern two-thirds up their length, are terminated with flowering capitals reminiscent of Egyptian architecture. Helena Vurnik was responsible for the painted designs of the interior; she drew on local iconography and predominately used a palette of white, blue, and red, the colors of the Slovene flag, with a touch of gold. The spandrels contain her version of a woman in traditional folk costume spinning while surrounded by arches of abstracted flowers below and pendulous bunches of grapes above, all rendered in intensely saturated colors (fig. 4.36).[101] In sum, the Vurniks' use of folk motifs both perpetuated the myth that they spoke to the core of Slovene identity and reinforced the cooperative bank's role in supporting Slovene self-determination.

∷ THE LANGUAGES of myth in the Austro-Hungarian Empire spread over and through other languages of architecture with varying degrees of intensity and articulation. We have seen the role played by mythic stories of Czech origins. Imperial architecture in Vienna also had a mythic dimension, associating the legitimacy of the Habsburgs with imperial Rome. For some Hungarians, the Huns, Arpad, and India provided a locus of origin. The Poles thought a unique identity could emerge from the historical legacy of the old capital of Cracow and the folk motifs and traditional construction of the mountainous outskirts. The Slovaks believed a unique Slovakian vernacular could be found in folk forms that in a few hands transcended their local identification. For Slovenes, Etruscan origins and folk art provided sources to create something distinctly Slovene. These convictions all shared a common necessity: for the language of myth to "speak" or to be "read," its listeners and readers needed both to recognize the stories they represented and to believe to some degree in their symbolic value. That condition lifts us beyond details and specifics back to the larger issue of the limits to architecture's "saying" what its makers intend. Even in western Europe, where modern architecture was emerging simultaneously with these developments, functionalism had its own myths of autonomy, efficiency, and truth expressed in materials and structure. In the late Austro-Hungary, few buildings spoke exclusively in a single language of myth, and myths permeated other architectural languages as well as those that defined a "hybridity" distinctive to the waning days of the empire.

FIGURE 4.36 Helena Vurnik, wall painting inside the Cooperative Bank, Ljubljana, Slovenia, 1921–22.

5

JUST AS the Austro-Hungarian Empire was multilingual, its modern architecture was polyglot. In their profusion and lack of "purity," these architectural languages suggest an eclecticism in which no single mode dominates. In its original sense in Greek, where ʽεκλέγ-ειν means "to select" and ʽεκλεκτικός means "selective," *eclecticism* referred to the class of philosophers who were not attached to any system, but selected the doctrines that pleased them.[1] The word *eclecticism*, however, has pejorative associations emanating from twentieth-century perceptions of nineteenth-century architecture; its practitioners appeared to pick pieces and parts of precedents, collaging them, often without a coherent organizing idea. The result was a pastiche. But the architects of Austria-Hungary created a different kind of eclecticism that reflected coherent motivations. The result was a hybridity whose purpose, like that in horticulture, was to graft differing elements to create a new, vigorous organism. Though the term is current in critical discourse, I use it differently from the way theorists of postcolonialism and multiculturalism use it, and emphasize hybridity's connotations of biological grafting.[2]

The language of hybridity in Austria-Hungary allowed the coexistence of languages of history, organicism, rationalism, and myth, in which no single mode dominated other tendencies. The many strands of modern architecture in the region could be rational, nationalistic, and folkloric at once, a condition of complexity that baffled and offended the polemicists of the modern movement.[3] One outstanding example of hybridity is the Chamber of Commerce and Industry in Galician Cracow, designed and built from 1904 to 1906 (fig. 5.1). It is the kind of building that historians often reduce to "national romanticism," dismiss as mere historicism, or ignore for its strangeness, lack of conformity to a style, and absence of monumentality and technical innovation. It is, however, a building of surprising complexity that defies easy categorization.

Polish chambers of commerce originated at the beginning of the nineteenth century as organizations intended to provide economic advice to state authorities on industry and craft.[4] Cracow's Chamber of Commerce and Industry was founded in 1850 along with those in Brody and L'viv, the two other principal towns in Galicia.[5] The founding moment was auspicious and necessary: When the Austrian monarchy absorbed Cracow in 1846, the city lost its free-trade status, suffering significant economic losses. Commerce with the kingdom of Poland diminished, and Austrian and Bohemian interests took precedence over Galician concerns. Unlike L'viv, which thrived with its metropolitan status in the mid-nineteenth century, Cracow was declining, suffering the absence of both specialists in areas of trade and capital. But at the same time, the city made some progress: the first railway to Cracow opened in 1847, the telegraph arrived, and a bridge linked Cracow with Podgorze on the opposite side of the Vistula.

FIGURE 5.1
Franciszek Mączyński and Tadeusz Stryjeński, Chamber of Commerce and Industry, exterior, Cracow, 1904–6.

Initially, the members of the Chamber of Commerce and Industry set out to promote mercantile interests and financial operations that provided the dual bases of the local economy. It sought not only to create ties with the kingdom of Poland, but also to establish a branch of the Bank of Austria, a commercial tribunal, and a commercial school, as well as to improve transportation and communications.[6] Tradespeople continued to dominate the chamber over industrialists, who were few in number, owing to the general weakness of the industrial sector. Only large landowners had substantial financial means, and because their wealth was rooted in agriculture, they were not particularly interested in industrial development. Nevertheless, industrialists began to emerge with the support of the Chamber of Commerce and Industry.

In 1868, the central Austrian government reorganized and re-regulated all twenty-nine chambers of commerce in the Dual Monarchy to conform to uniform requirements emphasizing commercial and industrial matters.[7] The local organization evolved into playing an important role in both forming and providing opinion as well as protecting the interests of western Galicia. It attempted to develop effective trading policies, new kinds of industry, credit institutions, public transport, and even vocational schools as well as deal with economic emigration. Furthermore, it took an interest in building a railway network and a modern system of waterways linking the Vistula with the Danube, Oder, and Dniester. Between 1881 and 1892, it created seventeen industrial supplementary schools, which it subsidized, and the Cracow Commercial College, a secondary school, with the assistance of local tradespeople and industrialists.

The growing importance of the chamber in Cracow culminated in plans for a new headquarters on the corner of Basztowa and Długa streets near Market Square (Rynek Główny), one of the largest municipal spaces of its type, dating from medieval Europe and the historic heart of the city. For what would be the first building dedicated exclusively to its own use, the chamber selected Franciszek Mączyński (1874–1947) and Tadeusz Stryjeński (1849–1943) to develop the architectural plans in 1904. Both were members of the Mloda Polska art movement and participants in the efforts to reestablish Polish identity, and both were experienced architects of reputation. In 1901, for example, Mączyński had designed the Palace of Art on Szczepanska Square where he rendered some details in an art nouveau idiom.[8] In addition to the architects, the chamber selected Stanisław Wyspianski (1869–1907) to design the interiors.[9] A multi-talented painter, designer, and typographer as well as a poet, dramatist, theatre reformer, and stage designer, Wyspianski was a leading figure of Mloda Polska.[10]

Called locally the "House under the Globe" for the ornament topping its spire, the chamber's new headquarters had four stories over an L-shaped plan on a trapezoidal site. The building served multiple functions, including retail stores on the ground floor, a large meeting room for the chamber, a variety of offices and subsidiary functional spaces on the second floor, and apartments on the third floor above the offices. Rental income from the stores and apartments would go directly to the chamber's coffers.

The exterior treatment of the building embodies the kind of linguistic complexity that drives historians to avoidance or dismissal, but exemplifies the language of hybridity. On the one hand, the House under the Globe recalls the guildhalls of Brussels, and invokes the Ruskinian neo-Gothic traditions of the nineteenth century, which emphasized the inclusion of color and pattern on surfaces, a "built-in polychromy" seen in the buildings of Alfred Waterhouse in Manchester and those of Edward Godwin. The chamber also recalls H. P. Berlage's Amsterdam Stock Exchange (1897–1903), which had just been completed to much acclaim. On the other hand, the House under the Globe speaks of local traditions and identity, and its specific role in promoting the city's business and industry to the world outside its limits. The inclusion of light stones into the dark masonry of the walls and the use of stone frames over windows recall with their contrasting colors and textures the exterior of the nearby monuments, St. Mary's Church and the historic Cloth Hall on Market Square; moreover, the Cloth Hall had a similar arrangement for its facilities, with stalls on the ground floor and rooms for the cloth guild above.

The most dramatic exterior element, the chamber's clock tower topped by a spire and a globe, also provides multiple references. Originally, it had a zodiacal ring and wings of Mercury to suggest symbolically the wide realm of the city's ambitions.[11] The tower recalls the civic importance of local heritage: at Cracow's Jagiello University, the so-called Jagiellonian Globe (circa 1510) was a treasure that displayed the first known representation of the American continents. The structure also refers to the two towers of the nearby St. Mary's Church, the taller of which received in 1666 a gilded crown and a gilded sphere that allegedly contains the city's written history.

The exterior and interior of the rest of the fabric speak for the building itself, connecting local history and tradition to commercial activity. The portal of the main entry of the Chamber of Commerce and Industry on Długa Street, with its two hermlike female allegories of Commerce and Industry, contributes to the message of the building. Under the gable above the entry, a model of a sailing ship symbolizes the global scope of Cracow's trade and renown. On the interior, the main stairwell has stained-glass medallions designed by Mączynski, with a locomotive as a symbol of transport, a figure of Mercury representing commerce, and views of the townscape and industrial landscape.[12] Throughout the building, floral forms, both literal and abstract, resonate with the organicism of nature and the traditions of Polish folk craft. The fabric of the building, therefore, connected the building's meaning to the traditions of local heritage and identity.

The chamber's meeting room provides the culminating dramatic representation of Polish national identity. Wyspianski supplied the initial designs, proposing an interior treatment that used color as the overall organizing principle: he wanted to express the entire composition in differing shades of red to animate the experience of the interior and to recall use of that color in folk art; his design was also rectilinear, clear, and rational in the mode of the Wagnerschule. Wyspianski, however, withdrew from the project because the chamber's councilors insisted on having a place for a bust of the emperor Franz Josef. To Wyspianski, the bust represented the occupying power, while his efforts at creating the image of the chamber emphasized the nation and the homeland. After he withdrew, the chamber asked Józef Mehoffer to provide furnishings and decorations for the meeting room. Mehoffer, a member of the artistic elite at whose home the Mloda Polska movement often met, had collaborated with Wyspianski at St. Mary's Church in Market Square.

The meeting room of the chamber provides an intense demonstration of the overlay of languages at the core of the building's hybridity (fig. 5.2). Located on the second floor at the rear of the site, it is at the end of a procession that begins at the main entry, then moves through a vestibule into a grand stair hall and up to the room itself. Mehoffer's designs encompass not only walls and ceiling, but also furniture. Instead of using variations of a single color, Mehoffer employed a rich palette. On the ceiling were painted plumes of a pheasant—an entire stylized peacock was rejected—resplendent in the colors of the rainbow, along with scintillating scales of wriggling

FIGURE 5.2
Józef Mehoffer, meeting room at the Chamber of Commerce and Industry, Cracow, 1904–6.

serpents, an allusion to Mercury's caduceus. By dividing the composition of the polychromed walls into two zones, Mehoffer referred directly to the composition, decoration, and color of traditional Cracowian painted chests and other regional artifacts, including embroidery. The woodwork of the wainscoting features the chiseling technique often found in folk woodwork, while the fan shapes on the panels recall the organicism associated with art nouveau. Further details, ranging from fascia to the gallery balustrade and desktops, exhibit similar treatments, including brass bosses that recall Cracowian folk jewelry. Chandeliers suspended from the ceiling and brass lights mounted on walls resemble the forms of flowering twigs.

The main focus of the meeting room is Mehoffer's canvas painting that hangs behind the dais of the presidium, a symbolic (and male chauvinistic) extravaganza titled the

Taming of the Elements. It shows a powerful young man subduing the elements of nature, symbolized by four women. Representing Genius, he overwhelms Earth, the female clad in a brown dress with corn in her hair. He also holds Water in one hand, a girl whose dress is the color of the sea. She is doubled over by his force, and her long, golden hair flows toward the ground. In his other hand Genius holds two winged creatures: the symbols of Fire, clad in purple, and Air, denoted by wings on her shoulders and ankles.

Not only does Mehoffer's painting represent the allegory of human effort in controlling the forces of nature, but it corresponds to the symbolist philosophy which he articulated in his *Notes on Art* published in 1897. Comparable to other followers of the movement, Mehoffer saw color in art as the carrier of symbolic meaning, to be used to reflect nature as a source of creative inspiration and to convey these feelings to viewers. The total impact of the ensemble raises the meaning of the meeting room to a quasi-sacred space. Accordingly, the rostrum of the chamber's chairman acts as the altar, the rows of desks correspond to the seats of a nave, and the public gallery above brings to mind a choir loft. In 1906, when it opened, the ensemble of the building and its objects "said" that the responsibilities of the members of the Chamber of Commerce and Industry, meeting in full session at their House under the Globe, fulfilled not merely a pragmatic purpose, but also a symbolic one at the center of the economic life of the Cracowian citizenry.[13]

:: ANOTHER EXAMPLE of the language of hybridity, with its multiple strands of identity and motif, found expression in the new Academy of Music in Budapest (1902–7; fig. 5.3). In establishing its role as a symbol of Hungarian cultural identity, the building juxtaposes the meanings of the music performed inside with the imagery of the façade outside in a strange dialogue that reinforces its hybridity. The establishment of a music academy in Budapest originally arose from broad efforts of Hungarians after the Compromise of 1867 to found their own cultural institutions; by paralleling those existing in Austria, they attempted to assert Hungarian autonomy. The effort also sprang from the perceived need to train musicians at home rather than send them abroad, and to lure back to Hungary the famous Franz Liszt.[14] In 1875, the composer, who was splitting time between Rome, Weimar, and Budapest, was named the Academy of Music's first president.[15] The school began in modest rented rooms, but moved to a new building on Budapest's grand Sugár út (Radial Avenue, later Andrássy út). By 1886 it had enough students to be named the Royal Academy of Drama and Music, and enrollments and teaching expended so much that a new building was needed. Up to this point, not only had the academy provided the locus of Liszt's master class, but it had developed an emphasis on establishing a Hungarian style in opera.

The academy chose the architects Flóris Korb and Kálmán Giergl, who began designing the building in 1903, testing alternative schemes before arriving at a final plan.[16] Korb (1860–1930) had been born in Kecskemét, just southeast of Budapest, studied

CHAPTER FIVE

FIGURE 5.3
Flóris Korb and Kálmán Giergl, Academy of Music, exterior, Budapest, 1902–7. From *Budapester Neubauten* (Vienna: Verlag Anton Schroll, 1910).

at the Berlin Academy of Architecture, and worked in Germany. Giergl (1863–1954) was born in Pest into a family of artists and architects, studied at the Academy of Fine Arts (Kunstakademie) in Berlin and the Technical University in Budapest, and, like Korb, worked in Germany for a year. Upon returning to Hungary, both young architects worked with Alajos Hauszmann, designer of the new neobaroque Palace in the Royal Castle in Buda (1890–1903). Korb and Giergl started their partnership in 1894, attracting official and royal commissions. Prior to receiving the commission for the Academy of Music, they had designed pavilions for the Millennial Exhibition of 1896, houses, shops, and a rental building for the royal court, and had also participated in ongoing work on the Royal Castle in Buda.[17]

The new academy building opened on May 12, 1907, an event marked by the renaming of the area in front of it Liszt Ferenc Square. (Only later, upon its fiftieth anniversary, did the academy rename itself in honor of Liszt.) The exterior of the building is a victory of exuberance over syntax. The front façade has a classicizing tripartite division with its base, middle with engaged columns, and top cornice, but the surface is partly covered with motifs and figures not found in Greco-Roman models. Laid upon the base of striated stone coursings are pylon forms at the entries that both recall the organic language of the Viennese Secession and also refer to a deeper antiquity, the gateways and entries of Egyptian architecture. Wreaths, swags, and an image of Nike all proclaim the victory of music, but abstracted ribbons and details bring to mind the chip carving of Hungarian folk art that had already entered the repertory of nationalistic motifs; the outdoor lamps next to the main entry integrate these forms. The looping forms of column capitals recall the organicism of Lechner, but studiously avoid any direct reference to the architect, who had been officially sanctioned.

The overall massiveness of the masonry façade is countered by the extensive inclusion of large windows, whose thin mullions provide an additional contrapuntal motif to the visual heaviness of the stone. At the ground floor, the mullions provide another layer within the horseshoe stone arches found in Eastern architecture, countering the classical forms. The somber effect of the building created by its large volume is also lightened by the inclusion of numerous plump and stubby putti, some of whom sing in small choruses, while others play an organ in accompaniment (fig. 5.4). The squatty columns above the glass entry canopy contrast with the attenuated proportions used by architects of the Wagnerschule. Above the cornice, four Atlantae support six heads, each with emblems of musical instruments. Above them sits the figure of Liszt, cast in bronze from the designs of sculptor Alajos Stróbl (fig. 5.5). The composer looks outward as if gazing over the whole Hungarian nation.

In addition to its great hall with organ, the new building includes a small recital hall; an "Artists' Room" illuminated with stained-glass windows; classrooms; and a library with a reading room. Its spaces come to life with sculptures and paintings designed and executed by members of the Gödöllő Artists Colony. Upon entering on the ground floor, a visitor first sees a sparkling fountain with a memorial tablet (fig. 5.6). Two pairs of figures with lyres flank the marble dedicatory panel that honors Liszt and, among others, the director of the academy and its architects. Above the panel is the royal Hungarian coat of arms and, flanking it, plant forms, abstracted and executed in the chip-carved floral motifs of folk art. Below, water flows from the mask of Tragedy into a brachiated pinkish marble basin. Two piers on either side of the fountain along with the tablet evoke studded leatherwork overlaid with gilt filigree of an oval-shaped lattice; the pier on the left has round relief, with faces of a singing man and woman, while the one on the right has a lyre. Gilding and gold tesserae create a scintillating impression of lush sensuality, as if music itself, expressed through Hungarian idioms, resonates with the vibrancy of life.[18] Even the newel post of the staircase in the foyer conveys sensuality with its lapis-colored ball, which is mounted on a disk surrounded by gilt spheres. Instead of balusters, stained-glass panels fill spaces between handrail and steps (fig. 5.7).

FIGURE 5.4
Flóris Korb and Kálmán Giergl, Academy of Music, detail of the front façade, Budapest, 1902–7.

FIGURE 5.5
Flóris Korb and Kálmán Giergl, Academy of Music, detail of the front façade, Budapest, 1902–7.

FIGURE 5.6
Flóris Korb and Kálmán Giergl, Academy of Music, fountain at the entry, Budapest, 1902–7.

FIGURE 5.7
(*Facing, top*) Flóris Korb and Kálmán Giergl, Academy of Music, detail of the staircase, Budapest, 1902–7.

FIGURE 5.8
(*Facing, bottom*) Flóris Korb and Kálmán Giergl, Academy of Music, main concert hall, Budapest, 1902–7. From *Magyar Épitõmûvészet* no. 7 (1907).

Elaborate treatments cover surfaces of the interior of the main concert hall (fig. 5.8). Friezes show figures playing music in the midst of pastoral scenes; vaults are covered with floral motifs; and panels of circles and squares create blank fields in the ceiling. Sumptuous chandeliers and the curving arches of a huge display of organ pipes above the stage provide constant visual stimulation. The modern use of reinforced concrete allowed the vastness of the space itself and its representational program. But the technology was a means to an end, not a material or system to be celebrated. The life of music dominates here in a complex relationship with the building that shelters it. The self-conscious use of antique, classical, and folk details presents a hybrid synthesis that is uncomfortable.

With the new building, more students and new faculty came, including Zoltán Kodály, who composed music and trained generations of students; and Béla Bartók, who continued Liszt's legacy and started pioneering research in Hungarian folk music. As the leading institution for music education in Hungary, the academy was not

only a memorial to Liszt and trained musicians, but a key player in promoting cultural identity, with its emphasis on Hungarian styles and folk music. As such, it had a role somewhat analogous to the Czech National Theater in Prague; in both buildings, iconography still played a critical role in telling the story of the building. On the one hand, the music played within and the history of the institution communicated a clear sense of national culture. On the other hand, the form language of the exterior presented an idiosyncratic hybridity. The result was an ambiguity and disjunction between form and identity.

While cultural institutions often needed complex representational programs, many ethnic and religious groups within the Austro-Hungarian Empire relied upon the languages of hybridity to express their diverse identities. One such group were the Hungarian Jews, whose amalgamated identity was itself hybrid: they were at once Hungarian and Jewish, assimilated and different. We have seen this paradoxical condition from the discussion of synagogues in Budapest and Szabadka, but it is also readable in the design of the new synagogue in Trieste (1903–12) that evolved in a different ethnic mix and in close physical and cultural proximity to Italy.

Trieste, the empire's main port on the Adriatic, had a long history of religious buildings representing its various settlers as the English, Germans, Greeks, Slavs, Swiss, and Jews all brought their own cultural traditions. The liberality of Empress Maria Theresia and the Edict of Tolerance in 1781–82 issued by her son, Joseph II, granted political and religious rights to religious minorities, except for Jews. As a result, much building activity moved forward, and varying architectural languages of history coexisted to represent various cultures and religions. Neoclassic, neo-Byzantine, and neo-Gothic vied with each other.

The fate of Triestine Jews ebbed and flowed depending on edicts and concessions, which either isolated them from or integrated them into the greater community.[19] In the late nineteenth century, the city's expanding Jewish population of 4,400 members needed more space for worship, and despite an unsuccessful attempt to build a new synagogue in the 1870s, the Ashkenazic and Sephardic communities agreed to collaborate and opened an international competition for a Tempio Israelitico in November of 1903.[20] Their site was on the Via Crocera (now Via Gaetano Donizetti) and the Piazza S. Francesco D'Assisi, amusingly inauspicious street names for a synagogue. The congregation's program called for a building with "a monumental character" and encouraged competing artists to search for aesthetic solutions with complete freedom as long as they followed the rules of Jewish tradition.[21] Needed were one thousand seats in a single space for male worshippers and four hundred seats in an upper gallery for females in the main synagogue, as well as a community building with school, weekday synagogue, service areas, and apartments for rabbi and caretaker.

Over forty architects from Austria, Germany, France, and Italy entered the competition, providing a cross section of the transnational approaches applied to the design of a synagogue. Among them, Oskar and Eugen Felgel, Viennese architects and former Wagner students, proposed a centrally planned domed structure that competed with the grand synagogues of Szeged, Szabadka, and Hódmezővásárhely in Hungary, as well as the one in Sofia, Bulgaria; Carol Krinsky describes their project as "Assyrian rococo."[22] The entry submitted by Oskar Marmorek, a Jewish architect and devoted Zionist, used the language of history filtered through ancient Near Eastern precedents to provide a severe and stark façade for the main temple and encompassing arches on the interior over the Ark of Covenant. Emil Hoppe and Otto Schönthal, the emerging young stars from Wagner's atelier, submitted a competition project that showed how members of the Wagnerschule turned organic and rational language into a language of hybridity (figs. 5.9–5.11).[23] Organic in its aesthetic, Hoppe and Schönthal's design was also rational in its technology, which used reinforced-concrete (occasionally called "ferro-concrete") framing supported by thin iron columns and a thin cementitious panel material, "Rabitz," for the ceiling.

FIGURE 5.9
Emil Hoppe and Otto Schönthal, synagogue, Trieste, competition entry, front elevation, 1903–4.

Despite the plethora of entries, the jury of seven Jewish engineers found all of them impractical, and a new building committee asked Franz Matouschek, an Austrian who had studied with Wagner but worked in Budapest with Emil Adler, to transform his own submission, which resembled a "railway terminal," into a suitable solution.[24]

WETTBEWERB FÜR DEN ISRAELITISCHEN TEMPEL IN TRIEST
QUERSCHNITT DURCH D. TEMPELSAAL
MOTTO: MÄRZ

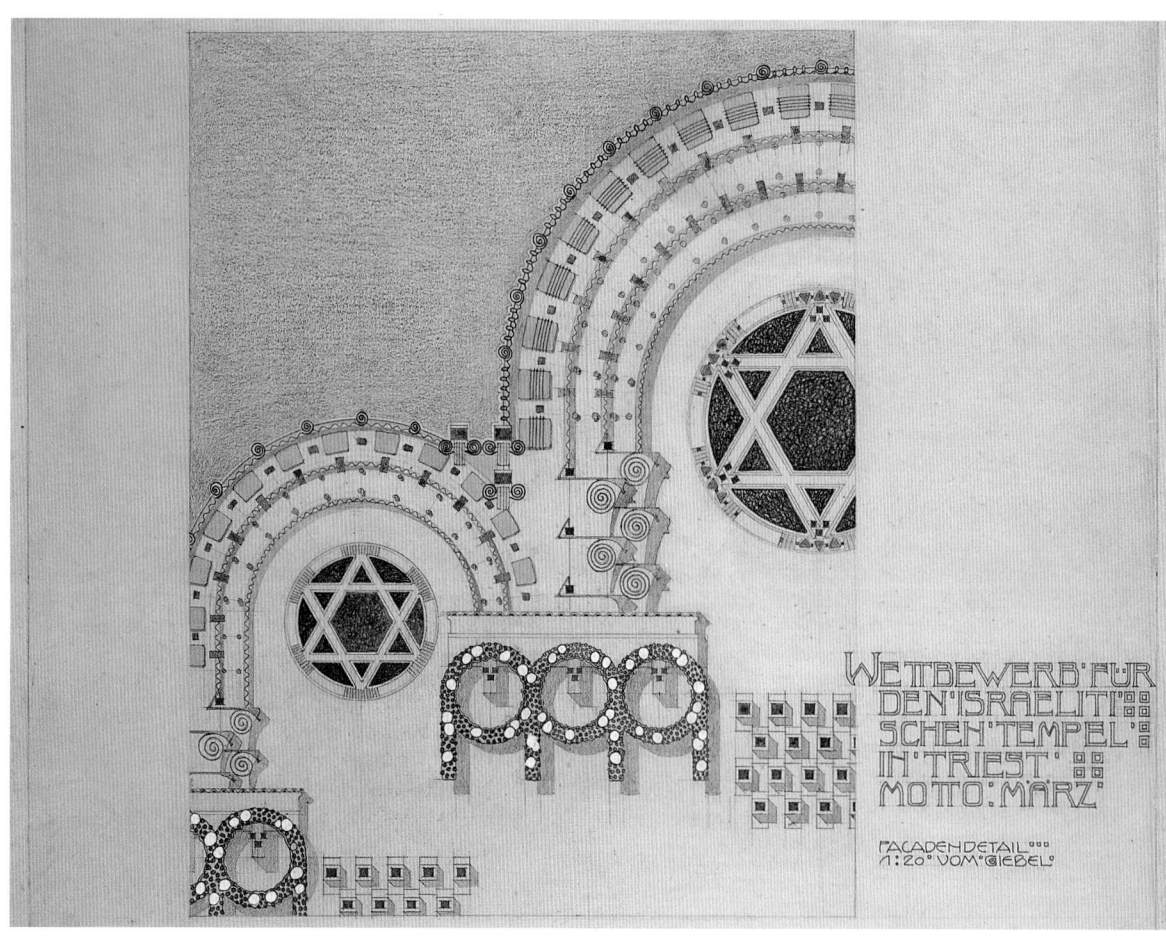

WETTBEWERB FÜR DEN ISRAELITISCHEN TEMPEL IN TRIEST
MOTTO: MÄRZ
FACADENDETAIL 1:20 VOM GIEBEL

FIGURE 5.10
(*Facing, top*) Emil Hoppe and Otto Schönthal, synagogue, Trieste, competition entry, section, 1903–4.

FIGURE 5.11
(*Facing, bottom*) Emil Hoppe and Otto Schönthal, synagogue, Trieste, competition entry, detail of the pediment, 1903–4.

FIGURE 5.12
(*Above*) Ruggero and Arduino Berlam, Tempio Israelitico, exterior, Trieste, 1903–12.

After Matouschek, working solo, could not produce the plans quickly enough, the committee gave the job in 1906 to the father-son team of Ruggero (1854–1920) and Arduino Berlam (1880–1946) of Trieste.[25] The two Christian architects were respectively the second and third generation of a family of Triestine architects who had played a significant role in the development of civic and domestic architecture in the city. When dedicated in 1912, the Berlams' synagogue represented a masterful combination of history and structural innovation in an architectural example of hybrid identity (fig. 5.12).[26] As the father and son explained in the *Corriere Israelitico*, they sought a style that "corresponded to the nature of the religion of Israel and respected historical-artistic traditions and material conditions of Palestine so that the building's intended use would stand out clearly at first glance."[27]

That standout design required the combinatory power of several sources. One was the late Roman, fourth-century architecture of Syria. It had the advantage of locating the origin of the Jews near the Holy Land without making them appear too Byzantine Christian or Muslim but still near the Habsburg Empire itself, Rome's great imperial successor.[28] Examples of this vocabulary could be seen in the paired mullioned windows above the entry portal, which recall Syrian precedents (fig. 5.13).[29] Research on Syria, including Palmyra and Baalbek, had been published as early as 1753 in Robert Wood's *The ruins of Palmyra, otherwise Tedmor, in the desert*; and numerous studies, including archaeological reports, had appeared subsequently. As seasoned professionals, the Berlams would have had such books in their library or had access to many of them.[30] More direct popular sources for Arduino are revealed in illustrations he

THE LANGUAGE OF HYBRIDITY

FIGURE 5.13
Ruggero and Arduino Berlam, Tempio Israelitico, detail of the entry portal, Trieste, 1903–12.

prepared that bear the influence of Josef Strzygowski, the Viennese professor of art history, who had been stimulating interest in post-Roman architecture of the Middle East.³¹ For more general references to the ever-elusive model of the synagogue, the Berlams had recourse to the Bible itself. Furthermore, they must have had at least some awareness of the latest modern trends in Europe, with their tendencies toward simplicity of line and massing, as well as their straightforward presentation of construction materials. H. P. Berlage's Stock Exchange in Amsterdam and contemporary synagogues in Germany, which emphasized central plans, domed roofs, and clear massing, provided immediate contemporary points of reference.³²

In their design of the Tempio Israelitico, the Berlams took the same urbanistic approach as other architects, including Hoppe, Schönthal, and Marmorek, responding to the configuration of the L-shaped lot by locating the temple on the vertical of the L, and the rabbi's apartment and the school on the horizontal. However, they reinforced the urban integration of the building within the square by locating its main portal entry and an immense rose window on the square (and at right angles to the main axis of the temple) and by incorporating a loggia on the ground floor of the annex. The annex brusquely butts against the temple with little tectonic transition except for the continuation of the pedestal bases, a string course, and repetition of the arch motif of the main temple. This directness underlies the architects' functional attitude, which uses the massing to express the spaces within the building. The functional approach is most obvious on the side street, where the interior corner stairs and towering apse are clearly expressed on the exterior. The expression of the apse also mitigated the huge mass of the central cube that contained the worship space.

In addition to expressing interior space, the exterior of the Tempio Israelitico presents a dialectic between the mass and the iconography of its surfaces, contrasting austerity with inflection, representation with abstraction. The exterior of the great main portal, with its lattice molding, seven concentric arches, and incised stone details, has multiple sources: the principal portal of the Duomo of Orvieto by Lorenzo Maitano, and the Armenian monastery of Spitavorok or a similar Middle Eastern precedent.[33] Using these precedents suggested the synthesis of Western and Eastern religions.

Once inside the temple, the visitor encounters a space whose imposing symmetry produces a monumental sobriety inflected with carefully elaborated imagery. The main axis terminates in the apse with its sacred ark, the *Aron ha-qodesh*, made of granite and marble (fig. 5.14). A splayed framing with descending curved volutes holds the gilt bronze doors of the ark, behind which sits the Torah. Above the ark are four short columns supporting an elaborate base holding the Tablets of the Law. Originally, towering one-story-tall menorahs flanked the ark. Two additional, widely branching menorahs framed the *bimah*, from which the scriptures were read. The apse behind the ark and *bimah* was intended to be clad in black marble but was executed in warm-colored stucco. Mosaics cover the moldings and basin.[34] Four massive piers above the center of the sanctuary support a dome and oculus (fig. 5.15). The combination of vegetal and geometric forms on the capitals of the big piers comes from descriptions of the Temple of Solomon found in the Old Testament; other images in mosaics and other surface patterns refer to biblical descriptions. Four palms on the surface of the dome's pendentives spread their branches as if supporting a golden orb of the sky. Between the piers on the entry side is the huge rose window, reinterpreted as a geometricized Star of David with tracery ribs (fig. 5.16).

Extraordinary technical achievements in concrete technology complement the interplay of functional massing and the nonfigural representational detail. Careful engineering, as the Berlams explained, had gone into all parts of the building's structure, from the foundation to the cupola.[35] Reinforced concrete was used in the structure of the gallery, the dome, the apses, and the head and foot of the altar. The galleries, in particular, spanned great distances with the thinnest use of materials. From the architects' perspective, the constructive means allowed uniting "the best of the new

FIGURE 5.14
(*Facing, top*) Ruggero and Arduino Berlam, Tempio Israelitico, interior, Trieste, 1903–12.

FIGURE 5.15
(*Facing, bottom*) Ruggero and Arduino Berlam, Tempio Israelitico, interior of the dome, Trieste, 1903–12.

FIGURE 5.16
(*Above*) Ruggero and Arduino Berlam, Tempio Israelitico, interior with the rose window, Trieste, 1903–12.

technology of reinforced concrete to the venerable and noble traditions of construction of Roman and Byzantine vaults."[36]

Not only does the dialectic between surface and mass create vibrancy, tension, and contrast, but the building as a whole speaks of hybridity. Although Austrian citizens, the Jews of Trieste related very much to the conditions of Italian Jewry and were aware of the calls to consider Italy a Jewish homeland in answer to the Diaspora that had dispersed Jews from ancient Israel. They also were aware of efforts to create a temple architecture that spoke of that Italian homeland, and they knew about the important new synagogue just built in Rome. But while both the synagogue in Trieste and the recently completed synagogue in Rome rejected Moorish schemes, they made reference to biblical Palestine, a Jewish land that contradicted the idea of a homeland in Italy or Austria. In Rome, a Greek-inspired model with Assyrian references appeared appropriate, while in Trieste the precedents of central Syria of the fourth century CE evoked the original and traditional space of the Hebrew people.[37]

::   THE HYBRIDITY of religious, national, cultural, and even personal identities found focus in the architecture of Hungarian Béla Lajta. A quintessential architectural polyglot, Lajta (1873–1920) worked in a variety of languages without apparent conflict.[38] After attending the Technical University in Budapest, he went on study tours of England, France, Germany, Russia, and Spain, documenting what he saw in photographs. In Berlin he worked for architects Alfred Messel, who had designed the Wert-

THE LANGUAGE OF HYBRIDITY

heim Department Store in 1896 (completed 1906), and then Eberhard Ihnen; in London he became friends with Richard Norman Shaw and M. H. Baillie Scott. In Vienna he met both Josef Hoffmann and Adolf Loos. Travel and collecting images of folk art in Transylvania and upper northern Hungary complemented Lajta's international experience with a study of Hungarian tradition.

Lajta opened an architectural office around 1901, which provided space for collaboration with Ödön Lechner in 1902–3. His early designs included sculpture, interiors, and private and public buildings, but he preferred designing tombs and even wrote about cemetery architecture.[39] In his architecture, he drew on the embodiments of Hungarian national identity associated with Lechner, the motifs of folk architecture, English free-style country house design, and Finnish architecture as a collateral expression of national identity, as well as emerging examples of German modern architecture. Lajta also drew on multiple personal cultural identities. Like many Jews who supported the Hungarian national movement, he magyarized his German family name, Leitersdorfer: in 1907, with the counsel of József Huszka, the promoter of Hungarian ethnology, he changed his surname to Lajta, which both sounded like the beginning of his own family name and was the name of a river on the border between Austria and Hungary.[40] With his new name, Lajta metaphorically bridged the worlds of Austria and Hungary as an assimilated Jew who supported national expression.

Starting as a follower of Lechner, Lajta developed his own continually evolving idiom that showed facility in responding to the requirements of particular building programs.[41] Some of his projects were loaded with obvious Jewish iconography, while others, such as his "Cabaret Parisiana" (1907–9), with its cornice of cherubim by the sculptor Geza Maroti, were generically biblical.[42] A grant from the Jewish philanthropic foundation of Ignac Wechselmann provided the commission for Lajta to design in 1905 the Institute for the Blind. Wechselmann, a famous master builder who had worked with the historicist architect Miklós Ybl, became the first Jewish member of the guild of master builders in Hungary.[43] His gift funded a nondenominational school for blind or visually impaired young people to receive special education in craftsmanship. Lajta provided a dense, four-story building of brick with a decided verticality (fig. 5.17). Two versions of the project date from the first months of 1905, when he was still signing his drawings as Leitersdorfer.[44] One scheme has arched windows at the ground level and rectangular windows elsewhere, but in the built version Lajta developed the theme of the three-centered arch throughout the façade while canting the upper corners of the remaining rectangular windows. The windows appeared as flat, punched, arched openings reminiscent of Messel's work, but the major focus was the undulating arched entry that sprung from rusticated stone bases. The cavelike character that this arch produced resonated with the works of Scandinavian nationalist architects of the time. Several of Lajta's designs of this period referred to the work of Eliel Saarinen, particularly his railway station in Helsinki (1904–4).[45]

The link to Finland, a common thread in Hungarian culture at the turn of the century, relied on the affinity between the Finnish and Hungarian languages, which

FIGURE 5.17
Béla Lajta, Institute for the Blind, exterior, Budapest, 1905–8. From *A Ház* [1908].

both belong to the small Finno-Ugric linguistic group. Equally important was the Finns' struggle for independence and for the retention of their genuine culture against the larger imperial force of Russia, efforts that Hungarians saw as parallel to their own struggle against Austria. Therefore, Finnish artists and architects offered a spiritual and aesthetic sense of camaraderie as models of self-determined independence, and were a major influence in Hungary along with Hungary's admiration for England.[46]

While the exterior of the institute recalls a Scandinavian connection, the interior is a functional and straightforward arrangement for which Lajta created an asymmetrical plan with a cross axis. The main entry, which focuses on the lobed entry portal, protrudes both as an elongated bay and as an arched portal. At one end of the building stands a tower that provides both secondary vertical circulation and a visual transition to what appears to be a small chapel with its own entry.[47] The corridors are singly loaded—with rooms only at one side of the hall—and the dormitory has large arched windows so that light pours into the interior from the sides of the building.

The infusion of light for the sighted and sightless provides a metaphysical dimension whose aesthetics and functions harmonize with the experience of touch. Where the blind and partially sighted could not see, they could feel the presence of their school in its textures: on the exterior, a base of rubble-rough ashlar stone and piers of

THE LANGUAGE OF HYBRIDITY

FIGURE 5.18
Béla Lajta, Institute for the Blind, entry, Budapest, 1905–8.

coarse stone with invented capitals flanking the broad stairs oddly recall Lajta's funerary monuments. The entry doors recapitulate the experience of texture with their flat, smooth surfaces resembling leather, with the opening date cut into them in a technique resembling the chip carvings of folk art. Rows of brads and elaborate wrought-iron handles and escutcheons add to the tactile experience while referring to folk treatments (fig. 5.18). Each door combines a pane of glass with etched, abstracted folk flowers. The concentric arches around the doors contain layers of bricks in alternating flat and protruding bands with smooth corners of molded bricks while the interplay of molded and flat bricks defines the edges of the arch.

The overall effect is a hybridity of Finno-Hungarian association but with its own character. The entry seems to say that those deprived of sight can feel their way into the world within. Touch is the theme, and in touching the surfaces of the portal, a person will feel the contrast of flat and jagged, while the tracings of traditional forms ensured a link to the Hungarian heritage. Beyond the portal and windbreak doors, textures shift: the wide foyer has plain but massive cylindrical columns on double plinths—all of smooth stone—flanking the carved tablet that honors the principal founders of the school and makes an obligatory nod to Emperor Franz Josef.[48] Further inside, motifs of Hungarian folk art—emblems of national identity—provide texture on floor paving and in the chip-carved details used with door-frame moldings. Smooth and textured surfaces persist throughout the interior, creating sensation to all who touch them. The building's success lay in its hybrid combination of form, details, and function.

A contemporary writer saw it as Lajta's first great work, demonstrating the young architect's talent, which included achieving brilliant solutions, such as ornaments with poetic inscriptions written in Braille. It was important not only in Lajta's development, but "even more in the vast whole of modern Hungarian architecture."[49]

Lajta's design for the Metropolitan Commercial School in Pest (1909–12) provides another example of hybridity, combining functional requirements with a contemporary symbolism of commerce and an expression of national identity in a powerful demonstration in the modern use of materials (fig. 5.19). The creation of the school resulted from Budapest mayor István Bárczy's efforts to update the educational system as part of an overall urban reform movement.[50] An admirer of Lajta's work, he secured the commission for him and later defended the architect against criticisms from conservatives.

FIGURE 5.19
Béla Lajta, Metropolitan Commercial School, exterior, Budapest, 1909–12.

FIGURE 5.20
Béla Lajta, Metropolitan Commercial School, entry, Budapest, 1909–12; exterior detail.

For the constrained site on the narrow Vas Street, Lajta devised an L-shaped plan anchored by two towers, which contain entries and stairs. The larger entry on the left is clearly identified as the main one, while the other tower provides secondary circulation and additional egress. Along the street side is a sports gymnasium on the lower floors, with a library, teachers' room, and offices above. The interior wing at a right angle to the street contains classrooms and offices. The arrangement breaks from the conventions of scholastic architecture, which grouped rooms in blocks, and represents a fresh interpretation of modern pedagogy.

Lajta's first studies for the building had towers terminated with domes and figures, a reference to Josef Hoffmann's Palais Stoclet. As built, the tower tops were flat, but they nevertheless add to the monumentality of the building. The soaring brick piers in the central section, vertical slots of the secondary stair tower, and a broad, glass-filled void above the main entry reinforce the effect. The austere quality of the towers recalls the image of industrialism found in Peter Behrens's contemporary work at the AEG Small Motors Factory in Berlin (1910–15), but Lajta's building differs in its use of color, patterns, and folk motifs transformed into symbols of technology and progress.[51]

At the entry, the brick mass of the tower appears to rest on a massive lintel, with the name of the school carved in the stone. Another inscription right above the doors reinforces the enormity of the task of education with the Latin phrase *Non scolae sed vitae discimus* (We learn not for school but for life). Surrounding the entry are panels of folk motifs, cut with a technique resembling chip carving. But interspersed in the bands of folk art are symbols of progress: a locomotive and a dirigible. From the outset, the building announced in its language a dialogue between craft—a carrier of tradition and bearer of identity—and the technology reshaping the modern world (fig. 5.20).

Light reflected off Zsolnay tiles illuminates the main entry hall. Using a strategy similar to that at the Institute for the Blind, Lajta maximized window openings to make the interior luminous. Clear and simple geometry defines the entire spatial organization, and generous hallways and broad landings in the main stair tower provide ample circulation (fig. 5.21). Translucent glass allows the library to fill with light. The interiors, especially in common areas, contain a rich profusion of patterns in a confrontation of abstract geometric patterns with figural folk motifs. During construction and shortly thereafter, from 1910 to 1914, Gyula Tálos and Lajos Kozma developed many of the details. Kozma, who was strongly influenced by the Wiener Werkstätte, contributed particularly to the interior of the director's office, and the student areas, door cornices,

FIGURE 5.21
Béla Lajta, Metropolitan Commercial School, interior, Budapest, 1909–12.

bands of revetment, and paving.⁵² He animated the surfaces with geometric and folk motifs with their coded colors of red, yellow, and black. Just as on the exterior, in the interiors tradition represented by folk motifs coexisted with symbols of modern progress, the geometric language of rationalism, and even with classical references, such as a statue of Athena. The result was a hybridity that produced a new modern idiom.

The critics responded with praise to the synthesis of form and function, the interplay of materials and light, the exemplary laboratories, and the superbly accommodating classrooms and offices for students and teachers. One writer in *Művészet*, who also lauded the stereometric treatment of the façade and the interior's luminosity, described the institute as "surely an ideal model for the school of the future."⁵³ Another writer reaffirmed the excellent accommodations while noting the systematic arrangement of spaces and "polyphony of materials" in a building that was "not merely a feat of sensibility or language or expression, but a form of thought."⁵⁴ Along with his other buildings, the Commercial School showed Lajta's linguistic versatility that made buildings at once modern, functional, geometric, and figural in his use of motifs that resonated with national culture. But the war would soon cut short opportunities for his innovative approach, and he fell ill and died in 1920. Fifteen years later, a critic described Lajta and his position in Budapest's prewar architectural scene as the "man of the future" around whom a school of other architects circled, benefiting from his example.⁵⁵

:: ALADÁR ÁRKAY'S design of a Calvinist church in Budapest (1912–13) represented another statement of Hungarian hybridity before World War I. Árkay (1868–1932) was born in eastern Hungary, in Temesvár (Timișoara, Romania), the son of an art metalworker.⁵⁶ He studied design at the national School of Decorative Arts in Budapest and painting and architecture in Paris. He spent some time working in Zürich and in the early 1890s was a manager in the office of Ferdinand Fellner and Hermann Helmer, the prolific designers of theaters throughout the Austro-Hungarian Empire; he worked on their theater in Salzburg and the Somossy Orpheum in Budapest. Like many of his peers, upon returning to Budapest, Árkay also worked in the office of Alajos Hauszmann on the building of the Royal Castle in Buda. Then in 1894 he started working in the office of his father-in-law, Mór (Moritz) Kallina, who formerly collaborated with Otto Wagner on the Rumbach Street Synagogue, and from 1900 he worked independently while also collaborating on a series of competitions with his brother-in-law, Géza Kallina. During this period, Árkay designed and built only five houses on his own, but around 1910 his commissions increased to include the designs of forty houses in Budapest's Twelfth District for a housing estate sponsored by a corporation of lawyers.⁵⁷

In 1911, Árkay won the commission to design the Calvinist church at Városligeti Allée 7 (City Woods) in Budapest's Seventh District; construction followed for two years.⁵⁸ The Calvinist church, known as the Allée Reformed Church (*Fasori református*

FIGURE 5.22
Aladár Árkay, Allée Reformed Church (*Fasori református templom*), exterior, Budapest, 1911–13; view ca. 1914.

FIGURE 5.23
Aladár Árkay, Allée Reformed Church (*Fasori református templom*), exterior, Budapest, 1911–13; contemporary view.

templom), became a pinnacle of hybridity, reflecting Árkay's interpretation of Finnish national romanticism, the Wiener Werkstätte, and the work of Otto Wagner, as well as the Hungarian vernacular.[59] It also represented a finale just before World War I of Gesamtkunstwerk, with the architect designing every detail of the building.

The church intertwined religious purpose with political statement. Folk motifs in its design again played a role as signifiers of Hungarian national identity, but, being associated with Protestantism in Hungarian life, they provided a subtle means of opposing the dominant and suppressive Catholicism. Calvinism in particular had a strong appeal in Hungary, because it resonated with early pre-Catholic forms of worship.[60] Before Stephen of Hungary (975–1038) had brought the Christianity of Rome to the Hungarians in 1001, they practiced a somewhat Manichean version of Christianity that represented a middle ground between the Eastern Orthodox Church and

THE LANGUAGE OF HYBRIDITY

the Roman Catholicism of the West. With Stephen's imposition of Catholicism, earlier practices were outlawed, along with the objects that represented them. These objects included a kind of runic writing and system of coding intimately connected with the earlier version of Christianity. The shepherds carved runes on their long wooden staffs as a means of keeping track of their flocks. In addition, villages and regions used a related system of symbols on grave markers to indicate the identity of the interred. A flower, a leaf, or an angular symbol could denote the gender of the deceased, his or her age, marital status, and so forth. The simple carving knife was the principal tool for inscribing in both the language and the symbol system, which resulted in distinctive kinds of rectilinear cuts, because curves were more difficult to execute with it. The imposition of western Christianity suppressed this system of codification, and people perpetuated it at great risk, with the result that few examples of its artifacts survived.

Sparking a memory of the old traditions, Protestantism took root around Hungary within a short time after its first appearance. By 1600, approximately 80 to 85 percent of Hungarians were Protestant: Calvinists predominated in western Transylvania, Lutherans were the majority in the German parts of eastern Transylvania, and Unitarians added to the mix. The simplicity of Calvinism provided an antidote to the liturgical elaborations of Catholic ritual and the complexity of its churches and cathedrals.[61] In such circumstances, it is not surprising that the Catholic Habsburgs strongly aligned with the Counter-Reformation. Their suppression of religious rivals caused Calvinism's decline from prominence to an oppositional role. To identify with the Calvinist faith automatically implied taking a political position adversarial to the Habsburg mainstream and against Roman Catholicism.[62] As a confirmation of its Hungarianness, the Reformed Church had more ethnic and linguistic Magyars than it did Germans, Slovaks, Croats, or Slovenes.[63]

In its early years, the Hungarian Reformed Church used preexisting Roman Catholic churches for architectural models, but it transformed them by taking away the altar, placing the communion table in front of the pulpit, and removing any sculptures or figural representations. Seating in the chancel faced the pulpit, communion table, and congregation. These alterations reflected the importance in the Reformed Church of the community hearing the Word of God and participating in singing God's praises, with a greater emphasis on preaching. As George Starr has shown, these changes resulted in the tendency of Calvinist churches not only to allow an interior asymmetrical arrangement, but to emphasize width in the floor plans, thereby creating transverse plans. The arrangement of seating mattered more than the floor plan itself, and a wider plan accommodated the community better than a narrow, longitudinal one. This transverse layout, which recalled centrally planned churches, became the norm for the Hungarian Reformed Church; longitudinal plans, which focused on the altar, were identified with Roman Catholic liturgy.[64] Furthermore, Calvinists preferred smaller churches over large ones, as their more intimate worship space fostered the spiritual closeness of the congregation.

When Calvinist churches began being built in Hungary, they proceeded from neo-classical models to neo-Gothic style and then to a reliance on the Hungarian vernacular at the beginning of the twentieth century. Once again, the pure sources were found in Transylvania, in the old Calvinist churches from the seventeenth and eighteenth centuries. Architects, particularly members of the "Young Ones," made pilgrimages to these sites, which to them encapsulated Hungarian identity. While the effort to rediscover national and regional styles was widespread throughout the empire and Europe, the use of earlier church motifs in Hungary had particular religious and political significance.

For his models, Árkay followed prototypes of Calvinist churches in Germany and Switzerland, a Calvinist stronghold. These churches had inscribed Greek cross plans that created symmetrical interior spaces and contrasting exterior massing that introduced asymmetry. The architect would have also known of the new types of German Lutheran churches designed by the firm of Curjel & Moser: responding to the new liturgy associated with the Ringkirche in Wiesbaden, the firm had recently designed churches in Karlsruhe, Basle, Zug, St. Gall, and Flawil.[65] Drawings in the Budapest Historical Museum indicate that Árkay explored alternative schemes and give a sense of the hybrid character of his design process.[66] In one version, the architect drew an asymmetrical front façade with a tall rectangular tower to the left of an arched main entry and a short circular tower to the right. Above the entry is a huge semicircular window and smaller windows under the eaves of the sanctuary's pitched roof. At the far left is an appended rectory. Most noticeable in this scheme is the conventional ashlar treatment of the façade, with contrasting smooth surfaces, and the folk character of the short circular tower, as if it could have come out of a sketchbook by Károly Kós. In a second scheme, Árkay flipped the arrangement so that the tower, now with a clock, and the rectory are on the right and the short tower is on the left. More significantly, he filled the flat surface under the eaves of the sanctuary with swirling, tightly wound curves reminiscent, on the one hand, of the surface motifs of Gustav Klimt and, on the other, of spiraling vegetations. Árkay's goal became clearer in a sketch he titled "Református Templom," where the curvy motifs now have migrated around the main arch and take the shape of floral arabesques resembling paisley patterns, but interspersed with abstracted geometric folk motifs. The final design amalgamates his studies: set back from the street to make a small urban forecourt, the front façade consists of a circular tower on the right, replete with national folk forms, a sanctuary with pitched roof in the center, and a tall tower on the left (figs. 5.22, 5.23).

While the basic morphology of the church connected it to other Calvinist examples, its treatment by Árkay was distinctively different. The layering of languages starts with the circular tower on the right of the front façade. In recalling Finnish architecture, the top turret refers to the Finno-Ugric affiliation. Beneath the turret, the short engaged columns connect to the architecture of Transylvania and its association as the locus of the purist forms of the Hungarian race. The central entry with the low arched form and short, thick columns repeats a reading of Scandinavian and

FIGURE 5.24
Aladár Árkay, Allée Reformed Church (*Fasori református templom*), entry, Budapest, 1911–13.

Transylvanian motifs. A patchwork of Zsolnay tiles with floral and geometric motifs clads the entry, but rather than conveying vague, abstract meanings, they specifically tie Calvinism to the earlier Christian practices of the Hungarians (fig. 5.24).[67] One motif on some of the tiles resembles a tower with its bottom slit, a direct reference to the carved wooden markers of the early Christian church and their biographical coding. Árkay transformed this motif at the tops of both towers that flank the main façade. Additionally, in a shorter format, he used it at the tops of capitals that mark the side gate to the church. A fourth version on a larger scale appears inside the small side courtyard, as if repeating that this church contains the memory of the ancient rites and rituals of the earlier Christian days of the Hungarian people.

The color coding of tiles, abstract reliefs, and contrasting surface textures adds to the iconic complexity of the exterior and interior. Gold and black predominate both on the façade and in the interior, establishing a continuity in the spirit of a Gesamtkunstwerk; secondary colors include shades of blue, green, and yellow. Gold, in two shades, is especially abundant in the interior of the church, which some historians see as a reference to the work of Otto Wagner, particularly his St. Leopold's Church at Steinhof. The tiles alternate with an abstract rhythm of blank and filled spaces to create a composition that is modern in its nonhierarchical organization, yet uses motifs that resonate with cultural identity. Panels with reliefs wrap around the sides of the entry, acting as an abstract billboard to promote the meaning of the church. Below the panels are short stone columns tightly grouped together. Above the panels, a semicircular window of concentric arches filled with glass panes hints at the arch motif to be found within the church. The tall tower uses ashlar stones at its corners for quoins, but its smooth contrasting surface has vertical stripes to accentuate its verticality. Its pyramidal roof is covered with undulating lines, resembling waves rendered geometrically.

The church is entered through dark doors with incised folk motifs and wrought-iron trim (fig. 5.25). Once inside, the visitor experiences a vast space crowned by a hemispheric dome over thirteen meters in width, and walls that are tinted light green and creamy yellow and articulated with bands of polychrome tiles (fig. 5.26). Gold bands and gold motifs on tiles accompany a variety of stones and materials with contrasting colors (fig. 5.27). The lower altar rests in front of the congregation. Behind it, a high altar pulpit, reached by symmetrical stone stairs, sits beneath an arched frame of tiles; the frame is flanked by tall, dark wooden chairs for the elders of the church (fig. 5.28). An array of tightly spaced cylindrical columns supports the altars, repeating the columnar theme of the exterior entry portal. Behind the high altar is a deeply recessed apse, covered with tiles and containing the church's organ. At the

FIGURE 5.25
Aladár Árkay, Allée Reformed Church (*Fasori református templom*), detail, entry doors, Budapest, 1911–13.

FIGURE 5.26
Aladár Árkay, Allée Reformed Church (*Fasori református templom*), interior, Budapest, 1911–13.

gallery level, the inside faces of the arches have floral folk motifs in gold, green, and blue. The ring on which the dome sits is also patterned, and from the center of the dome hangs a chandelier featuring a series of concentric polygons with pierced sides.

Not only does the church combine and transform the motifs associated with Hungarian nationalism and draw on Calvinist precedents, it also serves as a locus for the exploration of modern technology, notably concrete, harnessed to serve the ideological purpose of the building. Árkay paralleled the process of linguistic transformation embodied in the iconography of the interior with the radically innovative technology he developed in the ceiling structure. He made the connection of the rectangular plan of the perimeter walls to the circle of the dome boldly, without the traditional transition through pendentives. The thin reinforced-concrete shell of the dome sits directly on a concrete ceiling, and concrete columns support the entire ensemble, creating a daring structural statement. The economic efficiency of a single dome appealed to Árkay's clients, but the technology, as we have often seen in Austro-Hungarian modernism, served not as an end but as a linguistic means of representation.

The Allée Reformed Church opened with an enthusiastic reception in June 1913. One commentator saw it as a statement of "richly ornamented, powerful Hungarian language."[68] Others said its use of ceramics as ornament and wall covering would usher in a new époque, its "Asian" sources were not to be missed, and its innovative structural system, which featured a reinforced-concrete arch spanning 13.3 meters for the cupola, had produced the first modern church in Budapest. The journal *Magyar Építõmûvészet* published images of the church when it opened, and the structure re-

FIGURE 5.27
Aladár Árkay, Allée Reformed Church (*Fasori református templom*), detail of the interior, Budapest, 1911–13.

FIGURE 5.28
Aladár Árkay, Allée Reformed Church (*Fasori református templom*), detail of the interior, Budapest, 1911–13.

ceived not only local attention, but international note as well with its publication in *Der Architekt*.⁶⁹

Reading the building as a statement of national identity would have been straightforward, as people's associations of carved crosses and carved grave markers with the early religious practices was fairly common knowledge. The overt connection between Calvinism and the pre-Stephenian era would have been clear as well as the association of Calvinism with an anti-Habsburgian political statement. Árkay's appropriation of these themes represents quotation where the singularity of references indicating the specifics of gender, age, and marital status is subsumed in a broader association of ancient motif and contemporary life. The building alludes to folk motifs while transforming them from replications of the past to modern usage.⁷⁰ Technological sophistication and the prowess of the thin-shelled dome coexist with the picturesque quality of the façade, but Árkay made the syntax modern, creating a remarkable demonstration of hybridity.⁷¹

ISTVÁN MEDGYASZAY, another Hungarian architect, advanced the search for national identity in his hybrid synthesis of modern technology and myth in civic and religious buildings. For him, a Hungarian national architecture would be the product of combining rational forms, amazing technological innovation and skill, iconic figural imagery of mythic figures, and abstracted folk motifs—but all recast as a modern architecture. Medgyaszay (1877–1959) was born in Budapest with the surname Benkó to a father who was an architect and teacher at a technical school. He finished his studies at the Technical University in Budapest in 1896, and after 1900 attended the Technical University in Vienna and Wagner's master class, concluding his studies at the Polytechnic Institute back in Budapest in 1904. In 1906 he magyarized his surname to Medgyaszay as a testament of Hungarian identity.[72]

Medgyaszay's prescience as a designer and his grasp of the rationalizing principles of new technology could be seen early while he was still a student at the Wagnerschule. In a study for an apartment building in Vienna (1901–2), subsequently published in *Der Architekt*, he proposed a spectacular glass curtain wall façade.[73] But while this early Wagnerschule project explored an innovative use of glass, reinforced concrete eventually became Medgyaszay's specialty.[74] He studied its use in Budapest and later also in the Paris office of François Hennebique, a leading practitioner in reinforced-concrete technology. Having developed an expertise, Medgyaszay lectured at the Eighth International Congress of Architects Devoted to Artistic Solutions of Reinforced Concrete in Vienna in 1908. His technical knowledge allowed him to shape reinforced concrete in direct response to structural loads, according to laws of compression and tension. But he also stressed that the challenge of using reinforced concrete for modern architecture was in the interplay between its neutral form and the necessity of symbolic representation, a position opposite that of western European functionalists, who saw concrete as a means to achieve the rational expression of structural load.

Medgyaszay wanted not only to exploit technology, but to invest material with cultural meaning in the service of a Hungarian national style. Like other architects in a similar pursuit, he traveled the countryside and documented examples of Hungarian folk architecture and arts; they were published as part of Dezsö Malonyay's five-volume *A magyar nép művészete* (The Art of the Hungarian People). He also studied Asian art in western European collections, searching always for relics of the Huns, the ancestors of the Hungarians. Inevitably aware of Lechner's work, as well as that of Kós and Lajta, Medgyaszay sought to combine in his own way the latest developments of technology—particularly reinforced concrete—with iconography identifiable as distinctly Hungarian.

Medgyaszay's first efforts to create his own hybrid version of a national language of architecture could be already seen in 1902–3, when he proposed a national pantheon upon the Gellért Hill in Pest, one of the most prominently visible sites in the city (fig. 5.29). At the center of the scheme, he placed a towerlike mausoleum flanked

THE LANGUAGE OF HYBRIDITY

FIGURE 5.29
István Medgyaszay, national pantheon on Gellért Hill (project), perspective, Budapest, 1902–3. Reprinted from *Magyar Mérnök és Építész Egylet Heti Értesítője*, no. 30 (1908), n.p.

by two rectangular wings filled with niches. On top of the mausoleum sits a dome in the shape of the Hungarian Holy Crown of Saint Stephen, identified by a crooked cross that, according to legend, broke upon the death of the great Renaissance king Matthias Corvinus. In front of the tower, two canted pillars frame a vast stairway along which Hungarians would process in pilgrimage to their heroes. Mounted warriors, reminiscent of the figures at the Millennial monument, guard the way. Medgyaszay apparently intended the complex to be built of reinforced concrete, with the honorific niches taking on a form that blended folk detail with the simplified expression of concrete masses.[75] In his perspective of the pantheon, he painted a dark foreground and background to allow the complex itself to shine in light. The tone was dramatic and serious and, if built, would have dominated the landscape with its theme of national heroes.[76]

Medgyaszay's evolving hybrid language of myth and technology could be seen effectively in the theater complex he designed in 1908 for the Hungarian town of Veszprém, southwest of Budapest and north of Lake Balaton (fig. 5.30). A market center, rail hub, and county seat, Veszprém had existed since at least the ninth century and consequently contained a complement of historic buildings. Not merely a theater, but a complex with ancillary offices and spaces, Medgyaszay's structure was made of reinforced concrete, with prefabricated consoles supporting balconies of reinforced concrete, patented concrete window frames, pergolas, and invented column capitals—

all incorporating abstracted folk art motifs. His drawings indicate that he conceived of the roof of the theater as a thin concrete shell, which was highly advanced for its time.[77] From the roof hangs the thin Rabitz ceiling, which at its center has a complex lattice of interconnecting circles located directly above a light monitor. Light fixtures with globular shades hang from bases of abstracted folk motifs, and folk motifs surround the edges of the proscenium. Tall windows with round arches let daylight flood the theater. Austere, exposed, unadorned concrete beams, whose shapes corresponded to their loads, and concrete columns with patterned surfaces support the lower level below the theater, a space used for intermissions.[78]

Though forgotten now, Medgyaszay's prowess as seen in Veszprém had a surprisingly wide impact in the 1920s. In his book *The Ferro-Concrete Style*, a unique international study published in the United States on the potentialities of reinforced concrete, Francis Onderdonk described Medgyaszay's theater at Veszprém along with other buildings, noting at length Medgyaszay's report in 1908 and detailing the beautiful effects of his concrete tracery.[79] He also clearly grasped Medgyaszay's innovations:

> *The Veszprém Theater is ventilated by a centralized system and with few exceptions the windows need not be opened. The reinforced concrete forms a uniform network for the surface which is to be glazed and closed hermetically. The concrete ribs have on the inner and outer side rebates which are varnished several times and which form a frame for the glass planes;*

FIGURE 5.30
István Medgyaszay, theater complex, exterior, Veszprém, Hungary, 1908.

FIGURE 5.31
István Medgyaszay, Roman Catholic church and mausoleum, exterior, Rárósmulyad (now Mul'a, Slovakia), 1908–10.

they are caulked with oilputty [sic] which creates durable, cheap, easily formed and hermetically closed windows. The concrete web has no projections but very strongly curved Oriental-Hungarian outlines, the decorative effect of which is to enliven the big, smooth surfaces of the façade.[80]

Innovative concrete-shell roofs became one of Medgyaszay's specialties, and he used a sensational prefabricated shell, transported from Budapest in eight pieces, for the Roman Catholic church and mausoleum he designed at Rárósmulyad, on the border of Hungary and Slovakia (now Mul'a, Slovakia), in 1908–10 (fig. 5.31).[81] Entirely constructed of reinforced concrete, it was not only the first church in Hungary made entirely of this modern material, but its shell roof spans fifteen meters in diameter and is only eight centimeters thick.⁸² A sound reflector in the belfry has an even thinner shell of four centimeters. Octagonal in plan, the church has an extension that leads to a crypt below and joins a square-based tower with a prominent pointed spire. A viewing platform below the spire uses cast concrete for its columns and pierced railings. The base of the ensemble has stripes of alternating textures with smooth side walls above.

However, the purpose of the church was not to revel in technology per se, but to employ it for symbolic and iconographic purposes. The periphery of the shell dome is encircled with a continuous concrete frame, with cast-concrete angels mounted at each corner of the octagon (fig. 5.32). The interior surfaces of the church originally had a seamless continuity punctuated by bands of abstracted Hungarian folk motifs (fig. 5.33). A wrought-iron balustrade before the altar and pierced wood panels, as well as

FIGURE 5.32
István Medgyaszay, Roman Catholic church and mausoleum, exterior, Rárósmulyad (now Mul'a, Slovakia), 1908–10.

THE LANGUAGE OF HYBRIDITY

FIGURE 5.33
István Medgyaszay,
Roman Catholic church
and mausoleum, interior,
Rárósmulyad (now Mul'a,
Slovakia), 1908–10, from
Magyar Építőművészet,
no. 1 (1911).

the pulpit and the screen in front of the organ, literally alluded to Hungarian folk architecture. The church had a purity of expression that made it not only a technological marvel with its reinforced-concrete structure, but also an imposition of Magyar identity on an area populated by ethnic Slovaks.[83] Furthermore, the church's hybridity prevails, despite its claims for Hungarian identity, in its association with Viennese practices. While the tower does recall folk architecture, the angels surrounding the dome, the low arches, and some of the ornament reduced to primary forms, such as circles in windows, typify the Wagnerschule. Similarly, though Medgyaszay substituted folk motifs for abstract patterns, he applied them only on two-dimensional borders or otherwise flat surfaces in a manner that was more Viennese than Lechnerian.

WHILE MEDGYASZAY explored a mythic language of nationalism materialized through technical innovations in concrete, other, parallel efforts were under way to proclaim a language of national identity that was more myth than hybrid, and relied more on image and cultural artifact than on a new technology. One of those efforts to represent Hungarian national identity to the West came through exhibitions at international fairs.[84] The culmination of the prewar strivings to present the Hungarian nation to the world took place in 1911, when the buildings themselves at the International Exposition of Industrial Art in Turin operated at a grand scale to convey the idea of Hungarian nationhood and a unitary national culture. For the exposition, Móric Pogány and Emil Tőry designed a pavilion called King Attila's Tent Palace, which was based on a purported description of the king's wooden palace (fig. 5.34).[85] It was the great sensation at the exhibition, confirming, as one commentator noted, "a 'revived' culture of the steppes, albeit one that was purely imaginative."[86] Located along the banks of the Po River, the pavilion consisted of a massive conical tower rising from a blocky base flanked by two wings with conical roofs. Armed knights guarded the dome above the entry, which was shaped like a helmet and embossed with wrought iron. The view from the Po on the back side was even more fantastical, with two multicolored spires flanking the rear hall and framing the tall, conical tower (fig. 5.35).[87]

FIGURE 5.34
Emil Tőry and Móric Pogány, Hungarian Pavilion at the International Exposition of Industrial Art in Turin, exterior, entry side, Turin, 1911. Reprinted from *Magyar Iparmüvészet* 14 (1911), 261.

FIGURE 5.35
Emil Tőry and Móric Pogány, Hungarian Pavilion at the International Exposition of Industrial Art in Turin, exterior, back side toward the river Po, Turin, 1911. Reprinted from *Magyar Iparművészet* 14 (1911), 263.

Inside Attila's Tent, light flooded in from the top of the glass dome, and from the dome's perimeter hung two oversized folk ornaments used as bangles that alternated with ceramic hanging planters. Dots, another familiar folk motif, covered the flat surfaces of the ceilings. Instead of moldings to mediate the connection between walls, the architects supplied a stepped cornice covered with floral and abstract motifs. In addition, they treated the upper parts of doorways with canted sides and flat arches, another ensemble motif of national style. Cabinets, ceramic objects from Zsolnay, and furniture continued the use of nationalistic folk motifs. However, all attention focused on the center of the space, where, surrounded by a low ring, stood an equestrian figure of the revered and mythic Attila (fig. 5.36).

Instead of ingratiating Hungarian identity with the outside world, the nonhybrid language of myth presented in the exhibitions ultimately had the opposite effect. Ironically, as Terri Switzer has demonstrated, the effort to create a positive image backfired, and the West, including the United States, tended to focus on the primitivist aspects of the culture with its roots in the Huns, considering Hungarians backward and seeing them en masse as lusty and lazy, while ignoring their industrial prowess and extensive agricultural production. From the perspective of progressive western European architects, the imagery of Hungarian nationalism had reached an extreme of difference, uniqueness, and strangeness, a curious otherness. Such associations overwhelmed the technological innovations and explorations of concrete technology and its aesthetic possibilities in the work of Medgyaszay.

FIGURE 5.36
Emil Tőry and Móric Pogány, Hungarian Pavilion at the International Exposition of Industrial Art in Turin, interior, Turin, 1911, from *Magyar Iparmüvészet* 14 (1911), 266.

THE HUNGARIAN half of the empire had no exclusive claim to the language of hybridity, as it also appeared in the evolving work of progressive circles in Austria. Passing from the austere forms of his language of rationalism, Josef Hoffmann sought a clarification of the role of modern architecture by going back in history beyond the Baroque and its revivals to the roots of architecture itself. Much analysis of Hoffmann's work from the 1910s onward reduces his work simply to a return to classicism. But some of his efforts created a new syntax that extended beyond revivals or returns to a new hybridity, seen for example in the villa he designed for Josefine Skywa and Robert Primavesi in 1913–15 in the Heitzing district of Vienna (fig. 5.37). Primavesi was the cousin and brother-in-law of Otto Primavesi, an industrial magnate and banker from Olmüz in Moravia, for whom Hoffmann had previously remodeled a bank and designed a sumptuous country house.[88]

The villa in Vienna is a residence of immense complexity on a large lot. To the street, it presents a symmetrical façade articulated with a system of pilasters and projecting pediments that frame recessed slanting roofs with dormers. Entry is from the east through a porte-cochère (fig. 5.38) leading into a double-height, marble-clad entry hall and further to a darker, wood-wainscoted great hall. The west side of the building negotiates the sloping site with terraces and stairs. The mass of the building moves in and out restlessly as its form shifts to accommodate the functions within. The interior is organized around the great hall, with a library, dining room, salon, kitchen, winter garden, and terrace around two sides, and bedrooms, workroom, and baths off the street side.

FIGURE 5.37
Josef Hoffmann, Villa Skywa-Primavesi, south façade, Vienna, 1913–15.

FIGURE 5.38
Josef Hoffmann, Villa Skywa-Primavesi, porte-cochère and main entry, Vienna, 1913–15. Author photo.

Though little recognized as such, the Skywa-Primavesi Villa is parallel and comparable to Palais Stoclet in Brussels, with interiors that were once nearly as rich. The salon, for instance, has a lemon-wood floor with black inlaid strips, door frames of *arabescaosato* marble, and white stucco decorations on light-brown ground.[89] These stucco decorations are a floral motif variation on Roman traditions of grape clusters suspended from curving, stylized branches. Even the air vent in the small salon is treated with great complexity: its shield shape contains a blooming plant and an encompassing thin wire lattice as background. In the great hall, dark, polished oak is used for carved panels, which alternate with different plant treatments. The hall's ceiling is coffered in wood, and the striated motif of the exterior is repeated on portions of the interior walls.[90]

The scrutiny of a detailed view of the wall and pediment of the south façade shows the combination of classical and nonclassical motifs that permeate the entire villa (fig. 5.39). The pediment is abstracted and transformed into a tall, equilateral triangle, something that could be also found in the work of the Wagnerschule, but that in Hoffmann's interpretation was unique. Eduard Sekler describes the pediment with consummate precision: "[Its] cornice has, above a fillet an astragal, a large cyma with floral appliqués, followed by a vertically grooved fascia, crowned by a double ovolo with distinctive foliage which looks almost like an inverted egg-and-dart."[91] But some of these elements are distinctly nonclassical: "floral appliqués"—which alternate heavy buds with curious flower-and-fruit ensembles—cannot be related to any specific

FIGURE 5.39
Josef Hoffmann, Villa Skywa-Primavesi, detail of the south façade, Vienna, 1913–15.

classical ornament and resemble folk motifs. In the centers of the pediments are stiff, nonclassical, sculptured figures by Anton Hanak, a reclining male and female. The flutings of the pilasters below the roof again suggest a classical vocabulary and syntax, but the transition between pediment and wall is abrupt, without any kind of capital. The resulting effect turns the classical motif of flutings into an abstracted pattern. Moreover, the flutings have an unconventional "complex profile—concave, convex, concave between flat fillets—assuring a rich modulation of light and shade."[92] This system of grooves provides a subtle rhythmic movement of A-B-B-A mirrored by the compositional arrangement of the pilasters themselves. While the roots of some of these details are classical, their syntax is wholly inventive and characteristic of the hybridity that permeates the entire project.

ARCHITECTURAL DEVELOPMENTS in the Czech lands also began to generate a combination of design variants that resonated with the languages of history and of myth, but resulted in hybridity. Emerging from 1914 to the early 1920s, designs stylistically labeled "Rondo-cubism" uniquely transformed history into a program of mythic association that seized the public's imagination through a new synthesis of bold elements and colors. It took on a new organization of motifs, sometimes applied flat to surfaces and at other times laid three-dimensionally in dramatically deep reliefs.

The new style appeared in the wake of political change. The outbreak of World War I in the summer of 1914 impeded the development of Czech cubism as the new political conditions suppressed the variety of political expressions in Bohemia and revitalized the rise of Czech nationalism, whose proponents began to value traditional qualities of folk art over the originality represented by Czech cubism.[93] The Cubist Group of Visual Artists terminated its activities, and its members sought alternative directions as the tradition-oriented public reacted negatively to their innovations. Pavel Janák and Josef Gočár began to alter their work: from 1914 to 1916, Janák added rectangular shapes in thick layers onto his façades, and both he and Gočár introduced rounded forms of circles and sectioned rings.[94] They also turned to ornament as the means that would help them reconnect with the public and express the new call for national identity with traditional folkloric associations. Not only was a new language of form in order, but, according to Janák, so was an exuberant use of "strong full-blooded colors."[95] "Color to the façades!" Janák intoned at the time, as bold reds and yellows became appropriate expressions of the Czech national temperament and colors in harmony with the baroque and neoclassical Prague.[96] He articulated a program for the third battle of the new direction in architectural design in an essay published in *Volné Směry* in 1918: the first battle had been against historic styles, the second for a fresh vocabulary expressed in the language of folds and that allowed a triumph over matter, and now the third, to provide a Czech national architecture.[97]

When the Czech Republic emerged independent in October 1918, the new style, later called Rondo-cubism, took over the efforts to counter the reactions to cubism. Its name came from its combining round shapes with rectilinear "cubic" ones. The motifs of circles, strips, and rectangles recalled the motifs of leather strap work developed during the Renaissance that became an emblematic form of ornament applied to surfaces. By associating Rondo-cubism with this strapwork, its proponents were connecting the new Czechoslovakia with the days of glory and independence of its earlier Renaissance. While the language of history had also reemerged after the war in the form of a neoclassicism, it coexisted for a while with the new style.[98] In the early 1920s, leading art historians saw Rondo-cubism not merely as the accumulation of ornament, but also as a transformative mode "which subjects the mass of the building to imagination and turns the façade, as well as the space itself into a plastic body." The color schemes of the façades added to "the plasticity of the surface and its individual elements."[99]

FIGURE 5.40 (*Facing*) Josef Gočár, Czechoslovak Legiobank, exterior, Prague, 1922–23.

Jan Kotěra, the founder of Czech modernism, did not adapt well to the changes, as he experienced a series of crises after the end of the war. Not only did the new government deny him deserved commissions, but the new stylistic expressions countered his earlier language of rationalism.[100] Upon Kotěra's untimely death in 1923, Josef Gočár succeeded him as professor at the Academy of Fine Arts. Dividing his time between Prague and Hradec Králové, Gočár had already begun experimenting in 1920–21 with the new multicolored ornamental style, which led to his winning a design competition in 1921 for the Czechoslovak Legiobank on Na Poříčí Street; the building was constructed in 1922–23 (fig. 5.40).[101]

The bank's name, which was originally spelled out in capital letters on its façade below the mezzanine, commemorated the Czechoslovak voluntary legions organized in France, Italy, and Russia by Tomáš G. Masaryk during World War I. This memorial function of the building is a leitmotif on the façade. Gočár set the building back from the street front, creating a small plaza in the foreground. Built in contrasting colors of red and white stone, the façade has a classical subdivision of base, middle, and cornice. Though Gočár originally planned to have a tripartite triumphal arch, the base was built with four partly sunken columns. The columns hold sculptural reliefs by Jan Šturza that depict scenes of Czech soldiers and citizens struggling during the war and confronting its horrors. Above this relief runs a frieze by Otto Gutfreund which shows the interaction of legionaries with Czech citizens.

The façade of four stories above the frieze reinterprets and transforms the classical elements of columns and arches. Gočár replaced columns with semicircular drums. Recessed bay windows topped by semicircular arches alternate with the drums; at the level of these arches, the "capitals" of columns are transformed into cubes with rings on their fronts. Lacking entasis (classical curving to produce optical refinement), the columns extend the vertical emphasis upwards. Windows on the top floor have no arches above them, but the deeply projecting cornice has massive protrusions on its bottom side, as if the columns and arches were rotated forward to a horizontal position. Above the cornice is an attic, where the windowed arch motif is repeated, but at a smaller scale; pairs of stone cushions acting as drums replace the columns.

The interior of the banking hall shows similar transformations of motifs. It does bear some similarity to Wagner's Postal Savings Bank—both are top-lit and have banking operations on either side—but their surface treatments are entirely different (fig. 5.41). Gočár used strap-work patterning in variations on the floor, walls, and columns while sculpting the ceiling as a series of intersecting circles and partial circles. The whole is an integral composition of circles and rectangles, translated into round solids and cubes that comprise the fundamental elements of the style.

Simply equating the Legiobank building with a Renaissance revival is far too reductive. The building is, in fact, a transformation of the elements and morphology of classical language whose precedent might be found in the mannerism of Michelangelo and Giulio Romano. While Rostislav Švácha describes the façade largely in terms

FIGURE 5.41
Josef Gočar, Czechoslovak Legiobank, banking hall, Prague, 1922–23.

of platonic forms, it is an effective demonstration of the transformation of motifs.[102] Furthermore, the building design reengaged myth, associating the expression of national identity with the pinnacle of autonomy in an era that saw an efflorescence of Renaissance forms in Prague and Bohemia.

A parallel to Gočár's hybrid Rondo-cubism is seen in the work of Pavel Janák. Janák first designed a family villa in the Rondo-cubist style in 1920–21 and then a façade for the Juliš Patisserie in the Wenceslas Square in Prague. Even at this modest scale, these designs illustrated the use of abstracted strap work of Renaissance origins to associate the newly independent nation with its glorious past. In 1921, Janák became professor at the School of Applied Arts in Prague, and in collaboration with Josef Zasche, he began designing a major example of Rondo-cubism, a building for the Italian insurance company Riunione Adriatica di Sicurtà (fig. 5.42). Janák designed the façade, while Zasche was responsible for the building's plan.

Also called the Adrie, the building was constructed between 1922 and 1924. Housed in one of the many branches of a company that existed throughout the Austro-Hungarian Empire, the Riunione Adriatica di Sicurtà began in Trieste in 1826 as the Adriatico Banco.[103] By the beginning of the twentieth century, it conducted various activities in the insurance industry, with agencies in various European capitals and Italian cities. Though its new headquarters, a palazzo in Trieste by Ruggero and Arduino Berlam (1909–14), was described as "renewing the luminous nobility of Cinquecento Italy,"[104] the company allowed a wide range of architectural expressions: the Budapest branch, which Tőry and Pogány designed in 1913, included luxurious rental apartments and penthouses and used white stone panels to create a sheer façade, in total contrast with the Prague office.[105]

For its Prague headquarters, the insurance company combined commercial functions with a department store on a prominent corner site. The main entry was along the long façade on Jungmannova Street, and the retail section with two floors extended around the corner on the short side of the building facing Narodní Street. The challenging building program required that the upper stories containing apartments on

FIGURE 5.42
Pavel Janák, Riunione Adriatica di Sicurtà, exterior, Prague, 1922–24.

FIGURE 5.43
Pavel Janák, Riunione Adriatica di Sicurtà, exterior, Prague, 1922–24.

the side street be pulled back to allow an elevated terrace with café. The program also produced a massive volume that was lightened by six projecting pavilions with pitched roofs between them.[106]

The pitched roof on the short side of the building, which stills stands, contains a sculptural grouping of figures cast in bronze; at its center is a nude female, an allegory of the virtues of commerce and industry (fig. 5.43). For the façade, the architects rhythmically alternated triangular and arched pedimented windows.[107] All the details are transpositions of classical elements, referring to the architecture of Renaissance palazzi, but Gočár transformed them from curvilinear moldings to chopped rectangular sections. Not only were these pediments and arches an abstraction of classical forms, but the architects inverted their syntax by flipping the motifs along the first floor of apartments so that the pediment forms appear both at the top and at the bottom of the windows. While the details are generally abstracted, they still incorporate floral motifs associated with folk traditions. This free combination of elements and traditions confirms the building's hybridity, but so does its status as a modern, functional enterprise, effectively demonstrating mixed use of commercial and residential spaces.

Rondo-cubism, however, repulsed the young generation of an emerging avant-garde: it used ornament when ornament began to be castigated, and it emphasized surface and message over spatial innovations. The Adrie building in particular and Rondo-cubism in general also provided the avant-garde with competition for public acceptance and approval. Jaromír Krejcar claimed that Janák's works were submerged in "historicism, idle nationalist traditionalism, and eclecticism."[108] One critic described the bank in *Stavba*, the functionalist avant-garde journal, as the example of "the chaos of the time," and Karel Teige claimed disingenuously that the building had "no programmatic nationalism." He saw it as "clumsy, overcrowded . . . with a heaviness of its color-scheme and form."[109] Teige also denigrated Rondo-cubist interiors as "peasant cupboards and Baroque chests."[110]

The negative reactions to Rondo-cubism continue in the writings of today's modernist critics and historians. Ákos Moravánszky calls it a "bizarre architecture . . . a strange marriage of expressionism and attempts to create Slav style; the result lacked the dynamism of cubism and appeared more archaic than future oriented."[111] The language's unconventional fit does create discomfort, but that is often the nature of hybridity, and discomfort is no reason to exclude it from the history of modernism. Švácha dismisses Rondo-cubism's designs for never developing "[their] own type of architectural space."[112] But this criticism could equally be leveled at earlier Czech cubist developments. Furthermore, is it possible for architects to create a new concept of architectural space each time a style emerges? A new fashion in clothes does not remake the human body. From a historical perspective, only a few fundamental shifts in the concept of architectural space have occurred within the Western tradition.

Rondo-cubism was indeed short-lived, although its precise disappearance has not been charted.[113] Švácha claims that its enthusiasm depended on patriotic fervor, and when the fervor faded, so did the style. Not immune to criticism and the changing times in the 1920s, Janák himself moved from the historical references of Rondo-cubism toward a simplified functionalism expressed in a series of family villas, and also in a monumental direction, as seen in his administrative building of the Škoda works (1924–26). With the demise of Rondo-cubism, the language of hybridity that enriched it, along with its mythic overtones, disappeared from Czech modern architecture.

FIGURE C.1

Central Europe, 1918–23.

Conclusion: Continuities, Discontinuities, and Transformations

THE SPLIT within the Czech architectural movement in 1925 between Rondocubism and functionalism occurred in a world that had vastly changed over the previous decade. Not only had the Habsburgs abdicated and the Austro-Hungarian Empire dissolved, but the languages of architecture had changed. However, instead of a clear condition defining prewar and postwar differences, the course these languages ran was jagged and complicated, paralleling the history of the new nation-states that arose from the disintegration of the empire. Instead of linear developments, they too have ragged edges and shifting boundaries and are characterized by continuities and ruptures, dead ends and transformations—all factors that prevent its architecture from falling within the simplified categories of conventional historiography.

That jagged quality also contributed to the omission of many developments of Central European modern architecture from the early histories of the modern movement, which depended on conformity and categorization. After 1922, as different avant-garde movements of Dutch De Stijl, Le Corbusier's purism, Soviet constructivism, *Neues Bauen* (the "New Building," which stressed technology), and *Neue Sachlichkeit* (the "New Objectivity," which reacted against expressionist emotion) began to interact, a reductive functionalism emerged, giving rise to what would ten years later be called the International Style. As functionalism took hold, the definition of modern architecture shrank instead of expanded, and the uneven developments of the former empire found little place within it, except as demonstrations of the new functionalism. The marginalization of the region could be seen clearly in Gustav Adolf Platz's *Die Baukunst der Neuesten Zeit* (The Architecture of Most Recent Times), a synoptic study that appeared in 1927.[1] What on the surface appears to be an ecumenical and up-to-date sampling of the history of modern architecture as it had evolved over the previous forty years was in fact largely an account of German architecture: of the 150 architects with biographies in the text, only fourteen had been born in the lands of the former empire. The short list included Josef Hoffmann, Joseph Maria Olbrich, and Otto Wagner (the latter two had died in 1908 and 1918 respectively), but none of the young Czech modernists or Hungarian innovators.

The political restructuring over the last decade had been epochal and tragic, and reverberated throughout the rest of the twentieth century. Though the facts are well known, they still help clarify the context for architectural developments.[2] On June 28, 1914, Archduke Franz Ferdinand, heir to the Austro-Hungarian throne, and his wife were assassinated in Sarajevo, Bosnia, and the First World War began one month later. When Austria-Hungary declared war on Serbia, other European nations entered into the cataclysm. The conclusion of World War I marked the dissolution of the empire, and the need to redraw the boundaries of Central Europe (fig. C.1).

When the victorious Allies drew the new borders at the Paris Peace Conference in 1919, their guiding principle was to make new divisions according to the commonalities of language. The boundaries would collect into enclaves people who spoke the same language and exclude others who did not. Yet much of the entire region of Austria-Hungary was multilingual and ethnically mixed. Even in relatively homogenous regions there had often been pockets of speakers of other languages, such as Germans in the Sudeten region of Bohemia, or those residing in Hungary.[3] Formerly, diversity in the empire had contributed as much to its cultural richness as to political tension, but in its aftermath the cultural richness diminished in many domains while the tensions shifted from opposition against the hegemony of a single nation to internal conflicts. Ultimately, pressures came from several larger nations on the boundaries of the new countries: Germany, Russia, and Italy.

Austria experienced collective psychological trauma and a drastic physical reduction of its landmass. Its multinational population was reduced both in numbers and in the very diversity that had made it at once vibrant, brilliant, and fractious. In January 1919, during the final days of the Habsburg monarchy, the Austro-German members of the Imperial Parliament had created the Republic of German-Austria (Republik Deutsch-Österreich), outlining a new independent state. It was to include regions inhabited by the German speakers of the western part of the former empire, including the western edge of Bohemia, as well as the area to the east, called for the first time Burgenland, despite its being an ethnically mixed territory of Hungary. The founders of this short-lived state declared outright that their intention was to unite with Germany. The treaty of St. Germaine on September 10, 1919, however, recognized Czechoslovakia's claims to the former Austro-Habsburg provinces of Bohemia, Moravia, and Silesia while rejecting the demand for German-Austria to unite with Germany. Instead, the treaty recognized the existence of an independent Republic of Austria, Republik Österreich. Austria also became ethnically homogenous, with 97 percent of its inhabitants recorded as German speakers by 1934.[4] Not until March 1938 at the initiative of Adolf Hitler and the support of the local Nazis did Austria become the first territorial acquisition of greater Germany. It ceased to exist as an independent country following the merger—*Anschluss*—with Germany.

Vast reductions also struck Hungary in every sphere of social, political, and economic life. In November 1918, when the war ended, Hungary became a republic under the leadership of Count Mihály Károly, but it was short-lived, and a Soviet Hungarian regime followed on March 1919. It too collapsed in the summer of 1919, and the Hungarian Kingdom was restored under Miklos Horthy, a former Austro-Hungarian naval commander. He served as a regent in the absence of a ruling monarch. By 1920, when the accords of the Treaty of Trianon were final, Hungary had lost two-thirds of its former territories, with substantial portions going to the new Czechoslovakia; to Romania, which absorbed Transylvania and the Banat region below it; and to the new Kingdom of Serbs, Croats, and Slovenes, which absorbed Croatia, Slavonia, and Vojvodina. Hungary even lost a portion of the Burgenland to a much reduced Austria. Although

Hungary's boundaries would be redrawn many times during the twentieth century, it eventually moved toward an ethnolinguistic homogeneity, with the percentage of Magyars becoming nearly total.[5]

Czechoslovakia became independent on October 28, 1918. At the Paris Peace Conference of the following year, it pressed not only for the former Austrian provinces of Bohemia, Moravia, and Silesia, but for other areas to the west, south, and east: the former Hungarian territory of Slovakia as far south as the Danube, and a portion of the small Sub-Carpathian Rus' to the west. Treaties in 1919 and 1920 confirmed claims to historic Czech boundaries and to Slovakia and the Rus' lands, but not other areas along the fringes. Although the initial intention of the Paris Peace Conference had been to divide territories along ethnolinguistic lines, in the formation of the new Czechoslovakia, large Magyar minorities remained in both Slovakia and the Sub-Carpathian Rus'. Czechoslovakia's territorial limits remained unchanged until the Munich pact of September 29, 1938, when Hitler's Germany began revising all of its eastern neighbors' boundaries.[6]

At the close of the war, Austria lost all of Galicia to the resurrected Poland. Declared independent in November 1918, the country's boundaries became fixed between 1920 and 1923. Previously divided between Austria, Germany, and Russia, it collected the Polish-speaking population into a mononational state, though it still contained many German speakers.

The area that would become Yugoslavia along the southern tier of the Austro-Hungarian Empire comprised the most complex linguistic and ethnic assemblage in all Central Europe.[7] Not only would it include five south Slavic peoples, but other Balkan minorities would be encompassed as well. The territory had been ruled by four different countries before 1918, with four different currencies, railway networks, and banking systems. In the final months of World War I, the idea of creating Yugoslavia as a Slavic unity arose from three sources: a Yugoslav Committee formed in November 1914 by Croat, Serb, and Slovene exiles in the Habsburg Empire; a National Council created in Zagreb in October 1918, which declared independence for all south Slavic lands in Austria-Hungary; and the government of Serbia, which had regained control of its own territory in November 1918, at the onset of the war. On December 1, 1918, the Kingdom of Serbs, Croats, and Slovenes was proclaimed, uniting south Slavs. Besides the three officially recognized nationalities, it incorporated a complex diversity of ethnic and religious groups, which included Montenegrins, Macedonians, and Bosnians. The claimed boundaries of this new state were countered by other countries, particularly Italy, which acquired by treaty in 1920 Austria's former coastal provinces Gorizia-Gradiska, Trieste, and Istria, along with some eastern Adriatic islands and the city of Zadar. By 1921, the Kingdom of Serbs, Croats, and Slovenes had its international boundaries set, and they remained so for the next twenty years. It absorbed parts of the Hungarian Kingdom, including all of Croatia and Slavonia, as well as the western half of the Banat region, despite the protests of Romania. Belgrade became the capital. In 1929, the kingdom was renamed Yugoslavia, the "country of southern Slavs." Meanwhile, new administrative districts, all subordinated to the central government in Belgrade, were created completely independent of historical boundaries.

∷ WITH THIS sociopolitical context in mind, we can turn to the fate of the languages of architecture. Superficially, the language of history appeared to have been extinguished. As the modern movement evolved from the late 1910s into the early postwar period, the use of historical references, particularly among the avant-garde of Germany, France, and Russia, became not merely irrelevant but the object of repudiation. Responding to the horrors of world war and revolution, history's opponents saw it as the embodiment of political and social structures from the past that had only brought calamity to the present. In the midst of fervor that modernism would create a new, autochthonous world, blazing with ingenuity and nurturing liberty, the icons and procedures of historical practice appeared moribund. Naturalism and figural representation in painting and sculpture, patterns of ornaments, references to myth, and precedents from the old styles of Renaissance and Gothic began to disappear quickly. The severe economic crises and pressing social problems after the war demanded new solutions involving technology and new building types, which the language of history could not provide. As we have already seen, the historical associations attached to Rondo-cubism were a major source of critical reactions against it.[8]

While this trend against historical association dominated the evolving modernism of western Europe, the language of history did not totally disappear in the successor states of the former empire. It lay in the subconscious of the culture, erupting sporadically from the early 1920s into the years of World War II with differing significations. Though denied, history was a presence that architects could not fully escape. As scholars are finally exploring the history of interwar Austria, we now see reinterpretations of how the legacy of the Baroque affected designers like Josef Hoffmann, who continued to design in a classicizing mode, though not always with the brilliance of his earlier hybrid works.[9]

The language of history as filtered through classicism also emerged at times to legitimize new political authority. Eventually, classical forms became a representational vehicle of authoritarian and totalitarian regimes, from the Nazis in Germany and Fascists in Italy to Stalinist Russia and elsewhere. Moreover, whereas classical forms were appropriate for grand and monumental architecture of reactionary regimes, the vernacular idiom of the Heimatstil became the vehicle for a new, virulent nationalism. With classicism and Heimatstil associated with totalitarianism and fascism, it is hardly surprising that the negative views of the language of history persisted for decades after World War II until the reactions against orthodox modernism surfaced in the late 1960s. But there is no simplistic route to follow in studying the language of history in the twentieth century. Not only did it form an inescapable cultural background for many architects of the former empire and the new nation-states, but the most ardent leaders of the modern movement had assimilated a historical consciousness in their work. Le Corbusier stands out particularly for understanding the logic of classicism and the value of order, rhythm, and proportion. Furthermore, recent scholarship has recast how we regard the architecture of fascism; no one denies the heinous activities of its proponents, but we have started to look at its architecture in terms of its transformations and its means of connecting ideology to form, that is, how it does or does not function as a language.[10]

The language of organicism moved in divergent directions before and after the First World War. On the one hand, early in the first decade of the twentieth century, architects and designers left the languid forms of biomorphic organicism behind, but the connotations of feeling and emotion associated with their forms reemerged, transformed in "expressionist" architecture as it began to appear in the late 1910s and early 1920s.[11] Though biomorphic organicism (calling on nature for its inspiration), like history, appeared dead to modernists, the interest in it never vanished. One such indication of interest is the appearance in 1917 of D'Arcy Thompson's *On Growth and Form*, which brought together the rationalism of mathematics, biomorphism, and historicism in his references to Greek antiquity.[12] Expressionist architecture continued its existence unseen on the surface of events, reemerging in such works as Rudolf Steiner's Goetheanum in Dornach near Basel, Switzerland, built 1924–28 after an earlier version had burned in 1923. On the other hand, the practitioners of a language of organism that followed the logic of structural rationalism contributed to what would become the central theme of modern architecture: rationality and function. Its appeal lay in the logic and efficiency of organic organization, but not in any metaphorical representation of its logic. From the new radical and particularly German perspective, "ornament," even as a product of a rational organic system, had no place; it became a code name for the entire defunct language of history.[13] The pitched roof met a similar fate: equated with tradition and the Heimatstil, it too became a sign of the antimodern, even where function would require it to shed rain or snow.

Thus, while many languages of architecture had previously coexisted in the late Austro-Hungarian Empire, the language of rationalism became in the aftermath the dominant mode of discourse and production, as it most coincided with functionalism—the path that the early modernist theorists, polemicists, and historians presented as the only viable guide for the future.

At the most basic level, functionalism created the illusion of a psychological break with the past and expressed hopes of a better future, often overlaid with the dream of more liberal, equitable, and democratic societies. Efficiency, industrialization, new technology, and social ideology were its means—not history, ornament, myth, or figural representation. Most of the new nation-states had their own version of functionalism, continuing the many modernisms that had preceded the war but with different inflections. For instance, the language of rationalism had its proponents in Hungary, which was not immune to the inroads of the International Style.[14] But even though historians often appraise Bela Lajta's later work as functionalist, it remained very much a language of hybridity. While some young Hungarians attended or were associated with the Bauhaus, notably Laszlo Moholy Nagy, Farkas Molnár, Fred Forbát, and Lajos Kassák, the Bauhaus and its aesthetics had a problematic reception. Radical modernists accepted concepts of the Bauhaus, more moderate modernists toned down its aesthetics, and the conservative architects, still adhering to languages of history and myth, vehemently rejected it.[15] Molnár, one of the few non-Jews among the radicals, remained adamant and was able to build some projects, but the functionalist aesthetics of the Bauhaus did not dominate.[16] The new Czechoslovak Republic, however, produced some of the most outstanding examples of functionalist architecture found anywhere in Europe in the 1920s, along with vigorous theoretical and critical debates. Many of its innovators had passed through cubist and Rondo-cubist phases to pursue the functionalist idiom.[17] Among the architectural developments occurring in the aftermath of the empire, Czech functionalism, particularly with its focus in Prague, has received much attention in recent studies, especially after the proclamation of independence of the Czech Republic in 1993.[18] In the Moravian town of Brno, the founding of a school of architecture at the new Polytechnic after the war assisted in the development of a functionalist architecture in and around the city, providing a context for a rich, if too brief, outpouring by architects such as Bohuslav Fuchs, Josef Kalous, Jaroslav Valenta, and Arnošt Wiesner, among others.[19]

Developments of functionalism elsewhere are less well known outside their own regions, yet they demonstrate the complex issues of the transformation of the language of rationalism.[20] Bratislava, lying by the Danube downstream from Vienna in Slovakian territory, had its own vibrant functionalism.[21] One of the leaders of functionalism in the Slovak region was Emil Belluš (1899–1979).[22] He represented a generation of architects who were still students during the war and upon its termination entered a new world enthused about architecture and involved in political movements. Belluš began studying architecture at the Technical University in Budapest in 1918 and became a founding member of the Hungarian Socialist Party during the time of revolutionary fervor. With the change of borders, however, he left to continue his studies in Prague.[23] After graduating in 1923, Belluš returned to Slovakia to begin his career despite the region's adverse economic conditions. Ideas of modern functionalist architecture permeated the area from its centers in Germany, France, and the Netherlands, and Belluš's work soon reflected functionalist interests in ameliorating social conditions and exploring minimum dimensions for habitation. Living in Bratislava, he immersed himself in Slovak cultural life, becoming a founding member of the Association of Slovak Artists, which later became the Association of Slovak Architects, and a sensitive promoter of Slovak identity.[24] He also soon became a founding member of the Slovak Rowing Club in Bratislava; not merely a sports club, it was an important meeting place for Slovak intelligentsia. Belluš designed the group's clubhouse (1929–30) with the planar architecture of functionalism that took the lead in modernist progressive efforts throughout the international movement.[25] Stripped surfaces and asymmetrical massing of his design show a complete command of functionalist principles as they evolved over the previous five years. The Slovak Rowing Club was also a direct retort to the German Rowing Club (1930–31), located a short distance from it along the river and constructed in a traditional classicizing style.

FIGURE C.2
Emil Belluš, Spa Bridge, exterior, Piešťany, Slovakia, 1930–33.

Belluš deviated, however, from the increasingly spare international functionalism, as can be seen in other designs, but particularly in his colonnade bridge in Piešťany, designed 1930–31 and built 1931–32 (fig. C.2).[26] The bridge serves as a promenade—formerly for patients of the Piešťany Spa, which treated rheumatism and motor diseases and connected the town to an island in the Váh River, source of healing mud for the spa. One hundred and forty-one meters long and twelve to fifteen meters wide, the bridge stands on six piers. With its highly efficient reinforced-concrete structure, construction only took eleven months. When completed, the bridge was brightly colored, with all metal parts painted blue, and provided views of the river and outlying area. Originally built for cars and pedestrians (now pedestrians only), it also included small shops, one of which sold fresh water. The colonnade protected strollers from the weather; patients could walk or sit in the sun and air as part of their therapy. There were also several touches that added human scale, including wooden chairs with tubular steel frames for resting spots. Belluš also included etched-glass panes with Slovak nationalist motifs by native artist Martin Benka. At one side of the bridge, a figure, *Bartolámač* by the sculptor Kühmayer, stands atop a set of steps and holds a broken crutch, symbolizing the renewal of health promised by the spa (fig. C.3). Above the entry to the promenade at the town side are the welcoming Latin words *Saluberimi Pisteniensis termi* (The healthy baths of Piešťany); at the other end, *Surge et ambula* (Stand up and walk), a biblical quotation that adds to its hybridity. Glass and metal-framed windows provide necessary protection from the weather, while railings made from tubular steel—functionalist icons—visually extend the length of the bridge along the river. At intervals Belluš located low walls edged with brick moldings, and soaring tubular steel flagpoles, another unavoidable modernist element. The ultimate

FIGURE C.3
Emil Belluš, Spa Bridge, detail, Piešťany, Slovakia, 1930–33.

result was a bridge functional, logical, and rational in its use of building materials and construction, sincere in its dedication to a social program, and aesthetically light and ethereal. Belluš's later work continued to combine the rational with the humanistic and to show, increasingly, an underlying classicism in its use of proportions and massive piers in an undeniable language of history.

In Austria, the language of rationalism as filtered through functionalism appeared amidst a shattered cultural and political life and continuing crises of identity. The notion of architecture as *Baukunst*—the art of building—which held such promise at the beginning of the century, lost its power as functionalism became more important. Architects pursued diverse directions, but no sense of coherent vision directed them, as the *Zeitgeist* seemed elusive. Some young practitioners experimented with a version of cubism, others with expressionism, and both could be tracked in the schools of architecture and design in Vienna. Architects also attempted to align themselves with the new international dialect of the language of rationalism. But in Austria, functionalism was a problematic model, especially for the mass housing produced in the period of Red Vienna, when the city separated from Lower Austria to embark on its own political course under Social Democratic government.[27] Instead of being the ideal model, it turned out to be unsuitable in saying anything adequately specific for ideological purposes. Consequently, authorities turned to former students of the Wagnerschule, who had skills in creating an architecture that "speaks." In some ways, the situation paralleled the predicament of Soviet constructivism: the lack of ability to convey messages was, among other factors, a reason for its rejection and the promotion of historical languages, effective in asserting authority, power, and legitimacy.

The work of the firm Theiss & Jaksch conveys some of the variegated routes of the period before and after the war. Siegfried Theiss (1882–1963), born in Bratislava, and Hans Jaksch (1879–1970), born in Hennersdorf, northern Bohemia (now Dubnice, Czech Republic), crossed the gap that divided the last years of the empire from the new world, embracing the enforced hybridity of that journey.[28] They both studied with Karl Köning at the Polytechnic and with Friedrich Ohmann at the Academy of Fine Arts in Vienna, and in 1907 they started a partnership. Their prolific practice, which continued until 1961, began with numerous commissions, including those for Evangelical churches, which became their specialty. Theiss, a Protestant, was quite interested in church architecture, promulgating principles for the construction of churches that focused on the artistic treatment of interiors and an emphasis on color to create atmosphere. The firm of Theiss & Jaksch started turning theory into practice in 1910, when it won a competition to build a church in Traiskirchen in Lower Austria.[29] The result, finished in 1913, was unique for that country: simple in form, the church had an octagonal plan, wooden gallery with traditional folk carvings, pyramidal wooden ceiling, and an immense, blocky tower.[30]

After World War I, Theiss & Jaksch designed a planned workers' settlement (1921–23) in the Alpine Knappenburg bei Hüttenberg; it resembled the vernacular Wekerle housing estate in Budapest, but used a single-family type to promote the idea of democratic uniformity.[31] Built at a height of one thousand meters above sea level, it comprised 108 homes for miners, a store, a school, and a bathhouse, integrating landscape into a complete vision of the village. The entire concept is hybrid in its merging of a social ideology into a visual language that took into account the native building traditions of farmhouses. The firm also designed public housing for the municipality of Vienna, including a complex on Penzingerstrassse and Phillipsgasse (1924–25) in the Fourteenth District, where Theiss and Jaksch overlaid a flat network of overlapping circles onto one of the main façades. With its notched corner quoins, which recall battlements, and a sculpture of a worker, the building relied on the tradition of ornament and representation, but also used modern iconic elements such as ribbon windows along the entire top floor. The spare aesthetic of flat surfaces, metal railings, and large glazed openings increasingly appeared in Theiss and Jaksch's projects of the period, as seen in a series of single-family houses built from 1929 to 1931.

The culmination of Theiss and Jaksch's turn to modernism and the building that best represented the hybridity of their combining aesthetics, function, and sensitivity to site was the Hochhaus on Herrengasse, the first skyscraper in Vienna (fig. C.4).[32] The irregular site was at the confluence of three streets on land that had belonged to the Liechtenstein princes since 1497, with the longest part of the lot along the Herrengasse—the "Street of Lords"—which had a hallowed history. The site had been the location of the Liechtenstein Riding School, which was converted in 1872 to a concert hall for Ludwig Bösendorfer and a venue for world premieres of works by Anton Bruckner, Bruno Walter, and Arnold Schönberg. Though world famous for its acoustics, the hall was demolished in 1913.

FIGURE C.4
Siegfried Theiss and Hans Jaksch, Hochhaus Herrengasse, exterior, Vienna, 1932.

Locating a building for public housing and commercial use in the domain of former nobility had both political and aesthetic implications. Rudolf Frass had won the competition for the project in 1929 under the purview of the Social Democrats, but the new Christian Socialist Party, which took power in the following year, preferred the design by Theiss & Jaksch for its potential to refute the housing schemes of the defeated political rivals. Providing 60 percent of the construction costs, the federal government saw the project as politically significant. Instead of bare-bones accommodations, the sixteen-story building on a prestigious site contained 225 luxurious apartments, 105 of which were for single people and consisted of one or two spacious rooms. Residents could order food to be delivered, or they could eat at the rooftop restaurant. The construction of such a tall building, particularly on such a historic site, also generated much public debate about the use of skyscrapers, with architects writing in both daily newspapers and the professional journals.[33]

Theiss & Jaksch's design, which was first presented in a handsome model, divided the six-sided polygonal site into a perimeter building and two large interior courtyards, one of which was dumbbell shaped and the other almost square (fig. C.5). The eight-story mass along Herrengasse continued the cornice heights and used windows with proportions similar to those of the existing building. At the corner, the Hochhaus stepped back to relieve the long façade and let the central mass rise up two stories and then step backwards in a series of receding floors that diminished in area until they reached the top floor and glass-enclosed restaurant. The height of the building allowed extraordinary views: from semicircular glass-and-steel stairwells in the interior courts, through a framework of thin steel mullions, residents at the upper levels could see panoramas of the historic city, especially the venerable St. Stephen's Cathedral. Views from the café terrace were especially sumptuous. Eating outside, one had a panorama of the city with the venerable Peterskirche in the foreground and St. Stephen's Cathedral beyond (fig. C.6).

The message of the Hochhaus was that living in modern housing, subsidized by a willing regime, could provide all necessary bourgeois comforts in a new, spare, functional aesthetic that still harmonized with the historical fabric of the city by replicating its spatial volumes. Prominent citizens, doctors, and lawyers moved into this new building type called *Ledigenwohnungen* (singles' apartment building). It was not a freestanding object detached from its surroundings, like many examples of the emerging International Style, but a highly contextual integration into the urban fabric that linked the building to the city's historic core. At once functional, technically efficient, and responsive to contemporary needs, it still showed the ties to history and tradition that permeated the work of Viennese modernists. After the building was completed in 1932, Theiss and Jaksch lectured about it in Vienna, Budapest, and Bratislava. The aesthetics of their work, however, would soon change to more conservative idioms, as after 1938 they worked with the Nazis, who controlled Austria; Jaksch had long been a member of the National Socialist Party, while Theiss's sympathies, if any, for the Nazis are unclear.[34]

FIGURE C.5
Siegfried Theiss and Hans Jaksch, Hochhaus Herrengasse, model, Vienna, 1932.

FIGURE C.6
Siegfried Theiss and Hans Jaksch, Hochhaus Herrengasse, view from the stairwell, Vienna, 1932.

THE LANGUAGE of myth nearly ceased to be spoken after World War I. It found less and less relevance in the upsurge of interest in rationalism, the celebration of technology, and the challenging social conditions that required providing basic economic necessities, including shelter and minimal security. Priority shifted from forming national identity to an international one, at least in Czechoslovakia. In Austria, the imperial myths were bankrupt, and many people apparently preferred to blend into a larger German nation than consider themselves Austrians. Yet although myth combined with history as a prop to nationalism did not necessarily reinforce democracy, it could serve fascistic political ambitions. The Heimatstil in particular had its own mythic dimension as a vehicle of propaganda, claiming to embody the essence of the Fatherland.

There were also exceptions, as the language of myth persisted among some of its early proponents. Remnants of Lechner's architecture of national identity were still present in 1922 in the proposal that his nephew, Jenö Lechner (1878–1962), made for the international competition for a new *Chicago Tribune* building (fig. C.7).[35] With its pointed dome, lobed arches, and abstracted volutes, the entry of the younger Lechner seemed to say that the mythic language of Hungarian national identity had universal applicability, a rather implausible claim in the context of the business of American journalism.

The nationalist Hungarian István Medgyaszay retained an ardent devotion to his hybrid assemblages of myth and technological expertise. His designs for pavilions of military exhibitions held in L'viv in 1916 and in Budapest in 1918 further exemplified his use of Hungarian folk architecture as a national style. In the 1920s, he continued to advocate Turanism and, following the path launched earlier by Ödön Lechner, visited India as co-chair of the Hungarian-Indian Society. Not only did his subsequent work become further hybridized, with Indian motifs of scalloped arches forming a variation of his mythologizing efforts, but he retained his nationalist idiom of Hungarian details, even when it appeared to veer most toward functionalism, as seen in retention of ornament at the TÉBE apartment building in Budapest (1932–34).[36]

Most of those architects who had used the language of myth attempted to incorporate the planarity and flat surfaces of the new style into their own work. Dušan Jurkovič's mythic language of Slovak identity began to dissolve after the war; though steadfastly Slovak in heart, the architect pushed his work toward an international idiom. He kept the transformative character of his Galician cemeteries, turning regional motifs into abstract themes, in his design for the monumental sepulcher on top of Mount Bradlo (1927–28) for M. R. Štefánik, Slovak astronomer and military general who helped found the new Czechoslovak nation with Tomáš Masaryk and Edvard Beneš in 1918–19. But his design for the sanatorium of Dr. Koch in Bratislava (with Jindrich Merganc, 1928–30) took a functionalist approach, using flat walls, large punctured openings for light, and no mythic associations.[37]

Ivan Vurnik, who had sought to create a mythic language for Slovene identity, reached a dead end after the completion of his Cooperative Bank. By 1927, he began reexamining the approach of assembling various national motifs to create fashionable forms. He deduced that truer results would come from the study of tradition. Reconsidering his previous work, he left out the Cooperative Bank when he presented his own works in the journal *Dom in svet* (Home and World).[38] He subsequently never again managed to synthesize parts of a building into an organic unity and could not compete with his colleague Jože Plečnik.[39]

Plečnik was the only figure undeviating in his commitment to the language of myth as he continued to reconfigure the urban plan and landscape of Ljubljana.[40] Among the many examples of his use of myth, particularly as embodied in historical types, is his design for Žale Cemetery in Ljubljana, begun in 1936 and completed in 1940 (figs. c.8–c.11).[41] His interest in Ljubljana cemeteries began as early as 1927, when he sought to save an abandoned municipal cemetery attached to the Church of St. Christopher. In 1932, he proposed a cemetery next to St. Christopher's, which would be dominated by a monumental Slovene pantheon. In addition to his ongoing interest in cemeteries and churches, Plečnik designed numerous gravestones, including his own family grave, which he made in the form of a miniature antique cemetery featuring steles and an archaic urn rendered as a house with a lamp providing an eternal flame.[42]

Meanwhile, to accommodate the increase in Ljubljana's population, the municipality considered creating a central mortuary near the main cemetery in the 1920s. Nothing happened, but in 1936 Plečnik began proposing his own version of the mortuary. Its entry would be a dramatic columned portal, and its main theme would be that of a "sacred grove" or "sacred garden," a place where the living bade farewell to the dead. In addition, he wanted chapels to be dedicated to the patron saints of Ljubljana's parishes. In the 1930s, the scheme was considered far too idealistic and grand for realization. But when Stanko Sučnik, director of the Vzajemna Insurance Company, who had commissioned an office building from Plečnik, became chairman of the administrative committee of the municipal mortuary, he rescued the proposal. Despite being attacked as out of synch with contemporary developments, the project was ultimately begun in 1937. As construction proceeded, the design was altered, becoming more ethnic.[43]

Plečnik's proposed entry with flanking facilities became a grand portal recalling the archaic idea of the Propylea and was intended not to separate but to join the living with the dead (fig. c.8). The name of the cemetery also changed during the construction from Garden of All Saints to Žale, a traditional name for a place of mourning.

FIGURE C.7 (*Facing*) Jenö Lechner, *Chicago Tribune* tower, competition entry, perspective, Chicago, 1923. Reprinted from Jenö Lechner, *Jenö Lechner* (Geneva: Masters of Architecture, Ltd., 1930), 35.

CONTINUITIES, DISCONTINUITIES, AND TRANSFORMATIONS

FIGURE C.8
Jože Plečnik, Žale Cemetery (1936–40), main entrance, Ljubljana, Slovenia, 1938–39; with main chapel with catafalque at the center, 1939–40.

FIGURE C.9
(*Facing, top*) Jože Plečnik, Žale Cemetery (1936–40), Workshop, exterior, Ljubljana, Slovenia, 1939–40.

FIGURE C.10
(*Facing, bottom*) Jože Plečnik, Žale Cemetery (1936–40), Workshop, detail, Ljubljana, Slovenia, 1939–40.

The chapels were ultimately named after patron saints of some of the city's parishes, and also other beloved Slovenian saints; one was also named Adam and Eve, intended ironically for nonbelievers and people of other religions. Eventually, fourteen chapels were built, corresponding to the stations of the cross in a journey toward human salvation. Plečnik's panoply of antique references included Theodoric's mausoleum in Ravenna with its columbaria, Roman subterranean sepulchers with niches, urns in the shape of Egyptian ointment vessels, the Chapel of St. Maurus near Beuron from the 1860s, and the Tower of the Winds in Athens, as well as other Gothic, Byzantine, and Turkish references. In total, Plečnik created what Damjan Prelovšek has called "an encyclopedic treasury of architecture," recalling an acropolis with models of the history of architecture.[44] While remaining devoted to classic prototypes, the architect still relied exclusively on another version of the mythic origins of architecture: Semper's mid-nineteenth-century theories of cladding, particularly the transformation of textiles into building surfaces. As described by Prelovšek, the façade of the Workshop building represents this process, with klinker, pebble stone in geometric patterns, and gradations of color and a "wave-shape" surface giving the impression of a woven carpet (figs. C.9, C.10).[45] A final testament to Plečnik's belief in a language of myth is a tumulus based on the model of the Etruscan tomb (fig. C.11). It speaks of the grave of the ancestors of the Slovene people, a mound of earth covered in grass.

Plečnik's use of the language of myth reflected what he experienced privately as a conversation between himself and his vision of deity. After almost three years of construction, the Žale Cemetery was opened in summer of 1940 as war shook much

FIGURE C.11
Jože Plečnik, Žale Cemetery, (1936–40), "Etruscan tumulus," Ljubljana, Slovenia, 1939–40. Author photo.

of Europe. While Plečnik's language of myth relied on references to antiquity, it remained consistent with his own principles, but out of line with the world around him. Even his students felt bitter disappointment and criticized the work for lack of innovation in material or construction. The world and its architectural language had already dramatically changed into idioms that were far more abstract and spoke not of genius loci, but an architectural Esperanto, a single-form language purported to have international and universal validity.

∷   WHILE THE path of modernism in architecture became channeled into the narrow streams of functionalism and the International Style, the language of hybridity had a strange continuity in successor states to the Austro-Hungarian Empire unlike any developments elsewhere. The multiple viewpoints of the region's diverse population still reverberated among some architects in their efforts to join an evolving modernism with the past. In this sense, memory played a significant role, making precedent, history, and local context difficult to fully escape. The results were often divergent and at odds with the line emerging in western Europe.

One of the most striking manifestations of the continuation of hybridity was not in the work of a single architect, but in a building type: the crematorium. A subject of diverse interpretations, it spoke of a political position and a metaphor for the times that experienced the cataclysm of mass destruction. Consistent with the multiple layering of language we saw throughout the Dual Monarchy, the crematoria designed and built shortly after World War I synopsize a diversity of linguistic experiments.

Cremation was a controversial practice that had moved from the domain of religion to civic concern. For millennia, people had burned the bodies of their dead over open fires, but the practice of incinerating corpses in enclosed chambers began only in the nineteenth century as part of a century-long effort at social and religious reform. The reasons for an interest in cremation were different. For the reformers, long wakes over the dead prior to interments led to putrefaction of the corpse. For physicians and sanitary engineers, cemetery burial posed the risks of polluted burial grounds as corpses decomposed.[46] Cremation provided a sanitary, economical, and space-saving means of disposing of corpses as the supply of cemetery space became acutely short in cities. In the 1860s, the emerging advocates of cremation in Europe and the United States saw it as an efficient, modern, and rational development. It was in tune with the technical transformation and progress of modern life itself. Furthermore, because cremation was based in science and technology, it had, according to its proponents, its own beauty and the egalitarian power to unite humanity. Consequently, as Matthew Witkovsky has astutely observed, "as a building type, the crematorium is the very definition of a 'truly modern monument'—a functional structure of commemoration born in and to the modern age."[47]

The international momentum for cremation increased after 1874, when Queen Victoria's surgeon, Sir Henry Thompson, published *Cremation: The Treatment of the Body after Death*. The first modern cremation chamber was built in Italy in the 1870s, starting a trend in Europe and North America, and the British courts ruled cremation legal in 1884. But a position for or against the use and construction of crematoria not only was an ethical statement, but also had religious consequences. The Roman Catholic Church officially banned cremation in 1886 and threatened to excommunicate any church members who arranged cremations. The motivation for the ban was the conviction that bodies of the dead must be intact for the resurrection that would take place at the return of Christ. Orthodox Jews also adamantly forbade cremation, but Protestant churches tended to be more supportive of it.

The crematorium constituted a new, modern building type, and despite strictures from the Catholic Church, it had begun to emerge while the empire was still intact, if not in the built form, then as the idealized project of architects. The somewhat morose subject paralleled the frequent studies, particularly in the Wagnerschule, of funerary chapels.[48] Móric Pogány designed in 1904 an idealized project of a crematorium in a vocabulary of Hungarian nationalism (fig. C.12). His perspectival drawings showed a massive dome flanked by fantastic buttresses, and his model featured a front entry with double towers.[49] The entry resembled a dark, gaping mouth

consisting of compressed and lobed arches of Hungarian nationalist architecture, which, combined with other details, resembled a grim face. Paralleling Medgyaszay's project for the national pantheon, Pogány's crematorium would be encircled by a vast arcade in which the ashes of incinerated bodies would be placed. Lajos Kozma's design for a crematorium, published in *Der Architect* in 1909, took an antithetical approach, showing its adherence to the language of rationalism and the simple geometric forms of the Wagnerschule (fig. C.13).

After the war, the ensuing proliferation of crematorium designs was not so much an effort to dispose of a backlog of dead bodies, but rather a demonstration of mass opposition to the power of the church. The crematorium took on a symbolic role of resistance to a traditional institution that was aligned with imperial power and acted covertly as an agent of political suppression. In the Czech lands, a movement had begun earlier in 1899, and because cremation had been proscribed by the Catholic Church, it was seen conversely as an expression of the Hussite legacy of clerical reforms and an anti-imperialist gesture.[50] After the war, the engineer František Mencl, the founding president of the Crematorium Society and a devout Protestant, surveyed the existing crematoria across Europe to popularize them at home. He saw crematoria as "machines of commemoration."[51] The editors of the functionalist journal *Stavba* followed with interest the crematorium competitions held in various Czech cities.[52] In all, thirteen crematoria were eventually constructed in Czechoslovakia before the Second World War, with one-third of them showing the influence of functionalism. These new buildings mod-

FIGURE C.12
Móric Pogány, crematorium (project), model, 1904. Reprinted from *Magyar Építőművészet*, nos. 7–8 (1912).

FIGURE C.13
Lajos Kozma, crematorium (project), perspective, ca. 1909. Reprinted from *Der Architekt*, no. 15 (1909), plate 66.

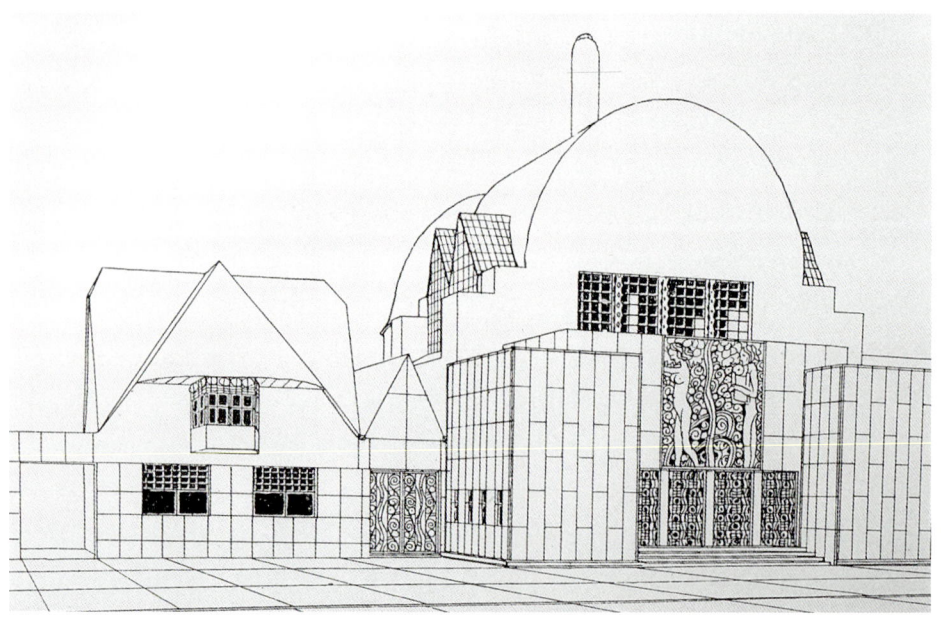

FIGURE C.14
Pavel Janák, crematorium, front façade, Pardubice, Bohemia, 1921–23.

ernized the practice of cremation, commemorated the arrival of modernism, and became, in some instances, paragons of hybridity.

In 1920, the City of Pardubice announced a design competition for a crematorium. Located east of Prague at the confluence of the Labe and Chrudimka rivers, the town took shape as a thirteenth-century trading center and had a historical legacy from prehistory to Gothic and Renaissance influences. By the beginning of the twentieth century, it had become an industrial center at the junction of railway and road, and after the war participated in the push for crematoria.[53] One competition entry came from Jiři Kroha (1893–1974), a member of the avant-garde Association of Artists in Prague. Kroha used the idiom of Czech cubism for his submission, producing one of the rare syntheses between the crystalline structure of the building's exterior massing and its interior conception. Angular forms that outlined voids in the building's mass became themes of the treatment of the interior.[54] However, Pavel Janák won the competition, and his design in the mode of Rondo-cubism was built between 1922 and 1923 (fig. C.14).

Janák's crematorium in Pardubice speaks directly through the colors and motifs of national identity. Red and white, its motifs refer to Renaissance rustication, arches, and details that are transformed, flattened, and abstracted. A visitor ascends a wide monumental stair flanked at the beginning by two female figures, each holding aloft

CONTINUITIES, DISCONTINUITIES, AND TRANSFORMATIONS

FIGURE C.15
Pavel Janák, crematorium, interior, Pardubice, Bohemia, 1921–23.

a cup. In the center of the open gable is a rose window allowing light into the interior. On the interior, Janák collated tradition, invention, and national iconography into a Gesamtkunstwerk (fig. C.15). The circular motif of the rose window is carried into the interior through the use of a barrel vault under the pitched roof. The vault's beams are covered in patterns and extend the full length of the space. Between the beams are sunbursts. The circle motif continues in the arches forming a niche that provides a space for services and houses an organ immediately overhead. The outer flat surface of the arch is painted with abstracted folk motifs of flowers and leaves in a color scheme of blue, red, and yellow.[55]

The overall massing of the Pardubice crematorium suggests a house for the dead on a base surrounded by an arcade of invented columns. But the images of a house for the dead and a temple with its domestic and religious associations hide the building's efficiency and subtle expressions of function in its massing: the base and a partial sub-

250   CONCLUSION

basement provide space for crematory preparations; the location of stairs behind the ceremonial ones are indicated by a lower roof; and a one-story extension at the rear of the building has its own form.

By the time of its completion in 1923, Janák's crematorium represented a high point of hybridity with its statement of color and ornament dedicated to ennobling the passing of the dead and promoting national identity. But its vocabulary of Rondo-cubism was already anachronistic. The idioms of both Czech cubism and Rondo-cubism had given way to the vigorous new developments of functionalism.

Another variant on the crematorium as a hybrid type can be seen in the Bohemian town of Nymburk, located some forty-five kilometers east of Prague on the Labe (Elbe) River and along the road to Hradec Králové (figs. C.16, C.17).[56] Bedřich Feuerstein (1892–1936), in collaboration with Bohumil Sláma, designed Nymburk's crematorium in 1921.[57] Not only an architect, Feuerstein also painted, designed for the theatre, and wrote essays. After briefly studying at the Polytechnic in Prague with Plečnik, he visited St. Petersburg to study Russian neoclassical architecture and during the 1920s lived in France, where he became familiar with Le Corbusier's purism and worked in the office of August Perret, a venerable innovator in the use of reinforced concrete. In his designs, Feuerstein combined primary forms of geometry, which had formed the basis of cubism, with a classicizing sense of proportion to produce elegant hybridity. Sláma's experience came from collaborations with others on designs for new apartment blocks in Prague.[58]

FIGURE C.16
Bedřich Feuerstein and Bohumil Sláma, crematorium, exterior, Nymburk, Bohemia, 1921.

FIGURE C.17
Bedřich Feuerstein and Bohumil Sláma, crematorium, interior, Nymburk, Bohemia, 1921.

The hybrid character of the crematorium lies in the union of its floating planes with primal volumes that have classical platonic associations. Its roof planes project as cantilevers floating parallel to the ground and are reminiscent of De Stijl, but instead of having the asymmetries of the avant-garde idiom, the building's solids maintain symmetry in the classical tradition. Using rectangles, circles, and semicircles, the plan of the crematorium pivots around a double-height ceremonial hall with apsidal extensions appended from it.[59] One apse off the hall provides a waiting room with windows; another at the opposite side is shifted behind the hall; and a third apse terminates the areas for incineration located at the rear. A porch with stocky cylindrical columns surrounds the ground floor and supports a flat roof. Purist abstractions of classical columns, each cylinder has a base but no capital. Stairs run along the full length of the front between the columns. A tall cylindrical drum provides the experiential center of the building. Layered planes, recalling the abstract overlays of purism, clad the exterior. The roof above is a thick, flat square that cantilevers over the drum's edges. Attached at the rear of the drum is a rectangular frame, opened to hold a bell, but mostly visible from the sides. On the interior, light from pierced openings pours in to contrast with the somber darkness of the exterior. The convex projections of a canopy and raised dais for memorial remarks animates the concave void of the interior. The building is at once modern and functional, yet recalls the traditions of platonic geometry and symmetrical order. It balances solid and void to speak of its purpose of commemorating the dead in solemnity while providing the light of hope for mourners.

After its completion, *Stavba* published four pages of illustrations of the crematorium, and Devětsil's anthology *Life* published drawings, recognition that confirmed Feuerstein's reputation as a leading architect of Czech modernism.[60] He had joined the group of avant-garde artists of Devětsil in 1922, bringing with him a perspective on international developments in art and architecture. Feuerstein's aesthetic sensitivity, however, soon led him to criticize in 1925 the "scientific functionalism" of some Devětsil members, particularly Karel Teige, its chief ideologue, whose position Feuerstein saw as "critical extremism."[61] His remarks in 1925 prompted other Devětsil architects to have their own doubts about a functionalism that ignored psychological and aesthetic needs, but this did not guarantee that they would find clients sympathetic to more aesthetic approaches.[62]

Arnošt Wiesner's crematorium in Brno presents another approach to hybrid design (fig. C.18). Wiesner (1890–1971), a Slovak born in Malacky near Bratislava, studied in Vienna at the Polytechnic and the Academy of Fine Arts under Friedrich Ohmann from 1908 to 1913. For a brief period he was the first assistant in Ohmann's atelier in the last years of former regime.[63] After serving four years in the war, he returned to Brno to open his own office in 1919.[64]

Designed and built between 1925 and 1930, Wiesner's crematorium sits a mile outside the city, overlooking low plains.[65] Constructed of brick, it has a plastered rectangular base on which sit the recessed walls of a double-height chapel and its sixteen pointed piers covered in gold-colored travertine. On the outside to the west of the complex is a columbarium and a courtyard with a pergola; a second pergola is located symmetrically on the east; behind the hall on the north are the preparatory and burning facilities. With its raised base, its encompassing arms, and the austere entry topped with spiky terminations, the ensemble conveys a somber, even threatening primordial quality, as if it speaks about the sharp pain of death. One contemporary commentator described the pyramidal tops of the piers as rocketlike.[66] *Stavba* editor Oldřich Starý regretted the spikes, calling them "unfortunate" Gothic stylizations.[67] Edwyn Heathcote has described the spikes as resembling a crown of thorns, a religious reference couched in a modernist language of "clear simplicity," resulting in a "startling building

FIGURE C.18
Arnošt Wiesner, crematorium, exterior, Brno, Moravia, 1925–30. Reprinted from *Horizont* (Brno), nos. 11–13 (1928).

which blurs the border of classification of inter-war architecture."[68] They also recall the steep spires used on churches throughout Moravia and Bohemia.

Opening on the south, a processional stair leads to the central entry and the ceremonial hall. A spare, white, planar, double-height space, the hall has a glazed pitched roof. Pattern exists only in the contrasting marbles on the floor and the flat grid of the suspended, flat glass ceiling, which floods the interior with muted light, creating a dramatic contrast with the totally enclosed volumes perceived from the exterior. Simply arranged benches, candelabra, plants, and glass doors, which open to reveal the catafalque, are the only furnishings in the chapel. In his own description of the building, Wiesner noted that while as a building type it had to appear churchlike, the crematorium's forms resembled Egyptian burial sites.[69] The building is hybrid in its stark modernity, idiosyncratic invention, and primordial archaic associations.

:: IN VIENNA, with the political separation of the city from Lower Austria and the rise to power of the Social Democrats, the proposition of a new crematorium became not only a municipal amenity but a political statement of opposition to the church. The City of Vienna announced a competition in 1921, open to Austrian and German architects, for a crematorium near the main cemetery, the Zentralfriedhof, on a site that had once been the summer residence of Emperor Leopold in the sixteenth century and a powder depot in the nineteenth century. The scheme of the first-prize winner was rejected, and the commission went to the third-prize recipient, Clemens Holzmeister.

Holzmeister's design appealed to the conservative tastes of the city planning director, who chose it over other entries, claiming that it referred to the ruins of a late Renaissance villa (fig. C.19).[70] Holzmeister (1886–1983) was born in Fulpmes, a small town in the Stubaier Alps of the Tyrol, and studied at the State Trade School in Innsbruck. A Tyrolean who carried with him a sense of the Alpine homeland, he continued his studies at the Polytechnic in Vienna under König and Ferstel.[71] He taught for a year in Vienna at the conclusion of the war and from 1919 to 1924 was a professor at his alma mater in Innsbruck. Teaching marked only one pole of his career, as he also became a designer of monumental and sacred buildings and set designs, as well as an interpreter of local building traditions balanced between simplicity and expressive gestures. With his sensitivity to site and tradition, Holzmeister differed from stricter modernists, as seen, for instance, in his designs for an Alpine hotel in South Tyrol or an occasional country house.[72]

Instead of exploiting the possibilities of advanced modern technology, Holzmeister used in his crematorium design traditional economical load-bearing masonry block walls covered with stucco. Quite aware of the historical use of the site, he uniquely combined motifs of crenellation, arches, and a watchtower to create a hybrid ensemble. On the basis of his sketches in black crayon or charcoal—the preferred media of architectural expressionists—and the building's strange appearance, historians have

FIGURE C.19
Clemens Holzmeister, crematorium, exterior, Vienna, 1921–22.

tended to describe it exclusively in terms of expressionism. Friedrich Achleitner, confirming the view of Austrian historians, cites the building as the most important expressionist building in Austria, noting the two prongs of its style: Gothic formal references with a mystical emotionality, and a modern antirationality that signals the immediate postwar condition in Austria.[73] These expressive qualities coincide with the ideological function of cremation itself as an anticlerical gesture. Though coming from a Catholic background, Holzmeister designed a building to fit perfectly with the current anticlericalism of Viennese socialism.

What is the language that communicates such powerful ideas through Holzmeister's crematorium? When we look closely, we see that the emotional qualities of the structure come from new uses of history: the pointed arch entry is the sign of Gothic, which alone as a detached fragment suffices to signify associations with pre-Renaissance times. Its character as a sign, and not a tectonic feature of building as the pointed arch was traditionally, lies in its replication as an organizing and unifying motif. On the exterior, it articulates the arcades and the main entry and terminates the narrow slit windows in the upper zone of the ceremonial hall (fig. C.20). On the

FIGURE C.20
Clemens Holzmeister, crematorium, entrance, Vienna, 1921–22.

FIGURE C.21
Clemens Holzmeister, crematorium, interior, Vienna, 1921–22.

FIGURE C.22
Clemens Holzmeister, crematorium, interior, Vienna, 1921–22.

interior, the arches form the four sides of the ceremonial hall, truncated and abruptly set on the floor, mediated only a by single molding (figs. C.21, C.22). The theme of the pointed arch is further repeated as punctures in the upper zones of the hall. Other motifs are transpositions or evocations of the language of history: planar surfaces of the upper reaches of the ceremonial hall resonate as if they are folded linens, suggesting textiles with associations of a tent and traditions of linen-fold woodwork; the zigzag of the exterior cornice molding recalls the pattern used extensively in medieval churches, often painted on surfaces or carved into columns.

When completed, the hybridity of the building, mistaken for a Roman ruin, met with such success that Holzmeister received an appointment in 1924 as director of the master class and rector at the Academy of Fine Arts in Vienna. He was expelled from his professorship, however, in 1938 for opposing the National Socialists.[74]

Crematoria were built in other Austrian cities, and as a topic they continued to stimulate architecture students in Vienna in the 1920s.[75] The theme of the mortuary served

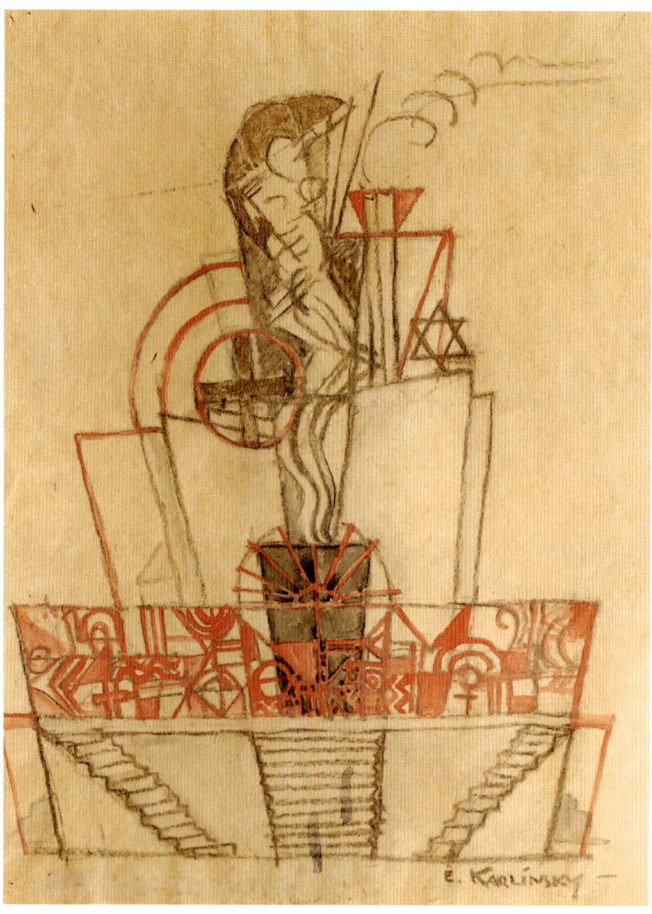

FIGURE C.23
Elisabeth Karlinsky, mausoleum (project), perspective, Vienna, 1924.

as a suitable subject, as seen in Elisabeth Karlinsky's design of 1924 (fig. C.23).[76] A coarse assembly of expressionist, cubist, and futurist motifs, the front façade collages concentric arches, an equilateral cross, and a Star of David with a swirling wraithlike figure that soars from the front entry and chimney, with smoke emerging behind. Another example is the diploma project of Ernst Anton Plischke (1903–92), a young Austrian who had studied from 1919 to 1923 under Oskar Strnad and Josef Frank at the State Trade School in Vienna and then continued in the master class of Peter Behrens at the Academy of Fine Arts. In 1926, for his thesis, Behrens asked him to develop the plans for a crematorium in Linz, which amounted to a counterproposal to Holzmeister's project.[77] Here in a hybrid approach Plischke used expressionist motifs and his imagination to create a poetic ensemble (fig. C.24). In contrast with the boxy massing of Holzmeister's crematorium, Plischke created an ethereal ensemble floating in water. Picking up the architectural themes of Fritz Lang's 1924 movie *Die Nibelungen*, he applied heavy shadows and broad washes of grays and blacks associated with expressionist architecture, but his forms are ephemeral and fragmentary. Intended for a site along the Danube, the crematorium is defined by ritual procession and organized by water. First the coffins awaiting cremation are placed in small wood-framed glass pavilions and are eventually transferred past water lilies to the crematory itself. The final rite for the dead occurs in a hall where organ music instead of human oration provides the ceremony. Plischke noted these rituals in his delicate drawings, indicating both the alliance of architecture with cinema and the tacit refutation of any conventional religious ceremony.[78]

A concluding example of the crematorium as an ideal type for a language of hybridity can be seen in Rudolf Perco's entry for the municipal competition in 1921, which Holzmeister ultimately built.[79] His entry not only adds a layer to this picture, but the circuit of his life and work displays the erratic movements that affected those trained before the war but who continued practicing after it. Perco (1884–1942) was born the son of a Slovene father and Italian mother in Görz (Gorizia in Italian) on the southern fringe of the Austro-Hungarian Empire, near the border with Italy.[80] After four years of school in Vienna, he entered the Academy of Fine Arts and studied with Wagner from 1906 to 1910, soon demonstrating tremendous proficiency and skill in mastering the idiom of the Wagnerschule.[81] His student work also showed a tendency

FIGURE C.24
Ernst Plischke, crematorium for Linz, thesis project, Academy of Fine Arts Vienna, perspective, Vienna, 1926.

towards monumental forms that would carry through into his later work, as seen in his *Idea for a Monumental Architecture*, designed in 1907 and published in 1909 in *Der Architekt*. The project was actually a mausoleum composed of a large block with inset multiple frames and a pyramidal roof pierced by a rotunda.

After working for other architects in Vienna during the 1910s, Perco began an independent practice, but during the war was held as an Italian prisoner of war. He pursued further architectural studies at the Polytechnic in Vienna from 1920 to 1923. During this time he entered a series of competitions, including the one for the *Chicago Tribune* building, for which he used the classic syntax of the language of history but transformed it by alternating façades of engaged columns with flat, unadorned planes.[82]

For the crematorium competition in 1921, Perco's entry, submitted under the code name Confessio, drew on the language of history at a moment when progressive architecture was casting it off (fig. C.25). The scheme is indeed a confession of Perco's own view of death and the architecture that accommodates it. Intended to fit into a site defined by axial pathways and circular gardens, his massive cubic form recalls the archetype of the ancient classical temple, but transforms its syntax. Though keeping the traditional base, arches, and stone treatments, Perco pierced the building's sides with tall slots of glazing and terminated it with massive piers from which the smoke of incineration moves skyward. The height of the interior space, its proportions, and the contrast between streaming light and the tall piers that project through the ceiling create an overwhelming impact of awe that engulfs the visitor (fig. C.26). Coffering of the ceiling continues the motifs of the language of history, but instead of using moldings in the coffers, Perco rejected classical decorum in favor of parallel rows of zigzags.

Unsuccessful in the crematorium competition, Perco continued to enter competitions as Red Vienna began to expand. By the end of the decade, the City of Vienna commissioned him to design an extensive housing complex, Engelsplatzhof (1929–33), in the city's Twentieth District. Intended to be a prototype of a superblock, Perco's complex

259   CONTINUITIES, DISCONTINUITIES, AND TRANSFORMATIONS

FIGURE C.25
Rudolf Perco, crematorium (project), perspective of exterior, Vienna, 1921.

would hold 2,300 apartments and communal facilities, including a cinema, kindergarten, laundry, and meeting rooms, and would have been even bigger than the widely published Karl Marx Hof housing complex by Karl Ehn (1926–30). But instead of becoming a new prototype, Perco's complex was the last phase of municipal planning under socialists. With the change of government, the project was only partially completed but showed the persistence of Perco's classicizing proportions and detail, including simplified molding courses, combined with the planarity and flat surfaces of international functionalism.

In the midst of the political changes that thwarted his most important commission to date, Perco took up to the study of law from 1929 to 1934 at the University of Vienna. He also continued to enter competitions, including one for a new bridge over the Danube to replace the old Crown Prince Rudolf Bridge (fig. C.27).[83] For the first stage of the competition, announced in 1933 by the Ministry of Trade and Transport, Perco's proposal showed the ongoing hybridity of his designs. At once functional and architectonic in expressing the electric poles that would support overhead cables, the scheme also used masonry bases abstracted from the language of history; a small study even included tryglyph motifs as column coverings.[84] Comparing Perco's project with Emil Belluš's Piešťany Bridge gives a sense of the range of hybrid approaches that emerged in the search for a viable language of modern architecture in the aftermath of the empire.

Perco continued to compete for commissions, particularly for a number of churches, beginning with his proposal for a new Roman Catholic cathedral in Belgrade (1930).[85] Again, monumental masonry forms defined the mass of the building, while the scale of the interior overwhelmed any sense of human scale. Shortly thereafter, he began turning to the political right, joining in 1932 the Union of Christian Art and the Fatherland Front, the corporate state-based fascist political party set up to replace Austria's other political organizations.

Within this right-wing political context, Perco conceived in 1933 a proposal for a Reunion Memorial Cathedral that he called David's Tent (fig. C.28).[86] It completely exemplified hybridity and provided a metaphorical statement of the complex conflation of

issues of identity affecting the languages of architecture in the period after World War I. Perco's intended site for the church had major historical significance as a termination of the former Kaiserforum, forming the end of an axis that begins at the imperial palace and follows between the venerable Museums of Fine Arts and Natural History. The cathedral would have been at least twice as large as both museums combined, occupying the equivalent of several city blocks, and would have required partial demolition of the imperial stables designed by Fischer von Ehrlach.[87] The "reunion" embodied in the proposal was for all Christian denominations in the world. It would take place in a building that transformed the idea of a moveable sanctuary, symbolized in the tent of the biblical David, into a fantastical assemblage of gabled masses with pointed arches recalling Gothic architecture but unlike any Gothic or neo-Gothic precedent. The spiky pinnacles covered the entire surface, providing a field of geometric stalactites, bewildering in their numbers but ever pointing upwards to the heavens. Mixing politics and apparent religious fervor, Perco designed all at once a combination of the Gothic style, a deeper ancient history of the Old Testament, and a statement about the unity of Christians as the select people, in an immense modern cathedral that defied the currents of international functionalism.

FIGURE C.26
Rudolf Perco, crematorium (project), perspective of interior, Vienna, 1921.

FIGURE C.27
Rudolf Perco, State Bridge (project), perspective, competition entry, Vienna, 1933.

Perco continued to pursue his particular historicity and monumental hybridity in church projects for the Ständestaat, the Austrian dictatorship in the so-called Austro-Fascism period launched under Engelbert Dollfuss, who, as chancellor of Austria from 1932 to 1934, had turned the Austrian Republic into an authoritarian regime based on conservative Roman Catholic and Italian Fascist principles. After the Anschluss, when Hitler's Germany annexed Austria in 1938, Perco applied to join the National Socialist

CONTINUITIES, DISCONTINUITIES, AND TRANSFORMATIONS

FIGURE C.28
Rudolf Perco, study for a Reunion Memorial Cathedral, "David's Tent" (project), perspective, Vienna, 1934.

Party, hoping, like others, to better his personal situation.[88] He traveled to Berlin in the summer of 1938, returned to Vienna, and worked for the next three years in the office of his former Wagner School classmate Franz Kaym, proposing buildings sympathetic to the Nazi cause.[89] In 1941, he was appointed to a post in the Planning Department, a center of Viennese National Socialist administration. Perco, however, soon had difficulties in his appointment, was fired without notice, and died totally isolated under curious circumstances on January 31 1942. According to Gestapo records, the cause of death was gas poisoning and officially an accident, but more probably it was a suicide.[90]

Brilliantly talented as a premier product of the Wagnerschule who in another time might have had immense success, Perco confronted historical and political conditions that dealt him a different fate as he became one of the "Forgotten Generation" of Austrian architects.[91] His early career spanned the end of the Dual Monarchy, he built housing for the Social Democrats, developed church projects for the Ständestaat, and ended creating what Ursula Prokop has called "Nazi megalomania."[92] Perco executed only seven buildings over a period of thirty years, but his work exhibited, through the language of hybridity, a fantastical—and tragic—utopianism combined with rationalist functionalism.

:: WITH THE language of hybridity freshly reviewed and a glance at the fate of other forms of architectural speech, we see the burden that the language of architecture had to carry to convey the cultural complexity of its time and place. This investigation of language and architecture posed questions of what architecture can and cannot say, and its means of communication, whether abstract or figurative, whether didactic or touching the depths of cognition. It explored who reads buildings and why, and the interplay between personal and national identity. It showed some of the multiple readings required to approach answers to these questions, and the paradoxical and contrary responses that often arose. Only within the realm of the Austro-Hungarian Empire and its successor nation-states were the challenges placed before the language of architecture so great. Despite the difficulty of reading these buildings, close attention to what they can and cannot say may deepen our understanding not only of history but also of the complexity of the region today. Despite its limitations, architecture as language may be more powerful than we realize as a manifestation of identity in all its dimensions.

Appendix

PLACE-NAMES

Names of cities in the text are those most familiar to western readings. However, many of the cities had multiple names under different languages during and the after the Austro-Hungarian Empire.

Bratislava [Sv], Pressburg [G], Pozsony [Mg]
Brno [C], Brünn [G]
Cracow [E], Kraków [P], Krakau [G], Krakkó [Mg], Krakov [C, Ru, Sv]
Hradec Králové [C], Königgrätz [G]
Görz [G], Gorizia [I], Gorica [Sl]
Liberec [C], Reichenberg [G]
Ljubljana [Sl], Laibach [G], Lubiana [I]
L'viv [U], Lwów [P], Lemberg [G, Y], Lvov [Ru], Ilyvó [Mg]
Prague [E], Praha [C], Prag [G, Y]
Prostějov [C], Proßnitz [G]
Plzeň [C], Pilsen [G]
Szabadka [Mg], Subotica [SC], Maria-Theresiopel [G]
Temesvár [Mg], Timișoara, [R], Temeschwar-Josephstadt [G]
Vienna [E], Wien [G], Bécs [Mg]
Zagreb [SC], Agram [G], Zágráb [Mg]

Source: Magocsi, *Historical Atlas of Central Europe*, rev. and expanded ed. [C] denotes Czech; [E], English; [G], German; [I], Italian; [Mg], Magyar; [P], Polish; [R], Romanian; [Ru], Russian; [SC], Serbo-Croatian; [Sl], Slovenian; [Sv], Slovak; [U], Ukrainian; [Y], Yiddish.

EDUCATIONAL INSTITUTIONS

Many educational institutions throughout the Austro-Hungarian Empire have had several changes of names in the course of their long histories. The following continue to the present.

Budapest

Budapest Technical University: Institutum Geometrico-Hydrotechnicum, in Buda, 1782; József Ipartanoda (named for the palatine governor of Hungary, the brother of the emperor Franz) established in 1846; united with the former institute, 1856, as Joseph Polytechnicum; became a university and established an architectural faculty and other technical faculties, 1871; Magyar Királyi József Műgyetem (Hungarian Royal Joseph Technical University) after 1871, when it moved to Pest, with its building erected in 1883; moved again to a bigger building complex in Buda, 1906–9; now Budapesti Műszaki és Gazdaságtudományi Egyetem (Budapest University of Technology and Economics).

Prague
Polytechnical institute: Pražská technika před březem, 1806 (known later as k. k. deutsche Technische Hochschule in German).

Czech Technical University: České vysoké učení technické, 1863, divided into German- and Czech-language universities, 1869.

Vienna
Academy of Fine Arts: Akademie, 1692; k. k. vereinigten Akademie der bildenden Künste, 1772; Akademie der vereinigten bildenden Künste, 1812; k. k. Akademie der bildenden Künste.

Polytechnic Institute: Polytechnisches Institut, 1815–75; k. k. Technische Hochschule, 1875–1918; Technische Hochschule, 1919–75; Technische Universität Wien (Technical University of Vienna), 1975.

School of Applied Arts: Österreichisches Museum für Kunst und Industrie, 1863; k. k. Kunstgewerbeschule (School of Arts and Crafts) des k. k. Österreichisches Museum für Kunst und Industrie, 1867; Staatliche Kunstgewerbeschule Wien, 1937; Reichshochschule für angewandte Kunst Wien, 1941; Hochschule für angewandte Kunst Wien, 1945; Akademie für angewandte Kunst Wien, 1948; Hochschule für angewandte Kunst, 1971; Universität für angewandte Kunst Wien, 1998. The museum is now Museum für angewandte Kunst (MAK).

State Trade School: Gewerblichen Zeichenschule (Commercial Drawing School), 1846; k. k. bau- und Maschinengewerbeschule, 1870; k. k. Staats-Gewerbeschule (State Trade School), 1880; Technische-gewerbliche Bundeslehranstalt, 1922/23; Höhere technische Bundes-Lehr- und Versuchsanstalt Wien 1, 1963; Höhere technische Bundes-Lehr- und Versuchsanstalt (Camillo Sitte Lehranstalt) Wien 3, 1982.

Sources: for Hungarian institutions, János Gerle to author, personal communication, August 4, 2005; for Czech institutions, Christopher Long, "East Central Europe: National Identity and International Perspective," *JSAH* 61, no. 4 (December 2002): 519–29; and for Austrian institutions, see http://www.azw.at/page.php?node_id=89&subnode_id=94 documentation by the Architekturzentrum Wien)"

TRANSLATION OF *SECESSION* THROUGHOUT THE EMPIRE

Secession	Vienna (*Sezession* in German)
secese	Bohemia (C)
secesija	Croatia (Cr)
szecesszió	Hungary (H)
secesja	Poland (P)

Notes

PREFACE

1. Roland Barthes, *Mythologies* (Paris: Éditions du Seuil, 1957); English translation by Jonathan Capet Ltd (New York: Hill and Wang, 1972).

INTRODUCTION

Works frequently cited have been identified by the following abbreviations:

M (1998): Moravánszky, Ákos. *Competing Visions: Aesthetic Invention and Social Imagination in Central European Architecture, 1867–1918*. Cambridge, MA: MIT Press, 1998.

M (1988): Moravánszky, Ákos. *Die Architektur der Donaumonarchie*. Berlin: Ernst & Sohn, 1988.

CNT: McCord, Olga Alexandra. "Nationalism and Its Expression in Architecture: The Czech National Theater and Its Legacy." Ph.D. diss., University of California, Berkeley, 1993.

JSAH: *Journal of the Society of Architectural Historians*

OW: Graf, Otto Antonia. *Otto Wagner: Das Werk des Architekten*. 7 vols. Vienna: Verlag Böhlau, 1985–2000.

1. The general tendency of scholars working in the field of modern architectural history in Central Europe has been to concentrate narrowly on an individual architect or to limit their investigation to a specific country. The pioneering architectural survey of the modern architecture of the Austro-Hungarian Empire is Ákos Moravánszky, *Competing Visions: Aesthetic Invention and Social Imagination in Central European Architecture, 1867–1918* (Cambridge, MA: MIT Press, 1998). Based on his two earlier works, *Die Architektur der Donaumonarchie* (1988) and *Die Erneuerung der Baukunst* (1988), this book takes a stylistic approach that is set against a cultural backdrop. Moravánszky has also looked at the relationship of architectural language to speech, particularly on façades; see his "Die Sprache der Fassaden: Das Problem des Ausdrucks in der Architektur der Donaumonarchie 1900–1914," in the exhibition catalogue *Österreich*, ed. Annette Becker, Dietmar Steiner, and Wilfried Wang, 12–21, Architektur im 20. Jahrhundert series (Munich: Prestel Verlag; Frankfurt am Main: Deutsches Architektur-Museum, 1995).

This study differs from Moravánszky's work by setting up a broad generic question about architecture itself—how buildings communicate—by looking in greater depth and with fewer examples, and by using the metaphor of language to provide an overall connective theme, instead of an episodic treatment. In addition, the scope of study includes some examples of buildings designed after World War I, so we shall see how those languages change with the cataclysm of war.

2. Literature on nationalism and the relationship between the nation and the state is enormous. For a comprehensive but approachable overview, see Eric J. Hobsbawm, *Nations and Nationalism since 1780: Programme, Myth, Reality*, 2nd ed. (Cambridge: Cambridge University Press, 1992). The themes of identity, nation-state formation, and architecture on the periphery of the Austro-Hungarian Empire have also been freshly pursued in Carmen Popescu, *Le Style National Roumain: Construire une Nation à travers l'architecture, 1881–1945* (Rennes, France: Presses Universitaires de Rennes, 2004).

3. For general historical studies, see Barbara Jelavich, *History of the Balkans: Twentieth Century*, vol. 2 (New York: Cambridge University Press, 1983); Lonnie R. Johnson, *Central Europe: Enemies, Neighbors, Friends* (New York: Oxford University Press, 1996); Robert A. Kann, *A History of the Habsburg Empire 1526–1918* (Berkeley and Los Angeles: University of California Press, 1974); Joseph Held, ed., *The Columbia History of Eastern Europe in the Twentieth Century* (New York: Columbia University Press, 1992); and Derek Sayer, *The Coasts of Bohemia: A Czech History* (Princeton, NJ: Princeton University Press, 1998). For a broader geopolitical study, see Eric Hobsbawm, *The Age of Extremes: A History of the World, 1914–1991* (New York: Vintage Books, 1996).

4. The complexity of regional names and identities is mirrored in areas like Vojvodina, which was so recognized before the Ausgleich, but absorbed in southern Hungary, and eventually made a province of Serbia.

5. For population statistics circa 1870 compared with 1910, see Paul Robert Magocsi, *Historical Atlas of Central Europe* (Seattle: University of Washington Press, 2002), 96.

6. The language belongs to the Finno-Ugric linguistic group and is spoken primarily in Hungary, but also in parts of today's Slovakia, Romania, Croatia, and Serbia. Ethnicity depended upon linkages to the Magyars, the ancestors who

came from the East to settle the region. In ethnographic terms, these proto-Hungarians were a mix of Ugric and Turkish peoples who lived in western Siberia, migrated by the early fifth century CE southwestward over the Khazar Empire, and centered near the Caspian Sea. By 830, they had arrived on the west banks of the Don River and comprised seven tribes. By the late ninth century, as they subjugated local Slavs and Huns, the Magyars had entered the region further west that took the English-language name Hungary.

7. See Friedrich Achleitner, "The Pluralism of Modernity: The Architectonic 'Language Problem' in Central Europe," in *Shaping the Great City: Modern Architecture in Central Europe, 1890–1937*, ed. Eve Blau and Monika Platzer (Munich: Prestel, 1999), 94–106; and Achleitner, *Wiener Architektur: Zwischen typologischem Fatalismus und semtantischem Schlamassel* (Vienna: Böhlau, 1996).

8. In Hungary, as Rudolf Klein has noted, pluralism was the "normal condition," while "monistic periods represented . . . crisis" (R. Klein, "Architecture and Identity: A Short Survey of Hungarian 20th Century Architectural Theory" [unpublished manuscript, n.d.], 2–4; quotation is from p. 2).

9. For a recent theoretical and stimulating approach to modern architecture, see Adrian Forty, *Words and Buildings: A Vocabulary of Modern Architecture* (New York : Thames & Hudson, 2000). For an earlier synopsis on linguistic analogies to architecture, see Peter Collins, *Changing Ideals in Modern Architecture, 1750–1950* (Montreal: McGill University Press, 1965; North American ed., 1967), 173–82. See also Jacques Guillerme, "The Idea of Architectural Language: A Critical Inquiry," *Oppositions* 10 (Fall 1977): 21–26; and Guillerme, "La colonna del discorso: Architettura e linguaggio," *Casabella* 54, no. 568 (May 1990): 36–39, 61. For a broad range of investigations on language and identity, see Michelle Facos and Sharon L. Hirsch, eds., *Art, Culture and National Identity in Fin-de-Siècle Europe* (Cambridge: Cambridge University Press, 2003).

10. For a brilliant investigation of how images of art evoke experience in their beholders, see David Freedberg, *The Power of Images: Studies in the History and Theory of Response* (Chicago: University of Chicago Press, 1989).

11. To begin this study with some clear common ground and to introduce the terminology of the assumptions subsumed in this text, it may be worthwhile to state some basic Saussurean concepts. I think of a *sign* as an object and idea that stand for something else, which they may or may not resemble. Classical examples are an arrow as a sign of direction or gray hair as a sign of old age. Signs have two parts: a signifier, which concerns physical appearance, sound, and so forth; and the signified, which concerns mental concepts. By *signification* I mean the process by which signs affect meaning; it is determined by the relationships and differences among signs, organized by codes, and their relationships to what they stand for. *Codes* here are the rules that allow the meaningful communication of symbols.

In some senses, relationships among signs may be analogous to relationships among people. That was certainly the position of Ludwig Wittgenstein, the Viennese linguistic philosopher, who tells us the sickness of life is the sickness of language. Just as when our personal relationships go well and are healthy, we feel that we understand the other. There is congruence in the exchange of information between signs. However beyond the personal realm the relationships between signs, which are organized by codes, are governed by conventions in a given culture, not by our private psyches. Therefore, semiological analysis ought to reveal meanings that are not exclusively a reflection of personal taste.

A variety of sign that will be particularly important here is the symbol. By *symbol* I mean a sign that by convention stands for something else. Its form and meaning may be arbitrary, but it is determined by a community using it, e.g. black as the color of mourning. While writers often create their own symbols, as do artists, the use of symbols in western European traditions has at times been codified: baroque artists, for example, could turn to a dictionary of symbols, such as Cesare Ripa's *Iconologia* (published in Siena in 1613 and in numerous editions through the mid-eighteenth century), to choose symbols that their community would understand. This reliance on convention for centuries broke down as the Enlightenment moved forward, and people ceased to believe in the values those symbols represented.

Studying the meaning of symbols through symbology, or through iconology in the arts, is yet one tool in the kit of semiologists. Other tools include the study of syntax, which generally deals with how some linguistic items are transformed into others, and pragmatics, which concern how context affects linguistic understanding. Using these tools pushes us beyond signification to semantics, the study and meaning of reference. While linguists may engage in such studies for their own sake, we are interested in them because they lead to the study of language. In this book these terms and concepts are assumed to be elements of the analyses under discussion.

12. See Georgia Clarke and Paul Crossley, eds., *Architecture and Language: Constructing Identity in European Architecture, c. 1000–1650* (Cambridge: Cambridge University Press, 2000); Moshe Barasch, *The Language of Art: Studies in Interpretation* (New York: New York University Press, 1997); and Sylvia Lavin, *Quatremère de Quincy and the Invention of a Modern Language of Architecture* (Cambridge, MA: MIT Press, 1992).

13. For my initial description of the interlocked interpretations in a net of meanings, see *Frank Lloyd Wright: The Lost Years, 1910–1922; A Study of Influence* (Chicago: University of Chicago Press, 1993), 6–8.

14. For a general introduction to the political and cultural context in Hungary in the nineteenth and twentieth centuries with an emphasis on art, see Steven A. Mansbach, "Introductory Thoughts on Hungarian History and Culture," in *Two Centuries of Hungarian Painters, 1820–1970* (Washington, DC: American University Press, 1991), 9–16.

15. A synoptic view of definitions of the region before the rise of nineteenth-century nationalism can be found in Thomas DaCosta Kaufmann, *Court, Cloister, and City: The Art and Culture of Central Europe 1450–1800* (Chicago: University of Chicago Press, 1995), 13–27.

16. For a review and update of the debates about the terminology of Central Europe and Mitteleuropa, see Timothy Garton Ash, "The Puzzle of Central Europe," *New York Review of Books* 46, no. 5 (March 18, 1999): 18–20, 22–23.

CHAPTER ONE

1. Ulrike Planner-Steiner and Klaus Eggert, *Friedrich von Schmidt, Gottfried Semper, Carl von Hasenauer*, vol. 8, part 2 of Die Wiener Ringstrasse, Bild Einer Epoche; Die Erweiterung der inneren Stadt Wien unter Kaiser Franz Joseph; Die Bauten und ihre Architekten, edited by Renate Wagner-Rieger (Wiesbaden: Franz Steiner Verlag, 1978), 24. The client for the Rathaus was the City of Vienna, acting under auspices of its mayor and Emperor Franz Josef.

2. Peter Haiko and Renata Kassal-Mikula, eds., *Friedrich von Schmidt (1825–1891): Ein gotischer Rationalist*, exhibition catalogue (Vienna: Historisches Museum der Stadt Wien, 1991), especially 94–134.

3. See ibid., 75.

4. In Reichensperger's words, "Yes, we believe firmly in the victorious power of Truth! That, in spite of all naysayers, this art of the Middle Ages will spring again to life, because it, like godly religion itself, streams back to us thousand fold, and is, above all and in keeping with its innermost being, true" (Monika Keplinger, "Zum Kirchenbau Friedrich Schmidts," in ibid., 21.)

5. Haiko and Kassal-Mikula, *Friedrich von Schmidt (1825–1891)*, 9. Reichensperger's conception of the neo-Gothic was inherently straightforward: "Above all, [the Gothic builders] built their houses not from the outside in, but from the inside out, so that the façade of the building became a product of the building interior, like the elevation grows from the plan. Over the dead Symmetry they placed Eurhythmy, and through the outer irregularity of their construction shines forth a deeply-rooted rule. There, everything grows naturally throughout, as if according to an organic Law" (August Reichensperger, *Die christisch-germanische Baukunst und ihr Verhältniß zur Gegenwart*, 2nd ed. (Trier, 1852), p. 14; quoted in Monika Keplinger, "Zum Kirchenbau Friedrich Schmidts," in ibid., 21).

6. Michael J. Lewis, *The Politics of the German Gothic Revival: August Reichensperger (1808–1895)* (New York: Architectural History Foundation; Cambridge, MA: MIT Press, 1993), 231, 233.

7. Ibid., 235.

8. M (1998), 74.

9. Lewis, *The Politics of the German Gothic Revival*, 235.

10. M (1998), 72–73. Reform Catholicism, led by Bernard Bolzano, sought to unify Germans and Czechs in Prague to combat secularization.

11. On the complex roles of architecture in nineteenth-century southern Bohemia, see Jindřich Vybíral, *Století dìdicù a zakladatelù: Architektura jižních Čech v obdobi historismu* (Prague: Argo, 1999), with English-language resumé, 198–202.

12. Letter, Friedrich von Schmidt to August Reichensperger, January 24, 1868; reprinted in Reichensperger, "Zur Charakterisirung des Baumeisters Friedrich Freihern von Schmidt," *Zeitschrift für christliche Kunst*, no. 4 (1891): 126–27; translation by Michael Lewis. Quoted in Lewis, *The Politics of the German Gothic Revival*, 235. For Rauscher, see Cölestin Wolfsgruber, "Rauscher, Joseph Othmar," *Catholic Encyclopedia*, vol. 12 (1908); transcribed by Douglas J. Potter online at http://www.newadvent.org/cathen/12660b.htm.

13. Planner-Steiner and Eggert, *Friedrich von Schmidt, Gottfried Semper, Carl von Hasenauer*, 33.

14. M (1998), 73.

15. Friedrich von Schmidt, quoted in Haiko and Kassal-Miklula, *Friedrich von Schmidt*, 100. Translation, author.

16. See Lewis, The Politics of the German Gothic Revival, 47, 147, 187.

17. See Haiko and Kassal-Mikula, *Friedrich von Schmidt*, figs. cat. 2.22 and cat. 2.24.

18. Lewis, *The Politics of the German Gothic Revival*, 236. Lewis also cites Florentine elements in the treatment of the façade as a means of pacifying objections to the neo-Gothic, but the persistence of pointed arches makes the claim difficult to maintain.

19. See M (1988), 50 for a redrawn plan of Rathaus as built.

20. For details of the competitions for sculpture and painting and symbols of the *Länder* (lands), see Planner-Steiner and Eggert, *Friedrich von Schmidt, Gottfried Semper, Carl von Hasenauer*, 42–45.

21. The festival hall ceiling was supposed to contain paintings of scenes of Vienna's triumphs: victory over the Turks in 1683 as well as contemporary victories, such as irrigation of the city, regulation of the Danube River, and construction of the city hall, but the ceiling was cross-vaulted instead. For the Mayor's *Repräsentation-Saal*, an allegory was planned of citizen virtues awakened by those of the city.

22. Planner-Steiner and Eggert, *Friedrich von Schmidt, Gottfried Semper, Carl von Hasenauer*, 45.

23. Haiko and Kassal-Mikula, *Friedrich von Schmidt*, 100. The laying of the keystone on September 12, 1883, marked the official completion of the building, though furnishing took another five years. One hundred and fifty-two meters long and one hundred and thirty-two meters wide, the Rathaus contained 18,700 square meters of floor space. Rathaus Park provided open space at the front entry facing the Ringstrasse; its surrounding gardens spread out around the building's edges, softening and making accessible a previously treacherous and soggy site. The rear entry along Rathausstrasse later became Friedrich Schmidt Square, where a bust of the architect was located.

24. The standard literature includes František Žákaveč, *Chrám znovuzrození* [Temple of the Resurrection]: *O budovatelích a budvê Národního divadla v Praze* (Prague: J. Štenc, 1918; 2nd ed., 1938); Antonín Matějček, *Národní divadlo a jeho výtvarníci* (Prague, 1933; updated, 1954); Mirolsav Korecký, "Sto let Zítkova projektu Národního divadla v Praze," *Umění* 14 (1966): 541–66; M (1988), 53; and Olga Alexandra McCord, "Nationalism and Its Expression in Architecture: The Czech National Theater and Its Legacy" (Ph.D. diss., University of California, Berkeley, 1993). For my study I rely heavily on McCord's excellent account of the building's history, subsequently cited as CNT.

25. CNT, 96.

26. See ibid., 91–98.

27. For a standard biography, see Eva Kritilová, *Architekt Josef Zítek* (Prague: Státni nakladatelství krásné literatury, hudby a umění, 1954).

28. For a summary of architectural education in the Austro-Hungarian Empire, see Christopher Long, "East Central Europe: National Identity and International Perspective," *JSAH* 61, no. 4 (December 2002): 519–29.

29. CNT, 69–71.

30. To accommodate the skewed angles of the site, Zítek slightly shifted the stage and seating; the semicircular termination of the seating allowed the shift without visitors noticing, and the use of *poché*—a thickening of walls—absorbed all irregularities. Multiple entries were required to deal with the site's slope; the major entry was perpendicular to the river, and a secondary entry with grand staircase opened from a ramp parallel to the river and provided access to the grand royal stair and ultimately to the Royal Imperial Lounge. A third entry was located facing the river and behind the Temporary Theater, which had been incorporated into the scheme. On the opposite side, an arcade extended along the exterior of the main auditorium.

31. Despite Emperor Franz Josef's optimism, the Prussians inflicted within seven weeks disastrous defeat on the Austrians at Hradec Králové (Königgrätz) in northern Bohemia. Regardless of the negative impact on the Czech economy, preparations for the theater resumed.

32. CNT, 204–6.

33. Ibid., 221–22.

34. Ibid., 220–21.

35. The statues were designed by Bohuslav Schnirch (1845–1901) after winning a commission announced in 1872 (ibid., 234–35).

36. Josef Václav Myslbek (1848–1922), whose work scholars saw as expressive of nationalism, received the commission for the allegorical figures in 1871. A specialist in figures representing Czech mythical history, he also designed the statue of Saint Wenceslas in Prague's Wenceslas Square (CNT, 233–34).

37. Antonín Pavel Wagner (1834–95), a sculptor from Dvůr Králové, the town where the manuscripts appeared, received the commission for the statues.

38. CNT, 236.

39. Ibid., 236–39. McCord's description is particularly cogent. She notes that Ženíšek also proposed to decorate the auditorium ceiling with eight allegories of Art.

40. Antonín Matějček, ed., *Národ Sobě: Národní Divadlo a Jeho Umělecké Poklady* (Prague:

Melantrich, 1940), 120–21. The book contains the programs for the paintings of the theater.

41. The painter Václav Brožik supplemented the program with a cycle illustrating the ruling dynasties of Premyslids, Luxemburgs, and Habsburgs. See ibid., passim.

42. Ibid., 112–13.

43. For Svatopluk, see http://www.wordiq.com/definition/Great_Moravia.

44. Quoted in CNT, 261.

45. Ibid., 245.

46. Tamara Bissell and Roman Prahl, "The 'Nation for Itself' and the Curtain for the Czech National Theater," *Umění* 44:6 (1996): 520–39.

47. Ibid., 529, quoting Hynais in Matějček, *Národní divadlo*, 260.

48. Bissell and Prahl, "The 'Nation for Itself' and the Curtain for the Czech National Theater," 530–31.

49. Ibid., 531n33.

50. CNT, 262–79.

51. Antonín Balšánek, "Slovo úvodem" [preface], *Štíty a motivy attikové v česke renessanci* (Prague: Česka matice techniká, 1902); quoted in ibid., 292.

52. See Isaiah Berlin, "The Romantics and Their Roots (Excerpt from the Mellon Lectures Delivered in Washington in 1965)," *Times Literary Supplement*, no. 5003 (February 19, 1999): 13–15.

53. For a synoptic monograph on the Rumbach Street Synagogue, see Ines Müller, *Die Otto Wagner-Synagoge in Budapest* (Vienna: Löcker, 1992). For a concise and insightful overview of synagogues in Budapest, see Carol Herselle Krinsky, *Synagogues of Europe: Architecture, History, Meaning* (New York; Architectural History Foundation; Cambridge, MA: MIT Press, 1985; New York: Dover, 1996), especially 154–63; Harold Hammer-Schenk, *Synagogen in Deutschland: Geschichte einer Baugattung im 19. und 20. Jahrhundert (1780–1933)*, 2 vols. (Hamburg: Hans Christians Verlag, 1981); and Géza Komoróczy, ed., *Jewish Budapest: Monuments, Rites, History* (Budapest: Central European University, 1999), especially 134–38. For a discussion on similar issues in America, see Olga Bush, "The Architecture of Jewish Identity: The Neo-Islamic Central Synagogue of New York," *JSAH* 63, no. 2 (June 2004): 180–201, especially 193–99 on neo-Islamic synagogues in German-speaking lands.

54. Friedrich Weinbrenner's design for the synagogue in Karlsruhe (1709–1806) used references to Egyptian pylons in the front façade along with Gothic and classical motifs. See Müller, *Otto-Wagner Synagoge*, 14.

55. Ibid., 21.

56. For Fleischer's examples, see his Bohemian (Budweis 1888) and Viennese (Schmalzhof-, Muellner-, and Neudeggergasse [1883–1903]) examples.

57. Müller, *Otto-Wagner Synagoge*, 21.

58. Dijana Alić and Maryam Gusheh, "Reconciling National Narratives in Socialist Bosnia and Herzegovina: The Baščaršija Project, 1948–1953," *JSAH* 58, no. 1 (March 1999): 8–9.

59. Müller, *Otto-Wagner Synagoge*, 20–22.

60. Owen Jones, *Plans, Elevations, Sections and Details of the Alhambra. Taken from Drawings by M. Jules Goury and by Owen Jones, Architect 1834 and 1837*, vol. 1, London, 1842; vol. 2, London, 1845.

61. Müller, *Otto-Wagner Synagoge*, 20.

62. Krinsky, *Synagogues of Europe*, 8–9.

63. In the rise of the Conservative movement, Zacharias Frankel (1801–75), rabbi and theologian, inspired its early ideas. He broke with modernizing extremists after a series of Reform conferences in Germany (1844–46). Born in Prague, he died in Breslau, Germany (now Wroclaw, Poland) (see *Encyclopaedia Britannica Online*, s.v. "Conservative Judaism").

64. Krinsky, *Synagogues of Europe*, 5–12.

65. Ibid., 157. Construction began in 1854.

66. Müller, *Otto-Wagner Synagoge*, 27.

67. Krinsky, *Synagogues of Europe*, 159.

68. See Komoróczy, *Jewish Budapest*, 132. The exact religious orientation of the group is somewhat ambiguous. One source (*Jewish Budapest*, 134) indicates the congregation was neither Orthodox (as the contemporary German Baedeker guide called them) nor Neolog, but closer to the *status quo ante* communities, though not officially linked to them (ibid., 154). Krinsky (*Synagogues of Europe*, 160) identifies the congregation as members of the "status quo" movement. Formally a part of the Neological movement, it distanced itself from the *Wiener Ritus*, a more reformed worship style, which embodied a compromise between tradition and contemporary practice and approached the radical German Reform movement. The 200,000 Neologists in Pest by the end of the century made it the largest such community in the world.

69. Komoróczy, *Jewish Budapest*, 135.

70. Müller, *Otto-Wagner Synagoge*, 33.

71. See ibid., 40–45, for further discussion of client issues and political setting.

72. The wealthy Vienna banker and trade advisor Gustav von Epstein may have recommended Wagner's invitation into the competition; Wagner was at the time engaged in a project for a villa in Vienna for von Epstein, and the patron's business

and religious interests were very much engaged in activities in Budapest (ibid., 43).

73. For the definitive catalogue and analysis, see Otto Antonia Graf, *Otto Wagner: Das Werk des Architekten*, 7 vols. (Vienna: Verlag Böhlau, 1985–2000). For the best biographical synopsis of Wagner, see Otto Antonia Graf, *Master Drawings of Otto Wagner*, exhibition catalogue (New York: The Drawing Center, 1987), 1–10; also *Macmillan Encyclopedia*, 4:357–361, s.v. "Wagner," by Carl Schorske.

74. Müller, *Otto-Wagner Synagoge*, 59, figs. 58–60. Contemporary Moorish synagogues in Germany were visible in Cologne, and in Gottfried Semper's example in Dresden. Centrally planned and designed in Romanesque style, Semper's synagogue had a main façade similar to that of Kait Bay Mosque, Cairo, and a gallery and interior stucco ornamental patterns in Alhambra colors; it also used an iron structural system. In addition, there were formal cousins to the Moorish style in sacred buildings in Vienna: the Greek Orthodox church by Theophil Hansen (1858–61) had a colorful brick façade, octagonal middle tower, and separation of profane (front) from sacred (back) spaces behind a representative façade; and Vienna's City Temple by Josef Kornhäusel (1824–26) featured a similar functional arrangement (ibid., 48). Contemporary profane Moorish examples in Vienna included Hansen's Weapon Museum. With a castellated cornice hiding the roof behind it, its closed, cubic building mass emphasized the central portion of façade with a triple-portal. Ornament defined façade walls and emphasized their "surface-ness," with sculptural terra-cotta relief tacked on that did not hint at any tectonic reality.

75. Ibid., 58, figs. 56, 57.

76. Ibid., 62–64.

77. Ibid., 30.

78. Krinksy, *Synagogues of Europe*, 191–95.

79. Müller, *Otto-Wagner Synagoge*, 27, 51.

80. Ibid., 54, 76, 78.

81. Krinsky, *Synagogues of Europe*, 160.

82. Müller, *Otto-Wagner Synagoge*, 34; Komoróczy, *Jewish Budapest*, 133.

83. Komoróczy, *Jewish Budapest*, 133.

84. For the dimensions of the building and an excellent description, see Krinksy, *Synagogues of Europe*, 161–62.

85. See Graf, *Otto Wagner*, 5:1285–1331, for the most complete graphical analysis of Wagner's design process. As Graf has noted, the processes of using rotational geometry and primary forms have roots in, among other sources, Wenzel Jamnitzer, *Perspectiva corporum regularium* (Nürnberg, 1568).

86. Müller, *Otto-Wagner Synagoge*, 12.

87. Ibid., 91. The card illustrated is dated 1911.

88. „Eine Jugendarbeit nach den damaligen Begriffen, aber mit einer Raumwirkung, die noch heute gilt"—from Ludwig Hevesi, "Wie soll man den Leopoldstädter Tempel bauen?—Ein Vorschlag zur Güte," in *Pester Lloyd* 7.4.1899 no. 877 (Feuilleton, 1899), 2; quoted in ibid., jacket overleaf; and "Man sieht ihn (in seiner Jugend) schon also Materialmenschen zum Beispiel im farbigen Ziegelbau einer Synagoge in Budapest," in Ludwig Hevesi, *Österreichische Kunst im 19. Jahrhundert* (Leipzig, 1906), 286; quoted in Müller, *Otto-Wagner Synagoge*, 12.

CHAPTER TWO

1. See, for instance, A. Bouillon, *Principes de Desin Linéaire*, 2nd ed. (Paris: Chez L. Hatchette, 1845); Jules Bourgoin, *Elements de l'art arabe. Le trait des entrelacs* (Paris: Firmin-Didot et Cie., 1879); and Bourgoin, *Théorie de l'Ornement* (Paris: A. Levy, 1873). Their work is part of my current research in the history of ornament. In America, Louis Sullivan represented biomorphic organicism, but Frank Lloyd Wright, his former apprentice, pursued rectilinear geometry and platonic shapes for his structural organicism. When united with innovative technology, it defines the conventional term, *structural rationalism*, with Viollet-le-Duc often cited as a principal proponent.

2. Van de Velde relied on Alois Riegl's ideas of the *Kunstwollen* and Theodor Lipps's empathy theory.

3. M (1998), 118.

4. For a brief synopsis of Olbrich's career, see *Macmillan Encyclopedia of Architects*, ed. Adolf K. Platzek, s.v. "Olbrich, Joseph Maria," by Robert Judson Clark (New York: The Free Press; London: Collier Macmillan Publishers, 1982), 3:315–19.

5. See Christian M. Nebehay, *Ver Sacrum 1898–1903*, 2nd ed (Vienna: Edition Tusch, 1981).

6. For Olbrich and Wright, and Moser's Egyptian mural at the Secession Building, see Alofsin, *Frank Lloyd Wright*, 35–41, 56–60, 104–7.

7. See Peter Noever, ed., *Der Preis der Schönheit: 100 Jahre Wiener Werkstätte*, exhibition catalogue (Ostfildern, Germany: Hatje Cantz, 2003); Werner J. Schweiger, *Wiener Werkstätte—Design in Vienna 1903–1932* (New York: Abeville Press, 1984); also, Michael Huey, ed., *Viennese Silver: Modern Design 1780–1918*, exhibition catalogue (Ostfildern-Ruit, Germany: Hatje Cantz Verlag, 2003).

8. For the Czech *Secese*, see Rostislav Švácha, *Architecture of New Prague 1895–1945* (Cambridge, MA: MIT Press, 1995), 46–62.

9. Variants of the "International Style" of art nouveau appeared in all parts of the empire. For

the situation in Slovenia, see Jelka Pirkovič-Kocbek and Breda Mihelič, *Secesijska arhitektura v Sloveniji* (Ljubljana, Slovenia: Ministrstvo za kulturo, Uprava Republike Slovenije za kulturno dediščino, 1997). For the situation in Croatia, see Damir Barbarić, *Fin de siècle Zagreb-Beč* (Zagreb, Croatia: Školska knjiga, 1997). See also Aleksander Laslo, "Lica moderniteta 1898–1918: Zagrebačka arhitektura secesijske epohe" [Faces of Modernity 1898–1918: Zagreb Architecture in the Age of Secession], in *Secesija u Hrvatskoj* [Art Nouveau in Croatia], exhibition catalogue, Muzej za umjetnost i obrt, Zagreb, 2003/2004, 22–41 and 228–51; and for the exhibition see http://www.muo.hr/secesija/html/2.htm; for the situation in Galicia, see *Lemberg/L'viv 1772–1918*, exhibition catalogue (Vienna: Eigenverlag der Museen der Stadt Wien, 1983). Igor Zhuk's ongoing and comprehensive studies of L'viv/Lemberg have contributed to our knowledge of art nouveau in the region.

10. Vidor (1867–1952) studied at technical universities in Budapest, Munich, and Berlin, and worked in the office of Miklós Ybl and later in the Budapest office of Oskar Marmorek. His house for Béla Bedö (1902–3) showed an influence of the French art nouveau and the Jugendstil in its wrought iron, stained glass, and furniture.

11. In their "Arkad-Bázar" toy store of Késmárky and Illés, Budapest (1909–10), the Vágó brothers used round brads signifying attachment of the veneer to the taut surface of the façade, similar to Wagner's façade of the Postsparkasse in Vienna. The floors and planters at the summer premises of the "Lipótváros" casino in the Leopold District of Budapest (1911) showed Hoffmann's signature square within a square, but the wall and ceiling treatments included folk floral motifs. József Vágó's design of the sumptuous Villa Grünwald (1914–16) was a Gesamtkunstwerk paralleling Hoffmann's Palais Stoclet in Brussels.

12. *OW*, 1:134–35, 215–20. For interiors of Wagner's railway pavilions, see Paul Asenbaum et al., *Otto Wagner: Möbel und Innenräume* (Salzburg: Residenz Verlag, 1984), 153–59.

13. Graf, *Master Drawings of Otto Wagner*, p. 45, fig. 14; and Masaaki Sekiya and Otto Antonia Graf, introduction to *Otto Wagner*, vol. 2 (Tokyo: Bunkensha, 1998), 67.

14. See *Allgemeine Bauzeitung* [65] (1900), p. 33, plates 10–12, figs. 488–89; cited in *OW* 1:324; see *OW* 1:324–25; and Friedrich Achleitner, *Österreichische Architektur im 20. Jahrhundert*, vol. 3, pt. 1, *Wien* (Salzburg: Residenz Verlag, 1900), 191–92. The builder was the Union Baugesellschaft.

15. See *OW* 1:102–7.

16. As seen in his drawings, the architect thought of the three buildings as one complex and designed their plans simultaneously with immense ingenuity. See *OW* 1:323, figs. 49, 89–91.

17. See: *OW* 1:322, fig. 487, no. 90.

18. Sekiya and Graf, *Otto Wagner*, 2:244.

19. For the involvement of Wagner's collaborators and students with the design, see Damjan Prelovšek, *Jože Plečnik, 1872–1957* (New Haven, CT: Yale University Press, 1997), 16. Jože Plečnik, working in Wagner's atelier, planned the corner entry at no. 38 Wienzeile.

20. See M (1998), 142.

21. Prelovšek, *Jože Plečnik*, 55.

22. Sekiya, *Otto Wagner*, 2:148–55, 244–45.

23. M (1998), 112–17. For a brief biography of Ohmann, see Christopher Long, s.v. "Ohmann, Friedrich," in Jane Shoaf Turner, ed., *The Dictionary of Art* (London: Macmillan Press, 1996).

24. For dates, see Johann Georg Gsteu, Otto Kapfinger, Ernst Mateovics, Wilfried Richter, and Dietmar Steiner, eds., *Architecture in Vienna*, 2nd ed. (Vienna: Georg Prachner Verlag, 1992), 75.

25. See Franco Borsi and Ezio Godoli, *Vienna 1900: Architecture and Design* (New York: Rizzoli, 1986), 237, 239. Laske, with Viktor Fiala, was involved with construction and possibly the design of the Tuchlaubenhof (1909–10/1912) in the First District of Vienna, a commercial project that included architects Ernst Spielman and Alfred Teller. By this time, the building surface had simple textured striations, and bands of windows with recessed and figural representation were totally absent. See ibid., 296–97; and Achleitner, *Österreichische Architektur im 20. Jahrhundert. Ein Führer in vier Bänden*, vol. 3, pt. 1, pp. 54–55. According to Achleitner, Laske left architecture to become a painter.

26. For Schönthal and his partners, see Iain Boyd Whyte, *Emil Hoppe, Marcel Kammerer, Otto Schönthal: Three Architects from the Master Class of Otto Wagner* (Cambridge, MA: MIT Press, 1989), 36–38.

27. *OW* 1:400–420; Asenbaum et al., *Otto Wagner*, 240–51. While this book was in production, a highly informative and stimulating essay appeared on the psychiatric hospital: Leslie Topp, "Otto Wagner and the Steinhof Psychiatric Hospital: Architecture as Misunderstanding," *Art Bulletin* 87, no. 1 (March 2005): 130–56. In a probing and thorough study, Topp looks at the "extra-architectural context" of the commission, particularly asylum reform. Her use of the words

linguistic metaphor in her conclusion reinforces my general approach, while she argues that Wagner only partially understood the goals of contemporary asylum planners and designed "am Steinhof" as a utopian environment apart from the city and "normal" people, whereas planners sought to integrate the mentally ill more closely into the "sane" world. Topp asserts that the ensemble emerged "from the interaction of two groups that, to use a linguistic metaphor, spoke two different but overlapping languages about their shared project" (ibid., 150). For Topp, architects' efforts to interpret clients' needs is perpetually problematic, so that she focuses on "'architecture' as a foreign language rather than as an accurate translation" (ibid., 151).

28. For the site plan, see Sekiya, *Otto Wagner*, 3:52, 58, 66–67. The client was the Lower Austrian Provincial Institutions for the Care and Cure of the Mentally and Nervously Ill "am Steinhof." The complex was the "largest mental hospital on the continent" (Topp, "Otto Wagner and the Steinhof Psychiatric Hospital," 131).

29. Quoted in Roberto Schezen and Peter Haiko, *Vienna 1850–1930, Architecture* (New York: Rizzoli, 1992), 148.

30. See M (1998), 162–67 for an overview of St. Leopold's Church.

31. Moser's composition includes a seated male figure with a halo of stars who extends an encompassing cloak. He is flanked by two frontal stylized angels; beside them are a kneeling nude male and a female in an attitude of prayer.

32. For Saint Leopold, see http://www.catholic-forum.com/saints/saintl20.htm; for Saint Severinus of Nordicum, see http://www.catholic-forum.com/saints/saints54.htm.

33. Stained-glass windows at the side of the baldachin, entitled with the theme of *The Fountain of Life*, were also by Koloman Moser; see Sekiya, *Otto Wagner*, 3:232.

34. Ibid., 3:112–13.

35. Compare the drawings in *OW* 1:402 (figs. 588, 106, 5) and 408 (figs. 594, 106, 17).

36. Sekiya, *Otto Wagner*, 3:102–4.

37. Ibid., 3:106–7.

38. Asenbaum et al., *Otto Wagner*, 244, 242.

39. See *Erläuterungen zur Bauvollendung der Kirche der Nieder Öst. Landes Heil- und Pflege Anstalten* (1907; Reprint: Vienna: Architektur- und Baufachverlag Gesselschaft m.b.H., 1983), n.p.

40. See M (1990), 166; Schezen and Haiko, *Vienna 1850–1930, Architecture*, 148; and Graf, *Master Drawings of Otto Wagner*, 7–9.

41. Joseph Rykwert, "Moist and Dry," in Huey, *Viennese Silver*, 370.

CHAPTER THREE

1. *Encyclopaedia Britannica*, 2003 CD-ROM version, s.v. "rationalism."

2. For the biography and catalogue of works, see Marco Pozzetto, *Max Fabiani* (Trieste: MGS Press, 1998). Earlier studies include Pozzetto's *Max Fabiani Architetto* (Gorizia, Italy: Commune de Gorizia, 1966), and his *La Scuola di Wagner, 1894–1912*, exhibition catalogue (Trieste: Commune di Trieste, 1979). For Fabiani's buildings in Vienna, see *Max Fabiani 1865–1962, Bauten und Projekte in Wien*, exhibition catalogue (Vienna: Architektur und Baufach Verlag, 1982).

3. Pozzetto, *Max Fabiani*, 128–31.

4. Moravánszky describes the façade as a woven pattern with lightness similar to a Venetian façade: M (1998), 155–56.

5. Ludwig Hevesi, "Portois & Fix," in *Kunst und Kunstwerk* 4 (1901): 321–22; quoted and cited in Pozzetto, *Max Fabiani*, 130–31.

6. The building was constructed for Berndt & Freytag, sellers of stamps and books, and Artaria, a firm of art dealers.

7. M (1998), 156.

8. Pozzetto, *Max Fabiani*, 114, 128–32, 139–43, 212–14.

9. *Macmillan Encyclopedia of Architects*, s.v. "Fabiani, Max," by Sokratis Dimitriou, 37.

10. Pozzetto, *Max Fabiani*, 22.

11. For the definitive monograph, see Eduard Sekler, *Josef Hoffmann: The Architectural Work*, trans. John Maas (Princeton, NJ: Princeton University Press, 1985); also *Macmillan Encyclopedia*, s.v. "Hoffmann, Josef," by Sekler.

12. See chap. 7, "A Lesson in Primary Forms," in Alofsin, *Frank Lloyd Wright*, 153–220; and Alofsin, "The Kunsthistorisches Museum: A Treasure House for the Secessionists," in *Jahrbuch der Kunsthistorischen Sammlungen in Wien* 88 (1992): 189–203. See also *OW* vol. 3, "Die Einheit der Kunst."

13. Sekler, *Macmillan Encyclopedia*, s.v. "Hoffmann, Josef," 399.

14. Ibid., 401.

15. For an introduction to Kotěra's work, see Vladimir Šlapeta, ed., *Jan Kotěra 1871–1923: The Founder of Modern Czech Architecture* (Prague: Municipal House and Kant, 2001); and Švácha, *Architecture of New Prague 1895–1945*, 46–54, 65–74, 462–63. See also M (1998), 204–6; and Marco Pozzetto, *Die Schule Otto Wagners 1894–1912* (Vienna: Verlag Anton Schroll, 1980), 234; and Marie Benešová, *Česká architektura v proměnách dvou století 1780–1980* (Prague: Státní pedagogické nakladatelství, 1984), 258. Earlier studies include Zdeněk Wirth and Antonin Matějček,

Česká Arhitektura 1800–1920 (Prague: Jan Štenc, 1922); and Otakar Novotný, *Jan Kotěra a jeho doba* (Prague: Státni Naklad. Krásné Literatury, Hudby a Umění, 1958).

16. M (1988), 218; Novotný, *Jan Kotěra a jeho doba*, 21.

17. Kotěra's return to Prague coincided with Ohmann's use of organicism. However, Kotěra represented a new parallel development of organicism within the Czech Secese. Kotěra was instrumental in bringing the teachings of Otto Wagner to Prague, and through his mediation the Czechs started applying Wagnerian vocabulary such as curvilinear wrought-iron elements, flat surfaces, and the iconography that mythologizes life, rebirth, and nature. His Mánes Pavilion (1902) for the local artists' association combined influences of Olbrich's Secession, contemporary English architecture, and the vernacular. On the other hand, Friedrich Ohmann blended influences of French art nouveau with reinterpretations of the local Renaissance and baroque heritage. These different strains of the Secese produced an architecture which was at the same time recognizable and complex in its many layers; see Švácha, *Architecture of New Prague 1895–1945*, 46–62.

18. For the extended list of Kotěra's students, see Novotný, *Jan Kotěra a jeho doba*, 141.

19. See Šlapeta, ed., *Jan Kotěra 1871–1923*, 107, 116.

20. For a concise history of the city, see http://www.hradecKrálové.cz/gbr/history–eng.htm.

21. Šlapeta, ed., *Jan Kotěra 1871–1923*, 181.

22. František Ulrich was associated with the Czech nationalist Lumír group of poets; see Rostislav Švácha, "Poznámky ke Kotěrovu muzeu" [Notes on Kotěra's Museum], *Umění* 34 (1986): 171.

23. Ibid., 171–79. My thanks to Matthew S. Witkovsky for his assessment of Švácha's article.

24. Švácha, *Architecture of New Prague 1895–1945*, 462–63. According to Švácha, this expression, with roots in the search for architectural truth found in Otto Wagner and John Ruskin, is a moralistic tendency of the advanced modern movement, and implicitly a testament to modern progress. Reinforcing this premise of modernism is the idea that modern architecture is defined by the evolution of new kinds of space (ibid., 74). Šlapeta has also suggested that during his visit to America for the installation of the pavilion he designed for World Exhibition in St. Louis in 1904, Kotěra became familiar with Frank Lloyd Wright's early work, and that the Town Museum showed Wright's "dynamic conception of space" (see Vladímir Šlapeta, s.v. "Kotěra," *Macmillan Encyclopedia* 2:579). Czech architects were aware of Wright's work as early as 1900, but Wright had built nothing in St. Louis itself, and Kotěra would have had to have seen his work elsewhere. But more to the point is the spatial experience of the City Museum dynamic in Wright's organic sense. Like Wright's Unity Temple of 1906, the museum has an expressive mass that shelters its interior spaces. The principal spatial drama occurs in the verticality of the recital hall, double-height top-floor gallery, and inner dome. In each case, space is verticality defined and contained by the walls surrounding it. In Unity Temple, the vertical spaces of the center, from the skylights to the ground floor, interconnect with the horizontal spaces of the seating areas, and Wright's dynamism is reinforced by an interconnected lattice of rectilinear lines connecting all surfaces. The total effect created the dynamism of the building, an experience Wright described as continuity and plasticity. While spatially dramatic, Kotěra's City Museum contains no such dynamic Wrightian space. Its impact comes from its integration of space and function, and its iconographic messages.

25. Rostislav Švácha, "The Culminating Years," in Šlapeta, ed., *Jan Kotěra 1871–1923*, 183.

26. Zdeněk Wirth, "Okresní dům v Hradci Králové," *Volné směry* 27, nos. 11–12 (1929): 252–68, 306.

27. For the site plan, see Novotný, *Jan Kotěra a jeho doba*, fig. 182.

28. The wings are not aligned, so that inside, a shift of movement would occur in the entry zone. The elevation reflects the tripartite organization; the wings are undefined, but the center entry has an arched portal, windows above, and a projecting central tower. The same sheet of sketches also contains a small perspective showing a curved gable; see a plan dated ca.1905–6 in Kotěra Collection, NTM (National Technical Museum), Prague.

29. By the time of the completion of a fully developed perspective in 1907, the use of a language of organicism for this early design phase is clear: vegetal curving forms define surface areas on the wings that appeared too blank. An apse with its masonry base and pierced windows on the short wing recalls the neo-Romanesque buildings of H. H. Richardson, which found their parallels in German and Scandinavian architecture. The center becomes an inward curve with scalloped edges at its tops, and curving tendrils and floral motifs on its surface. The tower has a dome supported by columns, with curvilinear forms filling the spaces

between the columns. For the perspective, see Novotný, *Jan Kotěra a jeho doba*, fig. 181.

30. Švácha ("The Culminating Years," 181) traces the evolution of formal ideas in the building to his early work. Noting that the apselike forms of the museum recall ecclesiastical architecture, he identifies it as a transformation into a temple to industry. While the forms have an industrial quality, though totally different from the *Industriekultur* that was evolving in Germany, the building also served to preserve memory of the past, of the pre-industrial history of the city.

31. Šlapeta, ed., *Jan Kotěra 1871–1923*, 263–64. In addition to Stanislav Sucharda, sculptor Jaroslave Horejc and painter Jan Preisler contributed to the building's iconography. See Švácha, "The Culminating Years," 181.

32. The distancing from the Viennese models comes from the fact that this is a City Museum whose central purpose is to preserve Czech memory and reinforce Czech identity.

33. See photograph identified by dimensions in Kotěra Collection, NTM, Prague, 18 × 23 cm.

34. Švácha, "The Culminating Years," 171.

35. Otto Wagner, *Einige Skizzen* 3 (September 1904), reprinted in *OW* 2:432–34.

36. Otto Wagner, "Erläuterungen zur Bauvollendung des k. k. Postsparkassen-Amtsgebäudes in Wien," *Jahrbuch der Gesellschaft österreichischer Architekten* (1907): 9–13, reprinted in *OW* 2:434–36.

37. Compare fig. 628 with fig. 629 in *OW* 2:439.

38. M (1998), 157.

39. See Kenneth Frampton, *Modern Architecture: A Critical History* (London: Thames and Hudson, Ltd., 1985), 83; also the introduction by Iain Boyd Whyte in *Otto Wagner: Vienna 1841–1918, Designs for Architecture*, exhibition catalogue (Oxford: Museum of Modern Art Oxford, 1985), n.p.

40. On Wagner's rosettes, see Emil Pichran, *Otto Wagner* (Vienna: Bergland Verlag, 1956), 19; quoted in M (1998), 157.

41. See Otto Wagner, *Modern Architecture: A Guidebook for His Students to This Field of Art*, introduction and translation by Harry Francis Mallgrave (Santa Monica, CA: The Getty Center for the History of Art and the Humanities, 1988), 94. Wagner's book appeared in four editions from 1896 to 1914; the Mallgrave translation is the edition of 1902.

42. *OW* 2:457–88.

43. Graf, *Master Drawings of Otto Wagner*, 9.

44. Wagner, *Modern Architecture*, 65.

45. For an example of the department store in Vienna designed under the influence of the Wagnerschule, see the project of the twenty-three-year-old Czech Johan (Jan) Chladek (1890–?), published in *Wiener Bauindustrie Zeitung* 35 (June 1914): 213.

46. Joseph A. Lux, "Das Hotel, ein Bauprobleme," *Der Architekt* 15 (1909): 17–20, reprinted in Marco Pozzetto, *Die Schule Otto Wagners* (Vienna: Schroll, 1980), 201–5, and quoted in Boyd Whyte, *Emil Hoppe, Marcel Kammerer, Otto Schönthal*, 48–49n44. For Lux (1871–1947), a much neglected but important early modernist historiographer and significant figure in *Heimatstil* developments, see Mark Jarzombek, "Joseph August Lux: Werkbund Promoter, Historian of a Lost Modernity," *JSAH* 63, no. 2 (June 2004): 202–19.

47. For the hotels of five Wagner students in 1907–08, see Pozzetto, *Die Schule Wagners 1894–1902*, figs. 223–232; and for 1912, see ibid., figs. 258–264. All were in the rational mode. For Wagner's own project for "Hotel Wien" on Kolwrat [Schubert] Ring, Vienna, 1907, see *Das ungebaute Wien: Projekte für die Metropole 1800 bis 2000*, exhibition catalogue (Vienna: Historisches Museum der Stadt Wien [1999]), 236–37.

48. For Schindler as a Wagner student, see David Gebhard, ed., *The Architectural Drawings of R. M. Schindler* (New York: Garland Publishing, 1994), no. 1378; and August Sarnitz, *R. M. Schindler, Architekt, 1887–1953* (Vienna: Edition Christian Brandstätter, 1986), 13–15.

49. Among the most successful was the trio of Emil Hoppe, Otto Schönthal, and Marcel Kammerer. Kammerer (1878–1969) worked as Wagner's assistant on his three major projects: the unbuilt Kaiser Franz Josef-City-Museum, the Postal Savings Bank, and St. Leopold's Church at Steinhof. The men's own work gained public attention, and in later 1909 Schönthal became editor of *Der Architekt*, a leading international architectural journal of the period. The trio started their own practice in 1910 on the basis of reconciling Viennese tradition with Wagner's architectural modernism. See Boyd Whyte, *Emil Hoppe, Marcel Kammerer, Otto Schönthal*, 8, 68; for biographical entries, see Pozzetto, *Die Schule Otto Wagners 1894–1902*, 228 on Emil Hoppe; 231 on Marcel Kammer; 247 on Otto Schönthal. World War I was disastrous for their practice; Kammerer left the firm in 1918, and eventually became a painter. His paintings appealed to the Nazis, and his involvement and support of them led to his exile from Austria. Hoppe and Schönthal continued after the war, contributing to city housing projects. See Boyd Whyte, *Emil Hoppe, Marcel Kammerer, Otto Schönthal*, 9, 86.

50. Boyd Whyte, *Emil Hoppe, Marcel Kammerer, Otto Schönthal*, 48.

51. For a short biography of Josef Hannich, see Pozzetto, *Die Schule Otto Wagners 1894–1902*, 226.

52. Novotný studied with Kotěra and at the Prague School of Applied Art, 1900–3, where he became a professor and taught 1929–53. He designed not only buildings inside and outside Prague, but also furniture. See Švácha, *Architecture of New Prague 1895–1945*, 466–67.

53. Ibid., 77.

54. Several exhibitions presented the phenomenon of Czech cubism to Europe: in 1966 in Paris, in 1969 in Prague, in 1984 in Japan, and in 1991/92 a traveling exhibition around Europe; see Alexander von Vegesack, ed., *Czech Cubism: Architecture, Furniture, and Decorative Arts 1910–1925*, exhibition catalogue (Princeton, NJ: Princeton Architectural Press, 1992), 7.

55. Janák (1882–1956) belonged to the Mánes Artists' Association and the avant-garde cubist Group of Visual Artists, 1911–14. He designed furniture, buildings, and ultimately town plans. For Janák, see Marie Benešová, *Pavel Janák* (Prague: NČVU, 1959); Olga Herbenová and Vladimír Šlapeta, *Pavel Janák 1882–1956: Architecktur und Kunstgwerbe*, exhibition catalogue (Vienna: Semper-Depot, 1984); Švácha, *Architecture of New Prague 1895–1945*, 461; and M (1998), 338–41.

56. For Gočár, see Marie Benešová, *Josef Gočár* (Prague: NČSVU, 1958). Gočár (1880–1945) was a member of the cubist Group of Visual Artists, 1911–14. He later became a professor at the Prague Academy of Fine Arts, 1924–45; chairman of the Mánes Artists' Association in the 1930s; and picture editor of *Styl*. He designed widely, and his buildings in Hradec Králové made his work a leading example of modern architecture in the 1920s; Švácha, *Architecture of New Prague 1895–1945*, 457–58.

57. Švácha, *Architecture of New Prague 1895–1945*, 108–13.

58. For Chochol (1880–1956), see *Allgemeines Künstlerlexikon* and www.archinform.net/arch s.v. (*Grove Dictionary of Art*, synopsized in www.artnet.com/library, s.v. "Chochol, Josef"). See also Švácha, *Architecture of New Prague 1895–1945*, 114–19, 455.

59. After 1914, Chochol gravitated toward the Czech version of purism, the aesthetic call to order using simple geometric shapes and primary colors first advocated by Charles-Eduard Jeanneret (later called Le Corbusier) and Amadée Ozenfant and allied with functionalism. He also became a member (1923–30) of Devětsil, an avant-garde group of artists, architects, and writers around Karel Teige. After 1926, he worked in the mode of Soviet constructivism. See Švácha, *Architecture of New Prague 1895–1945*, 455.

60. Pavel Janák, "Otto Wagner," *Styl* 1 (1908–9): 41–48; quoted in von Vegesack, ed., *Czech Cubism*, 35.

61. Pavel Janák, "From Modern Architecture to Architecture," *Styl* 2 (July 1910): 105–9; cited in von Vegasack, ed., *Czech Cubism*, 37 and 37n18.

62. Guillaume Apollinaire, *Les Peintres cubistes* (1913); quoted in Milena Lamarová, "Texts and Contexts, 1910–1914," in von Vegesack, ed., *Czech Cubism*, 12.

63. For some historic views of the interior and the building's contemporary use as a city museum, see Pavel Mertlík, *Wenkův Dům* (Jaroměř, Czech Republic: Vydalo městké muzeum v Jaroměří v roce, 1990). The building remained a department store until the start of World War II. From 1947 it became the city museum and was reconstructed and restored from 1985 to 1987.

64. See foreword by Helena Koenigsmarková in von Vegesack, ed., *Czech Cubism*, 7.

65. For Rondo-cubism, see the discussion of the Czechoslovak Legiobank, Prague (1921–23), in chapter 5 of the present text; and Nicholas Sawicki, "Writing the History of the 'Czechoslovak Official Modern': Karel Teige as Historian of the 'Cubist' Generation," *Centropa* 5, no. 1 (January 2005): 4–15. Marie Benešová originated the term *Rondo-cubism*, or a "rounded style," in her article "Rondokubismus," *Architektura ČSSR* 28 (1969): 303–17. Rondo-cubism preserved the plasticity of the prewar cubism, but introduced round and undulating shapes as a link to ancient Slav mythology; it also emphasized the national colors, red and blue. See Vegesack, ed., *Czech Cubism*, 73.

66. For correctives, see Christopher Long, "Adolf Loos's 'Trotzdem,'" *Harvard Design Magazine* 16 (Winter–Spring 2002): 64–66; and James Trilling, *Ornament: A Modern Perspective* (Seattle: University of Washington Press, 2003).

67. "Ornament and Crime" originally was only a lecture first delivered in 1910; it appeared in French in 1913 and finally in German in 1929. Because of its late and limited distribution, its impact may be more retrospective than contemporary with early developments of the modern movement in the 1920s; see Long, "Adolf Loos's 'Trotzdem,'" 64.

68. For the brief entry on the bank in the catalogue of Loos's work, see Burkhardt Rukschcio and Roland Schachel, *Adolf Loos: Leben und Werk* (Salzburg: Residenz Verlag, 1982), 509–10. The stonework was executed by Johan Cingroš from Pilsen, where he also did the stonework for Loos's Vogl residence. In 1973, the original space was

enlarged. In a sketch of the portal, Loos included a double eagle, symbol of the empire.

69. "Das Bankhaus Musz Sagen / Hier ist Dein Geld / Bei Ehrlichen Leuten / Fest und Gut Verwahrt."

70. See Damir Barbarić and Michael Benedikt, eds., *Ambivalenz des Fin de siècle: Wien-Zagreb* (Vienna: Böhlau, 1998), especially the chapters by Tonko Maroević, "Jugendstil, Sezession und Expressionismus. Der Nachklang in Zagreb," 261–66; and Olga Maruševski, "Architektonisch-urbanistische Verbindungen zwischen Zagreb und Wien um der Jahrhundertwende," 199–229.

71. My thanks to Aleksander Laslo for introducing me to this building and for his excellent documentation. See Laslo, "Lica moderniteta 1898–1918," 22–41 and 228–51; and his "Croatian Contributions, Preliminary Report" (unpublished manuscript, Zagreb, 1994). Now a hospital for children, the building's interior was completely altered and the exterior renovated in the 1950s.

72. Zsigmond Szikla (1864– ?) received his diploma from the Technical University in Budapest and designed a cinema in 1896 before receiving his commission for the department store, which is now called Divatcsárnok. (Source: János Gerle, "Biographies of Hungarian Architects," unpublished manuscript, 1996). Construction drawings are located in the Architectural Archives of the Budapest Town Council.

73. Árpád Gut (1877–1948) received his diploma in 1901 from the Technical University in Budapest and opened an office with Jenő Gergely. In 1921, Gut moved to Palestine, where he innovated the use of reinforced concrete in numerous engineering projects. See Gerle, "Biographies of Hungarian Architects," and Dávid Giladi, *Pesti Mérnökök—Izrael országépítői* [Architects of Pest—The Builders of Israel] (Budapest: Múlt és jövő, 1992).

CHAPTER FOUR

1. For the perspective of Austrian cultural identity at the turn of the twentieth century from the viewpoint of leading art critic Joseph A. Lux, see Jarzombek, "Joseph August Lux."

2. For overviews on the history of Hungarian architecture, see Dora Wiebenson and József Sisa, eds., *The Architecture of Historic Hungary* (Cambridge, MA: MIT Press, 1998), and in particular József Sisa, "Hungarian Architecture from 1849 to 1900," in ibid., 203–6. For a synopsis of Hungarian historicism, see Ilona Sármány, *Historizaló építészet az Osztrák-Magyar Monarchiában* (Budapest: Corvina, 1990).

3. M (1998), 218–22.

4. *Encyclopaedia Britannica* 2003, CD-ROM version, s.v. "Pan-Turanianism," s.v. "Turan."

5. See András Gerő, *Heroes' Square, Budapest: Hungary's History in Stone and Bronze* (Budapest: Corvina, 1990): 6, 13, 34–38.

6. Jenö Lechner, preface to *Jenö Lechner* (Geneva: Masters of Architecture, Ltd., 1930): xxvii–xlii. The author changed his name to Kismarty-Lechner in 1942.

7. See also figs. 235–36: Edit Fél, Tamás Hofer, and Klára K. Csilléry, *Hungarian Peasant Art* (London: Constable, 1971).

8. Welting could be used around garment openings to reinforce edges and became the equivalent of the embroidered edge. Piping was also an edge treatment for cloth and could thereby incorporate a different material into the folds at an edge. In addition, piping recalled the sinuous lines of pastry icing, thus pastry piping. Braiding comes from forming three or more strands into a cord or ribbon by crossing left and right, or by placing diagonally a woven and a crisscross pattern against each other.

9. For a discussion of the use of ethnographic sources in the creation of the national style in Hungarian architecture, see M (1998), 217–25; for Lechner's early career, see Ákos Moravánszky, "Nationale Bestrebungen in der ungarischen Architektur der Jahrhundertwende" [Hungarian National Architectural Efforts at the Beginning of the Twentieth Century], *Österreichische Zeitschrift für Kunst und Denkmalpflege* 33, nos. 1–2 (1979): 52–60. For an overview, see János Gerle, "Hungarian Architecture from 1900 to 1918," in Wiebenson and Sisa, *The Architecture of Historic Hungary*, 222–43.

10. For a brief biography and visual review of Lechner's work, see János Gerle, Attila Kovács, and Imre Makovecz, *A századforduló magyar építészete* [Hungarian Architecture at the Turn of the Century] (Budapest: Szépirodalmi Könyvkiadó-Bonex, 1990), 117–27; and M (1998), 217–41.

11. M (1998), 224; Moravánszky, "Nationale Bestrebungen," 52.

12. For detailed information on the history of the Zsolnay factory, see Éva Csenkey and Ágota Steinert, eds., *Hungarian Ceramics from the Zsolnay Manufactory, 1853–2001* (New York: The Bard Graduate Center for Studies in the Decorative Arts, Design, and Culture; New Haven, CT: Yale University Press, 2002).

13. Edmund [sic] Lechner, "Mein Lebens- und Werdegang," *Bildende Künstler* 12 (1911), 568; quoted in M (1998), 225.

14. Ödön Lechner, "A Magyar építőstílusról"

[On the Hungarian Architectural Style], text of an address published in the Hungarian daily newspaper *Magyar Nemzet*, June 29, 1902; quoted in János Gerle, "The Golden Age of Architectural Ceramics in Hungary," in Csenkey and Steinert, *Hungarian Ceramics from the Zsolnay Manufactory*, 191.

15. Ödön Lechner, "Magyar formanyelv nem volt, hanem lesz," *Művészet*, no. 1 (1906): 1–18. I have also consulted R. Klein, "Architecture and Identity." Klein's study contains the most extensive bilingual treatment of Hungarian architectural treatises, and I appreciate his generosity in sharing this material with me.

16. Ibid.

17. For a history of the museum, see Márta Nemes, *Museum of Applied Arts: History of the Building* (Budapest: Museum of Applied Arts, 1988).

18. János Gerle, *The Turn of the Century*, Our Budapest series (Budapest: Town Hall, 1992), 14.

19. See, for instance, Hungarian Ethnographical Museum, *Hungarian Decorative Folk Art* (Budapest: Corvina, 1954); Károly Gink and Ivor Sándor Kiss, *Folk Art and Folk Artists in Hungary* (Budapest: Corvina Press, 1968); and Fél, Hofer, and Csilléry, *Hungarian Peasant Art*.

20. M (1998), 225.

21. See the sectional drawing dated 1891 in László Pusztai and András Hadik, *Ödön Lechner 1845–1914*, exhibition catalogue (Budapest: Hungarian Museum of Architecture, 1991), 23.

22. Numerous examples of the Persian trefoil as surface pattern as well as detail of Indian ornament could be seen in Owen Jones's *The Grammar of Ornament* (1856). Plate 45, which Jones took from Persian manuscripts in the British Museum, shows in example no. 2 a running series of the patterns with flowers on stems inserted within the trefoil. There are also inverted plants between each trefoil. Jones's plate 46, examples no. 17 and no. 23, also from the British Museum, contains patterns of lobed shapes analogous to the arches Lechner used at the Museum of Applied Arts. Plate 46 also shows a band composed of two motifs, one convex at top and bottom and the other composed of an outline of curves with interlacing. The latter motif appears symmetrical but is not; it moves smoothly in and out as if made of two *cyma recta* profiles, while the bottom is cusped. This asymmetrically curving motif is similar to that of the *opaion* Lechner designed for the museum entry.

Following Jones's Persian plates are his nine plates of Indian ornament. These contain a wealth of floral patterns, some semirealistic, others abstracted. Plate 53 in particular is red-green with white and blue accents, the reproduction of a book cover. It uses lobed arches to structure the composition and allow a visual resonance between figure and ground.

23. See Moresque plate 42, no. 4, top, in Jones, *The Grammar of Ornament*.

24. See, for example, the remains of the Great Solanki temple from the twelfth century, the portico of Siddharpur Rudramala, and a *torana* (a ceremonial portal) of Vadnagar. Bulbous domes with semi-ogee versions of the cusped arch were principal elements of the Muslim Deccani kingdoms. Columns could have volutes, lotuses, or *muqarna*-capitals with foliate or bell-shaped bases and cannellated, balusterlike shafts, the latter taken from reed bundles. Column treatments at the Red Fort of Shahjahanabad, at Delhi, provided excellent models. The Lahore Gate had cusped arches supported by paired columns, and the *diwan-i-am* (court for public audiences) had semi-ogee arches on columns with collonettes around a central support. See Christopher Tadgell, *The History of Architecture in India: From the Dawn of the Civilization to the End of the Raj* (London: Phaidon Press, 1990), 109–12.

25. Márta Nemes, *Lechner Ödön Földtani Intézete Budapesten* [The Building of the Hungarian Geological Institute by Ödön Lechner] (Budapest: Lechner Ödön Foundation and the Hungarian Geological Survey, 1993), 5.

26. Nemes, *Lechner Ödön Földtani Intézete Budapesten*, 7.

27. Ibid.

28. Ibid.

29. For detail of the building, see M (1998), 231, fig. 6.10.

30. These sources would have included P. U. Botta and E. Flandin, *Monuments de Ninive*, 5 vols. (Paris, 1849–50); M. Dieulafoy, *L'Art antique de la Perse*, 5 vols. (Paris, 1884–1889); James Fergusson, *The Palaces of Nineveh and Persepolis Restored* (London 1851); A. H. Layard, *Monuments of Nineveh*, 2 vols. (London 1849) and *Nineveh and Its Palaces*, 2 vols. (London 1849); and G. Perrot and C. Chipiez, *History of Art in the Chaldea and Assyria, Persia, Phrygia and Judaea*, 5 vols. (London, 1884–92).

31. For a brief history of Austrian postal services, see http://www.post.at/english/content/unternehmen/geschichte/unternehmen_geschichte.html

32. János Gerle, *Palaces of Money* (Budapest: City Hall, 1994), 21.

33. M (1998), 230.

34. Ödön Gerö, writing in *Művészet* in 1908; quoted in Gerle, *Palaces of Money*, 25.

35. Columns treated with horned animals often refer to the Persepolis-type column, as found in the double "bull" capital of the Apadana, the great audience hall, executed by Xerxes I (486–465 BCE) at the Palace of Persepolis.

36. Gerle, *Palaces of Money*, 26.

37. Drawing 24744.Hrsz, "Main Elevation," Building Archives of the Town Council of Budapest.

38. Gerle, *Palaces of Money*, 25.

39. Gerle, *A századforduló magyar építészete*, 121.

40. Gerle, *Palaces of Money*, 24.

41. Lechner's nephew, Jenö, writing as an architect in 1930, claimed that the Lechnerian national style was regarded with abhorrence by both the official authorities and the conservative art establishment, which privileged western European art over homegrown Hungarian motifs. Lechner, *Jenö Lechner*, xxxiv.

42. Lajos Fülep, "Hungarian Architecture," *Nyugat*, April 16, 1918; quoted in Nemes, *Museum of Applied Arts*, n.p.

43. Károly Kós (1883–1977) was born in Temesvár (now Timisoara, Romania). An architect, book publisher, editor, and politician, he documented villages, farm buildings, towers, and grave markers throughout Transylvania and published his studies in hand-illustrated books, such as *Erdélyország népének építése* [Transylvanian Folk Architecture] in 1907 (facsimile ed., Budapest: Balassi Könyvkiadó; Kolozsvár: Polis Könyvkiadó, 1996). Kós studied engineering and architecture, receiving a diploma from the Technical University in Budapest in 1907. He began his first architectural surveying study tour to Kalotaszeg (Transylvania) in the summer of 1905. Kós collaborated with other members of "The Young Ones," designing pavilions for the Budapest Zoo with Dezső Zrumeczky (1909–12) and a school with Dénes Györgyi (1910–11). Moving in 1919 to a house he had built in 1910 in Sztána (Stana, Romania), Kós stayed in Transylvania after World War I when it was annexed to Romania. He promoted Hungarian cultural and intellectual life, as well as folk spirituality, until his death. See Károly Kós, "Nemzeti mûvészet," *Magyar Iparművészet* (1910): 141–57; translated with annotations in Rudolf Klein, "Architecture and Identity: A Short Survey of Hungarian 20th Century Architectural Theory" (unpublished manuscript), 15–33; and Anthony Gall, *Kós Károly műhelye, tanulmány és adattár* [The Workshop of Károly Kós, Study and Documentation] (Budapest : Mundus Magyar Egyetemi, 2002). For Károly Kós, see Anthony Gall, "Károly Kós (1883–1977)," in Burman, *Architecture 1900*, 156–60; Anthony Gall, "Kós in Budapest and Transylvania," *Domus*, no. 804 (May 1998): 117–24; Moravánszky, "Nationale Bestrebungen," 58; and Anthony Gall, "Domus itinerario n.145: Kós a Budapest e in Transilvania," no. 804, *Domus* (May 1998): [117–24].

44. See Károly Kós, *Erdélyország népenék építése*.

45. Kós designed a double-house at the main square of the Wekerle housing estate on the outskirts of Pest, bringing the familiar image of the country to the newly arrived migrants from the interior. See Gergely Nagy, *Garden Cities in Europe: Wekerle Estate, Budapest* (Budapest: Magyar Kepek, [2000]).

46. Gerle, *Századforduló magyar*, 84.

47. M (1998), 234.

48. The synagogue is also the largest of the Hungarian nationalist synagogues to have survived subsequent wars and postwar destruction, and was the first building in the style in an area that would later become part of Yugoslavia. See Rudolf Klein, "Pávatoll és építőművészet—Szabadka szecessziós épületei európai összefüggésben" [The Art Nouveau of Subotica in European Cultural Context], *Üzenet* 5–6 (Szabadka, Yugoslavia [Serbia], 1991): 411–22; R. Klein, "Sinagoga u Subotici—Uporedna analiza s krščanskim sakralnim objektima" [The Synagogue of Subotica—A Comparative Analysis with Christian Sacred Space], *Čovjek i prostor* 7–8 (Zagreb, Croatia, 1989): 15–17.

49. For a general introduction, see Jan Cavanaugh, *Out Looking In: Early Modern Polish Art, 1890–1918* (Berkeley and Los Angeles: University of California Press, 2000).

50. Witkiewicz had studied at the Academy of Fine Arts in St. Petersburg (1868–71) and the Academy of Fine Arts in Munich (1872–73).

51. See David Crowley, *National Style and Nation-State: Design in Poland from the Vernacular Revival to the International Style* (Manchester: Manchester University Press; New York: St. Martin's Press, 1992). Also, Stanisław Witkiewicz, *Styl zakopiański* [The Zakopane Style], 2 vols. (Lwów, 1904). Other buildings by Witkiewicz include the chapel in the Jaszczurowka district, Villa "Oksza" on Zamojski Street, the building of the Tatra Museum, the chapel of St. John the Baptist in the parish Church of the Holy Family on Krupowki Street, and the Kornilowicz family chapel in the Bystre district. The Zakopane style also found proponents among other outstanding architects, including Jan Witkiewicz-Koszyc (1881–1958), designer of the Villa "Witkiewiczowka" on Antalowka Street in Zakopane and the so-called

"Chaty" (Huts) in the resort town of Naleczow (erected for Polish writer Stefan Zeromski), as well as a number of villas in the towns of Wisla, Konstancin, and Milanowek (the latter two situated near Warsaw). See http://www.culture.pl/en/culture/wy_wy_styl_zakopianski_zakopane.

52. Stanisław Witkiewicz, quoted in ibid.

53. See ibid.

54. See http://www.culture.pl/en/culture/instytucje/muzea/in_mu_zakopane_tatrzanskie.

55. See Géza Hajós, "Heimatstil-Heimatschutzstil," *Österreichische Zeitschrift für Kunst und Denkmalpflege* 43, nos. 3–4 (1989): 156–57. The roots of such efforts are found in the landscape movements of the eighteenth century, when stylized constructions (e.g., *jardins fabriqués*) reflected vernacular tendencies in an effort to aestheticize a rural ideal. These expressions were seen as "bound to nature" in comparison with classical styles.

56. For Heimatstil, see Theodor Brückler, "Zur Geschichte der österreichische Heimatschutzbewegung," *Österreichische Zeitschrift für Kunst und Denkmalpflege* 43, nos.3–4 (1989):145–56; and Herbert Nititsch, "Heimatschutz in Österreich, in *Schönes Österreich: Heimatschutz zwischen Ästhetik und Ideologie*, ed. Österreichisches Museum für Volkskunde (Vienna: Österreichisches Museum für Volkskunde, 1995): 19–29.

57. This Heimatstil was not necessarily seen as atavistic; it was inherently the product of a modern industrial economy, the invention of urban industrial society, and relied on the connotations of traditional native forms—towers, fretwork, bay windows, asymmetry—to reinforce its potential for profit. A style of the upper and middle urban classes, it was urbane in the sense that it connoted a cultural "takeover" of rural regions by the city's elite. See Friedrich Achleitner, "Gibt es einen mitteleuropäischen Heimatstil?" *Österreichische Zeitschrift für Kunst und Denkmalpflege* 43, nos. 3–4 (1989): 166. The projects of Oskar Marmorek (as illustrated in the periodical *Neubauten und Konkurrenzen in Österreich und Ungarn*, of which Marmorek was editor) are good examples of the appearance of Heimatstil.

58. This movement was based in an attitude of defensiveness. It operated in direct opposition to all international tendencies, accompanied by frenetic research into folk art, dialect, music, and genealogy. Representing an escape from the visual, political, and economic forms of industrial society, it opposed the functionalism of the modern. In Austria, the Heimatschutzstil mentality sought expression through a revival of the forms of the Biedermeier from the early nineteenth century and the rural built landscape. See Hajós, "Heimatstil-Heimatschutzstil," 157. Wanting to connect building and landscape, its practitioners drew on the English cottage-style movement as well as the work of the German architect Hermann Muthesius. Joseph Maria Olbrich, Wagner's star student, designed not only as a Secessionist but also in the Heimatschutzstil mode. Ludwig Hevesi, the leading critic and proponent of the modern, described Olbrich's Haus Bahr as a "true country house . . . that appears to grow from the living ground itself, like farm houses and acacia trees do" (Andreas Lehne, "Heimatstil—Zum Problem der Terminologie," *Österreichische Zeitschrift für Kunst und Denkmalpflege* 43, nos. 3–4 [1989]; quotation is from p. 162). While the motifs of the Heimatstil decorated an otherwise unchanged set of urban types transplanted into the country, rural populations generally reviled this appropriation. The *kleinbürger* (petty bourgeois) and rural bureaucrat used it as fodder for their conservative crusades. A conservative movement began to respond not only to the homogenizing power of the Heimatstil, but also to perceptions of modern, industrial architecture. The influence of the German Heimatschutzbewegung (Movement for the Protection of the Homeland) grew in the late 1890s through the efforts of Berlin composer Ernst Rudorff, who was appalled at the condition of German landscapes, and the anti-industrial writings of Paul Schultze-Naumburg fueled this movement. The Heimatschutzstil also grew out of a general revival or renaissance of folk form, but distinguished itself from it.

59. Folk art was rediscovered around this time and found its place at international exhibitions next to works of modern industrial production. Vernacular crafts elicited scholarly interest, and were seen as an untapped source for artists and architects. Folk art was "a golden, until now unrealized treasure of unbelievable worth for future production"; it was seen as unpretentious, joyful, colorful, simple, and masterful and served as inspiration for Austrian architects to "regionalize" their work and combine it with strains of the fashionable art nouveau. See Lehne, "Heimatstil—Zum Problem der Terminologie," 161. *Heimatkunst* was defined as "an art that is obliged in theme, content, and form to vernacular traditions, without belonging to 'folk art'" (ibid., p. 159). The use of these two variants of the language of the vernacular shifted over time. After 1900, Heimatstil designers abandoned the colorful vernacular decorative motifs they had previously been

so intent on imitating and instead referenced the basic, powerful forms of rural architecture. The heroic, defensive qualities of this architecture became highly expressive, often through accentuated roofs. Around 1910, architects working in the Heimatschutzstil emphasized the context of their projects, taking the idea of linking building and landscape to the level of connecting new construction with historic built context. The necessity of documenting historic, rural contexts initiated a frenzy of research, as seen in the two volumes of Martin Gerlach's *Volkstümliche Kunst Ansichten von alten heimatlichen Bauformen, Land- und Bauernhausern, Hofen, Garten, Wohnraumen, Hausrat, etc.* (Vienna: Gerlach & Wiedling, 19??) and *Volkstümliche Kunst II: Österreich-Ungarn*, ed. Martin Gerlach (Vienna: Gerlach & Wiedling, 1911).

60. For Loos, rationality could conquer the excesses of the industrial age. Under the tutelage of forms shared in common, culture could be unified and reconstituted. Loos wanted to pave a new path toward modernism through a rejection of the aesthetic dictates of contemporary "innovative" design. See Christopher Long, review of *Fashioning Vienna: Adolf Loos's Cultural Criticism*, by Janet Stewart, *Harvard Design Magazine* 14 (Summer 2001): 81–83.

61. Adolf Loos, "Heimatkunst (1914)," in *Trotzdem: 1900–1930* (Vienna: Brenner-Verlag, 1931), 137, 144. Joseph-August Lux, critic of Otto Wagner and his circle, followed a less liberal line, but his interest, as expressed in his foreword to *Volkstümliche Kunst*, seems to be in maintaining a profound continuity between past and present as well, though with a much more romantic overtone.

62. See Dana Bořutová, Anna Zajková, and Matúš Dulla, eds., *Dušan Jurkovič: Súborna Výstara architekonického Diela* [General Exhibition of the Architectural Work] (Bratislava: Slovenská Národná Galéria, 1993); Dana Bořutová-Debnárová, *Dušan Samo Jurkovič: Osobnosť a dielo* (Bratislava: Pallas, 1993), English-language summary, 218–27; for an overview of Jurkovič's interest in nationalism, see Christopher Long, "'The Works of Our People'": Dušan Jurkovič and the Slovak Folk Art Revival," *Studies in the Decorative Arts* 12, no. 1 (Fall–Winter 2004–5): 2–29; on Heimatschutz, see Long, "'The Works of Our People,'" 28n22.

63. Walachians came in the fourteenth century from the area later known as Romania, passing through the Carpathian arch as they spread north and west, ultimately to northeast Slovakia and Silesia. They brought with them rustic timber-building traditions, and high-quality linens and embroideries in the nineteenth century. See http://www.czector.cz/?id_region=25.

64. Long, "'The Works of Our People,'" 13–14.

65. For the Chapel of the Way of the Cross of Saint Hostýne (1903), see Bořutová-Debnárová, *Dušan Samo Jurkovič*, 89.

66. Dušan Jurkovič, *Práce lidu našeho: Lidové stavby, zařízení a výzdoba obydlí, drobné práce—Slowakische Volksarbeiten: Volksbauten, Interieurs und Handarbeiten—Les ouvrages populaires des Slovaques: Batiments populaires, intéerieurs, ouvrages manuels* [The Works of Our People: Folk Buildings, Interiors, and Handicrafts] (Vienna: Kunstverlag Anton Schroll & Co., 1905–13). It was advertised in *Der Architekt* (January 1906) as "Hochinterresant für alle Freunde volkstümlicher Baukunst" (Highly interesting for all lovers of folk architecture).

67. Dušan Jurkovič, quoted in R. W. Seton-Watson, *Slovak Peasant Art and Melodies*, exhibition catalogue (London: The Doré Gallery, 1911), 10; cited in Long, "'The Works of our People,'" 24.

68. See Rudolf Broch and Hans Hauptmann, eds., *Die Westgalizischen Heldengräber aus den Jahren des Weltkrieges 1914–1915* (Cracow: K. u. K. Militärkommando Krakau, 1918).

69. Matúš Dulla, "Military Cemeteries of Western Galicia," in Bořutová, Zajková, and Dulla, eds., *Dušan Jurkovič*, 89–101; Matúš Dulla, *Military Cemeteries of Western Galicia, Dušan Jurkovič 1916/1917, Guide* (Bratislava: Vysoká Škola výtvarných umení, 2002). See also *Architektúra & urbanizmus, Časopis Pre Teóriu Architektúry a Urbanizmu* 30, nos. 1–2 (Bratislava, 1996).

70. Dulla, *Military Cemeteries of Western Galicia*, 95.

71. Ibid.

72. On the exact numbers, names, and further research on the cemeteries, see ibid., 99, 101. The huge cemetery at Łużna Pustki 123, in District 4, was Jurkovič's only cemetery outside the First District.

73. Ibid., 91–94.

74. Ibid., 94. Hans Hauptmann, coeditor of the 1918 publication on the cemeteries, also wrote the verses for the markers.

75. Ibid., 102–4.

76. Prelovšek, *Jože Plečnik*, 1.

77. See s.v. "Slovenia," *Encyclopaedia Britannica*, 2003 CD-ROM version.

78. Irish missionaries had arrived as early as the eighth century, and confessions and sermons were given in the Slovene language by the year 1000.

79. For a discussion of Slovene national awakening, see Steven A. Mansbach, *Modern Art in*

Eastern Europe from the Baltic to the Balkans, ca. 1890–1939 (New York: Cambridge University Press, 1999).

80. *Encyclopaedia Britannica*, 2003 CD-ROM version.

81. See Damjan Prelovšek, "Decoration in Early Vurnik's Architecture," in *Ivan Vurnik 1884–1971: Slovenski arhitekt* [Slovenian Architect], exhibition catalogue and special issue of *Arhitektov bilten* [Architect's Bulletin] 24, nos. 119–24 (December 1994): 67–68.

82. Also known as Aemona; see Steven Mansbach, "Jože Plečnik, and the Landscaping of Modern Ljubljana," *Centropa* 4, no. 2 (May 2004): 111–21, esp. 113.

83. Major works on Plečnik include Prelovšek, *Jože Plečnik, 1872–1957*; Peter Krečič, *Plečnik: The Complete Works* (New York: Whitney Library of Design, 1993); Jože Plečnik, *Architectura perennis; Napori; Ponatis s kazalom*, with text by Damjan Prelovšek, 3 vols. (Ljubljana, Slovenia: Dessa, 1993); Damjan Prelovšek, Zeděnek Lukeš, and Tomáš Valena, eds., *Josip Plečnik: Architect of Prague Castle* (Prague: Prague Castle Administration, 1997). See also Peter Krečič, "Architecture in the Former Yugoslavia," in *Impossible Histories; Historical Avant-Gardes, Neo-Avant-Gardes, and Post-Avant-Gardes in Yugoslavia 1918–1991*, ed. Dubravka Djurić and Miško Šuvaković (Cambridge, MA: MIT Press, 2003).

84. Semper's other work of importance for Plečnik was *Die Vier Elemente der Baukunst* (1851).

85. Prelovšek, *Jože Plečnik, 1872–1957*, 14.

86. Mansbach, "Jože Plečnik, and the Landscaping of Modern Ljubljana," 112n10.

87. Plečnik intended that the numerous churches he designed in Slavic lands of Slovenia, Bohemia, Croatia, Bosnia, and Serbia both elevate the spiritual life of the people and reinforce a sense of Slavic identity.

88. Mansbach, "Jože Plečnik, and the Landscaping of Modern Ljubljana," 112n15; Damjan Prelovšek, "Ideological Substratum in Plečnik's Work," in Prelovšek, Lukeš, and Valena, *Josip Plečnik, Architect of Prague Castle*, 99.

89. Prelovšek, *Jože Plečnik, 1872–1957*, 115–16.

90. For Plečnik and Hradčany castle and his effort to make democracy visible, see Tomaš Vlček, "Modernism as a Means to Achieve Democracy," in Prelovšek, Lukeš, and Valena, *Josip Plečnik, Architect of Prague Castle*.

91. For a brief history, see Prelovšek, *Jože Plečnik, 1872–1957*, 122–27.

92. Plecnik also designed the Sacred Heart Church in Prague in 1931.

93. Prelovšek, *Jože Plečnik, 1872–1957*, 39.

94. Ibid., 148. Prelovšek observes (ibid., 139) that the flagpole bases "recalled two gilt shaft rings with visible screw heads, which are a literal adaptation of Semper's thesis that the columns in the archaic antiquity were clad in metal."

95. Prelovšek has described the volutes as "rows of textile fitted between the abacus and the echinus," confirming his own interpretation of Plečnik as largely inspired by Semper's cladding theory (ibid., 6–10, 148).

96. Mansbach, "Jože Plečnik, and the Landscaping of Modern Ljubljana," 112.

97. See *Ivan Vurnik 1884–1971: Slovenski arhitekt*.

98. At the Polytechnic Institute in Vienna, Karl Mayreder, architect and urban planner, became Vurnik's mentor and sponsor. After four years of study, Max Fabiani, the Slovene architect of Portois & Fix and assistant to Karl König at the school, recommended that Vurnik enter Wagner's master's class at the Academy of Fine Arts, while he continued his technical courses. Vurnik spent three semesters studying with Wagner, who, nearing the end of his teaching career, had less impact on the young Slovene than he had on earlier students.

99. For a discussion of the pattern in Vurnik's early work, see Prelovšek, "Decoration in Early Vurnik's Architecture," 64–72; and Andrej Hrausky, "Notes on Vurnik's Cooperative Bank," in *Ivan Vurnik 1884–1971: Slovenski arhitekt*, 77.

100. Hrausky claims that use of a grape motif on the interior painting of the banking hall became an abstracted motif for the exterior façade. See Hrausky, "Notes on Vurnik's Cooperative Bank," 75.

101. Ibid.

CHAPTER FIVE

1. *Oxford English Dictionary*, 2nd ed., 5:56, s.v. "eclectic."

2. For the use of *hybridity* by Homi Bhabha as a "negotiation of identity" that lacks clear sources of singularity, see the writings of Homi K. Bhabha: "Postmodernism/Postcolonialism," in *Critical Terms for Art History*, ed. Robert S. Nelson and Richard Shiff, 3rd ed. (Chicago: University of Chicago Press, 2003), 435–51; and "Figures of Difference," in *Art in Theory 1900–2000: An Anthology of Changing Ideas*, ed. Charles Harrison and Paul Wood, 2nd ed. (Malden, MA: Blackwell, 2003). For other uses of the term in cultural and identity discourse, see Avtar Brah and Annie Coombes, eds., *Hybridity and Its Discontents: Politics, Science, Culture* (New York: Routledge, 2000); and Robert Mugerauer et al., *Discourses in Hybridity and Identity* (Berkeley, CA: Center for Environmental De-

sign Research, University of California at Berkeley, 2002).

3. See M (1998), "The Search for a National Style," 217–84.

4. See Zbigniew Beiersdorf and Jacek Purchla, *Dom pod Globusem: Dawna siedziba Krakówskiej Izby Handlowej i Przemyslowej/The Globe House: The Former Headquarters of the Kraków Chamber of Commerce and Industry*], trans. Jerzy Pilawski, exhibition catalogue (Cracow: Wydawn. Literackie, 1997). For the history of Polish chambers of commerce, see ibid., pp. 68–89.

5. The multinamed L'viv/Lvov/Lemberg saw a proliferation of buildings whose architects adapted the language of organicism. Igor Zhuk has thoroughly documented the city's turn-of-the-century buildings.

6. The purpose of a commercial school to train students for business reflected the broader need for institutions to support trade and industry throughout the Austro-Hungarian Empire. This need was particularly strong in the poor eastern reaches of the empire, where Austrians occupied western Galicia, formerly a part of Poland.

7. The reorganization included provision of data as requested by ministries and authorities; the assessment of bills affecting commerce and industry along with the provision of opinions on various issues; and debate as called for by the government. These large responsibilities were mirrored in a clearly defined internal structure of membership. During the 1870s, the Chamber of Commerce and Industry even had representation in the Galician parliament of L'viv and in the Austrian parliament in Vienna.

8. Although built as the headquarters for the venerable Society of Friends of the Fine Arts, founded in 1854, the institution intended to support the new movement with temporary art exhibitions.

9. For the detailed history of the building see Beiersdorf and Purchla, *Globe House*, 79–119.

10. Wyspianski launched his career with a restoration of the late medieval frescoes at Cracow's Holy Cross Church, where he added hints of organic art nouveau to flower patterns and to outlines of figures. He also designed stained-glass windows above the organ loft for the venerable twin-spired Gothic St. Mary's Church on the main Market Square.

11. Beiersdorf and Purchla, *Globe House*, 119.

12. Ibid., 61, fig. 62.

13. Ibid., 144–49. When substantially complete in June 1906, the Chamber of Commerce and Industry still lacked its furniture and Mehoffer's paintings. Its members were put off by the dramatic effects, claiming that the interior was "completely unsuitable for official meetings" (ibid., 112). Further complaints ensued about the furnishings: the aisles between the seats were too narrow and the benches too long. Alterations followed, including the shortening of the chairman's rostrum and a reorganization of some of the benches. The building officially opened on September 15, 1906, and to honor the day, a fund was created to provide vocational training for workers in industry, commerce, and craft. The big painting still had not been installed, and when councilors saw it, some of them strenuously objected, claiming it unsuitable for a meeting room, while others approved. Despite these quibbles, the building finally opened to extensive and positive press coverage. For subsequent transformations to the building after World War I, see ibid., 115–19. The idiom of Young Poland continued in its efforts to propagate a Polish national identity and cultural autonomy. After the construction of the House under the Globe, Stryjeński and Mączyński completed their remodeling in 1907 of the venerable Old Theatre on Szczepanska Square. Jozef Gardecki provided the design of the façade in the spirit of Young Poland, but not without visual connections to the Vienna Secession's language of organicism. Established in 1799, the theatre had a long history, and its renovation in the hands of designers of Young Poland further attests to local confidence in the justness of their cause.

14. For a history of the Ferenc Liszt Academy of Music, see http://www.musicacademy.hu/.

15. Ferenc Erkel became director and filled in during Liszt's absences; he was also responsible for the academy's emphasis on a Hungarian style in opera.

16. See drawings in the National Archives Department for Plans, Budapest.

17. Eszter Gábor, "Korb and Giergl," in *Magyar Művészet 1890–1919* (Budapest, 1981); cited in Gerle, "Biographies of Hungarian Architects" (unpublished manuscript). Korb had won the gold medal of the Hungarian Association of Engineers and Architects for his design of an art gallery.

18. The theme of the vitality of music is further emphasized by a fresco on the ground floor, *The Fountain of Art* by Aladár Körösfői-Kriesch.

19. For general sources on Trieste, see http://www.triestetourism.it/inglese/itinerari/itinerario6.html; and http://triestenet.tripod.com/juden.htm.

20. Krinsky, *Synagogues of Europe*, 372–73. In 1871 Trieste's Jewish population was 4,400; by World War II it had peaked at 6,000. The new Tempio Israelitico was closed in 1942 due

to racial laws, but reopened after the Second World War. For the synagogue competition, see Alberto Boralvi, "Il 'Tempio Israelitico' di Trieste: Storia di un concorso," in *Comunità Religose di Trieste: Contribute di conoscenza* (Trieste: Civici Musei di Storia e Arte di Trieste, Ed. Isituto per L'enciclopedia de Friuli Venezia Giulia, 1979), 5–28.

21. See also Markus Kristan, *Oskar Marmorek, Architekt und Zionist, 1863–1909* (Vienna: Böhlau Verlag, 1996), 239–41. For contemporary publications about the competition, see ibid., 240, and in particular "Konkurrenzprojekt zum Bau des israelitischen Temples in Triest," *Wiener Bauindustrie-Zeitung* (Vienna) 22, no. 10 (December 9, 1904): 71–75, plates 19–23.

22. Krinksy, *Synagogues of Europe*, 370.

23. For the Hoppe and Schönthal entry, see Boyd Whyte, *Emil Hoppe, Marcel Kammerer, Otto Schönthal*, 44–45 and catalogue entries 104–10, pp. 224, 225; *Der Architect* 9 (1903); and *Der Architekt* 11 (1905): 5, 6. A preliminary study used a circular-planned building; they changed to a rectilinear one. As Boyd Whyte has noted, they missed the opportunity of associating the circular plan with the circular motifs that they used on the façade and elevations, but the section of the building did repeat the shape of the plan, thus organically uniting the design: Boyd Whyte, *Emil Hoppe, Marcel Kammerer, Otto Schönthal*, 44.

24. Krinsky, *Synagogues of Europe*, 371.

25. For the definitive study of the Berlams, see Marco Pozzetto, *Giovanni Andrea, Ruggero, Arduino Berlam: Un secolo di architettura* (Trieste: MGS Press, 1999), 1–25, 35–249 for family history and biographies; 120–34 for the Trieste synagogue. See also "Projekt für einen israelitischen Tempel in Triest," *Der Architekt* 15 (1909): 48, and plates 38, 39; cited in Kristan, *Oskar Marmorek*, 240.

26. The new synagogue replaced four eighteenth-century predecessors. Arduino Berlam went on to design, with sculptor Giovanni Mayer (1863–1943), Trieste's Victory lighthouse, the second-tallest lighthouse in the world after the Statue of Liberty, during the 1920s to honor the sailors lost during World War I; see http://triestenet.tripod.com/vittoria.htm) and Pozzetto, *Giovanni Andrea, Ruggero, Arduino Berlam*.

27. R[uggero] and A[rduino] Berlam, "Notizie tecniche ed artistiche sul nuovo tempio, in Il nuovo tempio israelitico di Trieste," *Il corriere israelitico* 51, no. 2 (1912): 22; quoted in L. Scott Lerner, "The Narrating Architecture of Emancipation," *Jewish Social Studies* 6, no. 3, reproduced online at http://iupjournals.org/jss/jss6-3.html#f33.

28. Krinsky, *Synagogues of Europe*, 372.

29. Pozzetto, *Giovanni Andrea, Ruggero, Arduino Berlam*, 124, fig. 242.

30. Available sources on Syrian architecture included Louis François Cassas, *Voyage pittoresque de la Syrie, de la Phénicie de la Palestine, et de la Base Égypte/Gravée sur les dessins de Cassas* (Paris, 1799–1800); Charles Jean Melchior, marquis de Vogüé, *Syrie central: Architecture civile et religieuse du Ier au VIIe siècle* (Paris: J. Baudry, 1865–77); Emmanuel Guillaume Rey, *Étude sur les monuments de l'architecture militaire des croisés en Syrie et dans l'île de Chypre* (Paris: Impr. nationale, 1871); Rudolf-Ernst Brünnow, *Die Provincia Arabia auf Grund zweier in den Jahren 1897 und 1898 unternommenen reisen und der berichte früherer reisender beschrieben von Rudolf Ernst Brünnow und Alfred V. Domaszewski*, 3 vols. (Strassburg: K. J. Trübner, 1904–09); Howard Crosby Butler, *Ancient Architecture in Syria, Princeton University Archeological Expeditions to Syria in 1904–1905 and 1909*, Publications, Division 2 and 3, 2 vols. (Leiden: E. J. Brill, 1907–20); and Howard Crosby Butler, *Architecture and Other Arts, Publications of an American Archaeological Expedition to Syria in 1899–1900*, pt. 2 (New York: The Century Co., 1903).

31. Arduino prepared illustrations for the thesis that Attilio Tamaro, the young writer, nationalist, and future historian, had discussed with Josef Strzygowski (Pozzetto, *Giovanni Andrea, Ruggero, Arduino Berlam*, 128–29). Strzygowski's recent work pointing toward the East included *Kleinasien, ein Neuland der Kunstgeschichte, Kirchenaufnahmen von J. W. Crowfoot und J. I. Smirnov unter Benutzung einiger Ergebnisse der Expedition nach der asiatischen Turkei des Kais. Legationsrates Dr. Max Freiherrn von Oppenheim, der Isaurischen Expedition der Gesellschaft zur Forderung Deutscher Wissenschaft, Kunst und Literatur in Bohmen, Beitragen von Bruno Keil, Otto Puchstein, Adolf Wilhelm u.a.* (Leipzig: J. C. Hinrichs, 1903). Strzygowski had also linked Wagner's Majolikahaus to the architecture of the Middle East in his book, *Die bildende Kunst der Gegenwart* (1907), cited in M (1998), 234.

32. See Krinsky, *Synagogues of Europe*, 372.

33. Pozzetto, *Giovanni Andrea, Ruggero, Arduino Berlam*, 129.

34. Ibid., 127, figs. 251–55.

35. See Berlam, "Notizie," 22; quoted in part in Pietro Piva, "Il Tempio Israelitico di Trieste, Note sugli Elemnti Costruttivi," extract from *Archeografo Triestino* 54 (102 dell Raccolta), ser. 4 (1994): 147–65, offprint.

36. Ibid., 150; translation by author.

37. L. Scott Lerner deserves to be quoted here:

"In Rome (1904) and Trieste (1912), where 'Eastern' and 'exotic' styles also predominated in design competitions, Moorish plans were rejected. In both cities, winning designs instead made reference to another Jewish land still more fully in contradiction with the idea of a Jewish homeland in Italy: biblical Palestine. Lacking a 'sure guide to establish the true nature of the architectonic art flourishing in Palestine in the remotest age,' architects Vincenzo Costa and Osvaldo Armanni in Rome wished to adopt a style that brought to mind 'the historical period in which the religious system to which the building was to be consecrated had its origin.' Similarly, Ruggero and Arduino Berlam in Trieste sought a style that 'corresponded to the nature of the religion of Israel and respected historical-artistic traditions and material conditions of Palestine so that the building's intended use would stand out clearly at first glance.' In both cases, the declared style of the new temple—Greek-inspired with Assyrian elements in Rome, and predominantly central Syrian (fourth century c.e.) in Trieste—was supposed to evoke the original and traditional space of the Hebrew nation. Once again, the language of the architectural style contradicted the speeches with their message of a homeland in Italy. In these instances, the Diaspora argument could no longer be invoked" (from Lerner, "The Narrating Architecture of Emancipation").

38. For Lajta, see Marco Biraghi, ed., *Béla Lajta: Ornamento e modernità* (Milan: Electa, 1999).

39. For the Italian translation of Lajta's essay in *Magyar Iparművészet* 18 (1914): 112–22, see "L'arte del cimetero," in Biraghi, *Béla Lajta*, 159–61.

40. M (1998), 256–57.

41. See Biraghi, *Béla Lajta*, 98–100.

42. For the "Cabaret Parisiana," see ibid., 115–16. The cherubim of the cornice hold lanterns to light the night (like theatre itself); between them is blue majolica with white letters spelling the name Parisiana.

43. János Gerle to author, personal communication, August 27, 2004.

44. Drawings for the first scheme are in the Budapest Historical Museum. See nos. 63.33.1 and 63.34.1.

45. Lajta's complex three-centered shape at the entry arch of the institute approximates the type of parabolic arch found in works by Nordic architects, as seen in Carl Bergsten's Hjorhagen Church in Stockholm of 1909.

46. For the connections between Hungary, Ruskin, and the Pre-Raphaelities, see Katalin Keserü, "Art Contacts between Great Britain and Hungary at the Turn of the Century," in *Hungarian Studies* 6, no. 2 (1990): 141–54. The Finnish Pavilion at the Paris World's Fair in 1900 had fascinated Hungarian artists, and in 1908 the journal *Magyar Iparművészet* (Hungarian Arts and Crafts) devoted an entire issue to the Finns in which the art critic Elek Koronghi Lippich claimed that the Finns' learning from the people was a model for Hungarian painters, sculptors, and architects; but instead of mere copying, artists should "seek and find the soul of the People" (Moravánszky, "Nationale Bestrebungen," 56–57).

47. The institute was a day school. Students did not board but could attend religious services with their families. The role of the chapel remains unclear. (János Gerle to author, personal communication, August 27, 2004.)

48. Noted on the plaque are Fulop Weinmann, Zsigmond Kohner, Emperor Franz Josef (inevitably), and the architect.

49. Artúr Bárdos, "Béla Lajta," *Művészet* (1913): 285–94; quoted in Biraghi, *Béla Lajta*, 170, and translated from Italian by the author.

50. M (1998), 191–95; Biraghi, *Béla Lajta*, 54–56, 64, figs. 117–22.

51. As Moravánszky has noted, the verticality of the building also recalls Alfred Messel's Wertheim Department Store in Berlin in 1898: M (1998), 191.

52. A mosaic by the painter Bertalan Pó was installed under the principal stairs.

53. Bárdos, "Béla Lajta," 285–94; quoted in Biraghi, *Béla Lajta*, 170, and translated from Italian by the author.

54. Pál Nádai ["A Modern City Architect: The Art of Béla Lajta"], *Magyar Építőművészet* 3 (1915): 122–25; quoted in Biraghi, *Béla Lajta*, 172, and translated from Italian by the author.

55. Virgil Bierbauer, ["A Hungarian Pioneer of New Architecture: Béla Lajta"], *Nouvell Revue de Hongrie* 18 (January–May 1935), 156–60; quoted in Biraghi, *Béla Lajta*, 175, and translated from Italian by the author.

56. For Árkay, see Balázs Dercsényi, *Árkay Aladár* (Budapest: Akadémiai Kiadó, 1967); Imre Kathy, "Árkay Aladár," in *Magyar Művészet 1890–1919* (Budapest: Akadémiai Kiadó, 1981); Péter Farbaky, "A Fasori Református Templom," *Ars Hungarica*, no. 2 (1984): 263–67; Ákos Moravánszky, "Materialwahrheit und Bekleidungsästhetik: Árkay Aladárs reformierte Kirche in Budapest (1911 bis 1913)" [Material-Truth and Clothing-Aesthetic: Aladár Árkay's Reformed Church in Budapest], in *Die Wiener Jahrhundertwende: Einflüsse, Umwelt, Wirkungen*, ed. Jürgen Nautz and Richard Vahrenkamp (Vienna: Böhlau Verlag, 1993), 588–604; George Starr, "Hungarian Reform Church Architecture

and the Nineteenth and Twentieth Centuries," *Centropa* 3, no. 3 (September 2003): 208–24; and M (1998), 263–67.

57. "The most significant of his architectural works after World War I are his designs of churches which approach the modern style. With his son, Bertalan Árkay he designed a church of outstanding value of the 1930s, the Parish-church of the Városmajor. From 1894 Árkay's paintings were also exposed at some exhibitions. His furniture designs were issued in the specimen sheets for handicraftsmen and technical schools. The architectural heritage which he left behind and is still not studied can be found in the Budapest Historical Museum" (Gerle, "Biographies of Hungarian Architects" [unpublished manuscript]). In addition to the Reformed Calvinist church and vicarage, Városligeti Allée 7, 1912–13, his main works were the concert hall of Buda (with Mór Kallina), Corvin Square, 1897–98; Villa Babochay, Dózsa György Road 92/A and 92/B, 1905–6; a housing estate with 40 villas for the Lawyer's Corporation, 1910–13; Roman Catholic church, Csaba Street 5, 1923; Roman Catholic chapel, Keleti Károly Street 39, 1924; Mohács, town hall, 1927; Rákosszentmihály Calvinist Community House (with Rezsövel Csaba), Budapest, 1927–28; and Gyárváros Roman Catholic Church (with his son Bertalan Árkay), Györ, 1932 (tower 1935) (ibid.).

58. For details of the commission and church history, see Farbaky, "A Fasori Református Templom," 255–69, plates 31–56; and J. István Kováts, ed., *Magyar refomátus templomok* [Hungarian Reformed Churches] (Budapest: Athenaeum, 1942). See also Moravánszky, "Materialwahrheit und Bekleidungsäthetik," 598 for the competition, 588–92 for the building's critical reception. M (1998), 167, erroneously gives differing dates (1901–7) for the building.

59. My thanks to János Gerle for introducing me to the Calvinist church and for providing much detail in its interpretation.

60. Calvinism is named for French Protestant reformer John Calvin (1509–64), who developed his doctrines while living in Switzerland. Calvin's most important works are his *Institutes of the Christian Religion*, published in 1536, and a massive collection of commentaries on the Bible. Calvin originally signed the Lutheran Augsburg Confession in 1540, but thanks to Calvin himself and his followers, the doctrine eventually developed in a direction independent of Lutheranism. Calvinism is a common name for Protestant doctrines of non-Lutheran national churches and various minority reform movements—known as Reformed Churches—that formed outside Catholicism in the late sixteenth and seventeenth centuries. The main points of Calvinist doctrine are the sovereignty of God, the Bible as the sole rule of faith, and the doctrine of predestination.

61. For an overview, see Starr, "Hungarian Reform Church Architecture," 208–24. István Medgyaszay, a Calvinist, contemplated and wrote about the future of the Calvinist church, designing one in Budapest in 1927–29. See ibid., 217.

62. See ibid., 221n2.

63. See ibid., 216.

64. Lutheran churches also tended to use longitudinal plans, a factor that differentiates them from Calvinist churches.

65. For Karl Moser (1860–1936) and Robert Curjel (1856–1925), see *Grove Dictionary of Art*, 22:186, s.v. "Moser, Karl." Their firm, which had begun in 1888, was based in Karlsruhe; Moser's principal interest was in church design.

66. See Budapest Technical Museum drawings (BTM) 67.47.1; BTM 67.47.2; and BTM 67.47.15.

67. Moravánszky sees the façade as mediating between the world of the urban street and ritual space associated with the Byzantine. Following Semperian theories, he furthermore sees the façade as drapery supported on heavy stone columns, like a coat replete with motifs from peasant woodcarvings, particularly wooden grave posts: M (1998), 167. See also Moravánszky, "Materialwahrheit und Bekleidungsästhetik," 602–4. Whereas Moravánszky claims that Wagner's St. Leopold's Church at Steinhof was a model for the interior; Starr challenges the assertion for lack of proof: Starr, "Hungarian Reform Church Architecture," 223n37.

68. Gáspár Károlyi, "A fasori uj templom," *Magyar Iparmüvészet* 16, no. 6 (1913): 259f; quoted in Moravánszky, "Materialwahrheit und Bekleidungsästhetik," 588.

69. See *Magyar Építömüvészet* 6 (1913). The church was also published as late as 1931 in Dutch architectural critic J. G. Wattjes' book, *Moderne kirken in Europa und Amerika*.

70. Starr concurs with my analysis of the church, calling it a "curious hybrid": Starr, "Hungarian Reform Church Architecture," 216.

71. After the cultural, political, and social changes in Hungary following World War I and continuing through the Soviet domination of the country, reading of the church achieved an even more generalized level. Over time, the specificity of the idiom of the building became increasingly general and vague. How it is read in the future remains open to question. Will it be a marker on a tourist trail, or simply a mute object in a language undecipherable to the citizens of its future?

72. The standard monograph on Medgyaszay in Hungarian is Imre Kathy, *Medgyaszay István* (Budapest: Akadémiai Kiadó, 1979). For earlier literature, see István Medgyaszay, "A vasbeton művészi formájáról," *Művészet* 8 (1909); *Magyar Építőművészet* 1 (1909); *Magyar Építőművészet* 1 (1911). See also Ákos Moravánszky, "Hungarian National Architectural Efforts at the Beginning of the Twentieth Century," *Österreichische Zeitschrift für Kunst und Denkmalpflege* 33, nos. 1–2 (1979): 52–60; and Moravánszky, "Materiallandschaften," *Kritische Berichte* 28, no. 2 (2000): 20–28, on emphasis of early modernists on materials. For an overview, see Gerle, "Hungarian Architecture from 1900 to 1918," 222–43.

73. See Pozzetto, *Die Schule Otto Wagners 1894–1902*, fig. 128. Although this curtain wall façade represented a daring use of technology for its time, the project hinted at Medgyaszay's interest in Hungarian national expression. Wagner discouraged nationalism among his students, but Medgyaszay cleverly hid his nationalist inclinations in his project: the letters of the inscription he drew in the building's frieze could be regrouped to read in Hungarian as a challenge to German dominance (M [1998], 268). See also Moravánszky, "Hungarian National Architectural Efforts at the Beginning of the Twentieth Century," 52–60.

74. For the use of reinforced concrete by Wagner's students, see Marco Pozzetto, "Cemento armato, materiale nuovo nella scuola di Otto Wagner," *L'Industria Italiana del Cemento*, no. 6 (1981): 417–34.

75. See Zoltán Bartha's comments in the pamphlet *Family Memoriam of the Architect Medgyaszay* [Budapest: Privately published, n.p., n.d.]. For illustrations, see Kathy, *István Medgyaszay*, figs. 10–16; plate section unpaginated.

76. Medgyaszay's synthesis of the language of rationalism, the benefits of concrete as a quintessential modern material, and his embrace of Hungarian folk iconography took more realistic shape in the two studio villas he designed 1904–6 for members of the Gödöllő Artists Colony, the group of life reform movement advocates who shared similar sympathies for Hungarian tradition. The mass of each villa differed in volume depending on the function, while the use of brick for walls tied everything together, with concrete used for balcony and porch columns. See M (1998), 268, 272–73.

77. See Bartha, *Family Memoriam of the Architect Medgyaszay*, unpaginated. For illustrations, see Kathy, *István Medgyaszay*, figs. 10–16; plate section unpaginated.

78. Medgyaszay took the same approach in the theater he designed in Sopron in 1909.

79. Francis S. Onderdonk Jr., *The Ferro-Concrete Style: Reinforced Concrete in Modern Architecture* (New York: Architectural Book Publishing, 1928), 134. For Medgyaszay's remarks in 1908 on the use of concrete, see pp. 246–48.

80. Ibid., 134.

81. See Kathy, *István Medgyaszay*, figs. 21–25, for drawings and earlier views, particularly those of the original interior; published in *Magyar Építőművészet* 1 (1911). Drawings identify the church as Rk "templom." The client was Rudolf Körfy; see www.vandoriskola.hu/kozos/kirandulas/felvidek/kirandulas_2001_felvidek.htm.

82. Onderdonk described the walls as built of concrete blocks with all ornamental parts and tower of monolithic concrete (Onderdonk, *The Ferro-Concrete Style*, 248, fig. 375).

83. This message is no longer so clear: the panel above the wooden entry doors showing originally a single religious figure has been repainted with a strange scene of a man, a woman, and a child ascending toward heaven and supported in part by a nude figure. Two fallen figures lie at the bottom of the panel. The interior has been altered by the removal of the low altar screen and the addition of side altars that obscure the folk motifs.

84. Presenting itself as parallel to but different from Austria, Hungary exhibited a giant keg of wine and featured a Hungarian café with Gypsy musicians at the Paris exposition of 1878. Though the Hungarians wanted respectful recognition, the French thought the display was uncivilized. However, at the Barcelona exhibition of 1888, Spaniards praised the Hungarian exhibition, seeing it as evidence of a "rejuvenated nation." However, Hungary missed a big opportunity to present its culture to America when it skipped the 1893 Columbian Exposition in Chicago, where Hungarians were still regarded as strange outsiders, even curiosities. This gaffe was met with criticism at home, and the Hungarians set out to counter the loss. Borrowing exhibits shown in Budapest at the Millennial Exhibition of 1896, Hungary demonstrated its economic prowess at the Paris World's Fair of 1900. The elaborate display won awards, but Hungary was still seen as "belonging entirely to the East" and not as a western European nation. This exoticism was reinforced by the very exhibit that was intended to represent the pinnacle of national pride: *The Hall of Hussars*, a vast painted panel showing the history of the Hussars, herders on horseback on the iconic Great Plain of

the nation. Nonetheless, it helped recapture some international attention. Subsequently, members of the Gödöllő Artists colony contributed to the making of a Transylvanian peasant house for the 1904 Louisiana Purchase Exhibition in St. Louis. Hungary finally received its sought-after international recognition at the International Exposition in Milan on 1906. Among its various exhibits, the decorative arts section, which included a Home of the Artist, was a favorite of fairgoers, received international praise, and was called "the sensation of the furniture exhibition." Artists of the Gödöllő colony again contributed, and Medgyaszay assisted the exhibit designers. See Terri Switzer, "Hungarian Self-Representation in an International Context: The Magyar Exhibited at International Expositions and World Fairs," in Facos and Hirsch, *Art, Culture and National Identity in Fin-de-Siècle Europe*, 160–85.

85. The pavilion was published in *Magyar Építőművészet* 7–8 (1912) and *The Studio*, 1911. Photographs are in the National Archives, Budapest Department for Plans T-13.31. Móric Pogány (1878–1942) was born in Nagyenyed (Aiud) in central Transylvania, studied at a Transylvanian technical school, and worked on the reconstruction of castles in the region. His background thus gave him a rich source of imaginary architecture and contact with the deeper, less disturbed roots of Hungarian culture. Moving to Budapest, he entered design competitions until he joined the office of Emil Tőry (1863–1928), an architect and university professor. From acting as Tőry's office manager, he became Tőry's partner in 1908. Emil Tőry studied at the Technical University in Budapest and after that in Berlin; he worked in the office of Alajos Hauszmann in Budapest. See János Gerle, "Architecture at the Exhibitions," in *Lélek és Forma: Magyar művészet 1896–1914/A Golden Age: Art and Society in Hungary 1896–1914*, ed. Gyöngyi Éri and Zsuzsa Jobbágyi, exhibition catalogue (Budapest: Corvina; Miami: Barbicon Art Gallery, Center for the Fine Arts, 1990), 60.

86. Terri Switzer, "Hungarian Self-Representation in an International Context: The Magyar Exhibited at International Expositions and World Fairs," 179n64.

87. The interior vestibule contained friezes showing the wedding of Attila and the crowning of Saint Stephen as part of a program to reaffirm Hungarian origins in a mythology of the Huns. The soaring main cupola had folk motifs, stained glass, and wood construction to represent traditional architecture and crafts. The designers even provided written texts to explore to the significance of the imagery (Switzer, "Hungarian Self-Representation in an International Context," 180). The Attila legend had provided the program for an earlier presentation at the Venice Biennial of 1909, and the general themes were present in a second exhibition in 1911, the International Fine Arts Exhibit in Rome (ibid., 178, 180–81). Going back to the ideas of József Huszka, the Hungarian ethnographer, it drew attention to roots in "ancient Eastern, Parthian-Sassanid" cultures as well as "Hindu kinship," and its goal was to make the origins of Hungarians separate from Slavs, Austrians, and Germans, promoting a cultural superiority that through assimilation unified and controlled the population with its diverse minority ethnic groups; see ibid., 163.

88. For the remodeling of the Banking House Primavesi, Olmüz, 1913–14, see Sekler, *Josef Hoffmann*, 127–34; for the Primavesi country house, Winkelsdorf (Kouty), Czechoslovakia, 1913–14, see ibid., 127–31.

89. Ibid., 156, fig. 203.

90. For the definitive discussion and detailed description of Villa Skywa-Primavesi, see ibid., 150–59, 365–70, cat. 185.

91. Ibid., 367.

92. Ibid. Hoffmann explored in parallel with the Skywa-Primavesi villa this new device with grooves in the Austria House for the German Werkbund exhibition in Cologne in 1914. Like the villa, the pavilion also used a pyramidal roof, but it sat on a stacked base.

93. Švácha, *Architecture of New Prague 1895–1945*, 134–37, 187, 192–204.

94. Ibid., 134.

95. Pavel Janák, "Barvu průčelím!" [Color to the Façades!], *Venkov* 11 (December 3, 1916); quoted in Švácha, *Architecture of New Prague 1895–1945*, 136.

96. Švácha, *Architecture of New Prague 1895–1945*, 137n30.

97. Pavel Janák, "V třetině cesty," *Volné směry* 19 (1918): 218. I rely on Moravánsky's synopsis: M (1998), 359.

98. Švácha, *Architecture of New Prague 1895–1945*, 186–87.

99. Wirth and Matějček, *Česká Arhitektura 1800–1920*, 86; quoted in ibid., 187.

100. For his early work in the 1920s, see the ironworks Vítkovické on Olivova Street, 1921–24, and his proposed work for the Charles University Law School; see ibid., 192. Despite a retrospective exhibition of his work in 1926, Karel Teige, the polemicist of international functionalism, declared Kotěra passé and irrelevant. See Christopher Long, review of *Jan Kotěra 1871–1923:*

The Founder of Modern Czech Architecture, ed. Vladímir Šlapeta, *Centropa* 3, no. 2 (September 2003): 277–79.

101. For drawings and period photographs, see von Vegesack, *Czech Cubism*, 128–29.

102. Švácha, *Architecture of New Prague 1895–1945*, 194.

103. For a history of the Riunione Adriatica di Sicurtà, see Erminio Tedeschi, *Historical Notes, RAS: 1838–1988* (sic) (Trieste: Privately published by the RAS, 1989); and *Nel primo centenario della Riunione Adriatica di Sicurtà (1838–1938)* (Trieste, 1939). For the RAS's new building in Trieste, Amerigo Restucci, "Il palazzo della RAS a Trieste," extract from *Quaderni Giulinani di Storia*, no. 2 (1981): 73–92.

104. "Il palazzo dell RAS," *Il Picolo*, April 19, 1914; quoted in Restucci, "Il palazzo della RAS a Trieste," 73.

105. M (1998), 381–82, 389.

106. Švácha describes the building as being crowned with a "massive battlements" motif imitating the town halls of the Italian Renaissance city republics; Švácha, *Architecture of New Prague 1895–1945*, 198.

107. The rhythm is AA-BB-AA on the long side of the building, AA-BBB-AA on the short side.

108. Švácha, *Architecture of New Prague 1895–1945*, 204.

109. Ibid., 194.

110. Karel Teige, *MSA 2. Moderní architektura v Československu* [Modern Architecture in Czechoslovakia]; quoted in Švácha, *Architecture of New Prague 1895–1945*, 187.

111. M (1998), 359 quoted, 361–63.

112. Švácha, *Architecture of New Prague 1895–1945*, 187.

113. On the other hand, Czech cubism did not cease entirely; it went through its own developments, pursuing a pyramidal variety in the 1920s, as well as what some commentators have called a cubist expressionist line. It encountered what Švácha has called the "geometrical modern style" that represented an alternative to purism and functionalism which emerged in 1922. See ibid., 188–92.

CONCLUSION

1. Gustav Adolf Platz, *Die Baukunst der Neuesten Zeit* (Berlin: Propyläen-Verlag, 1927).

2. Among the numerous treatments of political history on the demise of the Austro-Hungarian Empire and the rise of the new nations, see Jelavich, *History of the Balkans*; Johnson, *Central Europe*; Kann, *A History of the Habsburg Empire*; Held, *The Columbia History of Eastern Europe in the Twentieth Century*; and for a broader study, Hobsbawm, *The Age of Extremes*. For a graphic view of the changing political boundaries and redistribution of people along ethnolinguistic lines, see Magocsi, *Historical Atlas of Central Europe*, 125–29.

3. See Magocsi, *Historical Atlas of Central Europe*, 104–5.

4. See ibid., 145.

5. See ibid., 147–48.

6. See ibid., 140.

7. For a brief synopsis, see ibid., 153–54.

8. See chapter 5, "The Language of Hybridity," in the present text.

9. For one of the most potent interpreters of the neobaroque in the 1920s, see Peter Noever, ed., *Dagobert Peche and the Wiener Werkstätte*, exhibition catalogue (New Haven, CT: Yale University Press, 2002).

10. See Dennis P. Doordan, "Architecture and Politics in Fascist Italy: Il Movimento italiano per l'architettura razionale 1928–1932" (Ph.D. diss., Columbia University, 1983); and Doordan, *Building Modern Italy: Italian Architecture, 1914–1936* (New York: Princeton Architectural Press, 1988).

11. For the classic text, see Wolfgang Pehnt, *Expressionist Architecture* (New York: Praeger, 1973).

12. D'Arcy Wentworth Thompson, *On Growth and Form* (Cambridge: The University Press, 1917).

13. Within the literature on the German debates about ornament in the 1920s, discussions of Frank Lloyd Wright highlight the issues. To many he appeared a pioneering modernist, but his use of "ornament" was unacceptable. See Anthony Alofsin, ed., *Frank Lloyd Wright: Europe and Beyond* (Berkeley and Los Angeles: University of California Press, 1999).

14. For the interwar years in Hungary, see András Ferkai, "Hungarian Architecture between the Wars," in Wiebenson and Sisa, *The Architecture of Historic Hungary*, 244–74; and András Ferkai, "*Neues Bauen* in Budapest," in Blau and Platzer, *Shaping the Great City*, 178–85.

15. Rudolf Klein's views provide this tripartite reaction; personal communication to author, August 24, 2004.

16. For Hungarians and the Bauhaus, see Monika Platzer, "Interlude: Ideas for a New World, 1919–27," in Blau and Platzer, *Shaping the Great City*, 167–77. For the interwar years in Hungary, see Ferkai, "Hungarian Architecture between the Wars"; see also *Avant-Garde Hongroise/Hongaarse Avant-Gard 1915–1925*, exhibition catalogue (Brussels: BBL and Brepols, 1999).

17. See Švácha, *Architecture of New Prague 1895–1945*, for a summary of architects who moved into functionalism.

18. For accounts of Czech functionalism, see ibid.; Vladimír Šlapeta and Gustav Peichl, *Czech Functionalism 1918–1938*, exhibition catalogue (London: Architectural Association, 1987); Vladimír Šlapeta, *Die Brünner Funktionalisten: Moderne Architektur in Brünn (Brno)*, exhibition catalogue (Innsbruck: Institut für Raumgestaltung der Technischen Fakultät der Universität Innsbruck; Vienna: Institut für Gebäudelehre und für Hochbau I der Technischen Universität Wien, 1985); Karel Teige, *Modern Architecture in Czechoslovakia and Other Writings*, trans. Irena Žantovská Murray and David Britt (Los Angeles: Getty Research Institute; and New York: Oxford University Press, 2001).

19. See Šlapeta, *Die Brünner Funktionalisten*.

20. For general histories of Slovak modernism, see Ladislav Foltyn, *Slovenská arhitektúra a česká avantgarda 1918–1939* (Bratislava: Vydateľstvo Spolku architektov Slovenska, 1993); also *Architektúra & Urbanizmus. Časopis Pre Teóriu Architektúry a Urbanizmu* 29, nos. 1–2 (Bratislava, 1995), whole issue.

21. See, for example, Slovak Artistic Club by Alois Balán and Jiří Grossmann in Bratislava (1924–26); *Architektúra & Urbanizmus. Časopis Pre Teóriu Architektúry a Urbanizmu* 29, nos. 1–2 (Bratislava, 1995): 14–17; and ibid., 26 (1992): 3–4.

22. *Architekt Emil Belluš, regionálna moderna/regional modernism*, exhibition catalogue (Bratislava: Spolok architektov Slovenska, 1992); Martin Kusý, *Emil Belluš* (Bratislava: Tatran, 1984); *Emil Belluš: Architektonické dielo*, exhibition catalogue (Bratislava: Slovenská Národná Galéria, 1989); Martin Kusý, *Architektúra na Slovensku 1918–1945* (Bratislava: Pallas, 1971); Matúš Dulla and Henrieta Moravčíková, "Kolonádový Most/Colonnade Bridge," *Architektúra & Urbanizmus. Časopis Pre Teóriu Architektúry a Urbanizmu* 29, nos. 1–2 (Bratislava, 1995): 88–93.

23. In Prague Belluš participated in the club Detvan, an association of Slovakian students.

24. Belluš's sensitivity to Slovakian culture and its efforts for political autonomy are seen in the little-known project he created in 1925, the tombstone to Slovak revolutionaries M. Jursa and J. Škápik in Bratislava. The two had initiated and led a revolt of an infantry regiment that had refused to leave for the Italian front in 1918 and met their deaths by a field military tribunal.

25. Belluš was an active member in the founding of the Slovak Technical University, which opened in 1937. He taught there until 1971, despite the fact that in the 1950s political conditions prevented him from actualizing any new architectural commissions.

26. The Spa Bridge in Piešťany paralleled in purpose the Sanatorium at Paimio by Alvar Aalto, whom Belluš much admired.

27. The literature on Red Vienna is extensive. For overviews, see Helmut Weihsmann, *Das Rote Wien* (Vienna: Promedia, 1985); and Eve Blau, *The Architecture of Red Vienna, 1919–1934* (Cambridge, MA: MIT Press, 1999).

28. For a history and catalogue of works, see Georg Schwalm-Theiss, *Theiss & Jaksch, Architekten 1907–1961* (Vienna: Edition Christian Brandstätter, 1986).

29. Ibid., 44–48.

30. In Catholic Austria, tall bell towers had been forbidden on Evangelical churches until the mid-nineteenth century, because the tower was considered a sign of protest and confirmation of conviction.

31. Schwalm-Theiss, *Theiss & Jaksch*, 62–65.

32. Ibid., 25–26, 94–99, 147.

33. See ibid., 95–96.

34. For the firm's involvement with National Socialists and their projects under the Nazis, see ibid., 31–45, 154–57. A much-needed complete study of the political positions of Austrian architects from 1933 to 1945 remains to be written.

35. Lechner, *Jenö Lechner*, 34–35. Lechner's entry received an honorable mention. The competition provided a cross section of diverse visions of modern architecture in 1922, precisely at the juncture before a single line began to dominate. The selection of Raymond Hood in collaboration with John Mead Howells as the winners over more progressive schemes, including Eliel Saarinen's influential entry, is often repeated as a claim of conservatism over innovation.

36. See M (1998), 274–75.

37. See "Kochovo Sanatórium/Koch Sanitorium," in *Architektúra & Urbanizmus. Časopis Pre Teóriu Architektúry a Urbanizmu* 29, nos. 1–2 (Bratislava, 1995): 64–69.

38. See "Vurnikova šola za arhitekturo," *Dom in svet* (1927): 291–331; see also Damjan Prelovšek, "Decoration in Early Vurnik's Architecture," in *Ivan Vurnik 1884–1971: Slovenski arhitekt/Slovenian Architect*, exhibition catalogue and special issue of *Arhitektov bilten/Architect's bulletin* 24, nos. 119–24 (December 1994): 70–71.

39. See Prelovšek, "Decoration in Early Vurnik's Architecture," 69–71.

40. For Plečnik after the war, see Prelovšek, *Jože Plečnik, 1872–1957*; Krečič, *Plečnik: The*

Complete Works; and Mansbach, "Jože Plečnik, and the Landscaping of Modern Ljubljana."

41. See Prelovšek, *Jože Plečnik, 1872–1957*, 300–9.

42. Ibid., 302.

43. Ibid., 308.

44. Ibid., 305, 309.

45. Ibid., 307.

46. For a discussion of crematoria and their role in Czech modern architecture, particularly the monument to national liberation and memorial to Jan Žižka on Vitkov Hill in Prague, see Matthew S. Witkovsky, "Truly Blank: The Monument to National Liberation and Interwar Modernism in Prague," *Umění* 49 (2001): 42–60.

47. Ibid., 44.

48. See the remarkable funerary chapel project by Rudolf Tropsch ca. 1902, published in *Der Architekt* 7 (1902): pl. 77; Karl Maria Kerndle's Sepulchral Chapel, 1903, illustrated in Pozetto, *Die Schule Otto Wagners 1894–1902*, 232; and Borsi and Godoli, *Vienna 1900*, 186–87.

49. Pogány's perspective view appeared in *Magyar Pályázatok*, no. 8 (1904); the main façade and model in *Magyar Építőművészet*, nos. 7–8 (1912).

50. For treatment of the cremation movement in Czech lands, see Witkovsky, "Truly Blank," 51–54.

51. Ibid., 52.

52. *Stavba* was interested in crematoria in Brno (1925) and Prague (1927). Its editors featured František Mencl's article, "Krematoria," (*Stavba* 1, no. 6 [June 1922]), which included Vlastislav Hofman's winning design for a crematorium in Moravian Ostrava (1922–25), as well as four pages of illustrations by Bedřich Feuerstein and Bohumil Sláma for the one in Nymburk. See Witkovsky "Truly Blank," 53, and n62.

53. Pardubice (Pardubitz in German) obtained civil rights in the mid-fourteenth century. By the end of the fifteenth century, the town was owned by the Pernštejns, a Czech family who remodeled it in a Renaissance style during the next century. Although Swedish troops razed the town in 1645, it retained in its central square a sixteenth-century Gothic castle, row houses of the upper class, and a distinctive Green Gate, built in 1507. Just on its outskirts to the northeast was a hill containing a prehistoric burial ground and ruined fifteenth-century castle. Pardubice was also known for the very secular activity of horse racing, and especially its Grand Steeplechase (*Encyclopaedia Britannica* CD-Rom edition, s.v. "Pardubice."

54. Kroha had studied 1911–16 at the Czech Institute of Science and Technology in Prague. After 1925, he became professor of architecture there. In 1927–31 he edited the newspaper *Horizont* [Horizon] and later became a founding member of Léva fronta [Left Front] and the first chairman of the Association of Socialist Architects in 1933. Between 1922 and 1928, he designed several buildings for the town of Mladá Boleslav. For his competition entries for the crematorium at Pardubice, see von Vegesack, *Czech Cubism*, 49, 77; also *Jiří Kroha: Kubist, Expressionionist, Funktionalist, Realist*, exhibition catalogue, ed. Architekturzentrum Wien (Vienna: Architekturzentrum Wien, and Sonderzahl Verlag, [1998]), 32. For biographical information on Kroha, see Blau and Platzer, *Shaping the Great City*, 255–56.

55. For the literature on the crematorium, see von Vegesack, *Czech Cubism*, 105, 134; Olga Herbanová and Vladimír Šlapeta, *Pavel Janák 1882–1956: Architektur und Kunstgewerbe*, exhibition catalogue (Vienna: Semper Depot, 1984), 35; Marie Benešová, *Česká architektura*, 297; Benešová, *Pavel Janák*, 13, 18, 19; and Novotný, *Jan Kotěra a jeho doba*, 95.

56. For the crematorium at Nymburk, see Benešová, *Česka architektura*, 303, 306; and Oldřich Dostál, Josef Pechar, and Vítězslav Procházka, *Moderní architektura v Československu* [Modern Architecture in Czechoslovakia] (Prague: Obelisk, Nakladatelství Umění a Architektury, 1970), 91.

57. See also Švácha, *Architecture of New Prague 1895–1945*, 215–16, 275–76.

58. On Sláma, see ibid., 158–59, 270, 273.

59. For Feuerstein's ingenious plan, see Dostál, Pechar, and Procházka, *Moderní architektura v Československu*, 91, fig. 96.

60. Witkovsky, "Truly Blank," 53.

61. Švácha, *Architecture of New Prague 1895–1945*, 275.

62. Feuerstein also designed the Geographical Institute in Prague (1921?–25), but receiving fewer commissions, he later worked in Japan for Antonin Raymond, the Czech-born architect who had been the assistant of Frank Lloyd Wright on the Imperial Hotel but had remained in Tokyo (ibid., 276).

63. For Arnošt Wiesner's brief biography and summary of works, see Šlapeta, *Die Brünner Funktionalisten*, 110–11. Wiesner emigrated from Czechoslovakia in 1939 to England, where he spent the rest of his career, practicing and teaching. His departure was one of many losses of a creative individual for the region. He died in Liverpool.

64. Wiesner practiced from 1919 to 1929 in Brno. In the interim, he became a member of the Union of Architects and collaborated with the Czechoslovak CIAM group.

65. See Arnošt Wiesner, "Über den Bau des Krematoriums," *Horizont* no. 11–13 (Brno, 1928); reprinted in Šlapeta, ed., *Die Brünner Funktionalisten*, 91–93; for illustrations, see Šlapeta and Peichl, *Czech Functionalism 1918–1938*, 46–48; and Vladímir Šlapeta, ed., *Arnošt Wiesner 1890–1971*, exhibition catalogue (Olomouc, Czech Republic: Gallery of Fine Arts, 1981). The crematorium is located at Jihlarská Street 1. For a view of the interior, see Šlapeta and Peichl, *Czech Functionalism 1918–1938*, 47.

66. Quoted from *The Master Builder* (1932) [sic] in Šlapeta, *Czech Functionalism 1918–1938*, 47.

67. Oldřich Starý, "K soutěži na pražské krematorium," *Stavba* 5, no. 9 (March 1927), p. 134; quoted in Edwin Heathcote, *Monument Builders: Modern Architecture and Death* (Chichester, West Sussex: Academy Editions, 1999), p. 61; cited in Witkovsky, "Truly Blank," 53.

68. Heathcote, *Monument Builders*, 61; cited in Witkovsky, "Truly Blank," 53n67.

69. Arnošt Wiesner, "Über den Bau des Krematoriums," reprinted in Šlapeta, *Die Brünner Funktionalisten*, 93.

70. Friedrich Achleitner, *Österreichische Architektur im 20. Jahrhundert*, vol. 3, pt. 1, *Wien* (Salzburg: Residenz Verlag, 1990), 294–95.

71. Georg Rigele and Georg Loewit, eds., *Clemens Holzmeister* (Innsbruck: Haymon, 2000); Freidrich Achleitner, Wilhelm Holzbauer, Herbert Muck, and Monika Knofler, *Clemens Holzmeister*, exhibition catalogue (Vienna: Akademie der Bildenden Künste, 1982); Clemens Holzmeister, *Architekt in der Zeitenwende: Clemens Holzmeister; Selbstbiographie, Werkverzeichnis* (Salzburg: Verlag Das Bergland-Buch, 1976); and Monika Knofler, "Clemens Holzmeister: Das architektonische Werk" (Ph.D. diss., University of Innsbruck, 1976). Holzmeister was initially invited to Turkey in 1927 to design buildings. For the exhibition of his Turkish contributions, see http://www.byegm.gov.tr/YAYINLARIMIZ/newspot/2001/sept-oct/n17.htm.

72. For Holzmeister's rural idiom, see his Hotel Tre Cime, Sexten-Moos in Sesto, Italy (1926–28), and his Haus Eichmann in Seewalchen (1927–28).

73. Achleitner, *Österreichische Architektur im 20. Jahrhundert*, vol. 3, pt. 1, *Wien*, 294–95.

74. Holzmeister moved to Istanbul in 1940 and operated an extensive architectural practice there until he returned to Austria in 1949. In 1954, he reassumed his professorship at the Academy of Fine Arts in Vienna. After 1957 he taught a master class near Salzburg.

75. The crematoria built elsewhere in Vienna and in other Austrian cities showed the divergence of interpretations: Schulte's Linz project demonstrated the move from expressionism toward the Neue Sachlichkeit, Wiedenmann's in Salzburg (1930/31) played on Secessionist motifs, and Erich Boltenstern's strong and severe crematorium at Alte Postraße om Vienna, which Achleitner has described as resembling Scandinavian modern classicism that led to a strong and impressive architectonic language: „einer starken und einprägsamen architektonischnen Sprache" (Achleitner, *Österreichische Architektur in 20. Jahrhundert*, vol. 2, *Ein Führer in drei Bänden* (Salzburg: Residenz Verlag, 1983), 348, 349.

76. Elisabeth Karlinsky (1904–94) was a student at the State Trade School in Vienna (1921–27) and made the project in the class of Franz Čižek. She also made a model of the scheme, which is in the collected of Wien Museum, inv. Nr. 171.592/2.

77. After the Anschluss in 1938, Plischke and his wife emigrated to New Zealand, where he worked as an architect, but returned to Vienna in 1963 where he became professor of architecture at the Academy of Fine Arts. For the thesis project, see August Sarnitz and Eva B. Ottlinger, eds., *Ernst Plischke: Modern Architecture for the New World; The Complete Works* (Munich: Prestel Verlag, 2004), 28–29; the catalogue entry for the crematorium, CR 5.9, appears only in the German edition: August Sarnitz, *Ernst Plischke: Das Neue Bauen und die Neue Welt* (Munich: Prestel Verlag, 2003). See also *Ernst Anton Plischke: Architekt und Lehrer*, essays by Friedrich Achleitner, et al. (Salzburg: Verlag Anton Pustet, 2003); *Ernst Anton Plischke*, exhibition catalogue (Vienna: Akademie der Bildenden Künste, 1983), 38–39; and Ernst Anton Plischke, *Ein Leben mit Architektur* (Vienna: Löcker Verlag, 1989), 70–71.

78. For Plischke's antithetical approach to his hybrid funerary project, see his project in line with the Neue Sachlichkeit, the Office Building "Zeho," in *Das ungebaute Wien*, 292–93.

79. For Perco's crematorium entry and his proposal for a crematorium in Graz (1930), see Ursula Prokop, *Rudolf Perco 1884–1942: Von der Architektur des Roten Wien zur NS-Megalomanie* (Vienna: Böhlau Verlag, 2001), 254–63, 384–85, 399.

80. For Perco's biography, see Prokop, *Rudolf Perco 1884–1942*, 423–26; Blau and Platzer, *Shaping the Great City*, 258; and Ursula Prokop, "Rudolf Perco 1884–1942: Architektur jenseits von

Tradition und Moderne" (Ph.D. diss., University of Vienna, 1997).

81. See, for instance, Perco's design for a thermal spa (1910), which won the Staatpreis in 1910 and was published in *Der Architekt* (1911), plates 6–11. The drawings for the project are located in the Perco Nachlaß, Wiener Stadt- und Landesarchiv (WSTLA).

82. Drawings for the project are located in the Perco Nachlaß, WSTLA.

83. For the Reichsbrücke competition, see Prokop, *Rudolf Perco 1884–1942*, 405. Hoppe and Schönthal won the first phase; the jury requested a chain or cable bridge. Theiss and Jaksch eventually built the bridge in collaboration with Holzmeister, but it collapsed in 1976.

84. Ibid.

85. For his religious buildings and memorials from the period 1930–33, see ibid., 266–84, and additionally for Belgrade, 399.

86. For "David's Tent," see ibid., 285–91, 406–07; also "Reuniongedächtnisdomanlage 'Zelte Davids'" in *Das Ungebaute Wien*, 320–321.

87. For Perco's *Sühnedenkmal* (Atonement Monument), 1918, for the world war, see *Das ungebaute Wien*, 286–87. Later in the twentieth century, the site was used as fairgrounds and, after much controversy, has been reconfigured with new buildings to create Vienna's Museums Quarter.

88. Prokop, *Rudolf Perco 1884–1942*, 353.

89. For a comment on the paradox of being liberal and anti-Semitic and for Perco's sympathy with the National Socialists, see ibid., 339–40.

90. For Perco's demise, see ibid., 363–64.

91. Ibid., 365; quotation is from p. 369.

92. Ibid., 369.

Selected Bibliography

Achleitner, Friedrich. "Gibt es einen Mitteleuropäischen Heimatstil? (oder: Entwurf einer peripheren Architekturlandschaft)." *Österreichische Zeitschrift für Kunst und Denkmalpflege* 43, nos. 3–4 (1989): 165–69.

———. *Österreichische Architektur im 20. Jahrhundert*. 4 vols. Salzburg: Residenz Verlag, 1990.

———. "The Pluralism of Modernity: The Architectonic 'Language Problem' in Central Europe." In Blau and Platzer, *Shaping the Great City*, 94–106.

———. *Wiener Architektur: Zwischen typologischen Fatalismus und semantischen Schlamassel*. Vienna: Böhlau, 1996.

Achleitner, Friedrich, Wilhelm Holzbauer, Herbert Muck, and Monika Knofler. *Clemens Holzmeister*. Vienna: Akademie der Bildenden Künste, 1982. An exhibition catalogue.

Achleitner, Friedrich. *Ernst Anton Plischke, Architekt und Lehrer*. Salzburg: Verlag Anton Pustet, 2003.

Adamek, Blahoslav, František Fröml, Dušan Janoušek, Pavel Marek, and Jaroslav Port. *Nová radnice v Prostějové*. Prostějov, Czech Republic: Městský národní výbor v Prostějové, 1990.

Alić, Dijana, and Maryam Gusheh. "Reconciling National Narratives in Socialist Bosnia and Herzegovina: The Baščaršija Project, 1948–1953." *JSAH* 58, no. 1 (March 1999): 6–25.

Alofsin, Anthony. *Frank Lloyd Wright: The Lost Years, 1910–1922; A Study of Influence*. Chicago: University of Chicago Press, 1993.

———, ed. *Frank Lloyd Wright: Europe and Beyond*. Berkeley and Los Angeles: University of California Press, 1999.

———. "The Kunsthistorisches Museum: A Treasure House for the Secessionists." *Jahrbuch der Kunsthistorischen Sammlungen in Wien* 88 (1992): 189–203.

Anderson, Benedict. *Imagined Communities. Reflections on the Origin and Spread of Nationalism*. London: Verso, 1991 (1983).

Anna, Susanne, ed. *Das Bauhaus im Osten- Slowakische und tschechische Avantgarde 1928–1939*. Ostfildern-Ruit, Germany: G. Hatje, 1997.

Architectural Heritage of Art Nouveau/Jugendstil: History and Conservation. Architecture and Protection of Monuments and Sites of Historical Interest Series, vol. 30, edited by Hans-Dieter Dyroff. Bonn: Deutsche UNESCO-Kommission, 1991. An exhibition catalogue.

Architecture and Avant-Garde in Poland, 1918–1939. *Rassegna* 18, no. 65 (1996).

Architekt Emil Belluš, regionálna moderna [Regional Modernism]. Bratislava: Spolok architektov Slovenska, 1992. An exhibition catalogue.

Architektúra & Urbanizmus. Časopis Pre Teóriu Architektúry a Urbanizmu [Architecture and Urbanism. Journal of Architectural and Town-Planning Theory] 29, nos. 1–2 (Bratislava, 1995); whole issue.

Architektúra & Urbanizmus. Časopis Pre Teóriu Architektúry a Urbanizmu 30, nos. 1–2 (Bratislava, 1996); whole issue.

Art in Theory 1900–2000: An Anthology of Changing Ideas. Edited by Charles Harrison and Paul Wood. 2nd ed. Malden, MA: Blackwell, 2003.

Art Nouveau/Jugendstil Architecture in Europe. Architecture and Protection of Monuments and Sites of Historical Interest Series, vol. 26, edited by Hans-Dieter Dyroff. Bonn: Deutsche UNESCO-Kommission, 1988. An exhibition catalogue.

Asenbaum, Paul. *Otto Wagner: Möbel und Innenräume*. Edited by Museum Moderner Kunst. Salzburg: Residenz Verlag, 1984.

Asenbaum, Paul, Stefan Asenbaum, and Christian Witt-Dörring, organizers and eds. *Moderne Vergangenheit 1800–1900: Möbel, Metall, Keramik, Glas, Textil, Entwürfe—aus Wien*. Vienna: Gesellschaf bildender Künstler Österreichs, 1981.

Ash, Timothy Garton. "The Puzzle of Central Europe." *New York Review of Books* 46, no. 5 (March 18, 1999): 18–20, 22–23.

Avant-garde Hongroise/Hongaarse Avant-Gard 1915–1925. Brussels: BBL and Brepols, 1999. An exhibition catalogue in French and Dutch.

Ballantyne, Andrew, ed. *What Is Architecture?* New York: Routledge, 2002.

Barasch, Moshe. *The Language of Art: Studies in Interpretation*. New York: New York University Press, 1997.

Barbarić, Damir. *Fin de siècle Zagreb-Beč*. Zagreb, Croatia: Školska knjiga, 1997.

Barbarić, Damir, and Michael Benedikt, eds. *Ambivalenz des Fin de siècle: Wien-Zagreb*. Vienna: Böhlau, 1998.

Barron, Stephanie, and Sabine Eckmann, eds. *Exiles + Emigrés: The Flight of European Artists from Hitler*. Los Angeles: Los Angeles County Museum of Art, 1997. An exhibition catalogue.

Bartha, Zoltán. *Family Memoriam of the Architect Medgyaszay*. Budapest: privately published, n.p., n.d.

Barthes, Roland. *S/Z*. Translated by Richard Miller. New York: Hill and Wang, 1974.

Becker, Annette, Dietmar Steiner, and Wilfried Wang, eds. *Österreich*. Architektur im 20. Jahrhundert Series. Munich: Prestel Verlag; Frankfurt am Main: Deutsches Architektur-Museum, 1995. An exhibition catalogue.

Beiersdorf, Zbigniew, and Jacek Purchla. *Dom pod Globusem: Dawna siedziba Krakówskiej Izby Handlowej i Przemysłowe/The Globe House: The Former Headquarters of the Kraków Chamber of Commerce and Industry*. Translated by Jerzy Pilawski. Cracow: Wydawn. Literackie, 1997. An exhibition catalogue.

Bellák, Gábor. "Folk Art, Art Nouveau and Historism at the Turn of the Century." In Éri and Jobbágyi, *A Golden Age*, 58.

Benešová, Marie. *Česká architektura v proměnách dvou století 1780–1980*. Prague: Státní pedagogické nakladatelství, 1984.

———. *Josef Gočár*. Prague: Nakladatelství československý výtvarných umělců, 1958.

———. *Pavel Janák*. Prague: Nakladatelství československý výtvarných umělců, 1959.

———. "Rondokubismus." *Architektura ČSSR* 28 (1969): 303–17.

Benson, Timothy O., ed. *Central European Avant-Gardes: Exchange and Transformation, 1910–1930*. Los Angeles: Los Angeles County Museum of Art; Cambridge, MA: MIT Press, 2002.

Benson, Timothy O., and Éva Forgács, eds. *Between Worlds: A Sourcebook of Central European Avant-Gardes, 1910–1930*. Los Angeles: Los Angeles County Museum of Art; Cambridge, MA: MIT Press, 2002.

Berend, Iván T. "From the Millennium to the Republic of Councils–Introduction." In Éri and Jobbágyi, *A Golden Age*, 53–56.

Berlam, R[uggero] and A[rduino]. "Notizie tecniche ed artistiche sul nuovo tempio, in Il nuovo tempio israelitico di Trieste." *Il corriere israelitico* 51, no. 2 (1912): 22. Quoted in Lerner, "The Narrating Architecture of Emancipation."

Berlin, Isaiah. "The Romantics and Their Roots (Excerpt from the Mellon Lectures Delivered in Washington in 1965)." *Times Literary Supplement*, no. 5003 (February 19, 1999): 13–15.

Bhabha, Homi K. "Figures of Difference." In *Art in Theory 1900–2000: An Anthology of Changing Ideas*, ed. Charles Harrison and Paul Wood, 2nd ed. (Malden, MA: Blackwell, 2003).

———. "Postmodernism/Postcolonialism." In Nelson and Schiff, *Critical Terms for Art History*, 435–51.

Biraghi, Marco, ed. *Béla Lajta: Ornamento e modernitá*. Milan: Electa, 1999.

———. "Bela Lajta e i suoi angeli." *Casabella* 60 (March 1996): 50–59.

———. "Ödön Lechner: La corona dell'architettura." *Casabella* 64, nos. 684–85 (December 2000–January 2001): 167–69.

Bissell, Tamara, and Roman Prahl. "The 'Nation for Itself' and the Curtain for the Czech National Theater." *Umění* 44, no. 6 (1996): 520–39.

Blau, Eve. *The Architecture of Red Vienna 1919–1934*. Cambridge, MA: MIT Press, 1999.

Blau, Eve, and Monika Platzer, eds. *Shaping the Great City: Modern Architecture in Central Europe, 1890–1937*. Munich: Prestel, 1999.

Boeckl, Matthias, ed. *Visionäre & Vertriebene: Österreichische Spuren in der modernen amerikanischer Architektur*. Vienna: Ernst & Sohn, 1995. An exhibition catalogue.

Bor, Ferenc. "Lignes courbes et vifs coloris: Art nouveau Magyar." *Monuments historiques*, no. 201 (March–April 1996): 70–74.

Boralevi, Alberto. "Il 'Tempio Israelitico' di Trieste: Storia di un concorso." In *Comunità Religiose di Trieste: Contributi di conoscenza*, edited by Civici Musei di Storia e Arte di Trieste. Udine: Istituto per l'Enciclopedia de Friuli Venezia Giulia, 1979.

Borsi, Franco, and Ezio Godoli. *Vienna 1900: Architecture and Design*. New York: Rizzoli, 1986.

Bořutová, Dana. "Dušan Jurkovič—The Architect of Genius Loci." *Architektúra a urbanizmus* 25, no. 3 (1991): 165–84.

———. "Kotázce národého stýlu v slovensky architektúre" [On the Problem of a National Style in Slovakian Architecture]. *Ars*, nos. 1–3 (1997): 167–73.

———. "Die Persönalichkeiten und Trends in der Architektur Bratislavasder zwanziger Jahre." *Ars*, no. 2 (1991): 97–109.

———. "The Slovak Contribution." In Burman, *Architecture 1900*, 64–75.

Bořutová-Debnárová, Dana. *Dušan Samo Jurkovič: OsobnosŤ a dielo*. Bratislava: Pallas, 1993.

Bořutová, Dana, Anna Zajková, and Matúš Dulla, eds. *Dušan Jurkovič: Súborna Výstara architekonického Diela* [General Exhibition of the Architectural Work]. Bratislava: Slovenská Národná Galéria, 1993.

Bösel, Richard. *Monumente: Wiener Denkmäler vom Klassizismus zur Secession: Eine Ausstellung des Kulturkreises Looshaus und der Graphischen Sammlung Albertina*. Vienna: Kulturkreis Looshaus, 1994.

Bösel, Richard, and Selma Krasa. *Monumente: Wiener Denkmäler vom Klassizismus zur Secession*. Vienna: Kulturkreis Looshaus, 1994. An exhibition catalogue.

Bouillon, A. *Principes de Desin Linéaire*. 2nd ed. Paris: Chez L. Hatchette, 1845.

Bourgoin, Jules. *Elements de l'art arabe. Le trait des entrelacs*. Paris: Firmin-Didot et Cie. 1879.

———. *Théorie de l'Ornement*. Paris: A. Levy, 1873.

Boyd Whyte, Iain. *Emil Hoppe, Marcel Kammerer, Otto Schönthal: Three Architects from the Master Class of Otto Wagner*. Cambridge, MA: MIT Press, 1989.

Brah, Avtar, and Annie Coombes, eds. *Hybridity and Its Discontents: Politics, Science, Culture*. New York: Routledge, 2000.

Breitwieser, T. M. "Krakau um 1900: Architektur im Wandel." Master's thesis, Paris-Lodron University, Salzburg, 1993.

Broch, Rudolf, and Hans Hauptmann, eds. *Die Westgalizischen Heldengräber aus den Jahren des Weltkrieges 1914–1915*. Cracow: K. u. K. Militärkommando Krakau, 1918.

Brückler, Theodor. "Zur Geschichte der österreichische Heimatschutzbewegung." *Österreichische Zeitschrift für Kunst und Denkmalpflege* 43, nos. 3–4 (1989): 145–56.

Brüderlin, Markus, ed. *Ornament and Abstraction: The Dialogue between Non-Western, Modern and Contemporary Art*. Basel: Fondation Beyeler, 2001.

Budapester Neubauten. Vienna: Verlag Anton Schroll, 1910.

Burkhardt, François. "Borek Šípek: Interventi al Castello di Praga [Work at the Prague Castle]." *Domus*, no. 786 (October 1996): 49–53.

———. "Károly Kós and the Hungarian Organic Movement." *Domus*, no. 826 (May 2000): 109–14.

———. "The Šípek School." *Domus*, no. 791 (March 1997): 106–10.

Burkhardt, François, Claude Eveno, and Boris Podrecca. *Jože Plečnik Architect: 1872–1957*. Cambridge, MA: MIT Press, 1989.

Burman, Peter, ed. *Architecture 1900*. London: Donhead, 1988.

Busek, Erhard. *Mitteleuropea, eine Spurensicherung*. Vienna: Kremayr & Scheriau, ca. 1997.

Bush, Olga. "The Architecture of Jewish Identity: The Neo-Islamic Central Synagogue of New York." *JSAH* 63, no. 2 (June 2004): 180–201.

Calvocoressi, Richard, and Keith Hartley. "Vienna, 1908–1918." In *Century City: Art and Culture in the Modern Metropolis*, edited by Iwona Blazwick, 224–49. London: Tate Gallery Publishing, 2001.

Cavanaugh, Jan. *Out Looking In: Early Modern Polish Art, 1890–1918*. Berkeley and Los Angeles: University of California Press, 2000.

Ceiner, Giovanni. "La sede della 'RAS' di Trieste tra disegno e innovazione." *Archeografo Triestino* 54 (1994): 167–85.

Charazinska, Elzbieta, and Lukasz Kossowski. *Fin-de-siècle: Polish Art, 1890–1914*. Warsaw: Narodowe w Warszawie, 1996.

Cherkes, B. S., Martin Kubelik, and Elisabeth Hofer. *Arkhitektura Halychyny XIX–XX st.: Vybrani materialy mizhnarodnoho sympoziumu 24–27 travnia 1994 r*. L'viv: Lvivska politehnika, 1996.

Chruscicki, Tadeusz, and Frantiszek Stolot. *Museums of Cracow*. Warsaw: Arkady, 1994.

Clair, Jean, ed. *Vienne 1880–1938: L'Apocalypse Joyeuse*. Paris: Editions Georges Pompidou, 1986. An exhibition catalogue.

Clarke, Georgia, and Paul Crossley, eds. *Architecture and Language: Constructing Identity in European Architecture, c. 1000–c. 1650*. Cambridge: Cambridge University Press, 2000.

Clegg, Elizabeth. "Budapest: The Nagyanya Colony." *The Burlington Magazine* 138 (October 9, 1996): 713–14.

Collins, Peter. *Changing Ideals in Modern Architecture, 1750–1950*. Montreal: McGill University Press, 1965; North American ed., 1967.

Cometa, Michele. "Architecture and Literature in Prague." *Abitare*, no. 363 (June 1997): 104–9.

Contemporary Slovene Architecture/L'Architecture contemporaine slovène/Die zeitgenössische slowenische Architektur. Ljubljana, Slovenia: DESSA and Ljubljana Society of Architects, 1995. An exhibition catalogue in English, French, and German.

Cook, Jeffrey. *Seeking Structure from Nature: The Organic Architecture of Hungary*. Basel: Birkhäuser, 1996.

Crowley, David. "Finding Poland in the Margins: The Case of the Zakopane Style." *Journal of Design History* 14, no. 2 (2001): 105–16.

———. *National Style and Nation-State: Design in Poland from the Vernacular Revival to the International Style*. Manchester: Manchester University Press; New York: St. Martin's Press, 1992.

———. "The Uses of Peasant Design in Austria-Hungary in the Late Nineteenth and Early Twentieth Centuries." *Studies in the Decorative Arts* 2, no. 2 (Spring 1995): 2–28.

Csenkey, Éva, and Ágota Steinert, eds. *Hungarian Ceramics from the Zsolnay Manufactory,*

1853–2001. New York: The Bard Graduate Center for Studies in the Decorative Arts, Design, and Culture; New Haven, CT: Yale University Press, 2002.

Csorba, László, József Sisa, and Zoltán Szalay. *Das ungarische Parlament*. Budapest: Képzőművészeti Kiadó, 1993.

Das K. K. Oesterreichische Postsparkassenamt in Wien. 1913. Reprint, Vienna: Architektur- und Baufachverlag Gesselschaft m.b.H., 1983.

Das ungebaute Wien: Projekte für die Metropole 1800 bis 2000. Vienna: Historisches Museum der Stadt Wien [1999]. An exhibition catalogue.

Dercsényi, Balázs. *Árkay Aladár*. Budapest: Akadémiai Kiadó, 1967.

———. *Calvinist Churches in Hungary*. Budapest: Hegyi, 1992.

———. *Lutheran Churches in Hungary*. Budapest: Hegyi, 1992.

Dluhosch, Eric, and Rostislav Švácha, eds. *Karel Teige 1900–1951: L'Enfant Terrible of the Czech Modernist Avant-Garde*. Cambridge, MA: MIT Press, 1999.

Doordan, Dennis P. "Architecture and Politics in Fascist Italy: Il Movimento italiano per l'architettura razionale 1928–1932." Ph.D. diss., Columbia University, 1983.

———. *Building Modern Italy: Italian Architecture, 1914–1936*. New York: Princeton Architectural Press, 1988.

Dostál, Oldřich, Josef Pechar, and Vítězslav Procházka. *Moderní architektura v Československu* [Modern Architecture in Czechoslovakia]. Prague: Obelisk, Nakladatelství Umění a Architektury, 1970.

Dulla, Matúš. "Military Cemeteries of Western Galicia." In Bořutová, Zajková, and Dulla, eds., *Dušan Jurkovič*, 89–101.

———. *Military Cemeteries of Western Galicia, Dušan Jurkovič 1916/1917, Guide*. Bratislava: Vysoká Škola výtvarných umení, 2002.

———. "Theoretical Thinking of Modernism in Slovakia." *Architektúra & Urbanizmus. Časopis Pre Teóriu Architektúry a Urbanizmu* 26, nos. 3–4 (1992): 145–56.

Dulla, Matúš, and Henrieta Moravčíková. *Architektúra slovenska v 20. storočí*. Bratislava: Vydavateľstvo Slovart, 2002.

———. "Kolonádový Most/Colonnade Bridge." *Architektúra & Urbanizmus. Časopis Pre Teóriu Architektúry a Urbanizmu* 29, nos. 1–2 (Bratislava, 1995): 88–93. In Slovak and English.

Eggert, Klaus, and Hermann Reining. *Die Wiener Ringstrasse: Das Kunstwerk im Bild*. Die Wiener Ringstrasse, Bild Einer Epoche. Die Erweiterung der Inneren Stadt Wien unter Kaiser Franz Joseph. Die Bauten und ihre Architekten, introduction by Renate Wagner-Rieger, vol. 1. Graz, Austria: Hermann Böhlaus Nachf., 1969.

Einhornova, Milada, and Erich Einhorn. *Zlatá Praha*. Prague: Panorama, 1989.

Emil Belluš: Architektonické dielo. Bratislava: Slovenská Národná Galéria, 1989. An exhibition catalogue.

Entz, Géza. *Budapest Matthias Church*. Tájak–Korok–Múzeumok Kiskönyvtára Series, no. 98. Budapest: TKM Egyesület, 1988.

Éri, Gyöngyi, and Zsuzsa Jobbágyi, eds. *A Golden Age: Art and Society in Hungary 1896–1914*. London: Corvina/Barbican Art Gallery; Miami: Center for the Fine Arts, 1990. An exhibition catalogue. Published in Hungarian under the title *Lélek és Forma: Magyar művészet 1896–1914* (Budapest: Idegenforgalmi Propaganda és Kiadó Vállalat, 1986).

Erläuterungen zur Bauvollendung der Kirche der Nieder Öst. Landes Heil- und Pflege Anstalten. 1907. Reprint, Vienna: Architektur- und Baufachverlag Gesselschaft m.b.H., 1983.

Ernst Anton Plischke. Vienna: Akademie der Bildenden Künste, 1983. An exhibition catalogue.

Ernyey, Gyula, ed. *Britain and Hungary: Contacts in Architecture and Design during the Nineteenth and Twentieth Century; Essays and Studies*. 3 vols. Budapest: Hungarian University of Craft and Design, 1999, 2003, 2005.

Ethnographic Art in Slovakia. Rome: Museo Nazionale delle Arti e Tradizioni Popolari, 2001. An exhibition catalogue.

Expresionismus a české umění 1905–1927. Prague: Národní galerie, 1994. An exhibition catalogue.

Facos, Michelle. *Nationalism and the Nordic Imagination: Swedish Art of the 1890s*. Berkeley and Los Angeles: University of California Press, 1998.

Facos, Michelle, and Sharon L. Hirsch, eds. *Art, Culture and National Identity in Fin-de-Siècle Europe*. Cambridge: Cambridge University Press, 2003.

Farbaky, Péter. "A Fasori Református Templom." *Ars Hungarica* 2 (1984): 255–69, pl. 31–56.

Fél, Edit, Tamás Hofer, and Klára K. Csilléry. *Hungarian Peasant Art*. London: Constable, 1971.

Ferkai, András. "Hungarian Architecture between the Wars." In Wiebensohn and Sisa, *The Architecture of Historic Hungary*, 244–74.

———. "*Neues Bauen* in Budapest." In Blau and Platzer, *Shaping the Great City*, 178–85.

———. "Recording and Preserving the Modern Heritage in Hungary." In *Modern Movement Heritage*, edited by Allen Cunningham, 44–49. London: E & FN SPON (Routledge), 1998.

Ferkai, András, and Márta Branczik. *Buda építészete a két viágháború között*. Budapest: MTA Művészettörténeti Kutató Intézet, 1995.

———. *Pest építészete a két világháború között*. Budapest: Modern Építészetért Építészettörténeti és Műemlékvédelmi Kht., 2001.

Folnesics, Joseph, ed. *Innenräume und Hausrat der Empire- und Biedermeierzeit in Österreich-Ungarn*. Vienna: Verlag Anton Schroll [ca. 1906].

Foltyn, Ladislav. *Slovenská arhitektúra a česká avantgarda 1918–1939*. Bratislava: Vydatel'stvo Spolku architektov Slovenska, 1993. Published in German under the title *Slowakische Architektur und die Tschechische Avantguarde 1918–1939* (Dresden: Verlag der Kunst, 1991).

Forty, Adrian. *Words and Buildings: A Vocabulary of Modern Architecture*. New York: Thames & Hudson, 2000.

Frampton, Kenneth. *Modern Architecture: A Critical History*. London: Thames and Hudson, Ltd., 1985.

Freedberg, David. *The Power of Images: Studies in the History and Theory of Response*. Chicago: University of Chicago Press, 1989.

Frojimovics, Kinga, Géza Komoróczy, Viktória Pusztai, and Andrea Strbik, eds. *Jewish Budapest: Monuments, Rites, History*. Budapest: Central European University, 1999.

Gábor, Eszter. *Budapesti villák: A kiegyezéstől a második világháborúig*. Our Budapest Series. Budapest: City Hall, 2001.

———. "Korb and Giergl." In *Magyar Művészet 1890–1919* (Budapest, 1981).

Gall, Anthony. "Domus itinerario n.145: Kós a Budapest e in Transilvania" [Kós in Budapest and Transylvania]. *Domus*, no. 804 (May 1998): [117–24.]

———. "Károly Kós (1883–1977)." In Burman, *Architecture 1900*, 156–60.

———. "Kós in Budapest and Transylvania." *Domus*, no. 804 (May 1998): 117–24.

———. *Kós Károly műhelye, tanulmány és adattár* [The Workshop of Károly Kós, Study and Documentation]. Budapest: Mundus Magyar Egyetemi, 2002.

Gans, Deborah, and Zehra Kuz, eds. *The Organic Approach to Architecture*. Chichester, England: Wiley-Academy, 2003.

Gebhard, David, ed. *The Architectural Drawings of R. M. Schindler*. New York: Garland Publishing, 1994.

Gellner, Ernest. *Nations and Nationalism*. Ithaca, NY: Cornell University Press, 1983.

Gerle, János. "Architecture at the Exhibitions." In *Lélek és Forma: Magyar művészet 1896–1914/ A Golden Age: Art and Society in Hungary 1896–1914*, edited by Gyöngyi Éri and Zsuzsa Jobbágyi, exhibition catalogue (Budapest: Corvina; Miami: Barbicon Art Gallery, Center for the Fine Arts, 1990), 60.

———. "The Golden Age of Architectural Ceramics in Hungary." In Csenkey and Steinert, *Hungarian Ceramics from the Zsolnay Manufactory*, 191.

———. "Hungarian Architecture from 1900 to 1918." In Wiebensohn and Sisa, *The Architecture of Historic Hungary*, 222–43.

———. "Ödön Lechner, Architect (1845–1914)." In Burman, *Architecture 1900*, 12–20. Previously published in *The New Hungarian Quarterly* 27, no. 101 (1986): 183–88.

———. *Palaces of Money*. Our Budapest Series. Budapest: City Hall, 1994.

———. *The Turn of the Century*. Our Budapest Series. Budapest: City Hall, 1992. Published in Hungarian under the title *Századforduló*. Budapest: Városnáza kiadása, 1993.

———. "Window Design." In Lőrinci, *Budapest in Detail*.

Gerle, János, ed. *Lechner Ödön*. Az építészet mesterei (Masters of Architecture). Budapest: Holnap Kiadó, 2003.

Gerle, János, Attila Kovács, and Imre Makovecz. *A századforduló magyar építészete* [Hungarian Architecture of the Turn of the Century]. Budapest: Szépirodalmi Könyvkiadó-Bonex, 1990.

Gerle, János, László Lugosi Lugo, and Katalin Keserü. *A szecesszió Budapesten*. Budapest: Magyar Könyvklub, 1999.

Gerle, János, et al. *Építeszeti kalauz: Budapest építészete a századfordulól napjainkig*. Edited by Zsuzsa Lőrinci and Mihály Vargha. Budapest: 6 Bt Kiadó, 1997.

Gerő, András. *Heroes' Square, Budapest: Hungary's History in Stone and Bronze*. Budapest: Corvina, 1990.

Gerő, László. *Magyar építészet a XIX. század végéig*. Budapest: Építésügyi Kiadó, 1954.

———. *Magyarországi zsinagógák*. Budapest: Műszaki Könyvkiadó, 1989.

Giladi, Dávid. *Pesti Mérnökök—Izrael országépítői* [Architects of Pest—The Builders of Israel]. Budapest: Múlt és jövő, 1992.

Gink, Károly, and Ivor Sándor Kiss. *Folk Art and Folk Artists in Hungary*. Budapest: Corvina Press, 1968.

Graf, Otto Antonia. *Master Drawings of Otto Wagner*. New York: The Drawing Center, 1987. An exhibition catalogue.

———. *Otto Wagner: Denkend zeichnen, zeichnend denken; Zur diagraphischen Methodologik*. Vienna: Böhlau Verlag, 1999.

———. *Otto Wagner: Das Werk des Architekten*. 7 vols. Vienna: Verlag Böhlau, 1985–2000.

———. *Die vergessene Wagnerschule*. Vienna: Schriften des Museums des 20. Jahrhunderts, 3. Band, Verlag Jugend & Volk, 1969.

Gravagnuolo, Benedetto. *Adolf Loos*. New York: Rizzoli, 1988.

Gresleri, Giuliano. *Josef Hoffmann*. New York: Rizzoli, 1985.

Grimme, Karl M., and Peter Behrens. *Peter Behrens and His Academic Master-School, Vienna*. Translated by Dozent L. H. Paulovsky. Vienna: Adolf Luser, 1930.

Gsteu, Johann Georg, Otto Kapfinger, Ernst Mateovics, Wilfried Richter, and Dietmar Steiner, eds. *Architecture in Vienna*. 2nd ed. Vienna: Georg Prachner Verlag, 1992.

Guillerme, Jacques. "La colonna del discorso: Architettura e linguaggio." *Casabella* 54, no. 568 (May 1990): 36–39, 61.

———. "The Idea of Architectural Language: A Critical Inquiry." *Oppositions* 10 (Fall 1977): 21–26.

Guth, Christine M. E., ed. *Art Journal: Japan 1868–1945; Art, Architecture, and National Identity* 55, no. 3 (Fall 1996).

Gyáni, Gábor. *Parlour and Kitchen: Housing and Domestic Culture in Budapest, 1870–1940*. Budapest: Central European University Press, 2002.

Haas, Hans, and Hannes Stekl, eds. *Bürgerliche Selbstdarstellung: Städtebau, Architektur, Denkmäler*. Bürgertum in der Habsburgmonarchie, vol. 4. Vienna: Böhlau Verlag, 1995.

Haiko, Peter, and Renata Kassal-Mikula, eds. *Friedrich von Schmidt (1825–1891): Ein gotischer Rationalist*. Vienna: Historisches Museum der Stadt Wien, 1991. An exhibition catalogue.

Haiko, Peter, and Mara Reissberger. "Quelques Réflexions à propos du débat sur l'ornement entre 1900 et 1910." In *Critique de l'ornement de Vienne à la postmodernité*, edited by Michel Collomb and Gerard Raulet, 123–31. Paris: Méridiens Klineksieck, 1992.

Hajós, Géza. "Heimatstil-Heimatschutzstil." *Österreichische Zeitschrift für Kunst und Denkmalflege* 43, nos. 3–4 (1989): 156–59.

Hammer-Moravčíková, Henrieta. "The Slovak Architecture in the Period 1918–1925." *Architektúra a urbanizmus* 26, nos. 3–4 (1992): 157–62.

Hammer-Schenk, Harold. *Synagogen in Deutschland: Geschichte einer Baugattung im 19. und 20. Jahrhundert (1780–1933)*. 2 vols. Hamburg: Hans Christians Verlag, 1981.

Hanák, Péter. *The Garden and the Workshop, Essays on the Cultural History of Vienna and Budapest*. Princeton, NJ: Princeton University Press, 1998.

Handžić, Adem. *A Survey of Islamic Cultural Monuments until the End of the Nineteenth Century in Bosnia*. Istanbul: IRCICA, 1996.

Harrod, Tanya, ed. *Obscure Objects of Desire: Reviewing the Crafts in the 20th Century*. London: Crafts Council, 1997.

Haupt, Herbert. *Das Kunsthistorische Museum: Die Geschichte des Hauses am Ring; Hundert Jähre im Spiegel Historischer Ereignisse*. Vienna: Christian Brandstätter Verlag, 1991.

Heathcote, Edwin. *Budapest: A Guide to Twentieth-Century Architecture*. London: Ellipsis; Cologne: Konemann, 1997.

———. *Monument Builders: Modern Architecture and Death*. Chichester, West Sussex: Academy Editions, 1999.

Hechter, Michael. *Containing Nationalism*. New York: Oxford University Press, 2000.

Heinrich von Ferstel (1828–1883), Bauten und Projekte für Wien. Vienna: Historischen Museums der Stadt Wien, 1984. An exhibition catalogue.

Held, Joseph, ed. *The Columbia History of Eastern Europe in the Twentieth Century*. New York: Columbia University Press, 1992.

Heller, Imre, and Zsigmond Vajda. *The Synagogues of Hungary: An Album*. Edited by Randolph L. Brandon. New York: World Federation of Hungarian Jews, 1968.

Herbenová, Olga, and Vladímir Šlapeta. *Pavel Jának 1882–1956: Architektur und Kunstgewerbe*. Vienna: Semper-Depot, 1984. An exhibition catalogue.

Herscher, Andrew. "Städtebau as Imperial Culture: Camillo Sitte's Urban Plan for Ljubljana." *JSAH* 62, no. 2 (June 2003): 212–27.

Hevesi, Ludwig. *Österreichische Kunst im 19. Jahrhundert*. Leipzig, 1906. Page 286 quoted in Müller, *Otto-Wagner Synagoge*, 12.

———. "Portois & Fix." *Kunst and Kunstwerk* 4 (1901): 321–22. Quoted in Pozzetto, *Max Fabiani*, 130–31.

Hilger, Wolfgang, Irene Nierhaus, Kristian Sotriffer, Viktor Matejka, Georg Eisler, and

Daniel Eckert. *Die Wiener Secession—Die Vereinigung bildender Künstler 1897–1985*. Vienna: Hermann Böhlaus Nachf., 1986.

Hobsbawm, Eric. *The Age of Empire 1875–1914*. History of Civilization Series. New York: Vintage Books, 1989.

———. *The Age of Extremes: A History of the World, 1914–1991*. New York: Vintage Books, 1996.

———. *Nations and Nationalism since 1780: Programme, Myth, Reality*. 2nd ed. Cambridge: Cambridge University Press, 1992.

Hoffmann, Hans-Christoph. *Die Theaterbauten von Fellner und Helmer*. Munich: Prestel, 1966.

Hofmann, Werner. *Gustav Klimt*. Greenwich, CT: New York Graphic Society, Ltd., 1971.

Holzmeister, Clemens. *Architekt in der Zeitenwende: Clemens Holzmeister; Selbstbiographie, Werkverzeichnis*. Salzburg: Verlag Das Bergland-Buch, 1976.

———. *Clemens Holzmeister*. Berlin: F. E. Hubsch, 1927.

———. *Clemens Holzmeister: Bauten, Entwurfe und Handzeichnungen*. Salzburg: A. Pustet, 1937.

Hrausky, Andrej. "Notes on Vurnik's Cooperative Bank." In *Ivan Vurnik 1884–1971: Slovenski arhitekt*, 77.

Huey, Michael, ed. *Viennese Silver: Modern Design 1780–1918*. Ostfildern-Ruit, Germany: Hatje Cantz Verlag, 2003. An exhibition catalogue.

Hungaria Regia (1000–1800). Fastes et défis. Brussels: Brepols, 1999. An exhibition catalogue.

Hungarian Ethnographical Museum. *Hungarian Decorative Folk Art*. Budapest: Corvina, 1954.

Irace, Fulvio. "Architettura Razionalista." *Abitare*, no. 363 (June 1997): 144–65, 245–46. Italian and English.

Ivan Vurnik 1884–1971: Slovenski arhitekt [Slovenian Architect]. Exhibition catalogue and special issue of *Arhitektov bilten* [Architect's Bulletin] 24, nos. 119–24 (December 1994).

Jaeger, Roland. *Heinrich de Fries und sein Beitrag zur Architekturpublizistik der Zwanziger Jahre*. Berlin: Gebr. Mann Verlag, 2001.

Jahn, Harald A. *Jugendstil in Budapest: Die Sezession in Ungarns Metropole um die Jahrhundertwende*. Dortmund: Harenburg Editions, 1995.

Jamnitzer, Wenzel. *Perspectiva corporum regularium*. Nürnberg, 1568.

Janák, Pavel. "From Modern Architecture to Architecture." *Styl* 2 (July 1910): 105–9.

———. "Otto Wagner." *Styl* 1 (1908–9): 41–48.

Jarzombek, Mark. "Joseph August Lux: Werkbund Promoter, Historian of a Lost Modernity." *JSAH* 63, no.2 (June 2004): 202–19.

Jelavich, Barbara. *History of the Balkans: Twentieth Century*. Vol. 2. New York: Cambridge University Press, 1983.

Jiří Kroha: Kubist, Expressionist, Funktionalist, Realist. Vienna: Architektur Zentrum Wien, and Sonderzahl Verlag [1998]. An exhibition catalogue.

Johnson, Lonnie R. *Central Europe: Enemies, Neighbors, Friends*. New York: Oxford University Press, 1996.

Jones, Owen. *The Grammar of Ornament*. 1856. Reprint, London: Studio Editions, 1986.

———. *Plans, Elevations, Sections and Details of the Alhambra. Taken from Drawings by M. Jules Goury and by Owen Jones, Architect 1834 and 1837*. 2 vols. London, 1842–45.

Jurkovič, Dušan. *Práce lidu našeho: Lidové stavby, zařízení a výzdoba obydlí, drobné práce/Slowakische Volksarbeiten: Volksbauten, Interieurs and Handarbeiten/Les ouvrages populaires des Slovaques: Batiments populaires, intéerieurs, ouvrages manuels* [The Works of Our People: Folk Buildings, Interiors, and Handicrafts]. Vienna: Kunstverlag Anton Schroll & Co., 1905-13. Ten-plate folio, Vienna: Verlag Anton Schroll, 1906.

Kafka, František. *Baedeker's Prague*. New York: Prentice-Hall, 1987.

Kann, Robert A. *A History of the Habsburg Empire 1526–1918*. Berkeley and Los Angeles: University of California Press, 1974.

Kapfinger, Otto, and Adolf Krischanitz. *Die Wiener Secession—Das Haus: Entstehung, Geschichte, Erneuerung*. Vienna: Hermann Böhlaus Nachf., 1986.

Kaplan, Wendy, ed. *Designing Modernity: The Arts of Reform and Persuasion, 1885–1945*. New York: Times and Hudson, 1995. An exhibition catalogue.

Kathy, Imre. "Árkay Aladár." In *Magyar Művészet 1890–1919* (Budapest: Akadémiai Kiadó, 1981).

———. *Medgyaszay István*. Budapest: Akadémiai Kiadó, 1979.

Kaufmann, Thomas DaCosta. *Court, Cloister, and City: The Art and Culture of Central Europe 1450–1800*. Chicago: University of Chicago Press, 1995.

Keplinger, Monika. "Zum Kirchenbau Friedrich Schmidts." In Haiko and Kassal-Mikula, *Friedrich von Schmidt (1825–1891)*, 9.

Keserü, Katalin. "Art Contacts between Great Britain and Hungary at the Turn of the Century." *Hungarian Studies* 6, no. 2 (1990): 141–54.

———. "The Idea of Nationalism in Nineteenth-Century Hungarian Architecture: From an International to a Regional Style." Typescript, n.d.

———. "Indian Influence on Hungarian Architecture." In *Hungarian Scholars on India Architecture and Indiology*, 56–5. New Delhi: Hungarian Information and Cultural Center, 1992.

Kish, John, ed. *The Hungarian Avant-Garde 1914–1933*. Storrs, CT: William Benton Museum of Art, 1987. An exhibition catalogue.

Klein, Dieter. "Architektonische Wechselbeziehungen zwischen Wien und Budapest im 19. Jahrhundert." *Wiener Geschictsblätter* 47, no. 2 (1992): 65–83.

Klein, Rudolf. "Pávatoll és építőművészet—Szabadka szecessziós épületei európai összefüggésben" [The Art Nouveau of Subotica in European Cultural Context]. *Üzenet* 5–6 (Szabadka, Yugoslavia [Serbia], 1991): 411–22.

———. "Sinagoga u Subotici—Uporedna analiza s kršćanskim sakralnim objektima" [The Synagogue of Subotica—A Comparative Analysis with Christian Sacred Space]. *Čovjek i prostor* 7–8 (Zagreb, Croatia, 1989): 15–17.

Klösz, György. *Budapest Anno . . . Photographies en atelier et à l'extérieur*. Preface by Lajos Mesterházi. Budapest: Corvina, 1984.

Knofler, Monika. "Clemens Holzmeister: Das architektonische Werk." Ph.D. diss., Innsbruck University, 1976.

"Kochovo Sanatórium/Koch Sanitorium." In *Architektúra & Urbanizmus. Časopis Pre Teóriu Architektúry a Urbanizmu* 29, nos. 1–2 (Bratislava, 1995): 64–69. In Slovak and English.

Komoróczy, Géza, ed. *Jewish Budapest: Monuments, Rites, History*. Budapest: Central European University, 1999.

Komoto, Shinji. *Panorama: Architecture and Applied Arts in Hungary, 1896–1916*. Kyoto: National Museum of Modern Art, 1995.

König, Tamàs, and Péter Wagner. "The Reconstruction of Two Theaters of the Turn-of-the-Century in Hungary." In Burman, *Architecture 1900*, 334–46.

Koós, Judith. *Kozma Lajos munkássága*. Budapest: Akadémiai Kiadó, 1975.

———. "Motifs in the Iconography of Art Nouveau." *Actes du XXIIe Congrès International d'Histoire de l'Art* 2, nos. 313–318, Budapest, 1972.

Koppelkamm, Stefan. *Exotische Architekturen im 18. Und 19. Jahrhundert*. Berlin: Ernst & Sohn, 1987.

Korecký, Miroslav. "Sto let Zítkova projektu Národního divadla v Praze." *Umění* 14 (1966): 541–66.

Kós, Károly. *Erdélyország népének építése* [Transylvanian Folk Architecture]. 1907. Facsimile ed., Budapest: Balassi Könyvkiadó; Kolozsvár: Polis Könyvkiadó, 1996.

———. "Nemzeti művészet." *Magyar Iparművészet* (1910): 141–57.

[Koubská, Vlasta, and Vlaďka Valchářová.] *Bedřich Feuerstein: Scénografie, architektura (1892–1936)*. [Prague: Národní muzeum,] 1996. An exhibition catalogue.

Kováts, J. István, ed.. *Magyar református templomok* [Hungarian Reformed Churches]. Budapest: Athenaeum, 1942.

Kravos, Marko, Marco Pozzetto, Milan Pahor, Sandi Volk, Bogomila Kravos, and Pavle Merkù. *Narodni dom v Trstu 1904–1920*. Trieste: Založba Devin, 1995.

Krečič, Peter. "Architecture in the Former Yugoslavia." In *Impossible Histories: Historical Avant-Gardes, Neo-Avant-Gardes, and Post-Avant-Gardes in Yugoslavia 1918–1991*, edited by Dubravka Djurić and Miško Šuvaković. Cambridge, MA: MIT Press, 2003.

———. *Plečnik: The Complete Works*. New York: Whitney Library of Design, 1993.

Krinsky, Carol Herselle. *Synagogues of Europe: Architecture, History, Meaning*. New York: Architectural History Foundation; Cambridge, MA: MIT Press, 1985; New York: Dover, 1996.

Kristan, Markus. *Adolf Loos: Läden & Lokale*. Vienna: Album, 2001.

———. *Die Architektur der Wiener Ringstrasse, 1860–1900: In zeitgenössischen Architekturphotographien*. Vienna: Album Verlag, 2003.

———. *Bauten in Style der Secession Architektur in Wien 1900–1910*. Vienna: Album, 2002.

———. *Carl König 1841–1915: Ein neubarocker Großstadtarchitekt in Wien*. Vienna: Verlag Holzhausen, 1999.

———. *Josef Hoffmann: Bauten & Interieurs in zeitgenössischen Photographien*. Vienna: Album, 2002.

———. *Joseph Urban: Die Wiener Jahre des Jugendstilarchitekten und Illustrators 1872–1911*. Vienna: Böhlau Verlag, 2000.

———. *Oskar Marmorek: Architekt und Zionist, 1863–1909*. Vienna: Böhlau Verlag, 1996.

Kritilová, Eva. *Architekt Josef Zítek*. Prague: Státní nakladatelství krásné literatury, hudby a umění, 1954.

Krstić, Boško. *Gradska kuća subotičko čudo/Városháza a szabadkai csoda/Town Hall the

Miracle of Subotica. Subotica, Yugoslavia: Globus, 2003.

Krysiak, Maria. *Secesja w Katowicach* [Art Nouveau in Katowice]. Bydgoszcz, Poland: Wydawn Unitex, 2001.

Krysztofowicz-Kozakowska, Stefania. *Art déco en Pologne.* Brussels: S. Krysztofowicz-Kozakowska, 2001.

Krzović, Ibrahim, ed. *Arhitektura Bosne i Hercegovine, 1878–1918.* Sarajevo: Umjetnička galerija Bosne i Hercegovine [1987]. An exhibition catalogue.

Kusák, Dalibor, Jiří Burian, Eva Križanová, and Ivan Muchka. *Hrady a zámky v Československu.* Prague: Panorama, 1990.

Kusý, Martin. *Architektúra na Slovensku 1918–1945.* Bratislava: Pallas, 1971.

———. *Emil Belluš.* Bratislava: Tatran, 1984.

Lamač, Miroslav. *Cubisme Tschèque.* Paris: Editions du Centre Pompidou and Flammarion, 1992. An exhibition catalogue.

Lambrichs, Anne. *József Vágó un architect hongrois dans le tourmente européenne.* Bruxelles: Archives d'architecture moderne, 2003. Published in Hungarian under the title *Vágó József* (Az építészet mesterei [Masters of Architecture]. Budapest: Holnap Kiadó, 2005).

Laslo, Aleksander. "Lica moderniteta 1898–1918: Zagrebačka arhitektura secesijske epohe" [Faces of Modernity 1898–1918: Zagreb Architecture in the Age of Secession]. In *Secesija u Hrvatskoj* [Art Nouveau in Croatia], Muzej za umjetnost i obrt, 22–41, 228–251. Zagreb, Croatia, 2003–4. An exhibition catalogue.

László, Gyula. *1910—ben születtem: Egy a XX. századot végigélt magyar ember emlékezései.* Szombathely, Hungary: Életünk, 1995.

———. *The Treasure of Nagyszentmiklós.* Photographs by I. Rácz. Budapest: Corvina Kiadó, 1984.

Lavin, Sylvia. *Quatremère de Quincy and the Invention of a Modern Language of Architecture.* Cambridge, MA: MIT Press, 1992.

Lechner, Jenö. *Jenö Lechner.* Geneva: Masters of Architecture, Ltd., 1930.

Lechner, Ödön. "Magyar formanyelv nem volt, hanem lesz." *Művészet,* no. 1 (1906): 1–18.

Lehne, Andreas. "Heimatstil—Zum Problem der Terminologie." *Österreichische Zeitschrift für Kunst und Denkmalpflege* 43, nos. 3–4 (1989): 159–64.

Lehne, Andreas, and Tamás Pintér. *Jugendstil in Wien and Budapest.* Vienna: Edition J & V Wien Verlag, 1990.

Lemberg/L'viv 1772–1918. Vienna: Eigenverlag der Museen der Stadt Wien, 1983. An exhibition catalogue.

Le Rider, Jacques. *Modernity and Crises of Identity.* Translated by Rosemary Morris. New York: Continuum, 1993.

Lerner, L. Scott. "The Narrating Architecture of Emancipation." Jewish Social Studies 6, no. 3. Reproduced on-line at http://iupjournals.org/jss/jss6-3.html#f33.

Lesnikowski, Wojciech, ed. *East European Modernism: Architecture in Czechoslovakia, Hungary and Poland between the Wars, 1919–1939.* New York: Rizzoli, 1996.

Letis, Caterina. "Giovanni Berlam 1823–1892: Architteture." *Archeografo Triestino* 53 (1993): 33–88.

———. "Ruggero Berlam (1854–1920). Architetture fino al 1905." *Archeografo Triestino* 54 (1994): 111–45.

Lewis, Michael J. *The Politics of the German Gothic Revival: August Reichensperger (1808–1895).* New York: Architectural History Foundation; Cambridge, MA: MIT Press, 1993.

Lieven, Dominic. *When Nationalism Began to Hate: Imagining Modern Politics in Nineteenth-Century Poland.* New York: Oxford University Press, 2000.

Linde, Helmut. *Baedeker's Budapest.* New York: Prentice-Hall, 1987.

Lisowski, Bohdan. *Modern Architecture in Poland.* Warsaw: Interpress, 1968.

Long, Christopher. "Adolf Loos's 'Trotzdem.'" *Harvard Design Magazine* 16 (Winter–Spring 2002): 64–66.

———. "East Central Europe: National Identity and International Perspective." *JSAH* 61, no. 4 (December 2002): 519–29.

———. Review of *Fashioning Vienna: Adolf Loos's Cultural Criticism,* by Janet Stewart. *Harvard Design Magazine* 14 (Summer 2001): 81–83.

———. Review of *Jan Kotěra 1871–1923: The Founder of Modern Czech Architecture,* edited by Vladímir Šlapeta. *Centropa* 3, no. 2 (September 2003): 277–79.

———. "'The Works of Our People': Dušan Jurkovič and the Slovak Folk Art Revival." *Studies in the Decorative Arts* 12, no. 1 (Fall–Winter 2004–5): 2–29.

———. "'Wiener Wohnkultur': Interior Design in Vienna, 1910–1938." *Studies in the Decorative Arts* 5, no. 1 (Fall–Winter 1997–98): 29–51.

Loos, Adolf. *Trotzdem: 1900–1930.* Innsbruck: Brenner-Verlag, 1931.

Lőrinci, Zsuzsa, ed. *Budapest in Detail.* Budapest: GBt Kiadó, 1999.

Lucarz, Christel. "Budapest, la choix du décor." *Beaux Arts Magazine*, no. 150 (November 1996): 112–13.

Lux, Joseph A. "Das Hotel, ein Bauprobleme." *Der Architekt* 15 (1909): 17–20.

Macsai, John. "Between Classicism and Modernism: Details of the Hungarian National Romantic Movement." *Threshold: Journal of the School of Architecture, University of Illinois at Chicago* 3 (Autumn 1985): 92–105.

Magocsi, Paul Robert. *Historical Atlas of Central Europe.* Seattle: University of Washington Press, 2002.

Mallgrave, Harry Francis, ed. *Otto Wagner: Reflections on the Raiment of Modernity.* Santa Monica, CA: The Getty Center for the History of Art and the Humanities, 1993.

Mansbach, Steven A. "Confrontation and Accommodation in the Hungarian Avant-Garde." *Art Journal* 49 (Spring 1990): 9–27.

———. "The 'Foreignness' of Classical Modern Art in Romania." *Art Bulletin* 80, no. 3 (October 1998): 534–54.

———. "Introductory Thoughts on Hungarian History and Culture." In *Two Centuries of Hungarian Painters, 1820–1970: A Catalogue of the Nicholas Salgo Collection*, 9–16. Washington, DC: University Press of America, 1991.

———. "Jože Plečnik, and the Landscaping of Modern Ljubljana." *Centropa* 4, no. 2 (May 2004): 111–21.

———. *A Legacy Envisioned: A Century of Modern Art to Celebrate Hungary's 1100 Years, 896–1996.* Washington, DC: World Bank, 1996.

———. *Modern Art in Eastern Europe from the Baltic to the Balkans, ca. 1890–1939.* Cambridge: Cambridge University Press, 1999.

Maroević, Tonko. "Jugendstil, Sezession und Expressionismus. Der Nachklang in Zagreb." In Barbarić and Benedikt, *Ambivalenz des Fin de siècle*, 261–66.

Maruševski, Olga. "Architektonisch-urbanistische Verbindungen zwischen Zagreb und Wien um der Jahrhundertwende." In Barbarić and Benedikt, *Ambivalenz des Fin de siècle*, 199–229.

Matějček, Antonín, ed. *Národ Sobě: Národní Divadlo a Jeho Umělecké Poklady.* Prague: Melantrich, 1940.

———. *Národní divadlo a jeho výtvarníci.* Prague, 1933; updated, 1954.

Max Fabiani 1865–1962: Bauten und Projekte in Wien. Vienna: Architektur- und Baufach-Verlag, 1982. An exhibition catalogue.

McCord, Olga Alexandra. "Nationalism and Its Expression in Architecture: The Czech National Theater and Its Legacy." Ph.D. diss., University of California, Berkeley, 1993.

Medgyaszay, István. "A Szent Gellért-hegy kiképzése és a nemzeti panteon" [The Artistic Development of the St. Gellért Hill and the National Pantheon]. *Magyar Mérnök és Építész Egylet Heti Értesítője*, no. 30 (1908). N.p.

———. "A vasbeton művészi formájáról." *Művészet* 8 (1909).

Mencl, František. "Krematoria." *Stavba* 1, no. 6 (June 1922).

Mencl, Václav. *Lidová architektura v Československu.* Prague: Nakladatelství československé akademie věd, 1980.

Merényi, Ferenc. *1867–1965, cento anni architettura ungherese: Appunti per una storia dell'architettura contemporanea ungherese.* Quaderni di documentazione, year 7, no. 1. Rome: Accademia d'Ungheria in Roma, 1965.

———. *A magyar építészet 1867–1957* [Hungarian Architecture 1867–1967]. Budapest: Műszaki könyvkiadó, 1970.

Mertlík, Pavel. *Wenkův Dům.* Jaroměř, Czech Republic: Vydalo městké muzeum v Jaroměří v roce, 1990.

[Meyer, Christian, ed.] *Josef Hoffmann/Sanatorium Purkersdorf.* New York: Galerie Metropol Inc., n.d. An exhibition catalogue.

Miller Lane, Barbara. *National Romanticism and Modern Architecture in Germany and the Scandinavian Countries.* Cambridge: Cambridge University Press, 2000.

Moderne Städtebilder. Abth. IV: Neubauten in Wien. Berlin: Wasmuth, 1900.

Mohos, Márta. *Regélö Kispest.* Budapest: Magyar Képek Kft., 1994.

Moravánszky, Ákos. *Competing Visions: Aesthetic Invention and Social Imagination in Central European Architecture, 1867–1918.* Cambridge, MA: MIT Press, 1998.

———. *Építészet az Osztrák-Magyar Monarchiában.* Budapest: Corvina Kiadó, 1988. Published in German under the title *Die Architektur der Donaumonarchie* (Berlin: Ernst und Sohn, 1988).

———. *Die Erneuerung der Baukunst: Wege zur Moderne in Mitteleuropa 1900–1940.* Salzburg: Residenz Verlag, 1988.

———. "Hungarian National Architectural Efforts at the Beginning of the Twentieth Century." *Österreichische Zeitschrift für Kunst und Denkmalpflege* 33, nos. 1–2 (1979): 52–60.

———. "Materiallandschaften." *Kritische Berichte* 28, no. 2 (2000): 20–28.

———. "Materialwahrheit und Bekleidungsästhetik: Árkay Aladárs reformierte Kirche in Budapest (1911 bis 1913)" [Material-Truth and Clothing-Aesthetic: Aladár Árkay's Reformed Church in Budapest (1911 to 1913)]. In Nautz and Vahrenkamp, *Die Wiener Jahrhundertwende*, 588–604.

———. "Nationale Bestrebungen in der ungarischen Architektur der Jahrhundertwende" [Hungarian National Architectural Efforts at the Beginning of the Twentieth Century]. *Österreichische Zeitschrift für Kunst und Denkmalpflege* 33, nos. 1–2 (1979): 52–60.

———. "Die Sprache der Fassaden: Das Problem des Ausdrucks in der Architektur der Donaumonarchie 1900–1914." In Becker, Steiner, and Wang, *Österreich*, 12–21.

———. "'Truth to Material' vs. 'the Principle of Cladding': The Language of Materials in Architecture." *AA Files*, no. 31 (Summer 1996): 39–46.

Mugerauer, Robert. *Discourses in Hybridity and Identity*. Berkeley: Center for Environmental Design Research, University of California at Berkeley, 2002.

Müller, Ines. *Die Otto Wagner-Synagoge in Budapest*. Vienna: Löcker, 1992.

Muñoz, Bernal, and José Luis. "Ödön Lechner: Arquitectura y nacionalismo en Hungría." *Goya*, no. 258 (May–June 1997): 352–60.

Nagy, Gergely. *Garden Cities in Europe: Wekerle Estate, Budapest*. Budapest: Magyar Kepek, [2000].

Nagy, Gergely, and Károly Szelényi. *Kertvárosunk, a Wekerle*. Veszprém, Hungary: Szelényi Ház, 1994.

Nagy, Ildikó. "The Character of Hungarian Art Nouveau as Reflected in Hungarian Research (1959–1981)." *Acta Historiae Artium* 28 (1982): 383–427.

Nautz, Jürgen, and Richard Vahrenkamp, eds. *Die Wiener Jahrhundertwende: Einflüsse, Umwelt, Wirkungen*. Vienna: Böhlau Verlag, 1993.

Nebehay, Christian M. *Ver Sacrum 1898–1903*. 2nd ed. Vienna: Edition Tusch, 1981.

Nelson, Robert S., and Richard Shiff, eds. *Critical Terms for Art History*. 3rd ed. Chicago: University of Chicago Press, 2003.

Nemes, Márta. *Lechner Ödön Földtani Intézete Budapesten* [The Building of the Hungarian Geological Institute by Ödön Lechner]. Budapest: Lechner Ödön Foundation and the Hungarian Geological Survey, 1993.

———. *Museum of Applied Arts: History of the Building*. Budapest: Museum of Applied Arts, 1988.

Németh, Lajos, ed. *Magyar Művészet, 1890–1919* [(Hungarian Art]. 2 vols. A magyarországi művészet története Series, vol. 6, edited by Nóra Aradi. Budapest: Akadémiai Kiadó, 1981.

Neubauten in Wien, Prag, Budapest: Facaden, Details, Haustore, Vestibule. Vienna: Anton Schroll & Co., 1904.

Nititsch, Herbert. "Heimatschutz in Österreich." In *Schönes Österreich: Heimatschutz zwischen Ästhetik und Ideologie*, edited by Österreichisches Museum für Volkskunde, 19–29. Vienna: Österreichisches Museum für Volkskunde, 1995.

Noever, Peter, ed. *Dagobert Peche and the Wiener Werkstätte*. New Haven, CT: Yale University Press, 2002. An exhibition catalogue.

———, ed. *Der Preis der Schönheit: 100 Jahre Wiener Werkstätte*. Ostfildern, Germany: Hatje Cantz, 2003. An exhibition catalogue.

Noever, Peter, and Oswald Oberhuber, eds. *Josef Hoffmann 1870–1956: Ornament zwischen Hoffnung und Verbrechen*. Vienna: Österreichisches Museum für angewandte Kunst and Hochschule für angewandte Kunst, 1987. An exhibition catalogue.

Noll, Jindřich. *Josef Schulz (1840–1917)*. Prague: Národní galerie, 1992. An exhibition catalogue.

Novotný, Otakar. *Jan Kotěra a jeho doba*. Prague: Státńi Naklad. Krásné literatury, Hudby a Umění, 1958.

Ödon Lechner 1845–1914. Budapest: Hungarian Museum of Architecture, 1988. An exhibition catalogue.

Ogata, Amy Fumiko. *Art Nouveau and the Social Vision of Modern Living: Belgian Artists in a European Context*. New York: Cambridge University Press, 2001.

Ohmann, Friedrich, ed. *Architektur und Kunstgewerbe der Barockzeit, des Rococo und Empires aus Böhmen und anderen österreichischen Ländern*. Vienna: A. Schroll, 1902.

Olszewski, Andrzej K. *An Outline History of Polish 20th Century Art and Architecture*. Warsaw: Interpress Publishers, 1989.

Onderdonk Jr., Francis S. *The Ferro-Concrete Style: Reinforced Concrete in Modern Architecture*. New York: Architectural Book Publishing, 1928.

Ostrowski, Jan. *Cracow*. Warsaw: Wydawnictwa Artystyczne i Filmowe, 1992.

Otto Prutscher 1880–1949: Architektur, Interieur, Design. Vienna: Hochschule für Angewandte Kunst in Wien, 1994. An exhibition catalogue.

Otto Wagner Möbel. Vienna: Österreichische Postsparkasse, 1991. An exhibition catalogue.

Otto Wagner: Vienna 1841–1918, Designs for

Architecture. Introduction by Iain Boyd White. Oxford: Museum of Modern Art Oxford, 1985. An exhibition catalogue.

Otto Wagners Postsparkasse. [Vienna: Zentralvereinigung der Architekten Österreichs, 1975.]

Pantelić, Bratislav. "Nationalism and Architecture: The Creation of a National Style in Serbian Architecture and Its Political Implications." *JSAH* 56, no. 1 (March 1997): 16–41.

Pehnt, Wolfgang. *Expressionist Architecture*. New York: Praeger, 1973.

Peichl, Gustav, ed. *Die Kunst des Otto Wagner*. Vienna: Akademie der bildenden Künste, 1984. An exhibition catalogue.

Péter, Márta, ed. *Historizmus és eklektika* [Revival Styles in the Nineteenth Century]. 2 vols. Az Európai iparművészet stíluskorszakai [Periods in European Decorative Arts]. Budapest: Iparművészeti Múzeum, 1992. An exhibition catalogue.

Pichran, Emil. *Otto Wagner*. Vienna: Bergland Verlag, 1956.

Pintér, Tamás K. *Budapest architectura 1900*. Budapest: Alma Grafikai Stúdió és Kiadó, 1999.

Pirkovič-Kocbek, Jelka, and Breda Mihelič. *Secesijska arhitektura v Sloveniji*. Ljubljana, Slovenia: Ministrstvo za kulturo, Uprava Republike Slovenije za kulturno dediščino, 1997.

Piva, Pietro. "Il Tempio Israelitico di Trieste, Note sugli Elementi Costruttivi." Extract from "Archeografo Triestino," 4th ser., 54 (CII dell Raccolta, 1994): 147–65, offprint.

Planner-Steiner, Ulrike, and Klaus Eggert. *Friedrich von Schmidt, Gottfried Semper, Carl von Hasenauer*. Volume 8, Part 2 of Die Wiener Ringstrasse, Bild Einer Epoche; Die Erweiterung der Inneren Stadt Wien unter Kaiser Franz Joseph; Die Bauten und ihre Architekten. Edited by Renate Wagner-Rieger. Wiesbaden: Franz Steiner Verlag, 1978.

Platz, Gustav Adolf. *Die Baukunst der Neuesten Zeit*. Berlin: Propyläen-Verlag, 1927.

Platzer, Monika. "Interlude: Ideas for a New World, 1919–27." In Blau and Platzer, *Shaping the Great City*, 167–77.

Plečnik, Jože. *Architectura perennis; Napori; Ponatis s kazalom*. With text by Damjan Prelovšek. 3 vols. Ljubljana, Slovenia: Dessa, 1993.

Plischke, Ernst Anton. *Ein Leben mit Architektur*. Vienna: Löcker Verlag, 1989.

Popescu, Carmen. *Le Style National Roumain: Construire une Nation à travers l'architecture, 1881–1945*. Rennes, France: Presses Universitaires de Rennes, 2004.

Potzner, Ferenc. *Medgyaszay István*. Az építészet mesterei (Masters of Architecture). Budapest: Holnap Kiadó, 2004.

Pozzetto, Marco. "Annotazioni per una storia dell'architectura moderna a Trieste." *Parametro*, no. 132 (1984): 14–49.

———. "Cemento armato, materiale nuovo nella scuola di Otto Wagner." *L'Industria Italiana del Cemento*, no.6 (1981): 417–34.

———. "La formazione degli ingegneri-architetti Triestini nella seconda metà dell'ottocento: Il caso di Giovanni Berlam." *Archeografo Triestino* 53 (1993): 23–31.

———. *Giovanni Andrea, Ruggero, Arduino Berlam: Un secolo di architettura*. Trieste: MGS Press, 1999.

———. *Max Fabiani*. Trieste: MGS Press, 1998.

———. *Max Fabiani Architetto*. Gorizia, Italy: Commune de Gorizia, 1966.

———. *Max Fabiani: Ein Architekt der Monarchie*. Vienna: Edition Tusch, 1983.

———, ed. *Max Fabiani: Nuove frontiere dell'architettura*. Venice: Cataloghi Marsilio, 1988. An exhibition catalogue.

———. "La saga dei Berlam: Arduino (1854–1920)." *Archeografo Triestiono* 54 (1994): 106–9.

———. *Die Schule Otto Wagners 1894–1902*. Vienna: Verlag Anton Schroll, 1980.

———. *La scuola di Wagner 1894–1912: Idee-premi-concorsi*. Trieste: Commune di Trieste, 1979. An exhibition catalogue. Published in German under the title *Die Schule Otto Wagners 1894–1912* (Vienna: Verlag Anton Schroll & Co., 1980).

Prague 1891–1941: Architecture and Design. Edinburgh: City of Edinburgh Museums and Art Galleries, 1994. An exhibition catalogue.

Prague, 1900–1938: Capitale secrete des avant-gardes. Dijon: Musée des Beaux-Arts Dijon, 1997. An exhibition catalogue.

Prague: Passages et galeries. Conceived by Michaela Brozová, Anne Hebler, and Chantal Saler. Paris: Institut français d'architecture and Norma, 1993. An exhibition catalogue.

Prazák, Václav. *Umění renesance východních Čech: Architektura, sochařství, malířství, umelecká remesla*. Hradec Králové, Czech Republic: Garamon, 2000.

Prelovšek, Damjan. "Decoration in Early Vurnik's Architecture." In *Ivan Vurnik 1884–1971: Slovenski arhitekt*. An exhibition catalogue and special issue of *Arhitektov bilten* [Architect's Bulletin] 24, nos. 119–24 (December 1994).

———. "Ideological Substratum in Plečnik's Work." In Prelovšek, Lukeš, and Valena, *Josip Plečnik, Architect of Prague Castle*.

———. *Jože Plečnik, 1872–1957*. Translated by Eileen Martin and Patricia Crampton. New Haven, CT: Yale University Press, 1997. Rev. ed. of *Architectura Perennis* (Salzburg: Residenz Verlag, 1992).

———. "Plečnik au chateau Hradčany." *L'Architecture d'Aujourdhui*, no. 305 (June 1996): 52–59.

———. Review of *Mladí mistře: Architekti ze školy Otto Wagnera na Moravě a ve Slezsku* [Young Masters: Otto Wagner's Moravian and Silesian Students], by Jindřich Vybíral. *Centropa* (September 2003): 274–76.

Prelovšek, Damjan, Zeděnek Lukeš, and Tomáš Valena, eds. *Josip Plečnik: Architect of Prague Castle*. Prague: Prague Castle Administration, 1997.

"Projekt für einen israelitischen Tempel in Triest." *Der Architekt* 15 (1909), p. 48, plates 38, 39.

Prokop, Ursula. "Rudolf Perco 1884–1942: Architektur jenseits von Tradition und Moderne." Ph.D. diss., University of Vienna, 1997.

———. *Rudolf Perco 1884–1942: Von der Architektur des Roten Wien zur NS-Megalomanie*. Vienna: Böhlau Verlag, 2001.

———. *Wien: Aufbruch zur Metropole; Geschäfts- und Wohnhäuser der Innerstadt 1910 bis 1914*. Vienna: Böhlau Verlag, 1994.

Purchla, Jacek. *Wien-Krakau im 19. Jahrhundert: Zwei Studien über die osterreichisch-polnischen Beziehungen in den Jahren 1866–1914*. Modling, Austria: Verlag St. Gabriel [1988].

[Pusztai, László.] *Árkayné Sztéhló Lily (1897–1959): Emlékkiállítása*. Székesfehérvár, Hungary: Magyar Építészeti Múzeum, 1981. An exhibition catalogue.

[———.] *Pákei Lajos (1853–1921): Felvételi rajzai Kolozsvár reneszánsz építészeti emlékeiről*. Székesfehérvár, Hungary: Magyar Építészeti Múzeum, 1983. An exhibition catalogue.

Pusztai, László, and András Hadik. *Ödön Lechner 1845–1914*. Budapest: Hungarian Museum of Architecture, 1991. An exhibition catalogue.

Reissberger, Mara, Peter Haiko, Christian Witt-Dörring, and Reingard Witzmann. *Moderne Vergangenheit: Wien 1800–1900*. Vienna: Künstlerhaus, 1981.

Rerrich, Béla. *Rerrich Béla*. Geneva: Masters of Architecture, Ltd., 1930.

Restucci, Amerigo. "Il palazzo della RAS a Trieste." *Quaderni Giuliani di Storia*, no. 2 (1981): 73–92.

Riedl, Dušan. *Brněnská architektura 20. století*. Brno, Czech Republic: Památkový ústav and ústav and Úrad města Brna, 1992.

Rigele, Georg, and Georg Loewit, eds. *Clemens Holzmeister*. Innsbruck: Haymon, 2000.

Rochard, Patricia. *Csardas im Quadrat: Ungarische Avantgarde (1919–1930) und traditionelle Bauenkultur*. Mainz: H. Schmidt, 1995.

Rukschcio, Burkhardt, and Roland Schachel. *Adolf Loos: Leben und Werk*. Salzburg: Residenz Verlag, 1982.

Rypson, Piotr. "The Protean Factor." *Domus*, no. 804 (May 1998): 4–6.

Sármány-Parsons, Ilona. "Entfremde Nachbarn: Ein Doppelporträt der Wiener und Budapester Kunst um die Jahrhundertwende." Lecture text (1985) published in *Kakanien: Aufsätze zur österreichischen und ungarischen Literatur, Kunst und Kultur um die Jahrhundertwende*, edited by Eugen Thurnher. Budapest : Akadémiai Kiadó; Vienna: Verlag der Österreichischen Akademie der Wissenschaften, ca. 1991.

———. *Historizáló építészet az Osztrák-Magyar Monarchiában*. Budapest: Corvina, 1990.

———. "The Influence of the British Arts and Crafts Movement in Budapest and Vienna." *Acta Historiae Artium* 33 (1987–88): 179–98.

———. "Ludwig Hevesi und die Rolle der Kunstkritik." *Acta Historiae Artium Hungaricae* 35 (1990–92): 3–28.

———. "Zum Einfluß der Wiener Architekten in Ungarn um die Jahrhundertwende." In *Wien und die Architektur des 20. Jahrhunderts*, edited by Tilmann Buddensieg and Elisabeth Liskar. *International Congress of the History of Art* 8:21–31, pl. 159–70. Graz: H. Böhlau, 1986.

Sarnitz, August. *Architecture in Vienna*. New York: Springer, 1998.

———. *Ernst Lichtblau Architekt 1883–1963*. Vienna: Böhlau Verlag, 1994.

———. *Ernst Plischke: Das Neue Bauen und die Neue Welt*. Munich: Prestel Verlag, 2003.

———. *R. M. Schindler, Architekt, 1887–1953*. Vienna: Edition Christian Brandstätter, 1986.

Sarnitz, August, and Eva B. Ottillinger, eds. *Ernst Plischke: Modern Architecture for the New World; The Complete Works*. Munich: Prestel Verlag, 2004.

Sawicki, Nicholas. "Writing the History of the 'Czechoslovak Official Modern': Karel Teige as Historian of the 'Cubist' Generation." *Centropa* 5, no. 1 (January 2005): 4–15.

Sayer, Derek. *The Coasts of Bohemia: A Czech History*. Princeton, NJ: Princeton University Press, 1998.

Schafter, Debra. *The Order of Ornament, The Structure of Style: Theoretical Foundations of Modern Art and Architecture*. New York: Cambridge University Press, 2003.

Scheuch, Manfred. *Historischer Atlas Österreich.* Vienna: Verlag Christian Brandstätter, 1994.

Schezen, Roberto, and Peter Haiko. *Vienna 1850–1930, Architecture.* New York: Rizzoli, 1992.

Schilling, Jürgen, ed. *Wille zur Form: Ungegenständliche Kunst 1910–1938 in Österreich, Polen, Tschechoslowakei und Ungarn.* Vienna: Hochschule für angewandte Kunst, 1993.

Schlöss, Erich. *Österreich moderne Architektur.* Vienna: Bundeskanzelaramt, 1988.

Schorske, Carl E. *Fin-de-siecle Vienna: Politics and Culture.* New York: Vintage Books, 1981.

———. *Thinking with History: Explorations in the Passage to Modernism.* Princeton, NJ: Princeton University Press, 1998.

Schwalm-Theiss, Georg. *Theiss & Jaksch, Architekten 1907–1961.* Vienna: Edition Christian Brandstätter, 1986.

Schwarz, Hans-Peter, ed. *Die Architektur der Synagoge.* Stuttgart: Klett-Cotta, 1988.

Schweiger, Werner J. *Wiener Werkstätte—Design in Vienna 1903–1932.* New York: Abeville Press, 1984.

Sekiya, Masaaki, and Otto Antonia Graf, text. *Otto Wagner.* 4 vols. Tokyo: Bunkensha, 1998.

Sekler, Eduard F. *Josef Hoffmann: The Architectural Work.* Translated by John Maas. Princeton, NJ: Princeton University Press, 1985.

Seton-Watson, R. W. *Slovak Peasant Art and Melodies.* London: The Doré Gallery, 1911. An exhibition catalogue.

Shaeffer, M. P. A. "Otto Wagner: *Entwicklung der Vaterstadt.*" In Burman, *Architecture 1900*, 125–37.

Shelley, Alexandra. "The Art Nouveau Glory of Szeged." *New York Times,* June 23, 1996, sec. 5.

Sik, Miroslav. "Modern Anti-Modernism: Bohemian Cubism, 1910–1920." *Domus,* no. 782 (May 1996): 64–69.

Sisa, József. *Antal Szkalnitzky: An Architect in Hungary at the Time of the Austro-Hungarian Compromise.* Budapest: Akadémiai Kiadó, 1994.

———. "Hungarian Architecture from 1849 to 1900." In Wiebensohn and Sisa, *The Architecture of Historic Hungary,* 203–6.

———. *Steindl Imre.* Az építészet mesterei (Masters of Architecture). Budapest: Holnap Kiadó, 2005.

Šlachta, Štefan. *Moderne Architekture in der Slowakei 20-er und 30-er Jahre.* Bratislava: Spolok architektov slovenska and Architektenverein der slowakei, 1991.

———. "Urbanistické sútaže v Bratislave (20. až 30. roky)." *Architektúra a urbanizmus* 28, nos. 1–2 (1994): 40–47.

Šlapeta, Vladímir, ed. *Arnošt Wiesner 1890–1971.* Olomouc, Czech Republic: Gallery of Fine Arts, 1981. An exhibition catalogue.

———. *Die Brünner Funktionalisten: Moderne Architektur in Brünn (Brno).* Innsbruck: Institut für Raumgestaltung der Technischen Fakultät der Universität Inssbruck; Vienna: Institut für Gebäudelehre und für Hochbau I der Technischen Universität Wien, 1985. An exhibition catalogue.

———. "Cubism in Prague." *Daidalos* 39 (March 15, 1991): 64–71.

———. "Domus itenerario n. 104: Fuchs and Brno." *Domus,* no. 763 (September 1994): 111–18.

———, ed. *Jan Kotěra 1871–1923: The Founder of Modern Czech Architecture.* Prague: Municipal House and Kant, 2001.

———. *Praha, 1910–1978: Průvoce po moderní architektuře.* Prague: Národni technické museum, 1978.

Šlapeta, Vladímir, with a foreword by Gustav Peichl. *Czech Functionalism 1918–1938.* London: Architectural Association, 1987. An exhibition catalogue.

Slesin, Suzanne, Stafford Cliff, and Daniel Rozensztroch. *Mittel Europa: Rediscovering the Style and Design of Central Europe.* Photography by Gilles de Chabaneix. New York: Clarkson Potter/Publishers, 1994.

Spurensuche-Czernowitz und die Bukowina einst und jetzt. St. Pölten, Austria: Niederösterreichisches Landesmuseum, 2000. An exhibition catalogue.

Starr, George. "Hungarian Reform Church Architecture and the Nineteenth and Twentieth Centuries." *Centropa* 3, no. 3 (September 2003): 208–24.

Stewart, Janet. *Fashioning Vienna: Adolf Loos' Cultural Criticism.* London: Routledge, 2000.

Stierlin, Henri, and Andreas Volwahsen. *Islamic India.* Architecture of the World Series, edited by Henri Stierlin, no. 8. [Cologne:] Benedikt Taschen Verlag GmbH, n.d.

Stritzler-Levine, Nina, ed. *Josef Frank, Architect and Designer: An Alternative Vision of the Modern Home.* New Haven, CT: Yale University Press, 1996. An exhibition catalogue.

Strzygowski, Josef. *Die bildende Kunst der Gegenwart.* 1907. Cited in Moravánszky, "Materialwahrheit und Bekleidungsästhetik," 234.

Sümegi, György. *A kecskeméti városháza.* Kecskemét, Hungary: Kecskeméti Lapok, 1996.

Švácha, Rostislav. *Architecture of New Prague 1895–1945.* Cambridge, MA: MIT Press, 1995.

Published in Czech under the title *Od moderny k funkcionalismu* (Prague: Odeon, 1985).

———. "The Culminating Years." In Šlapeta, ed., *Jan Kotěra 1871–1923*, 183.

———, ed. *Jaromír Krejcar 1859–1949*. Prague: Galerie Jaroslava Fragnera, 1995. An exhibition catalogue.

———. "Poznámky ke Kotěrovu muzeu" [Notes on Kotěra's Museum]. *Umění* 34 (1986): 171.

———. *The Pyramid, the Prism and the Arc: Czech Cubist Architecture 1911–1923*. Prague: Gallery, 2000.

———. "The Story of the 'Dancing House' in Prague." *Domus*, no. 790 (February 1997): 15–16.

Switzer, Terri. "Hungarian Self-Representation in an International Context: The Magyar Exhibited at International Expositions and World Fairs." In Facos and Hirsch, *Art, Culture and National Identity in Fin-de-Siècle Europe*, 160–85.

Szabadi, Judit. *Jugendstil in Ungaren*. Vienna: Ausgale Achen Scroll & Co, 1982.

———. "An Outline of Hungarian Art Nouveau Ideas." *Acta Historiae Artium* 28 (1982): 117–30.

Szegő, Győrgy. *Teremtés es átváltozás: Budapest szecessziós építészete a századfordulón* [Creation and Metamorphosis. The Art Nouveau Architecture in Budapest at the Turn of the Century]. Budapest: HG & Társa Kiadó, n.d.

Szendrői, Jenő, Lajos Arnóth, József Finta, Ferenc Merényi, and Elemér Nagy. *Neue Architektur in Ungarn*. Munich: Georg D. W. Callwey Verlag, 1978.

Tadgell, Christopher. *The History of Architecture in India: From the Dawn of the Civilization to the End of the Raj*. London: Phaidon Press, 1990.

Tedeschi, Erminio. *Historical Notes, RAS: 1838–1988*. Trieste: Privately published by the RAS, 1989.

———. *Nel primo centenario della Riuone Adriatica di Sicurtà (1838–1938)*. Trieste, 1939.

Teige, Karel. *Modern Architecture in Czechoslovakia and Other Writings*. Translated by Irena Žantovská Murray and David Britt. Los Angeles: Getty Research Institute; New York: Oxford University Press, 2001.

Templ, Stephan, Michal Kohout, and Vladímir Šlapeta, eds. *Prag Architektur des XX. jahrhunderts*. Vienna: Linde, 1996.

Thompson, D'Arcy Wentworth. *On Growth and Form*. Cambridge: The University Press, 1917; 2nd ed., idem, 1942.

Tisztelgés Lajta Béla emlékének: A Parisiana újjáépítése. Curated by András Hadik. Budapest: Magyar Építészeti Múzeumának Kiállítása, 1991. An exhibition catalogue.

Topp, Leslie. *Architecture and Truth in Fin-de-Siècle Vienna*. Cambridge: Cambridge University Press, 2004.

———. "Otto Wagner and the Steinhof Psychiatric Hospital: Architecture as Misunderstanding." *Art Bulletin* 87, no. 1 (March 2005): 130–56.

Traum und Wirklichkeit—Wien 1870–1930. Vienna: Museen der Stadt Wien, 1985. An exhibition catalogue.

Trevisiol, Robert. *Otto Wagner*. Edited by Giovanni Fanelli and Ezio Godoli. Rome: Editori Laterza, 1990.

Trilling, James. *Ornament: A Modern Perspective*. Seattle: University of Washington Press, 2003.

Vale, Lawrence. R. *Architecture, Power, and National Identity*. New Haven, CT: Yale University Press, 1992.

Vámos, Ferenc. *Lechner Ödön*. Budapest: Amicus kiadas, 1927.

Vegesack, Alexander von, ed. *Czech Cubism: Architecture, Furniture, and Decorative Arts 1910–1925*. Princeton, NJ: Princeton Architecture Press, 1992. An exhibition catalogue.

Verborgene Impressionen [Hidden Impressions]. Vienna: Österreichisches Museum für Angewandte Kunst, 1990. An exhibition catalogue.

Vitez, Zorica, and Aleksandra Muraj, eds. *Croatian Folk Culture at the Crossroads of Worlds and Eras*. Zagreb, Croatia: Gallery Klovićevi dvori and Budapesti Történeti Múzeum, 2000.

Volkov, Shulamit. *Jüdisches Leben und Antisemitismus im 19. und 20. Jahrhundert*. Munich: Verlag C. H. Beck, 1990.

———. *The Rise of Popular Antimodernism in Germany: The Urban Master Artisans, 1873–1896*. Princeton, NJ: Princeton University Press, 1978.

"Vurnikova šola za arhitekturo." *Dom in svet* (1927): 291–331.

Vybíral, Jindřich. "Friedrich Ohmann and Prague Architecture around 1900." In Burman, *Architecture 1900*, 173–78.

———. *Jiny Dům: Německá a rakouská architektura na Moravě a ve Slezsku v letech 1890–1938* [The Other Home: German and Austrian Architecture in Moravia and Silesia 1890–1938]. Prague: Národní galerie, 1993. An exhibition catalogue.

[———.] *Josef Maria Olbrich 1867–1908: Architektonické dílo*. [Brno, Czech Republic: Svaz českých architektů, Český fond výtvarných umění, and Pedagogická fakulteta Ostrava,] 1989. An exhibition catalogue.

———. *Století dìdicù a zakladatelù: Architektura

jižních Čech v obdobi historismu. Prague: Argo, 1999.

———. "Die Troppauer Jahre Josef Maria Olbrichs." *Österreichische Zeitschrift für Kunst und Denkmalpflege* 47, nos. 1–2 (1993): 80–84.

Wagner, Otto. *Einige Skizzen* 3 (September 1904). Reprinted in Graf, *Otto Wagner: Das Werk des Architecten*, 2:432–34.

———. "Erläuterungen zur Bauvollendung des k. k. Postsparkassen-Amtsgebäudes in Wien." *Jahrbuch der Gesellschaft österreichischer Architekten* (1907): 9–13. Reprinted in Graf, *Otto Wagner: Das Werk des Architecten*, 2:434–36

———. *Modern Architecture: A Guidebook for His Students to This Field of Art*. Introduction and translation by Harry Francis Mallgrave. Santa Monica, CA: The Getty Center for the History of Art and the Humanities, 1988.

Weihsmann, Helmut. *Das Rote Wien*. Vienna: Promedia, 1985.

Werkner, Patrick, ed. *Egon Schiele: Art, Sexuality, and Viennese Modernism*. Palo Alto, CA: The Society for the Promotion of Science and Scholarship, Inc., 1994.

Wibiral, Norbert, and Renata Mikula. *Heinrich von Ferstel*. Weisbaden: Franz Steiner Verlag GmbH., 1974.

Wiebenson, Dora, and József Sisa, eds. *The Architecture of Historic Hungary*. Cambridge, MA: MIT Press, 1998.

Wiener Neubauten im Stile der Sezession und anderen modernen Stilarten: Fassaden, Details, Haustore, Vestibule. 5 vols. Plates. Vienna: A. Schroll, 1902–[12].

Wiesner, Arnošt. "Über den Bau des Krematoriums." *Horizont*, nos. 11–13 (Brno, 1928). Reprinted in Šlapeta, *Die Brünner Funktionalisten*, 91–93.

Wirth, Zdenek. "Okresní dům v Hradci Králové." *Volné směry* 27, nos. 11–12 (1929): 252–68, 306.

Wirth, Zdenek, and Antonin Matějček. *Česká Arhitektura 1800–1920*. Prague: Jan Štenc, 1922.

Witkiewicz, Stanisław. *Styl zakopiański* [The Zakopane Style]. 2 vols. Lwów, 1904.

Witkovsky, Matthew S. "Envisaging the Gendered Center: Prague's Municipal Building and the Construction of a 'Czech Nation' c. 1880–1914." *Umění* 47 (1999): 203–20.

———. "Truly Blank: The Monument to National Liberation and Interwar Modernism in Prague." *Umění* 49 (2001): 42–60.

Wolfsgruber, Cölestin. "Joseph Othmar Rauscher." In *Catholic Encyclopedia*, vol. 12 (1908) Transcribed by Douglas J. Potter on-line at http://www.newadvent.org/cathen/12660b.htm.

Yeoman, Andrew. "Dear Reader: Reflections on Urban Renewal, Zagreb, Croatia." *RIBA Journal* 104 (April 1997): 122.

Zachwatowicz, Jan. *Polish Architecture*. Warsaw: Arkady, 1967.

Žákaveč, František. *Chrám znovuzrození: O budovatelích a budvě Národního divadla v Praze*. Prague: J. Štenc, 1918; 2nd ed., *idem*, 1938.

———. *Dilo Dušana Jurkoviče; kus dějin československé architektury*. Prague: Vesmír, 1929.

Illustration Credits

ABBREVIATIONS

ABK: Kupferstichkabinett, Akademie der bildenden Künste Wien (Print Collection of the library of the Academy of Fine Arts, Vienna)

HE: Photography by Hans Engels. Copyright Hans Engels

HM Vienna: Historisches Museum der Stadt Wien (formerly Historical Museum of the City of Vienna, now Wien Museum)

MS: Photography by Masaaki Sekiya. Courtesy of Masaaki Sekiya and Archimedia, copyright holders

NTM Prague: Národní technické muzeum v Praze (National Technical Museum, Prague, Architectural Archives)

UPM Prague: Uměleckoprůmyslové muzeum v Praze (Arts and Crafts Museum, Prague)

WSTLA Vienna: Wiener Stadt- und Landesarchiv (Vienna City and Regional Archive)

I.2. Reprinted from Robert P. Magocsi, *Historical Atlas of Central Europe,* revised and expanded edition (Seattle: University of Washington Press, 2002), p. 81, plate 25b.

I.3. Reprinted from Robert P. Magocsi, *Historical Atlas of Central Europe,* revised and expanded edition (Seattle: University of Washington Press, 2002), p. 119, plate 36.

I.4. Reprinted from Robert P. Magocsi, *Historical Atlas of Central Europe,* revised and expanded edition (Seattle: University of Washington Press, 2002), p. 99, plate 30.

1.1, 1.2. Reprinted from Klaus Eggert and Hermann Reining, *Die Wiener Ringstrasse: Das Kunstwerk im Bild.* Die Wiener Ringstrasse, Bild Einer Epoche. Die Erweiterung der inneren Stadt Wien unter Kaiser Franz Joseph. Die Bauten und ihre Architekten, edited by Renate Wagner-Rieger, vol. 1 (Graz: Hermann Böhlaus Nachf., 1969), fig. 143b. By permission of HM Vienna.

1.3. Reprinted from Peter Haiko and Renata Kassal-Mikula, eds., *Friedrich von Schmidt (1825–1891): Ein gotischer Rationalist*, exhibition catalogue (HM Vienna, 1991), p. 97, cat. no. 2.22.

1.4, 1.5. HE

1.6. By permission of HM Vienna.

1.7, 1.8, 1.9. HE

1.10. NTM Prague, Zítek fond. 30 5/8.

1.11. HE

1.12. Reprinted from Antonín Matějček, ed., *Národ Sobě: Národní Divadlo a Jeho Umělecké Poklady* (Prague: Melantrich, 1940), p. 121.

1.13. HE

1.14. Reprinted from Antonín Matějček, ed., *Národ Sobě: Národní Divadlo a Jeho Umělecké Poklady* (Prague: Melantrich, 1940), p. 27.

1.15. Reprinted from Antonín Matějček, ed., *Národ Sobě: Národní Divadlo a Jeho Umělecké Poklady* (Prague: Melantrich, 1940), pp. 71–72.

1.16, 1.17, 1.18. MS

1.19. Photographs courtesy of Dr. Antonia Graf.

2.1, 2.2, 2.3, 2.4, 2.5. MS

2.6. Rare Book Collection, American Institute of Architects Library. By permission of American Institute of Architects Library.

2.7, 2.8, 2.9, 2.10, 2.11, 2.12. MS

2.13, 2.14. HE

2.15, 2.16, 2.17, 2.18, 2.19, 2.20, 3.1. MS

3.2. Courtesy of Vladímir Kulić, photographer.

3.3. MS

3.4. Photograph courtesy of Asenbaum Collection.

3.5. Reprinted in Michael Huey, ed., *Viennese Silver*, exhibition catalogue (Ostfildern-Ruit, Germany: Hatje Cantz Verlag, 2003), p. 229, fig. 30. Photograph courtesy of Asenbaum Collection. © Asenbaum Photo Archive.

3.6. Reprinted in Michael Huey, ed., *Viennese Silver*, exhibition catalogue (Ostfildern-Ruit, Germany: Hatje Cantz Verlag, 2003), p. 222, fig. 126.

3.7. Reprinted in Michael Huey, ed., *Viennese Silver*, exhibition catalogue (Ostfildern-Ruit, Germany: Hatje Cantz Verlag, 2003), p. 222, fig. 119.

3.8. Reprinted in Michael Huey, ed., *Viennese Silver*, exhibition catalogue (Ostfildern-Ruit, Germany: Hatje Cantz Verlag, 2003), pp. 326–27, fig. 178. Photograph courtesy of Asenbaum Collection. © Asenbaum Photo Archive.

3.9, 3.10. Photographs courtesy of Asenbaum Collection.

3.11, 3.12, 3.13. MS

3.16. Reprinted from Zdenek Wirth and Antonín Matějček, *Česká Arhitektura 1800–1920* (Prague: Jan Štenc, 1922), 77.

3.17, 3.18, 3.19. HE

3.21, 3.22, 3.23, 3.24, 3.25. MS

3.28. Photograph courtesy of Jutta and Wolfgang Fischer.

3.29, 3.30. HE

3.31. Collection, Musée d'Orsay, Réunion des Musées Nationaux Paris. Photograph courtesy of Jutta and Wolfgang Fischer.

3.32. Photograph courtesy of Jutta and Wolfgang Fischer.

3.33. Photograph courtesy of ABK, no. 29.039.

3.34. Photograph courtesy of ABK, no. 29.041.

3.35. Photograph courtesy of ABK, no. 29.051.

3.36. Photograph courtesy of ABK, no. 29.052.

3.37. Photograph courtesy of ABK, no. 29.053.

3.38. Photograph courtesy of ABK, no. 29.054.

3.39, 3.40, 3.41. HE

3.42. NTM Prague

3.43, 3.44. HE

3.46. Photograph courtesy of Museum of Decorative Arts, Prague.

3.47, 3.48. HE

3.49, 3.50, 3.51. Collection Aleksander Laslo. Photograph courtesy of Aleksander Laslo.

3.53. Photography by József Hajdú. By permission of József Hajdú.

4.1. Reprinted from Edit Fél, Tamás Hofer, and Klára K. Csilléry, *Hungarian Peasant Art* (London: Constable, 1971), fig. 77. By permission of Corvina Books, Budapest.

4.2. Reprinted from *Hungarian Decorative Folk Art* (Budapest, 1954), fig. 109.

4.3. Reprinted from Edit Fél, Tamás Hofer, and Klára K. Csilléry, *Hungarian Peasant Art* (London: Constable, 1971), fig. 76. By permission of Corvina Books, Budapest.

4.4. Reprinted from Károly Gink and Ivor Sándor Kiss, *Folk Art and Folk Artists in Hungary* (Budapest: Corvina, 1968), n.p. Photography by Károly Gink. By permission of Judit Gink.

4.5. Reprinted from *Hungarian Decorative Folk Art* (Budapest, 1954), fig. 178.

4.6, 4.7. HE

4.8B. Photography by Vladímir Kulić.

4.9, 4.10, 4.11, 4.12. HE

4.13, 4.14. Collection of Cushing Memorial Library, Texas A&M University. Courtesy of Cushing Memorial Library.

4.15, 4.16. HE

4.19, 4.20, 4.21, 4.22, 4.23, 4.24. Photography by Rudolf Klein. Courtesy of Rudolf Klein.

4.25, 4.26, 4.27, 4.31, 4.32, 4.33, 4.34, 4.35, 4.36, 5.1, 5.2, 5.4, 5.5, 5.6, 5.7. HE

5.8. Courtesy of János Gerle Collection.

5.9, 5.10, 5.11. Photograph courtesy of Jutta and Wolfgang Fischer.

5.12, 5.13, 5.14, 5.15, 5.16, 5.18, 5.19, 5.20, 5.21. HE

5.22. Metropolitan Ervin szabó Library, Budapest Collection.

5.23, 5.24, 5.25, 5.26, 5.27, 5.28, 5.30, 5.31, 5.32. HE

5.37, 5.39. MS

5.40, 5.41. HE

5.42. NTM Prague

5.43. HE

c.1. Reprinted from Robert P. Magocsi, *Historical Atlas of Central Europe*, revised and expanded edition (Seattle: University of Washington Press, 2002), 126.

c.2, c.3, c.4. HE

c.5. From Georg Schwalm-Theiss, *Theiss & Jaksch, Architekten 1907–1961* (Vienna: Edition Christian Brandstätter, 1986), 94. Photography by J. Scherb. By permission of Georg Schwalm-Theiss.

c.6. From Georg Schwalm-Theiss, *Theiss & Jaksch, Architekten 1907-1961* (Vienna: Edition Christian Brandstätter, 1986), 98. Photography by Bruno Reiffenstein. By permission of Georg Schwalm-Theiss.

c.8, c.9, c.10, c.14, c.15. HE

c.16, c.17. NTM Prague

c.19, c.20, c.21, c.22. HE

c.23. HM Vienna 171.592/2.

c.24. Photograph courtesy of ABK, no. 30.213.

c.25, c.26, c.27, c.28. WSTLA Vienna, Nachlaß Perco. By permission of Magistrat der Stadt Wien.

Index

Aalto, Alvar, 291n26
abstract geometry, 77, 86
abstraction, 55, 78, 81, 86, 103, 119; and architecture, 1; in art, 11; and modernism, 87
Academy of Fine Arts (Vienna), 32
Academy of Music (Budapest), 182, 183, 186; description of, 184; Hungarian cultural identity, promoting of, 188; hybridity of, 185, 188; opening of, 184. *See also* Royal Academy of Drama and Music
Achleitner, Friedrich, 255, 293n75
Adler, Alfred, 5
Adler, Emil, 189
Adriatica Banco (Trieste), 227. *See also* Riunione Adriatica di Sicurtà
AEG Small Motors Factory (Berlin), 200
aesthetic fixations, 13
Alberti, Leon Battista, 55
Albrecht I, 26
Albrecht III, 26
Alcázar (Toledo), 46
Aleš, Mikoláš, 37, 38
Alhambra (Granada), 45, 46
Allée Reformed Church (Budapest), 287n69; description of, 207, 208; and Hungarian national identity, 203, 208, 210; hybridity of, 202–3, 210; motifs of, 206, 208, 210; reaction to, 209; and technological innovations of, 208, 209, 210
Allgemeine Bauzeitung, 48
Alpine Knappenburg bei Hüttenberg workers' settlement, 238
Alpine Slavs, 165
Amsterdam Stock Exchange, 179, 192
Angel Pharmacy (Vienna), 72, 73
Anglo-Austrian Bank (Vienna), 120
Anschluss, 232, 261, 293n77
antimodern: and pitched roof, 235
Antwerp, 22
Apollinaire, Guillaume, 116
Architectural Record, 132
architectural theory, 1
architecture, 8, 15, 120, 267n1; as Baukunst, 238; communication, means of, 1; as expressionist, 235; of fascism, 235; and geometry, 87; identity, expression of, 1, 43, 127, 133, 263; as language, 1, 8, 9, 10, 11, 81, 231, 234, 263; meaning, expression of, 1; and myth, 149; and national identity, 155, 161; and organicism, 55; polyglotism in, 125; postmodernism in, 10; and rationalism, 81; readability of, 90; social production of, 11; speech, as analogous to, 1; structural rationalism in, 55; style of, 9, 10; text, as analogous to, 1; as theory, 9; visual manifestation and historical context of, as inseparable, 11. *See also* buildings
Der Architekt, 106, 210, 211, 248, 259, 276n49, 282n66, 294n81
Árkay, Aladár, 203, 206, 208, 209, 210; background of, 202; Calvinist churches, prototypes of, 205; works of, 287n57
Árkay, Bertalan, 287n57
Ark of Covenant, 189
Armanni, Osvaldo, 285–86n37
Arpad, 129, 175
Artaria, 274n6
Artaria Building (Vienna), 84
art: ideology of, 11
art nouveau, 56, 61, 132, 181; as international, 62, 68; and organicism, 155
Arts and Crafts movement, 81, 85, 160
Ashbee, Charles Robert, 85
Ashkenazic communities, 188
association: and architecture, 1
Association of Architects, 114. *See also* Mánes Artists' Association
Association of Artists in Prague, 249
Association in Prague for Collecting Donations for the National Theater, 30, 32, 36, 39
Association of Slovak Architects, 236. *See also* Association of Slovak Artists
Association of Slovak Artists, 236. *See also* Association of Slovak Architects
Association of Socialist Architects, 292n54
Athens (Greece), 244
Attila's Treasure, 147. *See also* Nagyszentmiklós treasure
Augsburg Confession, 287n60
Augustus, 166
Ausgleich Compromise (of 1867), 2, 4, 6, 145, 182, 267n4
Austria, 1, 4, 8, 17, 19, 30, 42, 56, 140, 155, 159, 161, 165, 182, 188, 196, 197, 233, 234, 240, 242, 255, 261, 270n31, 288–89n84; bell towers in, 291n30; and Dual Monarchy, 2; as ethnically homogenous, 232; functionalism in, 238; Germany, merger with, 232; Heimatschutzstil mentality in, 281n58; hybridity in, 220; identity, as associative, 127; identity, crisis of, 238; neo-Gothic revival in, 21; size, reduction in, 232

Austria House, 289n92

Austria-Hungary, 231, 232, 233

Austrian Postal Savings Bank (Vienna), 276n49; aluminum, use of in, 101, 102; description of, 101, 102; rationalism, as example of, 101; reinforced concrete, use of in, 101

Austrian Republic, 261

Austrian Tyrolean folk architecture, 159

Austro-Fascism period, 261

Austro-Hungarian Compromise, 159

Austro-Hungarian culture: Jews in, 52

Austro-Hungarian Empire, 1, 2, 12, 14, 43, 44, 52, 59, 69, 74, 81, 99, 125, 133, 145, 155, 161, 202, 205, 227, 233, 235, 263; architectural polyglotism of, 8, 90, 177; commercial schools in, 284n6; dissolving of, 231; as dual monarchy, 13; eclecticism of, 177; hybridity in, 177, 188; and identity, 127; Jews of, 43; Jugendstil movement, influence of in, 56; language, and identity formation in, 6; and memory, 246; as multilingual, 177; multiple identities in, 13; myth, language of in, 175; nationalism in, 4; and Roman Empire, 17

Austro-Prussian War, 34

Baalbek (Syria), 191

Bahr, Haus, 281n58

Baillie Scott, M. H., 85, 160, 196

Balšánek, Antonín, 42

Banat region, 232

Bank of Austria, 178

Barcelona, 56

Bárczy, István, 199

baroque architecture, 127

baroque style, 84

Bartók, Béla, 129, 186

Bartolámač (Kühmayer), 237

Basle, 205

Battle of Königgrätz, 94

Bauer, Leopold, 168

Bauhaus, 125, 236

Bauhütte tradition, 19, 20, 24

Die Baukunst der Neuesten Zeit (The Architecture of Most Recent Times) (Platz), 231

Baukunst unserer Zeit (Architecture of Our Time), 105

Baumann, Ludwig, 170

Bavaria, 26

Beardsley, Aubrey, 63

Bedö, Béla, 273n10

Behrens, Peter, 200, 258

Belgium, 56, 63

Belgrade, 233–34, 260

Belluš, Emil, 236, 237, 238, 260, 291n23, 291n24, 291n25, 291n26

Bendlmayer, Bedřich, 69

Beneš, Edvard, 243

Benešová, Marie, 119, 277n65

Benka, Martin, 237

Benkó, Károly, 48

Benš, Adolf, 93

Berg, Alban, 4

Berlage, H. P., 179, 192

Berlam, Arduino, 191, 192, 193, 227, 285n26, 285n31, 285–86n37

Berlam, Ruggero, 191, 192, 193, 227, 285–86n37

Berlin, 48, 64, 195–96

Berndt & Freytag, 274n6

Biedermeier style, 4, 120, 281n58

biomorphic organicism, 55, 59, 61, 69, 74, 77, 78, 79, 101, 235

biomorphism, 56, 235

Blaník, 32

blob architecture: emergence of, 10

Bohdaneč spa, 118, 123

Bohemia, 2, 8, 30, 38, 39, 40, 42, 93, 95, 118, 223, 226, 232, 233, 254, 283n87

Boltenstern, Erich, 293n75

Bolzano, Bernard, 269n10

Bösendorfer, Ludwig, 239

Bosnia, 44, 283n87

Bosnia-Herzegovina, 2, 161

Bosnians, 233

Brahms, 4

Braque, 118

Bratislava, 13, 240, 291n24; functionalism in, 236; sanatorium in, 243

Breg, 172

Britain, 158. *See also* England

British domestic architecture, 160

British Museum, 279n22

Brittany, 129

Brno, 160, 236, 253

Brody, 177

Brožik, Václav, 271n41

Bruckner, Anton, 239

Bruges, 22

Brunner, Antonin, 118

Brussels, 22, 24, 56, 179, 221

Buda, 5, 6, 140. *See also* Budapest

Budapest, 4, 5, 17, 39, 49, 59, 122, 129, 130, 140, 145, 182, 188, 202, 209, 240, 242, 273n11; ethnic diversity in, 6; growth of, 6; Jews in, 6; urban reform movement in, 199. *See also* Buda; Pest

Budapest Historical Museum, 205

Budapest Zoo, 280n43

buildings, 1; history and culture, context of, 11; multiple meanings of, 12; and national identity, 1; and personal identity, 1; social roles of, 10. *See also* architecture

Bukovina, 2

Bulgaria, 189

Burgenland, 232
Burgess, J., 136
By the Black Madonna department store (Prague), 114

Cabaret Parisiana, 196
Café Corso (Prague), 69
Cairo, 48
Calvin, John, 287n60
Calvinism: doctrine of, 287n60; in Hungary, 203, 204, 206, 210
Calvinist churches: Lutheran churches, as different from, 287n64
Carniola, 165, 166
Catholicism: in Hungary, 203, 204
The Cave Temples of India (Fergusson and Burgess), 136
Central Europe, 9, 15, 233, 267n1; architecture of, as unfamiliar, 8, 231; modernism in, 160
Chamber of Commerce and Industry (Cracow), 177, 178, 284n7, 284n8; design of, 179, 181; Polish national identity, representation of, 180; opening of, 182, 284n13
Charlemagne, 17
Charles IV, 168
Chicago, 288–89n84
Chicago Tribune building, 242, 259
Chochol, Josef, 114, 116, 277n59
Christianity: in Hungary, 203, 204
Church of the Holy Spirit (Vienna), 167–68
Church of St. Christopher (Ljubljana), 243
Cingroš, Johan, 277–78n68
City Hall (Szabadka), 150
City Hall and Palace of Culture (Marosvásárhely), 150
City Museum (Hradec Králové), 94, 101, 275n24, 276n32; and Czech identity, 96; design of, 95, 96, 97, 98, 99; meaning of, 97, 98, 276n30
City Temple (Vienna), 272n74
Čižek, Franz, 293n76
classical architecture, 17
classicism, 120, 220, 235; and language of history, 234
Cloth Hall (Cracow), 179
codes, 268n11
Cologne (Germany), 272n74
Cologne Cathedral, 19
Cologne Circle, 19
Cologne Werkbund exhibition, 90
Congress of Czech Lands, 39
Congress of Vienna, 4
Conservative Jews, 45, 46, 271n63
context, 11, 12
contextual formalism, 11, 12
Cooperative Bank (Ljubljana), 170, 172, 173, 174, 243

Le Corbusier, 125, 231, 251, 277n59; and classicism, 235
The Corporeal Works of Mercy, 75
Corriere Israelitico, 191
Costa, Vincenzo, 285–86n37
Counter-Reformation, 204
Cracow (Poland), 155, 161, 175, 177, 179, 180
Crane, Walter, 129
crematoria, 257; church, as resistance to, 248; as modern, 247
Cremation: The Treatment of the Body after Death (Thompson), 247
cremation, 249; as controversial, 247; and Hussites, 248
crematorium (Brno, Moravia), 253; as hybrid, 254
crematorium (Nymburk, Bohemia), 251; hybrid character of, 252
crematorium (Pardubice, Bohemia): description of, 249, 250; hybridity of, 251
crematorium (Vienna): design of, 254, 255; hybridity of, 257
Crematorium Society, 248
Croatia, 165, 232, 267–68n6, 283n87
Croatia-Slavonia, 2
Croats, 155, 166
Csaba, Rezsövel, 287n57
cubism, 118, 238, 251; and Rondo-cubism, 223
Cubist Group of Visual Artists. *See* Group of Plastic Artists
cultural expression, 13
Curjel & Moser, 205, 287n65
Curjel, Robert, 287n65
Czech architecture: split within, 231
Czech cubism, 93, 119, 223, 229, 236, 249, 251, 277n54, 290n113; historical consciousness of, 118; individual expression, emphasis on, 116; meaning of, 118; and modernism, 114; political implications of, 118; and rationalism, 114, 116; and space, 116, 118; vocabulary of, 118
Czech functionalism, 236
Czech Lands, 40, 42, 56; hybridity in, 223
Czech language: nationalist movements, rise of, 6, 33; suppression of, 6
Czech modern architecture: hybridity, disappearance from, 229
Czech modernism, 114, 118, 119, 225, 252
Czech national architecture, 223
Czech national movement, 223; and language, 42
Czech National Theater (Prague), 17, 32, 78, 188; allegorical imagery of, 38; construction of, 35, 36; construction, halting of, 34; curtain, as national emblem, 40; Czech identity, as representation of, 30; design of, 33; and fire, 40; and identity, 42; inspiration for, 33; opening of, 39, 42; paintings of, 36, 37, 38; rebuilding of, 40; as sacred symbol, 35, 42; vocabulary of, 30, 42

Czech Renaissance, 42
Czech Republic, 223, 236
Czech Secese (Secession) style, 160, 275n17
Czechoslovak CIAM group, 292–93n64
Czechoslovak Legiobank (Prague): design of, 225, 226; memorial function of, 225
Czechoslovak Republic: functionalist architecture in, 236
Czech Theater, 32
Czechoslovakia, 1, 168, 223, 232, 242; crematoria, construction of in, 248; independence of, 233
Czechs, 6, 43, 155, 175; and national identity, 30, 94; and Secession movement, 59

Dalmatia, 2, 154
Danube canal, 105
Darmstadt Artists' Colony, 56, 59
Decline of the Arts (Ženíšek), 37
De Stijl, 231, 252
Detvan, 291n23
Devětsil, 252, 253, 277n59
dialectic realism, 11
didacticism: and architecture, 1
Divatcsárnok, 278n72
Dohány Street Synagogue (Pest), 46, 47, 48, 51, 132
Dollfuss, Engelbert, 261
Dome of the Rock (Jerusalem), 49
Dom pod Jedlami (the House under the Firs), 155
Dom in svet (Home and World), 243
Don Giovanni (Mozart), 5
Drayak, Alois, 69
Dresden (Germany), 34, 272n74
Dr. Jokovič's Sanatorium (Zagreb), 122, 278n71
Dr. Tytus Chalubinski's Tatra Mountains Museum, 157
Dual Monarchy, 2, 46, 47, 93, 95, 122, 124, 178, 247, 262
Dulla, Matuš, 162
Duomo (Orvieto), 193
Dvor, 172
Dvořák, Antonín, 5, 30
Dvořák, Max, 105
Dvůr Králové, 33, 270n37

Eastern Orthodox Church, 203
École des Beaux-Arts, 55
Edict of Tolerance, 188
Ehn, Karl, 260
Eighth International Congress of Architects Devoted to Artistic Solutions of Reinforced Concrete, 211
Elisabeth of Poland, 94
embroidery, 130, 159. 278n8
Emona, 166

Engelsplatzhof housing complex (Vienna), 259, 260
England, 19, 140, 167; modernism in, 160. *See also* Britain
English Arts and Crafts movements, 56, 84, 150
English cottage-style movement, 281n58
Enlightenment, 45, 268n11
Entwurf einer historischen Architektur (An Outline of Historical Architecture), 43
Erkel, Ferenc, 284n15
Etruscans, 167
Eugene, Prince, 26
Europe, 13, 15, 17, 28, 124, 125, 192, 205, 234, 236, 246, 247, 248; architecture of, 8, 9; and functionalism, 175; revolutions of 1848, 2, 166; Secessionist movements in, 56
expressionism, 238
expressionist architecture, 235, 258
expressive rationalism, 93

Fabiani, Max, 82, 84, 113, 170, 283n98
Fascists, 234
Felgel, Eugen, 189
Felgel, Oskar, 189
Ferdinand, Franz, 84, 168; assassination of, 231
Fergusson, James, 136
The Ferro-Concrete Style (Medgyaszay), 213
Ferstel, Heinrich von, 20, 26
Feszl, Frigyes, 48, 130
Feuerstein, Bedřich, 251, 252, 253, 292n52, 292n62
Fiala, Viktor, 273n25
Fiatalok (the Young Ones), 149–50, 280n43
Finland, 129, 158
Finno-Ugric linguistic group, 197, 267–68n6
Finns: Hungary, influence on, 197, 286n46
Fischer von Erlach, Johann Bernhard, 43, 105, 127, 261
Fischer, Ignjat (Ignatz), 122
Fix, Herr, 82
Flawil, 205
Fleischer, Max, 44
Flora Hof apartment block (Vienna), 72
folk architecture, 157, 158, 159
folk art, 14, 128, 130, 281–82n59
folk costumes, 133
folk craft, 14
folk motifs: as transnational, 158
Forbát, Fred, 236
form, 11, 12
formalism, 11
Förster, Ludwig von, 46, 48
The Fountain of Life (Moser), 274n33
France, 17, 19, 42, 55, 56, 63, 118, 129, 140, 188, 225, 234, 236; *architecture parlante* in, 1
Francis I, 25, 26

Francis II, Holy Roman Emperor (later Francis I, emperor of Austria), 4
Frank, Josef, 258
Frankel, Zacharias, 271n63
Frankfurt, 45
Franz Josef I (emperor, 1830–1916), 4, 19, 82, 103, 180, 198, 269n1, 270n31
Frass, Rudolf, 240
fretwork style (Laubsägestil), 158
Freud, Sigmund, 5
Friedrich III, 26
Fuchs, Bohuslav, 93, 236
Fülöp, Lajos, 149
functionalism, 10, 93, 175, 237, 242, 246, 251, 253, 260, 277n59, 290n113; and crematoria, 248; and rationalism, 235, 236, 238; and Rondo-cubism, 21
functionalist architecture, 236

Galicia, 2, 8, 59, 155, 159, 161, 165, 177, 178, 233, 284n6
Galicians, 155
Gardecki, Jozef, 284n13
Gaudi, Antoni, 56
Gehry, Frank, 10
Gellért Hill (Pest), 211
Geographical Institute (Prague), 292n62
geometry, 103
Georgia, 128
Gergely, Jenő, 124, 278n73
Gerle, János, 287n59
German-Jewish national style, 44
German Lutheran churches, 205
German neo-Gothic movement, 20
German Rowing Club, 236
German Werkbund, 85, 114, 289n92
Germany, 19, 20, 42, 52, 56, 127, 158, 188, 196, 205, 233, 234, 236, 261, 276n30; Austria, merger with, 232; Jews in, 43; Moorish synagogues in, 272n74
Gesamtkunstwerk, 78, 143, 170, 203, 206, 250
Geyling, Remigius, 78
Giergl, Kálmán, 150, 182; background of, 183
Gładyszów, 164
Gočár, Josef, 93, 114, 116, 223, 225, 226, 228, 277n56
Gödöllő Artists Colony, 150, 184, 288n76, 288–89n84
Godwin, Edward, 179
Goetheanum (Dornach, Switzerland), 235
Goldberg, Sámuel, 123
Golden Age of the Arts (Ženíšek), 37
Golden Age of Czech Renaissance, 14
Goldman & Salatsch store, 120
Gorizia (Italy), 82
Gorizia-Gradiska, 233

Gothic architecture, 17, 20, 44; as sacred idiom, 19
Graf, Otto, 105
The Grammar of Ornament (Jones), 55, 135, 279n22
Granada, 46
Grand Hotel Wiesler (Graz), 106
Grand Magasin Parisien (Pest), 123
Graz, 166, 167
Great-Father Czech, 34
Great Mosque of Cordoba, 48
Great Solanki temple, 279n24
Greenberg, Clement, 11
Group of Plastic Artists, 116, 223
Group of Visual Artists, 277n55, 277n56
guild system, 45
Guimard, Hector, 56, 63
Gut, Árpád, 124, 278n73
Gutfreund, Otto, 225
Gyarmathy, Etelka, 129
Györ Synagogue, 48
Györgyi, Dénes, 280n43

Habsburg Empire, 1, 14, 45, 191, 233; expansion of, 2
Habsburg, Rudolf von, 25
Habsburgs, 5, 17, 26, 28, 118, 129, 165, 175, 204, 232; abdication of, 231
The Hall of Hussars, 288–89n84
Hamburg, 22
Hanak, Anton, 222
Hannich, Josef, 108, 110, 116
Hansen, Theophil, 272n74
Hasenauer, Carl Freiherr von, 26, 57, 84
Haus Unger, 48
Hauszmann, Alajos, 183, 202
Heathcote, Edwyn, 253
Heimat ("homeland"), 158
Heimatkunst, 281–82n59
Heimatschutzstil ("homeland protection style"), 158, 281n58, 281–82n59
Heimatstil ("homeland style"), 158, 281n58; and nationalism, 234; and pitched roof, 235; propaganda, as vehicle for, 242; as urbane, 281n57
Hennebique, François, 211
Henry II Jasomirgott, 26
Henszlmann, Imre, 6, 128
Herzl, Theodor, 5
Hevesi, Ludwig, 51, 59, 84, 281n58
Hiram, 43
historicism, 235
History, 38
history, 177; and classicism, 234; and identity, 55; language of, 13, 43, 45, 52, 71, 84, 90, 223, 234; meaning, as repository of, 11
A History of Indian and Eastern Architecture (Fergusson), 136

Hitler, Adolf, 232, 233, 261
Hlávka Bridge (Prague), 114
Hobsbawm, Eric, 13
Hochhaus (Vienna), 239; design of, 240
Hodek's Apartment Building (Prague), 114, 116
Hódmezővásárhely (Hungary), 189
Hofburg Palace (Vienna), 71, 170
Hofburg Theater, 26
Hofman, Vlastislav, 114, 292n52
Hoffmann, Josef, 4, 57, 59, 79, 84, 89, 90, 98, 113, 119, 127, 160, 196, 200, 221, 231, 234, 273n11, 289n92; geometry, focus on, 86, 87; hybridity of, 220; influences on, 85
Hofmannsthal, Hugo von, 4, 105
Holland, 42. *See also* Netherlands
Holy Cross Church (Cracow), 284n10
Holy Land, 191
Holy Roman Empire, 4
Holzmeister, Clemens, 254, 255, 257, 258, 293n71, 293n74, 294n83
Homeland (Aleš), 37
Hood, Raymond, 291n35
Hoppe, Emil, 189, 192, 276n49, 294n83
Horejc, Jaroslave, 276n31
Horizont (Horizon), 292n54
Horta, Victor, 56, 63
Horthy, Miklos, 232
Hotel Central (Prague), 69, 73; description of, 70
Hotel Rong, 106
Howells, John Mead, 291n35
Hradčany, 32, 38
Hradčany castle (Prague), 42, 168, 169
Hradec Králové (Bohemia), 94, 95, 96, 270n31, 277n56
Hrausky, Andrej, 283n100
Hungarian Association of Engineers and Architects, 284n17
Hungarian folk music, 186, 188
Hungarian Holy Crown of Saint Stephen, 212
Hungarian-Indian Society, 242
Hungarian Jews: amalgamated identity of, 188
Hungarian Kingdom, 232, 233
Hungarian Railways Company, 150
Hungarian Reformed Church, 204
Hungarian Royal Geologic Institute, 140, 148, 150; design of, 141, 142, 143; opening of, 144
Hungarian Royal Postal Savings Bank (Budapest), 144; criticism of, 149; design of, 145, 146; as modern, 148; and national identity, 148; significance of, 148; and technology, 148; vocabulary of, 147
Hungarians, 155, 175; origins of, 129
Hungary, 1, 5, 13, 30, 39, 46, 56, 138, 148, 155, 159, 161, 165, 186, 189, 214, 267n4, 267–68n6, 287n71; and architecture, 133; Calvinism in, 203, 204, 206, 210; Calvinist churches in, 205; Catholicism in, 203, 204; Christianity in, 203, 204; and clothing, 130, 133; codification, system of in, 204; and Dual Monarchy, 2, 6; and embroidery, 130; ethnolinguistic homogeneity in, 233; Finns, influence on, 197, 286n46; folk architecture, as national style, 242; and folk art, 128, 129, 130; and folk costumes, 133; and folklore, 133; hussar cavalry uniforms, 130; hybridity in, 202; Jews in, 43; and identity, 149; language of, 133; Lutherans in, 204; and magyarization, 6, 8, 43; Millennial Celebration of, 129; myth, language of in, 128; and national identity, 4, 6, 127, 128, 129, 130, 205; national identity, and architecture, 133, 139, 198, 199, 203, 211; national identity, and clothing, 130; national identity, and international fairs, 217, 219, 288–89n84; and nationalism, 133; nationalism, and crematoriums, 247; national style, call for, 6, 128; pluralism in, 268n8; Protestantism in, 203, 204; rationalism in, 123, 128, 235; revolt in, 2; and Secession movement, 59, 60; size, reduction in, 232; Unitarians in, 204
Huns, 147, 175, 211, 219
Hussars, 288–89n84
Huszka, József, 128, 133, 196, 289n87
hybridity, 13, 175, 179, 182, 188, 189, 191, 195, 198, 199, 202, 203, 210, 220, 222, 223, 235, 237, 251, 257, 260; and biological grafting, 177; and crematoriums, 247, 249, 258; language of, 14, 246, 262, 263; nature of, 229
Hynais, Vojtěch, 38, 40

Iconologia (Ripa), 268n11
Idea for a Monumental Architecture (Perco), 259
identity, 13; and architecture, 1, 263; myth, as basis for, 133, 144
Ihnen, Eberhard, 196
Illyrian provinces, 165
Imperial Court station, 61, 63; description of, 62
Imperial Hotel (Tokyo), 292n62
Imperial Parliament building, 26
India, 139, 144, 175, 242
industrialization, 1, 24, 55, 140, 158; crafts, as threats to, 159; cultural identity, as threat to, 95; and modernism, 95
Industrial Revolution, 5
Institute for the Blind, 201; design of, 196, 197; hybridity of, 198
Institutes of the Christian Religion (Calvin), 287n60
International Exhibition of Industrial Art, 217
International Exposition (1906), 288–89n84
International Fine Arts Exhibit, 289n87
International Style, 56, 158, 159, 231, 235, 240, 246; variants of, 272–73n9
Iran, 128

Irish missionaries, 282n78
Islam, 52
Islamic architecture, 44, 45, 52
Israel, 191, 195, 285–86n37
Istria, 165, 233
Italian Jewry, 195
Italy, 19, 127, 140, 167, 188, 225, 232, 233, 234, 247, 285–86n37
Iveković, Ciril, 44

Jager, Ivan, 166, 167
Jagiello University: and Jagiellonian Globe, 180
Jakab, Desző, 150, 151
Jaksch, Hans, 238, 240
Janáček, Leoš, 5
Janák, Pavel, 114, 116, 226, 229, 249, 250, 251, 277n55; and Czech national architecture, 223
Janův dům (Jan's House), 160
Japonisme, 56, 62
Jeanneret, Charles-Eduard. *See* Le Corbusier
Jerusalem, 43, 49
Jewish places of worship, 43, 44, 46; and Islamic architecture, 45, 52; and synagogue architecture, transnational language of, 51
Jews, 191; Austro-Hungarian culture, assimilation in, 52; and Diaspora, 195, 285–86n37; in Hungary, 43; identity of, 45, 52; and Islamic architecture, 52; in Moorish Spain, 44; multiple identities of, 43; outsider status of, 43, 153; synagogue, design of, 45; synagogue, image of, 43; in Trieste, 284–85n20; in Vienna, 48
Jones, Owen, 45, 48, 51, 55, 135, 279n22
Judaism, 44; complexity of, 45; and Diaspora, 43
Jugendstil movement, 56, 59, 71, 93, 119, 132
Juliš Patisserie (Prague), 226
Jurkovič, Dušan: background of, 159; cemeteries, work on, 161, 162, 163, 164, 165, 282n72; folk traditions, knowledge of, 162; influences of, 160; international idiom, use of, 242; modernism of, 160; Slovak national identity, reviving of, 159, 160, 161; and rationalism, 160
Jursa, M., 291n24

Kafka, Franz, 5
Kaiser Franz Josef City Museum, 105, 276n49
Kallina, Géza, 202
Kallina, Mór (Moritz), 49, 202, 287n57
Kalotaszeg, 149; folk art in, 129
Kalous, Josef, 236
Kammerer, Marcel, 106, 108, 276n49
Karelia, 129
Karinthia, 165
Karl, Archduke, 26
Karli, 144

Karlín, 5
Karlinsky, Elisabeth, 258, 293n76
Karlsruhe, 205, 271n55, 287n65
Karlštejn castle, 32
Kärntner Bar, 120
Károly, Mihály, 232
Kassák, Lajos, 236
Kaym, Franz, 262
Kazakhstan, 128
Khazar Empire, 267–68n6
King Attila's Tent Palace, 217, 218, 289n87
Kingdom of Serbs, Croats, and Slovenes, 232, 233
kleinbürger, 281n58
Klein, Rudolf, 268n8, 279n15, 290n15
Klimt, Gustav, 4, 57, 59, 61, 90, 205
Knoblauch, Eduard, 48
Kodály, Zoltán, 186
Kokoschka, Oskar, 4
Komor, Marcell, 150, 151
Köning, Karl, 238, 283n98
Korb, Flóris, 150, 182, 183, 284n17
Körfy, Rudolf, 288n82
Kornhäusel, Josef, 272n74
Körösfőoi-Kreisch, Aladár, 129
Kós, Károly, 149, 160, 205, 211, 280n45; background of, 280n43. *See also* Károly Kosch
Kosch, Károly, 149. *See also* Károly Kós
Kotěra, Jan, 90, 95, 96, 97, 99, 101, 113, 114, 118, 167, 275n17, 275n24, 277n52, 289n100; background of, 93; death of, 225; and organicism, use of, 93, 94; rationalism, move toward, 94; students of, 110
Kottler, Helena, 170. *See also* Helena Vurnik
Kozma, Lajos, 201, 248
Kraus, Karl, 4, 120
Krejcar, Jaromír, 93, 229
Krinsky, Carol, 46, 49, 189, 271n68
Krisper, Valentino, 84
Kroha, Jiři, 249, 292n54
Kubin, Alfred, 4
Kunst und Kunstwerk, 84

lace-making, 159
Lajta, Béla, 199, 200, 201, 211, 286n45; as assimilated Jew, 196; background of, 195; early designs of, 196; hybridity of, 235; and Hungarian national identity, 196; versatility of, 202
landscape movements, 281n55
Lang, Fritz, 258
language, 268n11; and architecture, 1, 8, 9, 10, 11; and identity, 9; multiple meanings of, 9; political control, as powerful weapon of, 8
Lanner, Joseph, 4
Laske, Oskar, 72, 273n25
Laslo, Aleksander, 278n71

Lechner, Jenö, 242, 278n6, 280n41
Lechner, Ödön, 134, 135, 136, 140, 141, 142, 143, 144, 145, 146, 184, 196, 211, 242; background of, 132; death of, 149; modernism of, 138, 139; national identity, language of, 148, 149, 150; organic national style of, 147; theory of, 132, 133
Ledigenwohnungen (singles' apartment building), 240
Leipzig, 34
Leopold, Emperor, 254
Leopold I, 26
Leopold IV, 26
Lerner, L. Scott, 285–86n37
Léva front, 292n54
Libuše (Smetana), 42
Libuše, Princess, 33
Lichtwark, Alfred, 85
Liechtenstein Riding School, 239
Life (Devětsil), 252
Linz, 258
Lippich, Elek Koronghi, 286n46
List, Wilhelm, 103
Liszt Ferenc Square, 184
Liszt, Franz, 182, 184, 186, 188, 284n15
literalism, 160
Ljubljana, 166, 167, 243
Ljubljana castle, 173
London, 6, 196
Loos, Adolf, 4, 122, 158, 196, 277–78n68; background of, 119; coffering, use of, 120; as misinterpreted, 119; ornament, use of, 120; philosophy of, 120; pluralism of, 120; and rationality, 282n60
Louisiana Purchase Exhibition (1904), 288–89n84
Lower Austria, 39
Lower Austrian Provincial Institutions for the Care and Cure of the Mentally and Nervously Ill, 274n28
Ludwig, Ernst, 59
Lueger, Karl, 5
Luhačovice (Moravia), 160
Lutheran churches: Calvinist churches, as different from, 287n64
Lutheranism, 287n60
Lutherans, in Hungary, 204
Lux, Joseph-August, 106, 282n61
L'viv, 13, 177, 242, 284n5

Macedonians, 233
Mackintosh, Charles Rennie, 63, 85, 160
Mączyński, Franciszek, 157, 179, 180, 284n13
Magura, 163
Magyar Építőművészet, 209, 288n81
Magyar Iparművészet (Hungarian Arts and Crafts), 286n46
magyarization: goals of, 6, 8; and Jews, 8, 43
A magyar nép művészete (The Art of the Hungarian People) (Malonyay), 211
Magyars, 130, 133, 147, 204, 233, 267–68n6; foundation myth of, 129
Maison Domino, 125
Maitano, Lorenzo, 193
Malonyay, Dezsö, 211
Manchester (England), 179
Manicheanism, 203
Mánes Artists' Association, 93, 114, 277n55, 277n56
Mánes Pavilion, 275n17
Manuscripts of the King's Court and the Green Mountain: as fake, 33
Maria Theresia, 26, 188
Marmorek, Oskar, 189, 192, 273n10
Maroti, Geza, 196
Masaryk, Tomáš G., 168, 225, 243
mathematics, 235
Matouschek, Franz, 189, 191
Matthias Corvinus, 26, 212
Matthias Gate, 168, 169, 170
Maximilian I, 26
Mayer, Giovanni, 285n26
Mayreder, Karl, 283n98
Medgyaszay, István, 216, 219, 242, 248, 287n61, 288n73, 288n78, 288–89n84; as designer, prescience of, 211; and Hungarian national identity, 211, 212; and rationalism, 288n76; reinforced concrete, as specialty, 211, 213, 214
Mehoffer, József, 180, 181, 182, 284n13
Mencl, František, 248
Merganc, Jindrich, 243
Mesopotamia: vegetal forms in, 65
Messel, Alfred, 195–96, 286n51
Metropolitan Commercial School (Pest): design of, 200, 201, 286n51; hybridity of, 199; reaction to, 202
Metternich, Prince, 4, 20
Michelangelo, 225
Milan (Italy), 288–89n84
Millenary Exhibition (1896), 129, 150, 183, 288–89n84
Millennial Celebration (1896), 129, 133
mimesis, 55, 81
Mitteleuropa, 13
Mladá Boleslav, 292n54
Mloda Polska (Young Poland) art movement, 155, 179, 180
modern architecture, 105, 175, 231, 260, 275n24; basis for, 14; central theme of, 235; and function, 235; and modernist space, 11; and ornament, 120; and rationality, 235

modern culture, 11
Moderne Architektur, 105
modernism, 4, 10, 47, 55, 61, 66, 93, 119, 125, 128, 138, 139, 160, 170, 229, 246, 275n24, 282n60; and abstraction, 87; and Central European modern architecture, 231; and crematoria, 249; and Czech cubism, 114; historical association, trend against, 234; and historical consciousness, 234–35; and industrialization, 95; and monochromy, 87; signs of, 87; and technology, 133; and tectonic expression, 90
modernity, 81
modernization, 1, 13
Moldavia, 161
Molitorov castle, 160
Molnár, Farkas, 236
Moniteur des Architectes, 157
monochromy: and modernism, 87
Montenegrins, 233
Moorish architecture, 44; experimentation in, 45; and synagogue design, 45
Moravánszky, Ákos, 101, 135, 150, 229, 267n1, 286n51, 287n67
Moravia, 2, 8, 30, 38, 39, 42, 93, 118, 159, 232, 233, 254
Moravian Empire, 39
Morris, William, 85
Moser, Karl, 287n65
Moser, Koloman, 57, 59, 65, 74, 75, 78, 160, 274n31, 274n33
Mount Blaník, 38
Mount Bradlo, 243
Mount Radhošt, 159
Mount Říp, 34, 38
Mozart, Wolfgang Amadeus, 5
Müller, Ines, 45, 51
multiculturalism, 177
Munch, Edvard, 114
Munich, 34, 56, 160
Museum for Applied Art (Vienna). *See* Museum of Art and Industry
Museum of Applied Arts (Budapest), 133, 141, 142, 144, 148, 150; constructive techniques, as innovative, 134, 136, 138; design of, 135, 136; Indian motifs in, 135, 136; modernism of, 138, 139; reaction toward, 139
Museum of Art and Industry (Vienna), 134
Museum of Decorative Arts (Prague), 95
Muthesius, Herman, 85, 281n58
Művészet (Art), 132, 202
Myslbek, Josef Václav, 270n36
myth, 177; and architecture, 149; language of, 13, 128, 165, 170, 175, 242; and nationalism, 242; and ornament, 148; uniqueness of, 155

Nagy, Laszlo Moholy, 236
Nagyszentmiklós treasure, 147. *See also* Attila's Treasure
Napoleon, 4, 165
National Council, 233
National Exhibition and Fair (1885), 129
National House (Prostějov), 93
national identity, 11, 168, 217; and architecture, 155, 211; and craft traditions, 149; and ethnic and historical origins, 155; and myth, 148, 150; and organicism, 159; and technology, 140; and vernacular architecture, 159
nationalism, 234; and myth, 242; rise of, 13, 128
Nationalities Law, 8
National Museum (Prague), 95
nation-states, 14; and functionalism, 235
nature, 55; and organicism, 81
Nazis, 232, 234, 240, 261–62, 276n49
neoclassicism, 223
neo-Gothic architecture, 17, 19, 21, 44, 269n5; as antimodern, 20; and discipline, 20; in Germany, 20; as organic, 20; and politics, 20; support, lack of, 20
Neologist Jews, 46, 271n68
Netherlands, 236. *See also* Holland
Neue Freie Presse, 20
Neue Illustrierte Zeitung, 22
Neue Sachlichkeit (New Objectivity), 231, 293n75
Neues Bauen (New Building), 119, 231
Die Nibelungen (film), 258
nostalgia, 13
Notes on Art (Mehoffer), 182
Novotný, Otakar, 93, 110, 112, 113, 114, 277n52
Nymburk (Bohemia), 251

Óbuda, 5, 46, 140
Ohmann, Friedrich, 69, 70, 71, 84, 93, 170, 238, 275n17
Olbrich, Joseph Maria, 4, 56, 57, 59, 64, 84, 85, 231, 281n58
Old Czechs, 30, 32, 36
Old Theatre (Cracow), 284n13
Old Town Square, 32
Onderdonk, Francis, 213, 288n82
On Growth and Form (Thompson), 235
opaion, 139
Oranienburger Street temple (Berlin), 48
organic building, 20
organicism, 72, 77, 128, 177, 181, 275n17, 284n5, 284n13; and art nouveau, 155; language of, 14, 55, 56, 60, 64, 68, 71, 74, 82, 86, 93, 94, 95, 96, 106, 160, 235, 275–76n29; and national identity, 159; nature, as model of, 81; and rationalism, 81
organic organization, 74

organism, 235
ornament, 119, 120, 235; and myth, 148; and national identity, 223
Ornament and Crime (Loos), 120, 277n67
Orthodox Jews, 45, 46; and cremation, 247
Orvieto (Italy), 193
Ozenfant, Amadée, 277n59

Palace of Art (Cracow), 179
Palace in the Royal Castle (Buda), 183
Palais Stoclet (Brussels), 200, 221, 273n11
Palestine, 191, 195, 285–86n37
Palmyra (Syria), 191
Pan-Slavism, 129
Pan-Turanism movement, 128–29; and Ural-Altaic languages, 149
Pardubice (Bohemia), 249, 292n53
Paris, 56
Paris Peace Conference, 232, 233
Paris World's Fair, 288–89n84; Finnish Pavilion at, 286n46
Pártos, Gyula, 134
Pawlikowski, Jan G., 155
Pecz, Samu, 150
Les Peintres cubistes, 116
Perco, Rudolf, 258, 259, 260, 294n81; death of, 262; as Forgotten Generation, member of, 262; hybridity of, 262; Nazi sympathies of, 261, 262
Pernštejns, 292n53
Perret, August, 251
Persepolis, 144
Persia, 144
personal identity, 13
Pest, 5, 6, 47, 48, 140, 199, 211, 280n45; Jews in, 46. *See also* Buda; Budapest
Pest Redout, 48
Peterka, Franziska, 93
philosophy, 125
Picasso, Pablo, 118
Piešťany Spa bridge (Piešťany, Slovakia), 238, 260, 291n26; hybridity of, 237
Pinkas, Adolf Maria, 32
Plans, Elevations, Sections and Details of the Alhambra (Jones), 48
Platz, Gustav Adolf, 231
Plečnik, Jože, 166, 168, 169, 170, 172, 243, 283n92; Catholicism of, 167; language of myth, belief in, 244, 246; and Slavic identity, 167, 283n87
Plischke, Ernst Anton, 258, 293n77
pluralism, 120
Podgorze, 177
Podhale, 155
Pogány, Móric, 217, 227, 247, 248, 289n85
Poland, 1, 39, 161, 165, 177, 178, 233, 284n6; and folk architecture, 158; and national identity, 155, 158, 284n13; and Polish national movement, 157
Poles, 175
Polish national style, 159
politics, 13
Polívka, Osvald, 114
polyglotism: in architecture, 125
Portois & Fix building (Vienna), 113, 283n98; description of, 82; modernism of, 84
postcolonialism, 177
postmodernism, 10, 11
Postparkasse (Vienna), 273n11
Práce lidu našeho: Lidové stavby, zařízení a výzdoba obydlí, drobné práce (The Works of Our People: Folk Buildings, Interiors, and Handicrafts) (Jurkovič), 160
pragmatics, 268n11
Prague, 4, 17, 32, 33, 69, 95, 110, 113, 114, 116, 132, 159, 160, 167, 188, 223, 226, 236, 269n10, 275n17; architecture, and identity, as idiom for, 5; culture of, 5; Czech renaissance in, 5; growth of, 5; nationalism in, 5; revolution in, 5
Prague Symphony (Mozart), 5
Prague-Vinohrady, 99
Preisler, Jan, 276n31
Prelovšek, Damjan, 165, 169, 244, 283n94, 283n95
Primavesi house, 90
Primavesi, Otto, 220
Primavesi, Robert, 220
Prokop, Ursula, 262
Protestant churches: and cremation, 247
Protestantism: in Hungary, 203, 204
Prussia, 140, 270n31
psychology, 10
purism, 290n113; and Czechs, 277n59
Purkersdorf Sanatorium, 87
Pustevny, 159
pyrogranite, 132

Rathaus (city hall) (Vienna), 17, 18, 20, 29, 38, 78, 270n18; competition for, 19; completion of, 270n23; design of, 22, 23, 24; infrastructure of, 24; interiors of, 26, 270n21; language of, 28; sacral associations of, 26; sculpture of, 25, 26; as technically advanced, 28; and Vienna, 269n1
rationalism, 61, 84, 94, 96, 101, 105, 119, 123, 160, 177, 220, 225, 242, 288n76; and architecture, 81; breadth of, 125; complexity of, 89; and Czech cubism, 114, 116; emotion, as enemy of, 81; and functionalism, 235, 236, 238; images of, 106; language of, 14, 79, 110, 120, 122, 124, 125; meanings, multiplicity of, 81; and organicism, 81; premise of, 81; and reason, 81; and tectonic expression, 90

rationalist functionalism, 262
rational organicism, 77
Rauscher, Joseph Othmar, 21
Ravenna (Italy), 244
Raymond, Antonin, 292n62
reason: and rationalism, 81
Red Fort of Shahjahanabad (Delhi, India), 279n24
Red Vienna, 238, 259
Reform Catholicism, 269n10
Reform Jews, 45
Reform synagogue (Szabadka), 150, 151, 152, 280n48; otherness of, 153
Regetów Niżny, 163
Regional Authorities Building (Hradec Králové), 93
regional identity, 158
Reichensperger, August, 19, 20, 21, 22, 269n4, 269n5
reinforced-concrete technology, 211, 213
Renaissance, 9
Republic of German-Austria, 232
resonance: and architecture, 1
Resurrection of the Arts (Ženíšek), 37
Reunion Memorial Cathedral (Vienna), 261; hybridity of, 260
revolution of 1848, 30
Richardson, H. H., 275–76n29
Ringkirche, 205
Ripa, Cesare, 268n11
Riunione Adriatica di Sicurtà (Prague), 226; description of, 227, 228; hybridity of, 229; reaction to, 229
Roman Catholic Church, 165, 166, 167, 204, 248, 287n60; cremation, banning of, 247
Roman Catholic church and mausoleum (Rárósmulyad), 214; Hungarian folk motifs in, 215, 216, 288n83; hybridity of, 216
Roman Empire, 17
Romania, 1, 232, 233, 267–68n6, 282n63
Romanians, 155
Romano, Giulio, 225
Rome, 90, 127, 167, 175, 195, 289n87
Rondo-cubism, 119, 226, 234, 236, 249, 251; and functionalism, 231; negative reactions toward, 229; origin, of term, 277n65; as short-lived, 229; as transformative, 223
Royal Academy of Drama and Music, 182. *See also* Academy of Music
Royal Castle (Buda), 183, 202
Rudolf (crown prince), 39
Rudolf I von Habsburg, 26
Rudolf II, 30
Rudolph II, 168
Rudolf IV, 25
Rudolf, the Founder, 26
Rudorff, Ernst, 281n58

The ruins of Palmyra, otherwise Tedmor, in the desert (Wood), 191
Rumbach Street Synagogue (Budapest), 17, 52, 60, 202; commission of, 47; construction of, 49, 50; design of, 50, 51
Ruskin, John, 85, 275n24
Rus' lands, 233
Russia, 161, 197, 225, 232, 233, 234

Saarinen, Eliel, 196, 291n35
Sacred Heart Church (Prague), 283n92
Saint Leopold, 74
Saint Severinus, 74
Saint Wenceslas, 39
Salt Works, 30
Sarajevo (Bosnia), 44, 45, 231
Sardinia-Piedmont, 19
Sassanian culture, 128
Sassanids, 128
Scamozzi, Vincenzo, 169
Scheu house, 120
Schiele, Egon, 4
Schimkowitz, Othmar, 66, 103
Schmidt, Friedrich von, 17, 20, 21; background of, 19; and Rathaus, 22, 23, 24
Schindler, Rudolf, 106
Schnaase, Karl, 44
Schnitzler, Arthur, 4
Schoenberg, Arnold, 4, 239
Schönthal, Otto, 72–73, 189, 192, 276n49, 294n83
Schulz, Josef, 40, 42
Schultze-Naumburg, Paul, 281n58, 293n75
science, 81, 125
Scott, George Gilbert, 22
Secession Building, 57; description of, 59; reaction to, 59
Secessionist movements, 59, 93, 132, 133, 149; in Europe, 56
Second World War. *See* World War II
Sekler, Eduard, 90, 221
semantics, 268n11
semiotics, 10
Semper, Gottfried, 26, 34, 68, 101, 166, 167, 272n74; and theories of cladding, 244
Sephardic communities, 188
Serbia, 231, 233, 267n4, 267–68n6, 283n87
Serbs, 155
Shaw, Richard Norman, 196
Siberia, 267–68n6
Šič, Albert, 166
Sicardsburg, August, 32, 47
sign: parts of, 268n11
signification, 268n11
Silesia, 38, 39, 42, 232, 233, 282n63
Sitte, Camillo, 56

Skalica, 160
Škápik, J., 291n24
Škoda works, 229
skyscrapers: public debate over, 240
Skywa, Josefine, 220
Sláma, Bohumil, 251, 292n52
Šlapeta, Vladimír, 275n24
Slavia, 40
Slavonia, 232
Slavs, 129, 166; as God's elect, 167
Slovak embroidery: as Slovak national idiom, 159
Slovakia, 8, 39, 214, 233, 267–68n6, 282n63; national identity in, 159
Slovak Rowing Club, 236
Slovak Technical University, 291n25
Slovaks, 155, 175, 216; identity of, 159, 236; language of, 159
Slovene architecture, 166, 170
Slovene identity, 166, 172, 174; and Etruscans, 167, 175; language of, 282n78
Slovene nationalist movement, 166
Slovene Peoples' Party: and Roman Catholic Church, 166
Slovene provinces, 2, 165, 166
Slovenes, 175
Slovenia, 59, 283n87
Smetana, Bedřich, 5, 30, 42
Society of Friends of the Fine Arts, 284n8
sociology, 10
Sofia (Bulgaria), 189
Solomon's Temple, 43, 46. *See also* Temple of Solomon
South Kensington Museum (London), 134
Soviet constructivism, 231, 238
Spain, 45, 48; Jews in, 44
Spielman, Ernst, 273n25
The Spiritual Works of Mercy, 75
Spitavorok monastery (Armenia), 193
Staats-Oper (State Opera) (Vienna), 32
Stadtbahn (railway), 60, 61, 105
Ständestaat, 261, 262
Staroměstske Náměsti (Old Town Square), 42
Starr, George, 204, 287n67
Starý, Oldřich, 253
Statue of Liberty, 285n26
Stavba, 229, 248, 252, 253, 292n52
Štech, Václav Vilém, 118
Štefánik, M. R., 243
Steindl, Imre, 128
Steiner, Rudolf, 235
Steiner house, 120
Štenc House, 110, 112, 113
Štenc, Jan, 110
Stephanie (Belgian princess), 39
Stephen of Hungary, 203, 204

Sternberg, Jaroslav, 39
St. Gall, 205
St. Germaine: treaty of, 232
Der Stil in den technischen und tektonischen Künsten oder Praktische Aesthetik (Style in the Technical and Tectonic Arts, or Practical Aesthetics), 166
St. Leopold's Church at Steinhof (Vienna), 90, 122, 170, 206, 276n49, 287n67; description of, 74, 75, 76, 77, 78; reaction toward, 78, 105
St. Louis (Missouri), 275n24, 288–89n84
St. Mary's Church (Cracow), 179, 180, 284n10
Stoclet, Adolphe: grand villa of, 90
Strauss family, 4
Strauss, Johann, 4
Strnad, Oskar, 258
St. Stephen's Cathedral (Vienna), 20, 24, 26, 240
structural organicism, 55, 68, 74, 78
structural rationalism, 235
Stryjeński, Tadeusz, 179, 284n13
Strzygowski, Josef, 105, 192, 285n31
The Studio, 160
Stüler, Friedrich A., 48
Šturza, Jan, 225
St. Wenceslas statue (Prague), 270n36
Styl, 114, 165, 277n56
Styria, 165
suba, 130
Sub-Carpathian Rus, 233
Sucharda, Stanislav, 96, 98, 276n31
Sučnik, Stanko, 243
Sullivan, Louis, 57, 119, 272n1
Švácha, Rostislav, 95, 96, 225–26, 229, 275n24, 276n30, 290n106, 290n113
Svatopluk, 39
Swiss House, 158
Switzer, Terri, 219
Switzerland, 205, 287n60
symbol, 268n11
symbology, 268n11
syntax, 268n11
Syria, 191, 195
systems theory, 10
Szabadka (Hungary), 188, 189; Jewish community in, 150
Széchenyi, István, 6, 128
Szeged (Hungary), 6, 189
Székely people, 129
Sziklaí, Zsigmond, 123, 278n72
szűr, 130, 135

Tálos, Gyula, 201
Tamaro, Attilio, 285n31
Taming of the Elements (Mehoffer), 182
Tatars, 39

TÉBE apartment building (Budapest), 242
technology, 81, 148, 242; and modernism, 133
tectonic expression: and rationalism, 90
Teige, Karel, 229, 253, 277n59, 289n100
Teller, Alfred, 273n25
Tempio Israelitico (Trieste), 188, 284–85n20, 285n26; design of, 192, 193; hybridity of, 195; imagery of, 193; technical achievements of, 193
Temple of Solomon, 193. *See also* Solomon's Temple
Theater of the Estates, 32
Theiss & Jaksch, 238, 239, 294n83; Nazis, work with, 240
Theiss, Siegfried, 238
Thompson, D'Arcy, 235
Thompson, Henry, 247
Thun-Hohenstein, Leo, 19, 21
Toledo (Spain), 46, 48
Topp, Leslie, 273–74n27
Tőry, Emil, 217, 227, 289n85
Town Museum, 275n24
Traiskirchen (Lower Austria), 238
Transylvania, 2, 128, 129, 149, 196, 204, 205, 232
Treaty of Trianon, 232
Tree of Life, 65
Trieste (Italy), 82, 165, 170, 191, 227, 233, 285–86n37; Jews in, 188, 195, 284–85n20
Tuchlaubenhof (Vienna), 273n25
Turá Lúka, 159
Turan: Sassanian culture of, 128
Turanian Magyars, 129
Turanism, 242
Turin (Italy), 217
Turkey, 129
Turkistan, 128
Turkmenistan, 128
Turks, 129
Tychonova Street duplex (Prague), 114, 116
Tyrol, 161
Tyrolean House, 158

Ullmann, Ignác Vojtěch, 32
Ulrich, František, 95, 96
Union of Architects, 292–93n64
Union of Christian Art and the Fatherland Front, 260
Unitarians, 204
United States, 213, 219, 247
Unity Temple (Oak Park, Illinois), 275n24
University of Vienna, 26
Unter den Linden, 64
Ural-Altaic languages, 129, 149
Urania Theater, 84

utopianism, 262
Uzbekistan, 128

Vágó, József, 60, 273n11
Vágó, László, 60, 273n11
Valenta, Jaroslav, 236
Vállalkozók Lapja (Journal of Entrepreneurs), 150
van der Nüll, Eduard, 32, 47
van de Velde, Henri, 56
Venice Biennial (1909), 289n87
verisimilitude, 81
vernacular architecture, 14, 158; and national identity, 159
Ver Sacrum (Sacred Spring), 57
Veszprém (Hungary), 212, 213
Veszprém Theater (Veszprém), 212, 213, 214
Victoria and Albert Museum (London). *See* South Kensington Museum
Victoria, Queen, 247
Victory lighthouse (Trieste), 285n26
Vidor, Emil, 60, 273n10
Vienna, 2, 17, 18, 19, 25, 26, 30, 39, 48, 56, 61, 64, 66, 69, 71, 72, 85, 93, 118, 122, 132, 160, 167, 175, 196, 211, 220, 239, 240, 259, 269n1, 272n74; anticlericalism in, 254, 255; crematoriums in, 254, 293n75; cultural life of, 4; growth of, 5; identity of, changes in, 4; modernism, contributions to, 4; and Museums Quarter, 294n87; revolution in, 4; tension in, 5; and Otto Wagner, 105
Vienna Kunstschau, 90
Vienna River Regulation project, 71
Vienna Secession, 42, 56, 61, 64, 79, 84, 85–86, 93, 96, 167, 284n13; founding of, 57; and geometry, 57
Villa Grünwald, 60, 273n11
Villa Koliba, 155
Villa Skywa-Primavesi, 220, 289n92; description of, 221; hybridity of, 222
Vindobona, 17
Viollet-le-Duc, Eugène-Emanuel, 55, 56
Vitruvius, 9
Vojcsik, Ladislaus, 73
Vojvodina, 232, 267n4
Volné Směry, 223
von Epstein, Gustav, 271–72n72
Votivkirche, 26
Voysey, Charles F. A., 85, 160
Vsetín, 159
Vurnik, Helena, 174. *See also* Helena Kottler
Vurnik, Ivan, 168, 173, 243, 283n98; folk motifs, use of, 174; and myth, 170; and Slovene identity, 172, 174

Vyšehrad, 32, 38
Vzajemna Insurance Company, 243
Vzkříšení Umění (Resurrection of Art) (Ženíšek), 38

Wagner, Antonin Pavel, 270n37
Wagner, Otto, 4, 17, 48, 49, 50, 51, 57, 59, 62, 63, 64, 66, 68, 69, 71, 72, 73, 74, 75, 76, 77, 82, 84, 85, 90, 93, 110, 122, 127, 166, 167, 168, 170, 189, 202, 203, 206, 211, 225, 231, 258, 271–72n72, 273n11, 273–74n27, 275n17, 275n24, 276n49, 281n58, 282n61, 283n98, 285n31, 287n67; as apolitical, 103; death of, 105; modernism, theory of, 47, 78; nationalism, discouragement of, among students, 288n73; new construction methods of, 101, 103, 105; and organicism, 60, 61; and rationalism, 105, 114, 116; students of, 106, 108; Vienna, impact on, 105; Wagnerschule, creation of, 105
Wagnerschule, 105, 180, 184, 189, 211, 216, 221, 238, 247, 248, 258, 262
Walter, Bruno, 239
Walachian buildings, 159
Walachians, 282n63
War Graves Department of the Military Command, 161
Wärndorfer, Fritz, 59
Waterhouse, Alfred, 179
Weapon and Machine Factory Corporation, 124
Weapon Museum (Vienna), 272n74
Webern, Anton von, 4
Wechselmann, Ignac, 196
Weimar, 34
Weimar Museum, 34
Weinbrenner, Friedrich, 271n54
Wekerle housing estate (Budapest),150, 239, 280n45
Wenke Department Store (Jaroměř), 116, 277n63
Wenke, Joseph, 116
Wertheim Department Store (Berlin), 195–96, 286n51
Die Westgalizischen Heldengräber aus den Jahren des Weltkrieges 1914–1915 (The West Galician Heroes' Graves from the Years of the World War 1914–1915), 161
Whyte, Iain Boyd, 73, 106, 285n23
Wiehl, Antonin, 42
Wiener Werkstätte (Viennese Workshops), 59, 86, 87, 98, 113, 119, 127, 160, 201, 203
Wienzeile apartment building, 74; description of, 64, 65, 66, 68, 69

Wienzeile Bridge, 61
Wiesbaden, 205
Wiesner, Arnošt, 236, 253, 254, 292n63, 292–93n64, 293n65
Wirth, Zdeněk, 114
Witkiewicz, Stanisław, 155, 157, 280n50; works of, 280–81n51
Witkiewicz-Koszyc, Jan, 280–81n51
Witkovsky, Matthew, 247
Wittek, Alexander, 44
Wittgenstein, Ludwig, 268n11
Wood, Robert, 191
World Exhibition (St. Louis), 275n24
World War I, 14, 119, 125, 161, 202, 203, 223, 225, 233, 235, 242, 247, 260–61, 276n49; beginning of, 231
World War II, 1, 234
World's Columbian Exposition (Chicago), 288–89n84
Wright, Frank Lloyd, 57, 125, 132, 272n1, 275n24, 292n62; ornament, use of, 290n13
Wyspianski, Stanisław, 179, 180, 284n10

Ybl, Miklós, 48, 128, 196, 273n10
Young Czechs, 30, 32, 33, 36
The Young Ones. *See* Fiatalok
Young Poland, 284n13
Yugoslav Committee, 233
Yugoslavia, 1, 233, 234

Zacherl, Johannes, 167
Zadar, 233
Zagreb (Croatia), 122, 233
Zakopane (Poland), 155; and Polish national movement, 157
Zakopane style, 155; and folk architecture, 157
Žale Cemetery (Ljubljana), 243
Zasche, Josef, 226
Ženíšek, František, 37, 38, 270n39
Zeromski, Stefan, 280–81n51
Zhuk, Igor, 284n5
Zionism, 5
Zitek, Josef, 17, 34, 35, 36, 40, 42, 47, 270n30; background of, 32; and national identity, themes of, 33; and Young Czechs, 33
Zrumeczky, Dezső, 280n43
Zsolnay, Vilmos, 132
Zug, 205
Zum Roten Igel (At the Red Hedgehog), 84
Zurich, 34